PILGRIMAGE AND HOUSEHOLD IN THE ANCIENT NEAR EAST

In this book, Joy McCorriston examines the continuity of traditions over millennia in the Near East. Tracing the phenomenon of pilgrimage in pre-Islamic Arabia up through the development of the Haj, she defines its essential characteristics and emphasizes the critical role that pilgrimage plays in enabling and developing socioeconomic transactions. Indeed, the social identities constructed through pilgrimage are key to understanding the long-term endurance of the phenomenon. In the second part of the book, McCorriston turns to the household, using cases of ancient households in Mesopotamian societies, in both the private and public spheres. Her conclusions tie together broader theoretical implications generated by the study of the two phenomena and offer a new paradigm for archaeological study, which has traditionally focused on transitions to the exclusion of continuity of traditions.

Joy McCorriston is Associate Professor of Anthropology at The Ohio State University. She has published more than forty academic articles and book chapters on the origins of food production, the development of agricultural economies through the Bronze Age, and Southern Arabian pre-history. She currently leads the Ancient Human Social Dynamics in Arabia Project in Oman.

PILGRIMAGE AND HOUSEHOLD IN THE ANCIENT NEAR EAST

Joy McCorriston

CAMBRIDGE
UNIVERSITY PRESS

CAMBRIDGE UNIVERSITY PRESS
Cambridge, New York, Melbourne, Madrid, Cape Town,
Singapore, São Paulo, Delhi, Tokyo, Mexico City

Cambridge University Press
32 Avenue of the Americas, New York, NY 10013-2473, USA

www.cambridge.org
Information on this title: www.cambridge.org/9780521137607

First published 2011

Printed in China by Everbest

A catalog record for this publication is available from the British Library.

Library of Congress Cataloging in Publication Data
McCorriston, Joy, 1961–
Pilgrimage and household in the ancient near east / Joy McCorriston.
    p.   cm.
Includes bibliographical references and index.
ISBN 978-0-521-76851-1 (hardback) – ISBN 978-0-521-13760-7 (pbk.)
1. Pilgrims and pilgrimages – Arabian Peninsula – History.   2. Arabian
Peninsula – Antiquities.   3. Households – Iraq – History.   4. Iraq – Antiquities.
I. Title.
BL619.P5M43   2011
203′.50935–dc22   2010023543

ISBN 978-0-521-76851-1 Hardback
ISBN 978-0-521-13760-7 Paperback

To Kevin

CONTENTS

FIGURES

TABLES

PREFACE

Deep in the Syrian desert lies an ancient caravan city at Palmyra, still today some four hours drive from the last oasis. Until a few years ago, modern autos and traffic still followed an old route across the grand axis of the city. Camels and their drivers rest in the shade of a monumental arch, while on the southern rise Palmyra's Bel temple dominates the oasis ruins. Even stripped of its original marble cladding, cult statues, treasury, and solemn pageantry, the temple's central cella and huge colonnaded precinct embody a powerful idea. Like the greatest mediaeval cathedrals, the relict cella ceiling soars above the heavy pavement, built, like pavement and precinct, of massive exotic stone blocks hauled great distances through a barren desert. A visitor is dwarfed by its monumental proportions, imagery not lost on the Orientalist painter Gustav Bauernfeind, whose view of nearby Baalbek ruins accentuates the lost splendor with tiny bedouin shepherds. No visitor can come away without wonder – What god and purpose did this grandeur once serve?

The Bel temple was almost as impressive in scale and wealth as its contemporary rivals and neighbors – the Haddad temple in Damascus, Heliopolis temple at Baalbek, and the massive Jerusalem temple, to which every male Jew was enjoined to travel for a sacrificial offering at least once a year. Two thousand years ago, these sites formed the loci of interwoven economic, social, and ideological practice – pilgrimage – that is a distinctive and very significant motif in many latter Near Eastern complex societies. In material terms, the lavish and ostentatious construction of the massive temples that attracted pilgrims displays the core

1. First-century AD cella of the temple of Bel, Palmyra (Syria). Author's photo.

role that the ritual played in economic networks, in ideologies of human relationships to the natural and supernatural worlds, and, not least, in constituting a society of believers whose practice of pilgrimage affirmed their collective identity. This book is about the continuity of those core ideas and practices and their epochal inheritance from a Neolithic past before the dawn of history.

This project came to me on a return journey from Palmyra – a Road-to-Damascus conversion – where my family visited extraordinary archaeological ruins and my three-year-old son rode his first camel. On the bus home I finally wondered why peoples past had traveled to Palmyra. Was it indeed, as Yale historian Michael Rostovtseff (1932) claimed, a "Cavavan City" built and prosperous because of its historical location on trade routes? I mused over a phrase in Ross Burns's (2005) excellent guidebook that connected the imposing Bel temple at Palmyra with its

2. "Temple Ruins of Baalbak," Gustav Bauernfeind, 1880. Bildarchiv Preussischer Kulturbesitz/Art Resource, New York.

contemporaries. All Semitic cult centers sought to entice the maximum number of visitors through rival displays of wealth and scale.

But why would relatively small urban populations seek to draw in large numbers of visitors with a huge outlay of time and resources? The answer then seemed obvious to me – trade and the economic side benefits of pilgrimage. I was at once reminded of the controversy over Meccan trade before Islam – was trade or was it not still significant in Arabia? (Crone 1987) – and of the social contexts of pre-Islamic Arabian states and economic transformations that accompany the emergence of state societies. In the case of pre-Islamic Arabian states, the so-called Frankincense Kingdoms, archaeologists are still frustrated by very little real evidence, but they have a wealth of ideas and general models about what should have happened or could have happened to bring about the impressive urban centers that organized, authorized, and secured the caravans bearing incense to the Mediterranean world. Palmyra is in one sense but a northward extension. Suddenly the mechanisms evident in pilgrimage to Semitic cult centers in the northern kingdoms seemed key to me in understanding similar mechanisms in ancient Southern Arabia. Pilgrimage played a key role in Near Eastern societies for thousands of years and continued to do so as states rose and fell. And a closer look shows that pilgrimage was key before states arose.

What interests me so profoundly about pilgrimage is its resistance to change, its dramatic manifestation of meta-structure that seemingly lies outside a theoretical canon dedicated to the explanation of change. When we visited Palmyra as a family, I was co-teaching a seminar at Damascus University on the history of theory in Americanist anthropological archaeology. Class discussions revolved around the Marxist historical materialist model and the articulations of American archaeological theory with the general premise of that model – that tensions between economic base and ideological superstructure are the basis for the historical transformation of societies and cultures. In these most basic historical-materialist terms archaeologists have sought to understand and explain history, what some call "the science of change" (Knapp 1992: 16, Lyon 1987). Alongside evolution, historical materialism has underlain virtually all theoretical contributions in sociology and anthropology: Darwin and Marx set the stage for all that followed. And these great theories are all about change.

As I recognized the durability and longevity of pilgrimage as a core institution, I became increasingly interested in archaeologically revealed meta-structure itself and the explanation of its persistence. Some of what this project concerns, such as pilgrimage, has been studied by anthropologists under the rubric of ritual institutions and ritual practices and their roles in structuring social identities and history (Kelly and Kaplan 1990). But I am not interested in examining ritual itself, nor in the anthropological discussions about what ritual is and the roles it plays.

This project instead focuses on the meta-structures that ritual manifests, that is, core cultural ideas that endure over extremely long time frames, beginning in the Neolithic. Anthropologists and historians struggled with core cultural idea sets in the first half of the last century, calling such phenomena "Great Cultures" (Spengler [1922] 1926, Kroeber 1944), "Civilizations" (Toynbee 1934–1954, Bagby 1959), and "Great Traditions" (Redfield [1955] 1967, Redfield in Singer 1974). But the full duration of such institutions has been previously unrecognized and indeed continues throughout what earlier anthropologists differentiated into Primitive Cultures and Civilizations, Little and Great Traditions. Archaeological evidence unavailable in the last century now demonstrates extremely long temporal frames of meta-structural phenomena. With this new recognition comes new questions: why did meta-structures of ideas and their manifestation as practices persist across long time frames and how did they do so across tremendous social, economic, and ideological changes?

In the answers to these questions and the making of this book, I have many to thank, for this has not been a journey alone. First and foremost, I thank my friends in the Middle East who have transformed my lifetime of visits into true pilgrimage. When I look back at thirty years of exploring and documenting archaeology in the Near East, I appreciate above all the indescribable hospitality of strangers: the bedouin pickup-driver who detoured a pair of young hitchhikers in the Wadi Hasa to his family tent for full supper before driving us many midnight miles to our destination; the young woman met on a bus to Madaba who insisted we eat at her home while she and family stood by; Jerusalem Palestinians – one patriarch sheltering young, single American girls in a family apartment and providing safe escorts, or a family-run hotel that effaced distinction between client and guest; and Damascenes who are surely the most hospitable people on earth. When I think of ancient peoples, I see before me the faces of modern strangers, not as the changeless stand-ins for a Biblical Lot or living proof of an "Oriental Mind" but as the real inspiration for my lifelong reach to understand cultural differences and their broader humanistic meanings. With grateful acknowledgment of all who have helped me on my way, I humbly hope this effort honors my many hosts abroad. Among these I especially acknowledge the influence of 'Abdalazīz Bin 'Aqīl, Youssef Barkoudah, the 'Awad-Hanoush family from Damascus and Marmarita, the Tazas of Hasseke, and Thuwaiba Al-Riyami.

In a wider circle are the Bayt al-'Alī Humūm bedouin and the many Syrian, Yemeni, Jordanian, and Omani colleagues too numerous to name who have so patiently welcomed, aided, and tolerated my research and taught me so much. Mostly we met through the Syrian Directorate General for Antiquities and Museums, the General Organization of Antiquities and Museums in Yemen, the Jordanian Department of Antiquities, and the Ministry of Culture in the Sultanate of Oman, and I bear deep gratitude for the opportunities and trust they have offered me. My thinking has been heavily influenced through archaeological field research, and I thank the unstinting efforts, under very trying conditions, of the incredibly talented field team at the core of the RASA (Roots of Agriculture in Southern Arabia) and AHSD (Arabian Human Social Dynamics) Projects: Eric Oches, Michael Harrower, Tara Steimer, Remy Crassard, Catherine Heyne, Matthew Senn, Jennifer Everhart, and Kimberly Williams. The American Institute for Yemeni Studies has been critical to our success, as has been funding from the National Science Foundation and Wenner Gren Foundation. We are all enormously grateful to Canadian Nexen Petroleum Yemen and Canadian Nexen in Calgary for extraordinary logistical and financial support to us and to archaeology in Hadramawt.

Closer to home, I acknowledge the encouragement of friends and family. What are the odds that one would find forty crumbling cattle skulls in Yemen when one's intimate friend is a world expert on Neolithic Near Eastern cattle? Louise Martin always fires my enthusiasm and gave a memorable New Year's holiday to analyzing cattle skulls in Mukalla with conservator Lisa Usman. Robert Wenke has encouraged every step of this project from concept (with which he surely disagrees) to completion. Frank Hole taught me to think outside the paradigm of what everyone else is doing. I miss Michael Zwettler's deep knowledge and thank him posthumously for his patient gifts of time when he had so little left.

For illustrations and technical support I sincerely thank Manuel Clerc, Mac Gibson, Alexander Sedov, Mike Harrower, Herb Wright, Iris Gerlach and the Deutsches Archäologisches Institut, Allison Grimes, Matt Indrutz, and Jen Everhart. Robert Odenweller generously provided an index, for which I am most grateful. Kevin Johnston, David Wengrow, Norman Yoffee, and Michael Zwettler offered very helpful suggestions that improved the final manuscript, and I have been honored in my interactions with students who have read, commented, and drawn upon chapters in process. I have transliterated Arabic terminology using the Library of Congress (LoC) system with the following exceptions: where terms and places have a conventional Anglicized form, I have retained that form (e.g., "Mecca" not "Makka," "Wadi" not "Wādī") and for toponyms whose roots I could not guess, I have retained the transliteration used in the reference I cite. For authors' names, I use LoC except where an author has himself used or acquiesced in a different transliteration (e.g., "Ibn al-Mujawir," but "Alatas" not "Al-ʿAṭṭās"). Site names derived from Arabic but widely published in English likewise retain their published transliteration (e.g., "El-Geili" not "Al-Qailī"). Terms from Old South Arabian languages appear as consonants (e.g., "byt" not "bayt"), following convention. I acknowledge with gratitude Serge Frantsouzoff's vocalization of Old South Arabian places, divinities, and offices, but any error is mine.

At last my greatest thanks go to my beloved husband Kevin Johnston and son Keoki for the sacrifices they made while I wrote.

CHAPTER 1

INTRODUCTION

In the middle Wadi Sana of the highlands of Southern Arabia rises a
rock inselberg today named by the Al-'Alī bedouin nomads "Khuzma-as-
Shumlya." It takes its name from the nose-ring of a camel that pierces
the nasal septum, and indeed geographically, the isolated mountain does
serve as a septum severing the watercourse of the Wadi Shumlya as it
feeds into the main drainage. Evidently people thought so long ago, for
on the Khuzma's eastern face, a caravaneer scribbled "Khuzmūm" (or
"Place of Khuzma") in Old South Arabic (AD 300) alongside a few camel
pictographs. But the place was significant for far longer. Close archaeological scrutiny has revealed a concentration of platformed structures,
each with a standing stone before it and evidence of ritual sacrifice dating
back 6,500 years. Before Khuzma was the septum, it probably housed
a god, and the location was the site of tribal gatherings, sacrifices, and
feasts in Arabia's oldest and certainly most important meta-structure,
here called Pilgrimage.

A substantial part of this book documents Pilgrimage as one example
of a wider phenomenon of long-term cultural continuities. Household
is another example. Pilgrimage and Household are convenient terms in a
new nomenclature for meta-structures that persisted through the emergence of social complexities and despite transformational changes in
societies, economies, and ideologies. The core of Pilgrimage (Chapter 2)
can be traced through the historical and archaeological records of
Arabia and endured for most of the time Arabia is known to have
been continuously occupied (Chapters 3 and 4). With 6,500 years of
practice, Pilgrimage represents a persistent phenomenon that outspans

the gaze of most anthropological inquiry (except for archaeology), yet its very persistence raises some interesting anthropological issues for which new theoretical approaches need to be explored.

Anthropology, Archaeology, and Theories of Change

It is perhaps surprising that there remain obvious meta-structural cultural phenomena like Pilgrimage that require description and explanation in a region as richly studied as the Near East, but the gaps can be traced to an epistemological focus on change. Study of change has been the engine driving most anthropological, sociological, and historical theory. Influential archaeologists like Gordon Childe, who set the agenda for Near Eastern pre-history, have been deeply influenced by wider sociological debates, including subjective and discursive Orientalist perspectives that framed Near Eastern pre-history as the precursor to European. But Childe, like his successors, above all sought explanation in the great biological and historical theories of Darwin and Marx, all about change.

Pre-historians came to the Near East looking for evidence of change. Their agenda for studying the ancient Near East was set by Gordon Childe, himself deeply influenced by the writings of Karl Marx. Marx transformed Lewis Henry Morgan's (1877: 3–18) model for the passage of societies through a complex of social stages – "Savagery" preceding "Barbarism" preceding "Civilization" (attained by Europeans). Morgan had suggested that humans acquired social graces for communal living and manifested social development at each stage. After a 1935 sojourn in the newly formed Soviet Union, Childe adopted a materialist focus on an economic base for societies (Klejn 1994: 76) and, in deference to Morgan's influential scheme, suggested that the economic attributes of hunting and foraging characterized Savage society; agriculture was associated with Barbarism and craft production with Civilization (Morgan 1877: 41, Childe [1936] 1951, [1942] 1950). Childe's scheme appropriated one of the great biases of his time – an Orientalizing narrative that situates European civilization at the climax of human achievement (Said 1979). Thus, his works highlighted great transitions that led through economic "revolutions" (the term stems from Marxist praxis rather than actual archaeological data) to European civilization. Childe established a theoretical agenda drawing on historical materialism with the result that intervening periods and cultures in the Near East have merited scientific study only as they contributed to greater themes – the Neolithic Revolution, the Urban Revolution, Civilization Comes to Us. History is the "science of change" (Knapp 1992: 16, after Bloch in Lyon 1987), and by setting the tone with Marx's theoretical model explaining history, Childe wedded pre-history to an explanation of change. There has been considerably less curiosity about explaining continuity.

Long dominated by the Childean agenda and by questions about the emergence of modern humans rooted in biological evolution, prehistorians have inherited a research agenda focused on change. Most of this work has been conducted by Western scholars with more recent and significant entry of Israeli, Arab, and Asian researchers. Theoretical approaches in archaeology followed different traditions in Anglo-American and Continental European scholarship. For example, French archaeology in the Near East has remained largely independent from anthropological traditions and ironically also shows little influence from the important structural and poststructural French contributions to sociological and anthropological theory. German archaeologists in Europe and abroad similarly regard archaeology as historical science for the reconstruction of the history of Mankind (Bittel 1980: 277). Biblical archaeologists, searching for wider context in which to interpret Biblical text, have also played a significant role in generating culture histories in the Near East (Dever 1990, Finkelstein and Silberman 2001), but ultimately such studies are rooted in humanism as an outgrowth of exegetic literary analysis. Such archaeological area studies, while deeply informative about the past, often lack the generalizing perspective attached to anthropological and sociological theory and are firmly rooted in a humanistic epistemology, one that seeks to describe Great Traditions but not to explain them as phenomena of a universal human experience. On the other hand, North American and British approaches have been notably more directly influenced by social theory. And of this, much social theory, despite an era of functionalism and structuralism (1950s–1960s), has been dedicated to the explanation of culture change (e.g., Marx 1973, Steward 1968, Sahlins and Service 1960, Renfrew, 1973, Giddens 1979, Boyd and Richerson 1985, Knapp 1992, Sewell 1992, 1996).

Anthropology and sociology draw theoretical models from two great sources: history (historical materialism) and biology (evolution). Both models inimically and intrinsically focus on change, so there is little surprise that explanation of change, rather than explanation of continuity, has dominated explicitly scientific anthropological archaeology.

Pilgrimage and Household as Continuities

This book argues that long-term cultural continuities existed as Pilgrimage and Household in the Near East and that they have not been adequately recognized or described as meta-structures worthy of scientific, anthropological study. In the past, anthropologists have characterized practices like pilgrimages as "ritual" and have examined them in the context of studying ritual (ideology) and its role in social identity and history (Kelly and Kaplan 1990). Anthropologists have recognized a durability of ideas and have struggled to define what pilgrimage, as a ritual, really signifies. Ritual is "ancient and unchanging," yet it is dynamic and transposable as actors chose from a repertoire of forms to engage in present circumstances (Sahlins 1985, Gell 1992, Bell 1992, Kertzer 1988). It is difficult to classify ritual, and the effort has raised many questions. What is ritual and what is not? Is all social identity structured by ritual? Is ritual designed to assimilate the shocking, the disjunctive, and the paranormal violations of daily life (Boyer 2001, Burkert [1972] 1983, Mack 1987, Turner 1974a, 1974b)? Is ritual a universal of human experience (Van Gennep 1909, Eliade [1949] 1954)? Maurice Bloch (1989: 18) defined as ritual everything epiphenomenal to socioeconomy; then he argued that ritual does not matter to social life (Kelly and Kaplan 1990: 125). But others disagree and have sought in ritual the key organizing principles of social life (e.g., Durkheim 1915, Valeri 1985). Is ritual an ideology – a set of common ideas socially shared for the maintenance of social order (Leone 1982)? Is ritual practice (Bell 1992, Bourdieu [1972] 1977)? What about routine practices that structure social order, like living in houses and sharing food? How does one separate ritual from the practical (cf. Turner 1969)? Or should it be done at all (Bell 1992)?

These are interesting questions but not the ones that this book addresses. Such approaches to ritual have sidelined a larger issue that is the extremely long continuities of some cultural traditions – like pilgrimage – as meta-structures over long time frames and throughout major changes in process and history. This book focuses on such continuity and the problems in explaining it. Everyone recognizes something quintessentially Egyptian in the 3,000-year-old culture that flourished in the Nile valley and delta areas of modern-day Egypt, but Egyptologists seldom seem to feel a need to explain why Egyptian culture is distinct or why it continued for so long (cf. Wengrow 2006). That such continuity existed and can be readily appreciated through linguistic, iconographic, religious, and epigraphic traditions is evident in even the most casual visit to any museum gallery or textbook. Likewise Mesopotamia persisted as a civilization writing cuneiform and holding a "Great Tradition" of city-dwelling for about 3,000 years. Norman Yoffee (1988, 1993, 2005: 53–90) has made a persuasive case that changing political circumstances – the rise and collapse of empires and dynasties – cannot be viewed as a truncation of essential Mesopotamian culture. Yet of what abstract features did these civilizations consist? What made Mesopotamia recognizably Mesopotamian and Egypt Egyptian? That question has been largely overlooked by social and behavioral scientists obsessed with the explanation of culture change but can be addressed through understanding their core cultural meta-structures like Pilgrimage and Household.

This project therefore focuses on Pilgrimage and Household not only because they persist, but because they do so as enduring frameworks for social, economic, political, and ideological constitution despite changes in all these aspects. In some respects, Pilgrimage and Household resemble theoretical constructs of culture already identified – by Bourdieu ([1972] 1977: 72) as "structuring structures," by Giddens (1984: 35) as "institutions," and as "structures" in history (Sahlins 1985, 1981, Knapp 1992). But as revealed through archaeological analysis, the longevity of Pilgrimage and Household over more than 5,000 years and the evolution of complex societies are meta-structural beyond the intergenerational or even historical span envisioned by sociologists and anthropologists. As such, these meta-structures deserve a new nomenclature, which here is introduced and captures the epochal integrity of their duration (Chapter 7).

The Science of Culture

Of course a study of long-term cultural traditions has anthropological and historical precedence. In the first half of the last century, many explored the Great Traditions or Great Civilizations of world history (e.g., Spengler [1922] 1926, Kroeber 1944, Toynbee 1934–1954, Redfield [1955] 1967, Redfield in Singer 1974, Bagby 1959), usually setting them off from lesser, more primitive societies whose trajectories truncated or fed into present-day stagnations (Yoffee 2005, Service 1962). The criteria of what makes a Great Civilization have differed according to historian or epistemological bias (yet they always include Western European Civilization) (Bagby 1959: 159–182). With its long temporal reach, archaeology has unique potential to document and describe long-term cultural traditions, yet where archaeology follows anthropological and sociological theoretical agendas, it has focused on change. For the past half-century, anthropological archaeologists with a disciplinary commitment to a universal human condition have relied on neo-evolutionism (derived from the historical materialist model) and biological evolution to define their objects of study. Therefore, scientific archaeology has dismissed meta-structures, which do not change, as epiphenomenal and not significant explanatory factors of a universal human condition.

Are Pilgrimage, Household, and other meta-structures indeed worthy of such study? That they are becomes evident when one compares meta-structures across time and space, invoking the well-practiced observational science of cross-cultural comparison. This has long been an epistemological mainstay of anthropological method (e.g., Kroeber 1944, Murdock 1981, Trigger 2003). In contemporary scientific anthropology, long-term developmental cases drawn from archaeology have been compared to discriminate pattern from noise in the process of change. A cross-cultural comparative approach argues that the structural regularities underlying common patterns of change can be elucidated through comparison and that they reveal universal aspects of the human condition (Gibbon 1984: 311–312, e.g., Nichols and Charlton 1997, Trigger 1993, 2003, Joyce and Gillespie 2000, Yoffee and Cowgill 1988, Kirch 1994, Beck et al. 2007). For example, Bruce Trigger (1993, 2003) argued that Egypt and Mesopotamia emerged as different types of state – territorial and city – differentiated by underlying geopolitical frameworks in broader global patterns.

Nevertheless there remain long-term and distinctive continuities – usually discarded as noise – that differentiate these cultures into diversities not so easily parsed (cf. Trigger 2003: 658–661, Boyd and Richerson 1985: 95–116). One city-state is not like another. Although both were city-states, Mesopotamian culture cannot be confused with Greek; indeed the advent of Hellenism best defines the end of Mesopotamian civilization (Yoffee 1988, cf. 2005: 53). Too often the cross-cultural observational science approach discards as explanatorily irrelevant what appears as difference. The aesthetics that separate diverse cultures are usually left to the descriptive and emotive realm of humanistic studies. For example, both the Classic Maya and Sumerians inhabited competing city-states with wealth-based social hierarchies and extracted wealth from an agricultural surplus. It seemingly matters little in explaining the evolution of city-states that the Maya thought themselves made of corn or preferred textiles to tattoos while Mesopotamians descended from clay and attached little significance to the body alive or dead. Thus, anachronistic cultural adhesion to idiom has seemed but a quirk of historical inheritance, and as such belongs to the realm of culture studies but not to scientific explanatory anthropology.

A comparative approach is not everywhere averse to historical idiom (e.g., Kirch 1994). In biology, neo-Darwinian evolutionary ecology makes full use of comparison between similar ecosystems and shows that no ecosystem functioning, nor mutualistic interaction, nor adaptive trait, nor population diversity can be divorced from the influence of historical contingency (Gould 1986). The comparison of structurally comparable ecosystems has underscored the significance of history in explaining differences in organisms and in their natural contexts, as can be readily grasped from the many case studies of mediterranean-type ecosystems worldwide (Raven 1973, Aschmann and Bahre 1977, Mooney and Dunn 1970, Naveh 1975, Trabaud 1981, Pignatti 1979, McCorriston 1992). The point is not to suggest that cultures are like plants and animals but to emphasize the importance of historical constraints on the processes of change. One must recognize and treat as significant the historical traditions of cultures. In evolutionary ecology, history has infused environmental determinism with explanatory power, a point not lost in the historical ecology approaches in archaeology (Crumley 1994, Crumley and Marquardt 1987, Knapp 1992, Kirch 1994). Yet in many cross-cultural comparative studies, archaeologists have taken an alternative path, focusing not on the historical contingencies that explain differences but on the structural parameters that produce similar social frameworks. Historical contingency – wherein lies the continuity of ideas and cultural practices – is long overdue for similar scientific treatment in archaeology (Kirch and Green 2001: 1–9).

Some have turned the lens of cross-cultural comparison on cultural idiom. Observational methods of cross-cultural comparison pointed the way for Trigger (2003: 656–660) to recognize "idiosyncratic patterns" as a regularity of cultures. He explained these different cultural traditions with the observation drawn from evolutionary theory (Boyd and Richerson 1985: 95–116, 276) that they are ideas that change slowly because of the slower rate of change in preindustrial societies (e.g., Urban 2001) and that the ideas themselves were adaptive outcomes of selective processes. Despite its rich use of archaeological time frames, Trigger's study is nevertheless relatively static in its comparison of structure and detail in fully emerged and emergent states. What Trigger did not emphasize was that the archaeological record shows a duration of cultural traditions reaching far back to the Neolithic. Moreover, such duration may prove difficult to explain with theories of change. Nevertheless, the cross-cultural comparative method is a valuable approach and will be used here to study the problem of epochal meta-structure.

Explaining Continuity

This book compares meta-structures in Arabia and Mesopotamia under the nomenclature of Pilgrimage and Household (Chapters 5 and 6). When one engages in cross-cultural comparison of a long duration of ideas that is epochal and meta-structural, it becomes evident that there is indeed something worthy of anthropological study – that is, these are significant universal aspects of the human condition – but the very definition of *ethnoepochs* (Chapter 7) opens the problem of how to explain them. A new theoretical foundation apart from theory focused on change is essential if one is to understand the causality and meaning of such meta-structures.

Where will such a theoretical foundation be found? The second major point of this book is a theoretical one, arguing that one can only explain the persistence of long-term cultural idiosyncratic patterns – Pilgrimage and Household – through the approaches of landscape analysis. "Landscape" has been called "a usefully ambiguous term" (Gosden and Head 1994), and the multiple disciplinary contributions to landscape analysis are here acknowledged and embraced (Crumley 1994). Landscape by its very definition(s) across the social sciences and beyond embraces an interplay of space, time, and bodily experience. In this interplay, the notion of landscape interweaves temporal and spatial perspectives of differing scales (Knapp 1992, Tilley 1994) and is an appropriate starting point for understanding the adherence of specific Near Eastern societies to long-term cultural traditions.

The relatively long time frames of archaeological cultures call for long-term perspectives on cultural continuity not found in the ethnographic approaches of sociocultural anthropology. Of course there exists significant and diverse sociological and anthropological theory dedicated to explaining the maintenance and transmission of culture (e.g., Durkheim 1915, Bloch 1977, Bourdieu [1980] 1990, [1972] 1977, Giddens 1979, 1984, Boyd and Richerson 1985, Connerton 1989). One inevitable outcome of the short-term temporal perspective afforded by traditional ethnographic fieldwork and participant observation, the core tools of anthropological method, is that cultural transmission is for the most part dedicated to short-term maintenance and change. Consequently, long time frames are outside the perspective of the observer. It is one thing, and an essential one, to understand how practices and ideas are transmitted from one generation to another in the microcosm of an ethnographic experience. It is quite another, and yet not unrelated problem, to explain the persistence of culturally distinct worldviews across many thousands of years, a perspective that only unfolds, moreover, with archaeological study and time depth (e.g., Crumley and Marquardt 1987, Barker 1991, Kirch 1994, cf. Hodder 1990). One may suggest along scientific principles that processes observable in the short term are the only processes that may account for long-term cultural continuities, but such arguments have not been specifically advanced because the long-term cultural frameworks in question have not been widely recognized as phenomena requiring explanation. (Perhaps exceptionally, the question of whether "function" (that is, the necessities of maintaining societies) or "structure" (that is, the way the past shapes or controls the present) best accounts for long-term continuities has characterized debates about archaeologically manifest Pacific political systems (Kirch 1994, Kirch and Green 2001, Terrell 1986: 222).)

Where can theoretical explanations be found? It is possible to modify two sets of theory: poststructuralist theory and landscape theory (which in turn relies on poststructuralist theory). Landscape analysis does offer important insights for explaining long-term persistence in cultural diversities and continuities. The concept of landscape has generally been used as a tool or analytical approach in archaeology, often as the spatially organizing principle or perspective for field research and analytical description (e.g., Higgs and Vita-Finzi 1972, Butzer 1982, Cherry et al. 1991). Nevertheless landscape has a theoretical sense to which archaeology has been successfully applied (Crumley 1994, Kirch and Hunt 1997, Knapp 1992, Butzer 1996, Leone 1984, Anschuetz, Wilshusen, and Scheick 2001, Tilley 1994, Bradley 2006). This theoretical concept of landscape has the sense envisioned by Pierre Bourdieu ([1972] 1977: 72) when he defined "habitus" as the durable and transposable dispositions that generate and are reproduced by practice. The relationship between Bourdieu's habitus and landscape is largely but not entirely moderated by temporal parameters, an idea to be explored in greater detail. Chapter 7 introduces into theoretical nomenclature the term "ethnoepoch" to represent the essential temporal and especially cultural coherence of what *Annales* historian Ferdinand Braudel historically and empirically recognized as a qualitatively integral *"longue durée"* (Knapp 1992: 13). Braudel's ([1966] 1972) conceptual *longue durée* has been heuristically melded with landscape in archaeological approaches (e.g., Barker 1991, Kirch 1994, Butzer 1996), but there is good reason to insist upon a new terminology. Braudel's *longue durée* is objectively described and implies a universality of perception (Moreland 1992: 115), whereas an ethnoepoch is bodily translated, a quality fundamental to its long continuity.

Pilgrimage, Household, and the Social Constitution of Near Eastern Societies

To address the problem of how ethnoepochs endure while civilizations rise and fall, one must first describe and document some examples. In

Near Eastern context there existed very different and very important organizing frameworks that persisted through the emergence of social complexity. "Pilgrimage" and "Household" belong to a new nomenclature, and each term receives extensive treatment here. Definition and recognition of the long-term continuities of these cultural meta-structures are necessary foundations for explaining Near Eastern cultural diversity and its maintenance throughout long time periods, major social and political changes, and sustained contact with alien cultural groups. The core practice of Pilgrimage can be traced through the historical and archaeological records of Arabia from the Neolithic roots of Southern Arabia's early pastoral peoples. Household was for Mesopotamian society a strikingly different but equally long-lived cultural tradition. Pilgrimage and Household as distinctive, long-term, cultural meta-structures, seemingly enduring outside history, ultimately offer a significant approach to understanding the development of diverse complex societies across the Near East.

Pilgrimage is known the world over, but Near Eastern and specifically Arabian pilgrimage presents a distinct and enduring tradition that conveys through its very longevity an important insight into Near Eastern societies and cultural continuities. Among scholars, the significance of pilgrimage rites for the maintenance of human relationships with other humans was grasped over a century ago. In the late 1880s, religious scholars like Julius Wellhausen (1887) and William Robertson-Smith (1907a, [1885] 1907b) analyzed the religious texts of ancient Hebrew and other Western Semitic speakers in search of the cultural origins of Judeo-Christian religious practices. What their generation understood, so implicitly that they hardly mentioned it directly, was that pilgrimage with its attendant rites endured as a core religious tradition and ideological necessity throughout great social, economic, and political changes – including for Biblical scholars the emergence of a unified monarchy, rival Judean and Israelite kingdoms, Conquest, Exile, and the Messianic traditions culminating in Christianity.

That continuity in pilgrimage practices, well understood in theological and historical scholarship, has been nearly overlooked by anthropology. Archaeology does describe culture history and document cultural diversity past and present, albeit often through area studies and regional approaches largely unconcerned with scientific explanatory frameworks. Classical archaeology, Biblical archaeology, and indeed more recently Islamic archaeology, have embraced a largely descriptive and documentary approach to the societies of the ancient Near East. This approach, while invaluable to humanistic and historical perspectives, offers explanation neither for the maintenance of distinct historical patterns of cultural diversity nor for the long-term cultural continuities that sustain them.

But long-term cultural continuities are empirically evident. Pilgrimage rites have long persisted in Southern Arabia with traditions that continue to this day. For example, French epigrapher Jacqueline Pirenne traveled widely in the two Yemens of the revolutionary 1960s and 1970s, newly recording ancient rock-cut inscriptions and building an historical context for the materials surfacing from pioneering excavations of great Southern Arabian caravan cities. High up the Wadi Bayhān, stream source for the irrigated lands of Qataban's ancient capital at Timna, Pirenne (1991) discovered a notable inscription at the base of a solitary ("mammelon" or breast-shaped) conical outcrop. The inscription described the "'Arbay Āmm of Labakh," an epithet Pirenne interpreted as naming two tribal groups (the two 'Arb) who were entitled to the beneficence of the god of the place, Āmm of Labakh. That the inscription was carved in high Old South Arabian letters in a script few if any of the 'Arbay could actually read or replicate suggests the intervention of the Qatabanian ruler whose political power rested on the maintenance of tribal confederacies and reciprocal obligations between tribes and gods. Labakh represents the place name wherein Āmm may be visited on an annual basis. The Qatabanian state appropriated to itself through an inscribed declaration the authorization to visit the beneficence of Āmm of Labakh.

It was only on her second visit that Pirenne discovered the nature of that beneficence connecting the annual visit to Labakh by the 'Arbay to the deep-rooted traditions of Arabian pilgrimage. Climbing the mammelon, Pirenne espied against the skyline a line of betyls, once naturally upright standing stones deliberately toppled in iconoclasm as representations of the house of the god. Presumably there was Āmm with all attendant divinities, probably revered by tribes people millennia before Qatabanian authorization. One might, although Pirenne did not, even suggest that the mammelon itself was Āmm's natural betyl. (Mammelon is but an evocative term for an unattached rock mountain with rounded peak, a huge natural stone upright like Khuzmūm.) The beneficence of Labakh now lay spread before Pirenne, spring and pools and grazing land for flocks that she had not noted on her first visit. On that second visit she also saw the tents of modern Arabian pastoralists, possibly the descendents of the ancient 'Arbay, gathered closely in an annual visit to take in lush pastures and spring at a strategic season.

Pirenne recognized that the rural sanctuary at Labakh marked strategic resources that allowed tribes (the two 'Arb) to gather and furthermore that this even-then-ancient tradition had both been appropriated by the Qatabanian state and continues to this day. Pirenne never expressly referred to Pilgrimage. Yet the long-term practices of tribal gatherings and attendant religious rites (betyls, sacrifices, feasts) in the service of social maintenance (two 'Arb tribes peacefully convening, a gathering of usually scattered folk, their purported integration into the state) well exemplify the pattern of Pilgrimage that was and remains an organizing framework for Arabian societies. The roots of Pilgrimage can be found in the Arabian Neolithic, already evident in Neolithic ritual practices newly documented in recent excavations.

Household is a cultural tradition categorically like Pilgrimage, and it is well understood that Household practices served as an organizing framework for Mesopotamian societies. Excavations at the temple of Inanna at Nippur have revealed the plan of the late third-millennium BC sanctuary, the house of the goddess, including the apartments of administrative personnel, workshops and craft areas, and most important, a rare in situ temple archive of cuneiform-inscribed clay tablets complemented by more than a thousand associated administrative records dumped into the backfill of a Parthian foundation. An archaeological treasure trove, the find of a temple archive within the temple itself allowed an unprecedented view of the functioning of the household of the god and the political economy it represented (Zettler 1992, Pollock 1999, Postgate 1992), tied closely to the actual places the householders once trod. Excavations revealed the residential quarters of several generations of administrative personnel in a family connected to the secular ruling elites (Zettler 1992: 64–65, 72, 82–86, 200–213). Ovens for baking bread, weights and clay sealings for measure and authentication point to the administrative functions of the temple in supplying and allocating stored

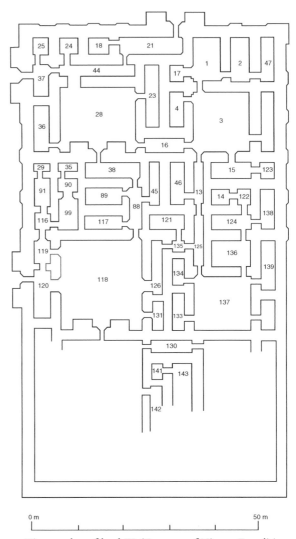

3. Ur III temple of Inanna at Nippur, plan of level IV. (Courtesy of Nippur Expedition, Oriental Institute)

grain. The storage of grain itself was attested in tablets (Zettler 1992: 59–62) and the rooms in which they were found. The archive abandoned in the northeastern sector of excavations details the administrative oversight by the family of Ur-Meme in the last centuries of the third millennium BC (Ur III period). From these and similar accounts, Assyriologists have learned the exact offerings to the gods and goddesses, how and where grain was stored in temple storehouses, how much wool and flax were woven into textiles, how much barley and cloth were rationed to workers, how many animals were maintained for the god's household, how the temple distributed or loaned its resources including silver, land access, and consumables, the holdings and working of temple land, and how many people labored in the temple confines and what work they performed.

This labor was performed by participants in the god's or goddess's household, which was a social milieu physically symbolized by the temple itself. The temple provided rations to designated millers, brewers, bird catchers, singers, doorkeepers, courtyard sweepers, reed workers, leather workers, fullers, potters, carpenters, weavers (women), plowmen, ox-drivers, gardeners, water carriers, sheep-pen workers, herdsmen, shepherds, grass carriers, guards, watchmen, temple workers, orphans, blind, elderly, given, and slave individuals (Zettler 1992: 158–160). Belonging in households was something Mesopotamians understood, for the practice and its significance for the identity of individuals and social groups stretched far back in time before the differentiation of Mesopotamian society into class groups based on access to material resources (Diakonoff 1991, 1975). By the time that the secular rulers of Mesopotamian cities vied for power through public demonstration of their support for city gods and the physical institutions supporting the god's maintenance, belonging to the household of a god was already an ancient device. In a famous limestone plaque now in the Louvre, Ur-Nanshe, ruler of Lagash, was shown carrying a basket of mud to rebuild the temple. The ruler thus derived and demonstrated ruling authority through participation in the god's household. As the physically and symbolically largest participant in the reconstruction of the god's house, Ur-Nanshe used such self-representation to proclaim his membership with other citizenry in the social institution that linked Lagash dwellers and at the same time his hierarchical status as first citizen.

Inhabited by the rich and the poor, free and not-free, rulers and ruled, Mesopotamian cities were home to people knit into a shared society of the god's household and performance of temple service, for which they received rations or access to land or both. The practice mirrored social obligations in kin-related households into which people were born in families. This fits few definitions of "ritual" and underscores the mundane nature of much socially-constituting practice (Bloch 1989, Giddens 1984). Scholars differ over the relative significance of temple society as a political and economic sector of Mesopotamian states at any one or different time periods (e.g., Pollock 1999, Stone 2000, Renger 1995, Van de Mieroop

4. Limestone relief of Ur-Nanshe of Lagash (Early Dynastic III) building the temple (household of a god) and participating in a banquet around 2500 BC. © Erich Lessing/ Art Resource, New York.

1997). Sometimes, in some places, the temple was more significant than others, but the temple household was without doubt an ever-present and influential idea in social constitution.

Just as Pilgrimage was not new to Arabian states, so did Household exist long before the mud of Mesopotamia was shaped to temple bricks in cities. The roots of Household as an organizing principle for social constitution lay in the Near Eastern Neolithic and most specifically in village societies dwelling in some of the first multigenerational houses of all time. It is now possible to trace the long-term continuity of Household practice over at least 5,000 years in the Fertile Crescent. Such a long time frame captures the endurance of cultural tradition across regional and temporal sequences in a way that only archaeology can do. Much detail has necessarily been abbreviated, culled, and summarized as the only possible approach to the rich archaeological data of Levantine-Mesopotamian pre-history. The cases examined here show that Household was a persistent practice and dominant paradigm for societies, even those practicing – as may have indeed been the case – pilgrimages to special places at special times. Pilgrimage societies could and did live in houses and maintain households. The point here is that in different cultural traditions in the Near East, Pilgrimage and Household long persisted as the dominant practical framework for social constitution and did so in spite of the massive social changes that have captured the attention of anthropological archaeology.

Ethnoepochal Meta-Structures

Archaeological inquiry needs to be expanded to cover meta-structure like Pilgrimage and Household, as described in the following chapters. Much of what this book will accomplish is simply to point out the existence of ethnoepochs and argue that while not changing over long time frames they nevertheless continue to function as socially constituting frameworks. In their unchanging aspects, they defy the assumptions of functionalism (Radcliffe-Brown 1952, 1958), while in their bodily translation, they are practically transmitted structures (e.g., Sahlins 1981, 1985) of previously unrecognized duration. If such meta-structures are common to all cultures, as seems to have been nevertheless grasped by earlier anthropologists and historians lacking the long perspectives afforded by archaeological evidence, poststructural theory suggests that they are subjectively perceived. But poststructural theory alone has not provided sufficient time depth to grasp and explain enduring meta-structures. Those who study long-term structure (e.g., Sahlins 1985, 1995, Braudel [1966] 1972) are stuck with the tools of ethnography and written history and try to explain it through devices and processes that have a short-term range and short-term view (e.g., Bourdieu [1972] 1977, [1980] 1990, Giddens 1984). It is like looking at an elephant with a microscope.

If meta-structures – ethnoepochs – exist, then a historical-materialist model with its focus on change brought about through dialectic tension in structural contradictions (material and ideological), offers incomplete explanatory power for meta-structures that endure across dialectic change. The model emphasizes both change and shared (objective) perception. These are both conditions that seem incompatible with ethnoepochal meta-structures, for if "the past is a foreign country," which one can hardly understand (Hartley in Knapp 1992: 9), then shared perception among ancients and their successors seems incredible over five millennia. Furthermore, if change is the outcome of dialectical incompatibilities, then how can one explain the persistence of core institutions across change, the persistence of structure outside of history? Ethnoepoch embraces a longer cultural context than the *structure-event-structure* of history (e.g., Sahlins 1985, Knapp 1992) and resists definition using the language of change. The conundrum of how ethnoepochs outside history coexist with history (change) is an important problem that can only be addressed once the subject of its inquiry – an archaeologically evident long duration of core ideas and practices – is fully recognized. Pilgrimage and Household over five millennia require new synthesis and new theoretical explanation in Near Eastern archaeology.

CHAPTER 2

WHY PILGRIMAGE?

In Jerusalem, and I mean within the ancient walls,
I walk from one epoch to another without a memory
to guide me.

Mahmoud Darwish [2003] 2007

Anthropological Approaches to Pilgrimage

Pilgrimage is a journey to a sacred place to participate in a system of sacred beliefs. The experience of pilgrimage can be both temporary – a punctuation in linear or cyclic time – and a transformation associated with life passages (including but by no means limited to healing, death, or metaphorical rebirth). Pilgrimage entails a spiritual quest and is in its essence an ideological phenomenon, but pilgrimage can also enable economic and social transactions with the constitution of a community of pilgrims and the encounters of a physical journey. Because there are so many dimensions to the practice and experience of pilgrimage around the world, pilgrimage as a phenomenon has a wide literature ranging across religious studies, geography, anthropology, sociology, history, psychology, political science, and literature. Geographers have sought to characterize the spatial and temporal dimensions of pilgrimage with studies of sacred space and the circulation of people to and from them (Deffontaines 1948, Sopher 1967, Park 1994). The great pilgrimages of Christianity, Hinduism, and Islam have attracted much study and commentary (Rinschede and Sievers 1987, Shair and Karan 1979, Shair 1979, King 1972, Rutter 1929, Sopher 1987, Morinis 1984, Nolan and Nolan 1997, Elsner and Rutherford 2005), both from dispassionate observers and in the narratives of pilgrims themselves (Ibn al-Mujawir [1204/5–1291/2] 1986, Ibn Baṭūṭah, [d. 1354] 1971, Burton 1964, Doughty [1936] 1979, Kinglake [1888] 1908, Morton 1964). There are also lesser pilgrimages, which attract fewer people, are reiterative, and attach to a wide diversity of events and places (e.g., Dubisch 2004, Prorok 1997, Eickelman 1976, Eickelman and Piscatori 1990).

Pilgrimage crosscuts disciplinary boundaries and has geographical, historical, sociocultural, economic, psychological, and religious dimensions (Preston 1992: 42). Chaucer's well-known *Canterbury Tales* captures some of the essential experiences of pilgrimage, including the constitution of a temporary society of pilgrims, the individual motivations for pilgrimage, the convergence of pilgrims at one place, and the new context for economic exchange that pilgrimage fosters. Chaucer's fictive pilgrims met in April at The Tabard Inn in London's Southwark at the start of a walking and riding journey to Canterbury's shrine of St. Thomas à Becket. Chaucer goes to some length to describe the differences among the pilgrims – some are elites (the Knight, the Squire, the Prioress), some from the burgher and guild class (the Merchant, the Haberdasher, the Dyer, the Carpenter, the Skipper, the Weaver, the Carpetmaker), and a Plowman represents the agricultural laboring class (which could not, as serfs, usually choose a pilgrimage). All are differentiated by tastes, mannerisms, and piety. Their Host enjoins them to embark upon a storytelling competition, for which there will be economic consequences (a prize) and which provides the vehicle for Chaucer's social commentary (Chaucer [Coghill] 1977).

Chaucer's device brings together disparate members of society with common purpose and highlights both the temporary society of pilgrims and their social discourse (Wheeler 1999). The new and temporary society more than any other dimension of a pilgrimage experience (e.g., healing, transformation and life process, the physical journey) links the ideological and ritual practice of pilgrimage to its cultural context and most appropriately concerns us as we examine the leitmotif of pilgrimage constituting Arabian social and economic life through the ages.

Religion, Society, and Pilgrimage

Pilgrimage is a ritual found in the practice of religious belief and its social and economic effects must be understood foremost in this context. In anthropology, the greatest theoretical contributions to understanding the significance of pilgrimage in human societies stem from the works of Émile Durkheim, Victor Turner, and, as we shall see later, Pierre Bourdieu. Only Turner explicitly addresses pilgrimage itself, and none of these are works rooted in ethnographic studies of pilgrimage. (Turner's work came from visits – but not as a pilgrim – to pilgrimage centers and historical/literature studies of medieval and modern Christian pilgrimage contrasted with his own ethnography in tribal initiation rites.) Such ethnographic work on pilgrimage itself has provided a powerful critique and informative empirical context for testing their ideas.

While not specifically addressing pilgrimage, Durkheim wrote extensively about religion and its relationship to society and social order. Arguing that the socially shared representations of elements like time and space trump individual perception and intellect, Durkheim (1915: 28–31) placed higher emphasis on the social condition of human existence than on the individual in understanding culture. Therefore understanding the working of social life and the consciousness born out of social existence is the best key to understanding the range of cultural diversity in religious practice. Durkheim (1915: 16) explicitly rejected the notion that one could explain differences in religion by tracing historical threads of development from a putative and unproven original (and universal) concept like animism. Instead, he argued that religions, and by inference religious practices, all play the same role in human societies regardless of the differing details of practices across different cultures. Through cross-cultural comparative method and recognizing common elements in different religions, Durkheim identified the function of religion as affirming social allegiances and codes by worshiping society itself in the metaphor of divinity. As Victor Turner (1974a: 57) put it, "in the last analysis, men have never worshipped anything but their own society." Durkheim maintained that "religion is something eminently social" (1915: 22) and that the causes of religious thought and practice are situated within the social constitution and social conformity of human existence.

This essentially functionalist approach has some important implications for understanding the ideological phenomenon of pilgrimage and its relationship to economic and social dimensions of culture. If ritual practices "function to strengthen the bonds attaching a believer to his god, i.e., to his society, since god is only a figurative representation of society" (Durkheim 1915: 257–258), then pilgrimage reflects and strengthens existing social bonds. In Arabian societies organized and maintained through the metaphor of segmentary kin-based lineages (as "tribes"), ritual practices, including pilgrimage, would therefore serve to reify and express community of tribe and clan. As others have argued (Evans Pritchard 1940: 142–150, Gellner 1969, Caton 1990, Lancaster and Lancaster 1999a: 56–68) such allegiances are contextual and, like pilgrimages, can coalesce a large social group into a common identity not expressed in mundane practice. Of course explaining how pilgrimage functions explains neither its origins (Boyer 2001: 23–28) nor the motivations behind why people practice pilgrimage from one generation to the next.

Other anthropologists have examined pilgrimage as "an enactment of the social order" (Morinis 1984: 246–249). By the act of people performing pilgrimage and associated rituals that reflect their social roles, the drama of pilgrimage can reinforce those roles, as in cases in Sri Lanka (Obeyesekere 1966), the Central Andes (Sallnow 1981), and Naples (Lahti 1994) and, significantly, in Muslim minor pilgrimages in Morocco (Eickelman 1976) and Palestine (Hecht and Friedland 1996). Pilgrimage can manifest and strengthen close association between the political order (kings) and divine order, thereby shoring up political authority. In several cases, political authority has invested itself through the appropriation and monopoly of religious places, relics, or roles associated with pilgrimage (e.g., Hecht and Friedland 1996: 342). By projecting state authority over or incorporating sacred places or objects of pilgrimage into state iconographies and identities, the social norms are re-affirmed to maintain the state (Morinis 1984: 247, Kertzer 1988). Pilgrimage can serve as an integrating force for national identity (Wolf 1958), the enactment of national ideology. But we are still left with the task of explaining the participation of non-elites in pilgrimage as it becomes the locus of elite authority.

A different contribution to understanding the relationships between social order and pilgrimage comes from the work of Victor Turner and Edith Turner, whose model of pilgrimage was based on medieval and modern Christian pilgrimages contrasted with tribal initiation rituals.

Turner argued that pilgrimage was a social process in which the actors leave their secular social contexts and conjoin in a new "communitas," an antisociety that breaks with society and that is at once simple, egalitarian, and transitional (1977:24, 1974a: 202, 243, Turner and Turner 1978:32). Pilgrimage is a voluntary break with social order and is marked by "liminality," a mid-transition in a rite of passage in which none of the familiar cultural markers (including social hierarchies) apply (Turner and Turner 1978: 249). Turner's model therefore emphasizes the opposition between social structure and the "potentially subversive" antistructure of communitas (1974a: 32, 1974b: 317). Always latent with social structure, communitas emerges full-blown in pilgrimage, making the pilgrimage process an important locus for social change.

Although I ultimately reject most of Turner's Christianity-based model (as have many anthropologists working on other pilgrimage contexts after Turner), Turner's contributions have been highly influential and merit paraphrasing here. The Turners' work has served especially to provoke examination of the social milieu of pilgrimage, setting the pilgrimage process aside from its geographic qualities of time and space. Turner's model affirms the potential of pilgrimage to constitute new social bonds but rejects the notion that pilgrimage enacts an existing social order. The model emphasizes a break with social order and a break with individual life experience.

Turner's work emerged from his interest in ritual, its association with rites of passage (Turner 1974a: 47, Winkelman and Dubisch 2005: xii), and a rejection of Durkheim's ideas on the relationship between society and religious practices. Turner (1974a: 43, 269) charged that Durkheim's method had "limited itself to a-temporal forms and structures, to the products of man's social activity abstracted from the processes in which they arise, and having arisen, which they channel to a varying extent." Durkheim's concept that society in essence worships itself "never had much appeal to the mass of ordinary mankind" (Turner 1974a: 57), which embraces and even creates new foci of sacred pilgrimage in a post-medieval world of scientific rationalism. In studying these emerging symbolic systems, Turner instead emphasizes the multiple meanings of ritual symbols and especially the ways in which they instigate social action (Turner 1974a: 55, Turner and Turner 1978: 245). Where Durkheim's approach is highly functional and static, Turner manifests an interest in process and temporal change and conceives the ritual as a safe template for change.

One might characterize Turner's concept of temporal change (processualism) as stepwise. Processualism engages a social drama that can move society from one institutionalized social structure to another or can stabilize social order through the venting of conflict (Turner 1974a: 44, 237–238). This social drama has four constituent phases, the third of which, "redressive action," engages mechanisms like pilgrimage and the performance of public ritual to ease the crisis in norm-governed social relations (Turner 1974a: 37–42). During redressive action, society is in a transition phase, experiencing liminality as spontaneous, existential, homogeneous society and iconoclastic counterculture (Turner and Turner 1978: 237, 250–251). An antisociety, communitas, is then required to pass to phase four, "reintegration" or resolution (Turner 1974a: 41, 48). Recognizing their emphasis on conflict, social drama, antisociety, and communitas, one might observe that the Turners experienced the social upheavals of the American 1960s (for example, students occupied the Administration Building at the University of Chicago and campus buildings at Cornell University) and that the appearance of the commune, counterculture hippies, and free love is clearly reflected in their model of pilgrimage as a fundamentally social process.

Although the phenomenon of pilgrimage conjoins Turner's interests in processual units (social drama), social antistructure (communitas), and the semantics of religious symbols (Turner 1974a: 166), it is the concept of communitas that most closely concerns us here. Communitas is a "bond uniting . . . people over and above any formal social bonds" (Turner 1974a: 45 quoting Znaniecki 1936). Communitas at the same time implies a new social formation – a communion of pilgrims with its implicit qualities of egalitarian, temporary, undifferentiated social status – as it revolts against the old. Communitas as antisociety in its structural opposition to social order is difficult to reconcile with the notion of Arabian pilgrimage practice as constituting and reaffirming notions of social order.

But it turns out that communitas need not always be experienced as a full disruption of normal social order. Turner (1974a: 49, 1974b: 325, Turner and Turner 1978: 252) defines different types of communitas, among them "normative" communitas, as "the attempt to capture and preserve 'spontaneous' communitas in a system of ethical precepts and legal rules." Spontaneous communitas is something everyone has someway encountered and is "richly charged" and "pleasurable" and conveys a feeling of "endless power" (Turner and Turner 1978: 251). Under conditions of normative communitas, the group [of pilgrims] is organized into a community that strives toward the experience of communitas while observing ethical and legal codes that ensure its continuity as a community (Turner 1974a: 169). A number of the Christian pilgrimages express normative communitas (Turner and Turner 1978: 196), as do many formally organized pilgrimages worldwide. Furthermore, social order is not always upended in pilgrimage: Turner himself (1974a: 171) cites a Hindu pilgrimage in which "the distinctions of caste are maintained during the pilgrimage journey" and the notion of communitas as an ideal paradigm in the Islamic *ummah* (Turner and Turner 1978: 191).

Others have iterated this as critique. As ethnographies of pilgrimage have proliferated, anthropologists have noted many instances where pilgrimage activities offer a theatre to enact the fractious and contested social relations of participant communities and individuals (e.g., Sallnow 1981, Eade and Sallnow 1991, Wheeler 1999) as well as to enact a social order (Morinis 1984: 246–249, Lahti 1994). Part of the problem is a notion that there even exists one established social order or dominant discourse (Wheeler 1999: 28) as assumed by Turner and Durkheim. The Turners applied a theoretical framework of social process (social drama) to their analysis of pilgrimage, but their model shoehorns pilgrimage and social change into a rigid structure (Sallnow 1981: 179, Winkelman and Dubisch 2005: xiii). If the structure is not universally valid, then its components, including communitas, are equally particularistic and therefore lack theoretical universality. Instead of communitas, Wheeler (1999: 29) suggests that contestatory and competing discourses are "confluent" on pilgrimage so that pilgrim groups accept – even judge – difference and commonality in common space and the connective community that pilgrimage offers.

Other critiques have emerged, also from the wider contexts of pilgrimage offered through fieldwork in different religions and culture. A range of individual motivations may prompt people to go on pilgrimage (Morinis 1984: 249–255, 1992: 9), only one of which may be a "desire to experience the religious communities of the shrine" (Rinschede and Sievers 1987: 215). Inductive study of numerous cases of pilgrimage also shows that there are significant dimensions unexplored by Turner, including healing (Dubisch and Winkelman 2005), individual motivations, tourism (Cohen 1992), and the territorial and economic arrangements that pilgrims and pilgrimage negotiate.

Most cases do not conform to the Turners' (1978: 17–18) fourfold classification of (Christian) pilgrimages based on time periods. Morinis (1992a: 10) suggests a new typology that considers different pilgrimage practices, including "normative" pilgrimage, one that "takes place as part of a ritual cycle, either life or calendrical celebrations." Journeys to a sacred center (Cohen 1992: 50, Eliade [1949] 1954: 12–17) engage geography and the notion of a socially constructed landscape in which the convergence of pilgrims into a new, if temporary, physical community in socially sanctified space constructs a new, if temporary, society. In this sense, I will argue that group solidarity is a very important aspect of the pilgrimage, albeit quite different from communitas and always negotiated in discourse with individual and factional identities.

Another problematic component of Turner's model lies in the assumed dichotomy between tribal initiation and (Christian) pilgrimage (1974b: 367), an outcome of structuralist classificatory analytical method.

> I distinguish pilgrimage from initiation as a locus of liminality by saying that it is like many features of life in large-scale, complex societies, rooted in optation, in voluntariness, whereas initiation is founded in obligatoriness, in duty. Initiations fit best in societies with ascribed status, pilgrimages in those where status may not only be achieved but also rejected. In tribal societies men and women have to go through rites of passage transferring them from one state and status to another: in post tribal societies of varying complexity and degree of development of the social division of labor, people can choose to go on pilgrimage. This is true even when . . . pilgrimage was held to be of obligation; a variety of mitigating circumstances and get-out clauses made pilgrimage virtually a matter of optation rather than of duty. (Turner 1977: 29)

The analytically derived structural differentiation between initiation rites and pilgrimage has other oppositional qualities besides the voluntary-obligatory one. Pilgrimage is hazardous; initiation rites are protected. Pilgrimage is motion; initiation is stasis. Pilgrimage liminalizes time; initiation liminalizes space (Turner 1977: 31). The analysis is overtly – and overly – structural.

A classificatory dichotomy between tribal initiation and pilgrimage severely inhibits anthropology's understanding of pilgrimage and its role in social negotiation and identity. Turner himself (1974a: 175) recognized the blurring of voluntary and obligatory motivation over the history of specific pilgrimages, calling into question the historical and temporal relationship between voluntary and obligatory ritual forms. One may stem from and intersect with the other in a generative historical process that may in some instances lead from tribal rites to pilgrimage practice, perhaps even at the same sacred spot. I will argue in a later chapter that this was probably the case in ancient Arabia.

Furthermore, Turner's conceptualization of initiation rites closely followed the model stemming from the work of Mircea Eliade and Arnold van Gennep, which marries a mystical death and resurrection to the articulation of the life cycle in stages, producing a widely applied presumption that initiation rites involve a transition, or liminal stage, before symbolic rebirth into new status is achieved (Grimes 2000: 100–105). Numerous case studies have shown that this model lacks universality and is perhaps only best suited to Australian Aboriginal male practices (Grimes 2000: 131). Liminality, it would seem, is not for everyone.

No one would consider the Turners' work bankrupt: it has had enormous influence in the field of ritual studies. But it rests upon a conceptualization of processualism as change in the prevailing social order of societies. This definition in turn serves as the foundation for Turner's particular interest in and model of pilgrimage. Such conceptualization of change retains little interest in a postmodern and poststructural disciplinary focus (a) that contests that there should be one perceived social order, (b) that disputes that societies transition from one order to the next, (c) that rejects a universalizing structural divide between social and antisocial order, and d) that negates that social groups widely share the same meaning for specific symbols.

For the purposes of this study, I therefore emphasize the enduring association between pilgrimage and society and especially recognize the incontrovertible fact that once engaged in the pilgrimage process, pilgrims form new social groupings that "honor both the division and the connection between individuals and their larger communities" (Wheeler 1999: 29). I disagree most strongly therefore with the concept of communitas, preferring instead to recognize a potential for new social constitution and enactment of existing social discourse. I also reject Turner's structural opposition of tribal initiation and pilgrimage, for as we shall see, the one can grow into the other in historical context.

Pilgrimage and Economic Transactions

One aspect largely ignored by Turner's studies of pilgrimage but quite evident in anecdotal accounts, subsequent ethnographies, and wider literature is the integration of economic transactions in pilgrimage practice. Chaucer's Pardoner – peddler of faked relics and indulgences – is a greasy character whose venal motivations and equally unflattering physical description embody Christian professed ideals against mixing worldly wealth and divine grace. And yet the character of the Pardoner epitomizes an inevitable intersection of economic and religious practice. More often than not, economic activity and significant socioeconomic transactions are enabled during pilgrimage. Such activity is seldom anathematized even in Christian tradition and may be celebrated and openly acknowledged as an important motivation and outcome of pilgrimage.

Medieval pilgrim fairs, a Catholic tradition reproduced in contemporary Mexican pilgrimages, drew not only pilgrims with professed religious devotion but also dance and theatre troupes, peddlers, traders, and vendors (Turner and Turner 1978: 36–37, 98) and allowed taverns and inns to prosper. In the relict Christmas markets sponsored in Cathedral squares all across modern France, one can still detect the fair tradition associated with high holy days. Pilgrims were an attractive source of additional revenue for the townsfolk and way-stations that sponsored them, for pilgrims often carry sufficient coin or goods to finance a journey. Under Ottoman rule, the annual pilgrim caravans departing Damascus and Egypt traveled with military escort to deter bedouin attacks, motivated in large part by the wealth in caravan baggage (Shair and Karan 1979: 600, King 1972: 65), and the surrounding populations of Damascus profited from the rental and sale of camels and provisions (Barbir 1980: 187, 198, Rafeq 1987: 129–130). Elite Crusaders – essentially militant pilgrims en route to Jerusalem at the end of the eleventh century (Edbury and Rowe 1988: 152) – crossed Byzantium and Anatolia with coin and assets to pay for provisions en route. Once ensconced in the Holy Land, they quickly discovered the

5. The annual Christmas market before Rouen Cathedral (France). Photo by Manuel Clerc.

economic benefits of pilgrimage (Bowman 1992: 163). To medieval hajjis (Muslim pilgrims) in Mecca, the profusion and diversity of exotic goods brought by pilgrims across the (wide) Islamic world was especially striking. One finds abundant Persian carpets in Damascus, brought and sold by Iranian Shia pilgrims to finance pilgrimage deflected from Iraq's holy sites to Syria's as an outcome of modern politics. There are hundreds if not thousands of other examples of the economic transactions and flow of goods fostered by pilgrim traffic.

Significantly, the economic opportunities presented by pilgrimage resonate not only with pilgrims themselves, but with the sponsors and residents of sacred sites. Although Wheatley (1971: 225–226) and Mumford (1961) argued that cities began as sacred centers and the Turners' emphasis on liminality would seem to suggest that pilgrim centers should be set apart from secular concerns (Eliade [1949] 1954: 12–18, Sopher 1997: 183), geographers have resoundingly argued that pilgrimage centers defy easy

6. "Pilgrims Going to Mecca," Léon Belly, 1861. Réunion des Musées Nationaux/Art Resource, New York.

spatial classification such as center and periphery (Park 1994: 250–253, Bhardwaj 1973, Sopher 1987). Cities may not have begun as sacred centers but could quickly appreciate the economic benefits that accrue to becoming one. Medieval cities competed to build imposing cathedrals – Amiens and Beauvais vying to outdo each other for the highest nave – and to stock them with sacred relics (which attract pilgrims). The incentives for such efforts, while rhetorically emphasizing devotion, stewardship, and divine protection, also included economic prosperity, a link not lost on the wealthy burghers who consecrated funds to the building of a city's cathedral.

Mecca, locus of Haj, the paramount pilgrimage in Islam, apparently enjoyed modest prosperity and very little nonpilgrimage trade as one of Arabia's many pre-Islamic centers (Crone 1987). This was to change dramatically with the influx of medieval hajjis (King 1972: 64), and in the early twentieth century, before the advent of oil revenues, the influx of wealth with pilgrims was the economic mainstay of the nascent Saudi Kingdom (King 1972: 67, 71). (The Kingdom now spends more than it takes in to support Haj and lesser pilgrimage; Saudi Arabia derives great prestige as the host country to Islam's most sacred shrines (King 1972, Noakes 1999)). There has always been a link between devotions at and around Mecca and the economic benefits that accompany an influx of pilgrims. Today catering to the needs of pilgrims employs about 16 percent of the area's labor force (Rowley 1997: 147) and draws volunteer and part-time labor from across the Kingdom. Although pre-Islamic trade at Mecca was insignificant compared to other Arabian cities, the pre-Islamic rituals were accompanied by an annual trade fair that remained an important aspect of early Islamic Haj (Lammens 1926: 143, 147–148). Kister (1980: 37–38) argues that pre-Islamic tribes refrained from trade activities during their pilgrimage and that trade was expressly permitted as an innovation of Islam, but the texts in question (ritual prayers) may also be read as emphases on the devotional aspects of pilgrimage rather than prohibition of trade. Temporary markets were and are significant in many lesser and pre-Islamic pilgrimages throughout Arabia.

The economic benefits that accompany pilgrimage constitute an important aspect of this study because as we shall see, ancient Arabian states attracted pilgrims for and with both religious and economic reasons. The intertwined socioeconomic activities and devotional aspects of pilgrimage can be traced throughout Arabian history and pre-history as a leitmotif for the constitution of Arabian society.

Muslim Pilgrimages: Haj and *Ziyārāt*

Pilgrimage constitutes a significant religious practice for all Muslims as one of the five pillars of faith and as a social and economic activity in a variety of Muslim contexts and cultures today. The diversity of lesser Muslim pilgrimages in Iran, Morocco, India, and Turkey for example (e.g., Eickelman and Piscatori 1990) lies beyond the scope of this study. Here we are concerned with the long history and pre-history of Arabian pilgrimages, both the major pilgrimage to Mecca, Haj, and local visits, or *ziyārāt*. These pilgrimages have been practiced through Islamic and pre-Islamic times, and their histories demonstrate that in Arabia, ritual practices were fused and syncretized to new cultural expressions, retaining as the wellspring of new pilgrimage the chrysalis of the old.

7. Haj pilgrims stoning the devil at Minā. Courtesy of Samia El-Moslimany/Saudi Aramco World/SAWDIA.

Haj is the greater Muslim pilgrimage, arriving in Mecca in the Islamic (lunar) month of *Dhū al-Ḥijjah* and ideally accomplished at least once in each Muslim's lifetime. As the site of the *Ka'bah*, a pre-Islamic shrine revered in Islam as the sanctuary built by Ibrahim (Abraham) (Thayer 1992: 170, Lammens 1926: 51, 56, 68–69) (also ascribed in pre-Islamic times to Adam (Kister 1980: 45)), Mecca is the holiest of Islamic shrines. Muslim practice of Haj involves a series of rites that take place over six days after pilgrims arrive in Mecca. Haj is definitively different from the lesser Muslim pilgrimage to Mecca, *'Umrah*, which is not obligatory and involves different rites (Din and Hadi 1997: 163, Rowley 1997: 144), probably deriving from separate pre-Islamic practices for separate townsfolk and bedouin (Lammens 1926: 167–169, 1919: 64, Peters 1994: 32, Chelhod 1955: 65).

Upon arrival, hajjis don a pair of white unstitched cloths to signify their state of *iḥrām* (ritual consecration). Henceforth until the end of Haj, the pilgrim neither shaves nor combs hair and abstains from sexual contact. Nowadays shelter and transportation are organized on a massive scale to permit the movement of millions of pilgrims across the Meccan

8. Muslim pilgrims circling the *Ka'bah* (Mecca). Kazuyoshi Normachi/Corbis.

landscape, for the next few days require extensive journeying back and forth from Mecca itself. On the second day, pilgrims arrive in 'Arafāt before midday, perform the midday prayer, and spend the afternoon standing (*wuqūf*) in prayer facing Mecca. After sunset, the pilgrims move again, this time to Musdalifah and a new set of campsites (Rowley 1997: 144).

On day three, the pilgrims move again, this time to nearby Minā where they symbolically stone the devils by throwing a set number of pebbles at three stone pillars. Pilgrims then perform Al Ādkhā, the Sacrifice, when all Muslims (whether performing Haj or at home) who can afford it sacrifice an animal in commemoration of God's substitution of a ram for Abraham's sacrifice. Meat is distributed to the poor – accomplished today through a massive meat-packing facility in the Saudi Kingdom. There remains the *tawwāf* (circling) of the *Ka'bah* at Mecca, kissing the black stone within *Ka'bah*, and a ritual commemoration of Hagar's frantic efforts to find water for Ismael (pilgrims running to and from the sacred well of Zamzam, which was revealed by Allah for Hagar and Ismael) (Rowley 1997: 144). Most of these practices were syncretized and adapted to Islamic Haj from preexisting polytheistic rites (Peters 1994, Lammens 1926, 1919).

Muslims returning from Haj speak of the transcendent experience of pilgrimage, setting aside earthly comfort (it is hot, most do not bathe, some pilgrims die from heat exhaustion or crushing crowds) and status to express common identity as members of a single Muslim society in which social ties and commonalities overwhelm individuality and differences. Although women hajjis commonly retain their national or traditional dress (providing appropriately modest covering), men doff outward signs of status and ethnic affiliation in deliberate enactment of *tawḥīd*, which professes at the same time the Oneness of Allah and the harmony of the Faithful. No jewelry is worn, and pilgrims carry no money – the Haj experience recognizes no rich or poor man. During Haj, pilgrims enact a social and political ideal. *Tawḥīd* showcases, albeit briefly, an ever-present social identity common to all Muslims and through which they affirm a common social constitution. Many non-Muslims (including those who advocate transformation of Islamic societies into Western-style democracies) forget that Islam is the sociopolitical system commanded by Allah as governance for Believers. Haj enacts this system through its subvention of individuality to social order, the leveling and suppression of wealth and status, and the provision for the poor through the bounty of sacrificed meat. Pan-Muslim society is at once enacted and established through the practice of Haj by pilgrims from all over the Islamic world.

Of course there have been changes to the Haj journey in the course of nearly 1,400 years. The journey itself, with its motif of motion (physical, metaphorical, and ideological) constitutes an important aspect of pilgrimage (Coleman and Eade 2004: 16–17) and, in the case of Haj, has been transformed by political, geographical, and technological factors over the ages. In the earliest years of Islam, Haj principally attracted pilgrims drawn from the non-urban Arabian bedouin (Lammens 1926: 164) who traveled on foot or mounted on camels and other animals. From Tangiers to Tashkent, by the medieval era, Haj drew widely upon multiple cultures, languages, and sects, whose principal encounter with the Other occurred during pilgrimage as confluent self-identification within the Muslim *ummah*, or community of believers. From the time of the Umayyids, Damascus served as the official collecting point for the Syrian caravan, and under Mameluke and Ottoman rulers, caravan campgrounds and facilities were both institutionalized and improved as state projects (Burns 2005: 205, 211, 227–229, 231–233). Cairo too served as a collecting

9. House decorated to commemorate return of a Haj pilgrim (Egypt). Author's photo.

point for a second great caravan, with pilgrims traveling along the Red Sea coast and later, in boats from Suez to Yanbu (King 1972: 65). Geographers have remarked on the centripetal site of Mecca and its influence on cohesive Islam (Rowley 1997: 145–146), the length of time some pilgrims (especially West Africans who spent 2, 8, or even 20 years crossing the Sahara) took to arrive at Mecca (Shair and Karan 1979: 600, Rutter 1929: 272), and the increase in circulation with modern transport (King 1972, Rowley 1997). Though the history of Haj clearly shows that the circumstances of the actual journey have changed, mobility of pilgrims to enact an ideal and create a temporary physical community remains a constant motif from the earliest Arabian practice of Islamic Haj. In this respect Haj, like many other anthropologically observed pilgrimages (e.g., Morinis 1992b), provides an important locus for "the rhetorical, ideologically charged assertion of continuity, even fixity, in religious and wider social identities" (Coleman and Eade 2004: 15, Eickelman and Piscatori 1990: 4).

There are lesser Islamic pilgrimages, including *'Umrah* in Mecca, Al-Ziyara – the visit to the Prophet's burial site and mosque in Medina (a visit that many add to Haj) (Rowley 1997: 143) – and *ziyārāt*, or localized visits to the shrines of Muslim saints. These latter provide important occasions for temporary social gatherings, community, economic exchange, and expression of social identities in Arabia, Morocco (Gellner 1969, Eickelman 1982, 1976, Geertz 1968); Iran (Lapidus 1990); Iraq, Syria, Israel, Palestine (Marx 1977, Weingrod 1990, Hecht and Friedland 1996); Turkey (Tapper 1990); and India (Morinis 1984: 38–42). The diversity of *ziyārāt* across the Muslim world is beyond this study and reflects historical traditions outside of Arabia (Geertz 1968). In Arabia itself, there remain to this day important local *ziyārāt* with long historical traditions, especially in Yemen.

Ziyārāt in Yemen

Yemen today is an amalgam of two very different cultural groups. Northern Yemen, by far the more populous region, is home to highland agricultural villages built on agriculture from perennial spring flow (*ghayl*) and now, deep diesel wells. Northern Yemen's tribes people are mostly Zaidi sect Shia Muslims whose dialects and customs contrast markedly with their Southern co-nationalists, only recently incorporated with the North into a modern nation-state (1991–1993). Along with differences in modern and ancient histories of Northern and Southern Yemen are profound differences in the expression of Islamic faith. In Southern Yemen, there is to this day a strong practice of *ziyārāt* built on a long history and, as we shall later see, pre-historic pilgrimage.

Southern Yemen consists of three vast and sparsely populated arid provinces: Mahra, Hadramawt, and Shabwa. Mahra lies along the border with Oman's Dhufār Province, with which it shares ethnographic and cultural traditions and the Mahri dialect of Southern Arabian language (Johnstone 1975, Simeone-Senelle 1991). In Hadramawt and Shabwa provinces there flourished ancient pre-Islamic states using massive agricultural irrigation works, collecting frankincense, and transshipping other aromatics from city centers along the caravan routes to Mesopotamia and the Eastern Mediterranean. The incense trade and these states collapsed prior to Islam (Crone 1987, S. Smith 1954). But as Islam and the customs and language of Northern Arabian Arabs spread into Hadramawt (Chelhod 1984: 33), religious and cultural practices were adopted and adapted to existing local traditions, including local seasonal pilgrimages. Local seasonal pilgrimages were familiar across much of pre-Islamic Southern, Western, and Northern Arabia (J. Ryckmans 1975: 453).

Hadramawt today is peopled by Muslims of predominantly Shafiitic tradition (a Sunni school of Islamic jurisprudence). There is an important center of Sufi learning in the Wadi Hadramawt city of Tarīm, and there existed populations of native Yemeni Jews (Arabian converts to monotheistic Judaism in the sixth century AD) for example in Ḥabbān (Shabwa province) and within the Wadi Masila of Hadramawt. In the tenth century AD, an Iraqi descendent of the Prophet Muhammad, Aḥmad bin ʿIsā Al-Muhājir, moved to Hadramawt with his family and companions and became progenitor of Hadramawt's Alawi *sāda* (singular *sayyid*, a descendent of the Prophet), the upper class in Hadramitic society (Bin ʿAqil n.d., Sergeant 1981, Bujra 1971, Hartley 1961, Ingrams [1936, 1937] 1939).

Several years ago, I took a group of archaeologists as tourists to Aḥmad bin ʿIsā's tomb outside of Saywūn in the Wadi Hadramawt. Formerly led there myself by native associates from Hadramawt – one an ethnographer from a tribal background and the other from an important *sayyid* family in Saywūn – I had expected no opposition to our making a visit to the domed site, which incorporates other early tombstones (Aḥmad bin ʿIsā's early descendants) and an interesting elongated tomb for Bin ʾIsā himself, stretching about 10 meters up the hill slope. The entire site is remarkable for its location up away from typical Muslim cemetery locations (always on the wadi floor, close to agricultural land and modern settlement). But on this occasion we were denied access to the tomb by a multi-generational group of men and women *sāda* dressed beautifully (one could see the men, male children, and infants had on crisp, festive clothing). There were about twenty people milling about waiting for others to arrive, and I think there were musicians in attendance but not yet set up to play. We asked if we might see the interior and were refused, even though tourist-bearing convoys pull up and visit frequently at other times. The reason given was that the descendants of Aḥmad bin ʿIsā were making a visit (*ziyārāh*) to his tomb, and it was clear from preparations underway that this would also involve a feast.

I asked if one of our party, an Iraqi Muslim who had come far, might at least see the tomb, and he was waived inside although not invited to

10. Tomb of Aḥmad bin ʿIsā Al-Muhājir, Hadramawt (Yemen), including a long, plastered grave. Author's photo.

participate with the visiting party or offered a tour. While we waited for him to reemerge, I explained to our group the historical and political significance of Aḥmad bin ʿIsā in English and in Arabic. As I spoke, more cars arrived and a larger crowd of men gathered. By this time, women had moved aside to wait separately, and I exchanged some pleasantries and information about their children and my own with a small group of them. The visit was clearly for a community we would not be invited to join – despite my speaking Arabic, knowing the history and importance of Aḥmad bin ʿIsā Al-Muhājir, the presence of at least eight Muslims in our party, our mutual interest in each other, and the usual generous welcome of Hadramitic people. It ran counter to my experience to be thus excluded, even at a local religious site, but I think we could not have joined the visit, coming as tourists to what was clearly a local pilgrimage.

The sacred nature of the space and beliefs about the purpose of our journeys was what separated us, as well as an expectation of who belonged to the temporary community forming at the ancestral tomb. Although I cannot elaborate further on the visit to Aḥmad bin ʿIsā's tomb (we left), there are other sites of local pilgrimage in Hadramawt, some associated with local saints and others with proscriptive traditions. In Hadramawt today there are still many *ḥāwṭah* or sanctuaries that at specific times or occasions draw a mix of tribes people and other social classes. *Ḥāwṭah* provide physical and social space in which to negotiate intertribal conflict and the conflict between tribes and state authority as well as a violence-free locus for economic exchange (Alatas 1997, Al-Ṣabbān 1998: 18, Caton 1990: 95, Knysh 1993, 1997, Sergeant 1962). At *ḥāwṭah*, the obligations of blood feud between tribesmen are expressly prohibited; therefore, members of one tribe can come to meet and trade with members of another. Sometimes *ḥāwṭah* are specific days in otherwise ordinary space, like the city of Shibām (Wadi Hadramawt). Other *ḥāwṭah* exist at the tombs of widely venerated figures at which annual pilgrimage and fairs occur.

Pilgrimage to Qabr Nabi Hūd

Perhaps the best known of these is the pilgrimage to Qabr Nabi Hūd (Tomb of the Prophet Hūd). The site of Hūd's tomb is at the beginning of Wadi Masila, a region associated with the pre-Islamic land of ʿĀd, whose people ignored Hūd's exhortations to recognize Allah and were destroyed in retribution (Al-Qurʾān Sūrah xi, "Hūd," Al-Ṣabbān 1998: 6–7). Hūd's tomb is an elongated, whitewashed grave that extends upslope from the white dome that covers a cleft rock at the lower end of the tomb. Like Aḥmad bin ʿIsā Al-Muhājir's, the tomb itself is between 10 and 12 meters long and situated apart from customary Muslim burial sites. Downslope from the tomb of Nabi Hūd are a mosque, a well-constructed, stepped approach that enshrines a "footprint" in the rock, and a shaded court built against an enormous rock called Hūd's She-Camel. The complex lies at the upslope end of an entirely deserted village with numerous houses shuttered and bolted throughout most of the year. Usually only a few goats roam the village and a decently clad and reverent small group of tourists can climb unshod to Nabi Hūd's tomb.

Once a year, in the lunar month of Shaʿbān, people of Hadramawt conduct a pilgrimage to Qabr Nabi Hūd. The pilgrimage takes about a week, involves women and men, and is accompanied by a market fair for two to four days at Qabr Nabi Hūd, which is a *ḥāwṭah*. Sergeant (1954)

11. Tomb of Nabi (prophet) Hūd, Hadramawt (Yemen) with elongated, whitewashed grave perpendicular to the slope. Author's photo.

and Al-Ṣabbān (1998) provide detailed descriptions of the pilgrimage originating in western Hadramawt and visiting other saint's shrines en route. The houses at Qabr Nabi Hūd are owned by prominent families who return annually or may rent them for the duration of the pilgrimage. The majority of pilgrims have undertaken the pilgrimage before (Al-Ṣabbān 1998: 29–30): it is an annual event that draws a local crowd who reach the ḥāwṭah after walking eastward only a few days. There they perform bathing, recitation, and prayers; engage in evening festivities and dance; and meet bedouin tribes people from the Manāhil (Al-Ṣabbān 1998: 34) who arrive mostly from the east and north, and from whom many townsfolk purchase goats, traditionally in exchange for cotton cloth (Sergeant 1954: 135). Prominent families (*sāda*) in Hadramawt present dates and rice to pilgrims en route to assist them and encourage the pilgrimage (Sergeant 1954: 135), a role consistent with the intertribal mediations traditionally performed by *sāda* (Knysh 1997: 201–203, Sergeant 1962). (Indeed there is some suggestion that the *sāda* appropriated a link with the preexisting *ḥāwṭah* as a means of consolidating their political authority in Hadramawt (Al-Ṣabbān 1998:12)). Camel races take place on the next day. At the end of the visit, pilgrims butcher goats and prepare special types of food for a feast (Al-Ṣabbān 1998: 34) before returning to their homes.

Among the details of the history and ritual attached to the Qabr Nabi Hūd pilgrimage, several in particular concern us here. There are significant associations with fertility and reproduction: women apply spittle to pieces of thread or clothing and attempt to stick them to the *qubbah* or dome interior. If they stick, the woman will conceive. Sergeant (1954: 163–164) reports that such intercession may encompass many wishes, but also reports a fellow pilgrim's remark that Hūd can help a woman conceive. The tradition of providing an *'arūs*, perhaps a covering for the tomb of Hūd (Sergeant 1954: 141), may echo the provision of a new covering annually for the *Ka'bah* in Mecca (King 1972: 63), but the term *'arūs*, or bride, suggests fertility and also the social relationships and bonds that can be facilitated in the temporary gatherings and confluence of pilgrimage. The *ḥāwṭah* provided by Nabi Hūd's tomb visit, the contact among different groups sharing common purpose, beliefs, and ritual activities; the feast; associations with reproduction; evening dance and festivities; and the economic exchanges these enable are persistent motifs of pilgrimage in Arabia.

Pre-Islamic Pilgrimage in Arabia

As a key ritual enacting and reproducing society, pilgrimage has a long pre-Islamic history in Arabia. In the next chapter, the archaeological and epigraphic sources for Iron Age (first millennium BC) Southern

Arabian civilization support my thesis that pilgrimage played a critical ideological role in the economic and social functioning of Southern Arabian city-states. Pilgrimage probably also was critical in the growth of states because its practice to sites under elite control facilitated elites' appropriation of the means of production as the labor of mobile tribal pastoralists. In Hadramawt pilgrimage probably also enabled the flow of frankincense both as extraction and accumulation of a wealth surplus and through the peace imposed through pilgrimage rites. These are issues for later discussion, but here it is important to establish the continuity of pilgrimage from pre-Islamic times, both in local contexts such as Hadramawt, and in the wider Arabian context. Pilgrimage continuity is arguably most evident in the syncretization of pre-Islamic Meccan rites to Haj. Written sources, modern shrines, the histories of *ziyārāt* in Arabia, and the history of Haj show that pilgrimage has passed into Islam as a persistent practice stemming from preexisting Arabian cultures. This continuity appears very clearly when one compares modern practice to the written sources from the earliest years of Islam, some of them documenting earlier, pre-Islamic traditions. Among these sources are passages from Qur'ān, Ibn al Kalbī's (d. AD 819) "Book of Idols" (*Kitāb al-Asnām*), and works by Al-Baghdādī, Al-Jāhiz, Ibn Hishām, Ibn Sa'ādah, Mas'ūdī, Al-Tabarī, Yāqūt (G. Ryckmans 1951: 8), Al-Hamdānī, and Ibn al-Mujawir. Some of these sources are *tafsīr*, or commentary on Qur'ān with its enigmatic passages and injunctions (e.g., Al-Tabarī 1987 [J. Cooper trans.]), *sīrah*, or biography of the Prophet Muhammad (e.g., Al-Tabarī 1970, Al-Tabarī 1879–1901 [de Goeje et al., ed.]), history and geography (e.g., Al-Hamdānī 1986, 1989, Mas'ūdī 1965), and *riḥlah*, or early travelogue, often inspired during Haj (e.g., Ibn al Mujawir 1986). Analysis and interpretation of these medieval Arabic texts has engaged both Western and Islamic scholars who have approached these texts from differing perspectives. Because I draw predominately on English and French scholarship, the history of Western interpretations deserves some comment.

It has not always been easy to see the influence of pre-Islamic Arabian polytheistic indigenous rituals on Islamic practice. In what Edward Sa'id (1979: 209) eschewed as classically Orientalist scholarship, many Western scholars emphasized in the emergence of Islam the influences of Christian and Jewish monotheistic communities already in the Arabian peninsula during the sixth and seventh centuries AD (e.g., Margoliouth 1905, Hirschberg 1939, Henninger 1951, cf. Waardenburg 1963, Lüling 1981). If Arabian cultures and the Orient could generate nothing new (I leave aside in this discussion divine revelation as the ultimate source of Islam), then Jewish traditions (Wensinck 1914, Torrey 1933) familiar to the early Muslim *ummah* (community following the Prophet's call) at Yathrib/Medina or the influence of Christian monotheists in Arabia and Byzantium (Bell 1926) must have inspired the Prophet Muhammad. This discourse also neglects substantial evidence that the notion of a single paramount divinity had deep indigenous roots in Arabian cultures, for which the epigraphic and archaeological evidence has amassed in the latter decades of the twentieth century (J. Ryckmans 1973a: 90, 107–108, Robin 2000). Another fallacy has been the "abiding predilection [of Western scholars on the centuries prior to Islam] for nomad ways" (Smith 1954: 467 cited in Eickelman 1967: 24, Harrison 1924: 42), a romance with the bedouin Other that ignores the dynamic integration of *ḥaḍārah* and *bādiyah* ([inhabitants of] civilization and wilderness) (Ibn Khaldūn [d. 1406] 1967: 91–151) that characterized Arabian political economies and societies (Obermeyer 1999). A modern reader of the secondary literature on the emergence of Islam cannot escape the strong impression that Islamic ritual practices (including pilgrimage) stem in large part from existing rituals in and around early seventh-century Mecca.

Pre-Islamic sixth and seventh century Arabs included both settled, urban peoples and bedouin, and both groups practiced rituals that were incorporated and syncretized into Islam. Further – and this is important – these rituals, while not identical for urban dweller and bedouin nomad (Lammens 1926: 164, 167–169), were highly complementary and interwoven, bringing bedouin into sanctuaries maintained by the urban elite for sponsored rites and inclusive prayer. Pilgrimage to sacred sites (although not all were in settled areas) knitted the tribes into a state-sponsored affirmation of common identity while permitting social and economic activities that benefited bedouin nomads and urban dwellers alike (Caskel [1954] 1988: 36, Henninger [1981] 1999: 111). In the highly competitive interactions between city-states and surrounding tribal political groups (cf. Caton 1990, Crone 1987, Gellner 1969, Ibn Khaldūn [d. 1406] 1967, Tapper 1990) one medium for establishing centralizing authority was the control of a *ḥarām*, or sacred enclosure, in which blood feuds and other tribal disputes could be settled by the shrine's guardian (Sergeant 1962), chosen from a holy family like the *Quraysh* at Mecca. The *Quraysh*, the urban tribe of Muhammad, had acquired guardianship of the *Ka'bah* generations before Muhammad's time, and had maneuvered to elevate the sanctity of the *Ka'bah* over sanctuaries controlled by *kāhin* (divining adjudicators, El Tayib 1983: 32–34) from other tribes (Lammens 1926: 163–165, Dostal 1991).

The situation at Mecca and in the Hejaz just prior to and during Muhammad's life is reasonably well understood (especially compared to the rest of seventh-century Arabia). At Mecca, there were multiple sacred sites (Lammens 1926: 42–26, 59–60, 65–66, 71, 115, Dostal 1991: 195) with the principal sacred site as the *Ka'bah*, or *Maqām Ibrāhīm* (Lammens 1926: 44, Rubin [1990] 1999: 338). Other sites, such as Dār an-Nadwah, Hajar, Zamzam, were (recently become) dependencies of the *Ka'bah* itself (Lammens 1926: 78, 142), while nearby were other sanctuaries (As-Ṣafa, Al-Marwah, 'Arafāt, Minā) and holy sites on the mountaintops around Mecca, each associated with a divinity (Lammens 1926: 71, Dostal 1991: 195). Visits to high places were especially important for petitioning a divinity for rain, as at the summit of Abū Qubays (Lammens 1926: 60, Rubin [1990] 1999: 336). Lammens argues that the *Ka'bah* itself was a betyl (*bayt-al*, or house of Him) that uniquely took architectural form but served, as did hundreds of standing stones, as the house of a divinity (Lammens 1926: 78–81, Pirenne 1976: 197), while containing idols to many other divinities, such as Al-Lāt, Al-'Uzzā, and Manāt. The names of sacred sites As-Ṣafa and Al-Marwah essentially mean "stone" or "rock," relict from the betyls once ensconced there (Lammens 1919: 73). Tribes people coming to Mecca would therefore find enshrined many divinities (Lammens 1926: 71–73, 117–118, G. Ryckmans 1951: 8–9), familiar in persona and to which supplication could be made for personal motives or under self-imposed punition (Kister 1982: 28–29).

Tribes people from Mecca itself performed separate and different rites from the pilgrims. The citizens of Mecca practiced *'Umrah*, which consisted of processional visits among multiple local sanctuaries that moved from quarter to quarter, halted to revere the betyl, practiced a ritual circling, mounted races or gymnastics between betyls, ritually halted before the place of sacrifice, and took part as a community in a feast after sacrifice (Lammens 1926: 46, 55, 99, 167–169). Haj was pilgrimage

practiced during consecrated months (Peters 1994: 32), when safe passage was assured, often by the same bedouin guarantors that protected
trade caravans (Lammens 1926: 161). Pre-Islamic Haj attracted bedouin
and non-Meccan tribesmen from the Hejaz, Tihamma, and the region
adjacent to Mecca (Lammens 1926: 162–164). Pilgrimage and commerce
were deeply intertwined. For example, one of the lesser sanctuaries at
Mecca was Dār an-Nadwah, associated with the rites of departure and
arrival of caravans (Lammens 1926: 65–66) and later secularized as a
meeting house. The pilgrimage coincided with annual trade fairs (*mawā-
sim*) at Mecca, 'Arafāt, and Minā. Lammens (1926: 149), in agreement
with most authors (e.g. Peters 1994: 31) argues that there was neither Pre-
Islamic nor Islamic injunction against commerce (quite the contrary)
during pilgrimage. (Kister's [1980] 1990 I: 37) view to the contrary may
be a conflation of the pre-Islamic separation of Haj and *'Umrah*, the latter
a Meccan rite that did carry injunctions against trade (Peters 1994: 31).)
The confluence of different tribes people during pilgrimage provided an
important platform for commerce (Lammens 1926: 143), for enactment
of tribal identities (races and poetry competition) (see Lammens 1926:
149, El Tayib 1983: 29–30), and for other social negotiations such as the
exchange of prisoners, the conclusion of treaties and truces, the arbitration of differences, and tribal confederation, all accompanied by rites of
sacrifice (Lammens 1926: 149–150).

Pilgrimage was sponsored by Meccan leaders who provided feasts and
banquets for pilgrims as well as food and water for animals (Lammens
1926: 152, Hawting [1990] 1999: 244, 246, Dostal 1991: 195). Sacrificed
animals were included in these feasts, of course (Lammens 1926: 99,
G. Ryckmans 1951: 13, Atallah 1969: 16), but other provisions came from
the Meccans themselves who stood to profit from the commerce that
attends pilgrimage (Sergeant 1962: 53). There were surely Meccans and
kinsfolk from surrounding districts who participated in Haj rites and
feasts, and the differentiation of Haj and *'Umrah* in pre-Islamic times
surely did not entail neat and complete separation of urban and nomadic
practitioners, some of whom were linked by kinship if separated by
attributes of class, wealth, and economy. Lesser pilgrimages – *ziyārāt* –
were practiced in the vicinity of Mecca itself (Lammens 1926: 137), and
Mecca had largely achieved its prestige as a unique center of multiple
sanctuaries (Lammens 1926: 143). Nevertheless, it is clear that the elite

Meccan, urban families jealously maintained the sanctuaries and offices for their maintenance, and these families derived both social prestige and economic benefit from sponsoring pilgrimage with a large influx of bedouin nomadic tribes people (Sergeant 1962: 53, Dostal 1991).

Other sanctuaries existed in pre-Islamic Arabia, typically with a sacred enclosure established by a holy man or member of a holy family whose descendents guarded his shrine with attendant prestige and obligations of providing feasts and arbitration to pilgrims and security to residents (Sergeant 1962: 43–44). To pay for these obligations, the guardians collected contributions from the settled population whose security and economic prosperity the sanctuary ensured (Sergeant 1962: 55, Kister [1986] 1990 II: 53). Significantly, the caravans bearing trade goods from urban enterprises passed unmolested across the lands of bedouin tribes whose *shaykhs*, or leaders, were feted at banquets organized by the urban elites (Sergeant 1962: 55, Lammens 1926: 152), but where the caravans crossed tribal lands not sending pilgrims to the sanctuary, a protection toll or *khafarah*, was paid (Sergeant 1962:55). Eickelman (1967: 24–25) argues that the system of rise and fall of urban centers closely connected to the pastoral nomadic tribal society through mutual use of the *ḥarām* was a persistent pattern that characterized Arabia throughout the centuries in which Islam emerged as a single monotheism and that there was no fundamental break in social and political life in Arabia after the Hijra (Muhammad's move to Medina, where he established a new *ḥarām* (Sergeant 1962: 55, also Sergeant 1983: 152, Korotayev, Klimenko and Proussakov 1999)).

Apart from the Prophet Muhammad's new *ḥarām* at Medina, other pre-Islamic sanctuaries competed with the Meccan *ḥarām*. Sanctuaries are known to have existed at At-Ta'if (Chelhod 1958: 95–96, cited in Eickelman 1967: 25), Al-Yamanah where a contemporary prophet to Muhammad, Musālimah bin Ḥabīb established a *ḥarām* at Al-Hadjr (Sergeant 1962: 48, Eickelman 1967), and at Al-'Ukkāz (Lammens 1926: 152, 162). The Banu Murra tried to establish a new sanctuary patterned on the *Ka'bah*, As-Ṣafa, and Al-Marwah at Mecca: this new *ḥarām* drew pilgrimage away from Mecca and ultimately brought down a destructive raid from Mecca. Other similar incidents include a sanctuary established by Abraha (invading Ethiopian general in the sixth century) and a sanctuary erected in Qawdām (Kister [1986] 1990 II: 43–44,

Dostal 1991: 215–216). G. Ryckmans (1951: 16–17) mentions sanctuaries established for the divinities Al-Lāt, Al-ʿUzzā, or Manāt at Ḥurāḍ (on the route between Mecca and Iraq), at Quḍaīḍ on the coast between Mecca and Medina (Atallah 1969: 9), and sanctuaries of lesser divinities in Yemen.

Finally, Nabi Hūd's *ḥāwṭah* in Hadramawt deserves mention again as one of many pre-Islamic sanctuaries. Hūd's very long plastered gravesite, extending straight up a steep slope, has a parallel not only at Aḥmad bin ʿIsā Al-Muhājir's grave, but also in the hundreds of uncounted, long, unplastered cairns that mark the hill slopes of ancient Hadramawt (the wadi between Nabi Hūd and Tarīm). These monuments are widely recognized by modern archaeologists to predate Islam, perhaps by 2,000 years or more. Certainly early Muslims of Hadramawt also thought so, as recorded by Ibn al-Mujawir ([1204/5–1291/2] 1986: 258–260) during his thirteenth-century travels. The *ḥāwṭah* of Nabi Hūd has great antiquity and may indeed have been functioning during the Prophet Muhammad's time and many centuries beforehand.

Nor is the *ḥāwṭah* of Nabi Hūd singular as a pre-Islamic pilgrimage site in Hadramawt and Yemen. Annual fairs, which often accompany pilgrimage, sacrificial rites, social discourse, and confederacy among tribes, took place throughout Hadramawt and have been recorded by early Muslim geographers and historians (Sergeant 1954: 124, Knysh 1993: 141). There exist many other long graves of named prophets in Hadramawt, including the grave of Nabi Mawlā Maṭar (The Prophet Lord of Rain) whose role and origin surely harken to pre-Islamic *istiqāʾ* (intercession for rain) at high places like Abū Qubays near Mecca (Rodinov 1997: 108–109, Knysh 1993: 143). Mawlā Maṭar is beside Hadramawt's highest mountain, and Mawlā Maṭar's modern sanctity among the bedouin may stem from its "relic as one of the old sanctuaries of the pre-Islamic nature gods" (Ingrams 1936: 531, Sergeant 1954: 160, 174–175). When Ingrams visited Mawlā Maṭar in 1936, the bedouin still held an annual fair. Today ritual ibex hunts in the high mountains continue the long-held Hadramitic practice of *istiqāʾ* within a lightly veneered Islamic context, and the tradition has clear pre-Islamic roots (J. Ryckmans 1976, Sergeant 1976, ʿAbdalrahman Bin ʿAqil 2004), as it seems, does the pilgrimage to the "White Dune" at Abyan and

12. Pre-Islamic stone alignments run perpendicular on the lower slopes of Wadi Hadramawt (Yemen). Note the vertical alignment at the base of the slope (center) and another at middle left. Refer to Figure 13 for illustration. Author's photo.

divination at the shrine (Sergeant 1971). Other sites with fixed *ziyārāt* in Hadramawt include Nafḥūn in Wadi 'Amd, Al-Mashhad, Qaydūn, Ṣīf, and Al-'Arsamah, all in Wadi Daw'an, Buḍah, Hadūn, Al-Qurayn, and Ar-Ribāṭ, all in Wadi Layman, outside Al-Ribāṭ, and a site near the Shitnah pass (Rodinov 1997: 107); ethnographer Alexander Knysh (1993: 139) counted between 20 and 200 such sites. A pre-Islamic Arabian tradition focused upon the burial places of eponymous ancestors; thus *bayt* (*byt*, an Arabic term for house, tomb, or even idol) can indicate the tomb of an elder, which receives reverent treatment (Lammens 1919: 88–95) and is a custom perpetuated today in many of

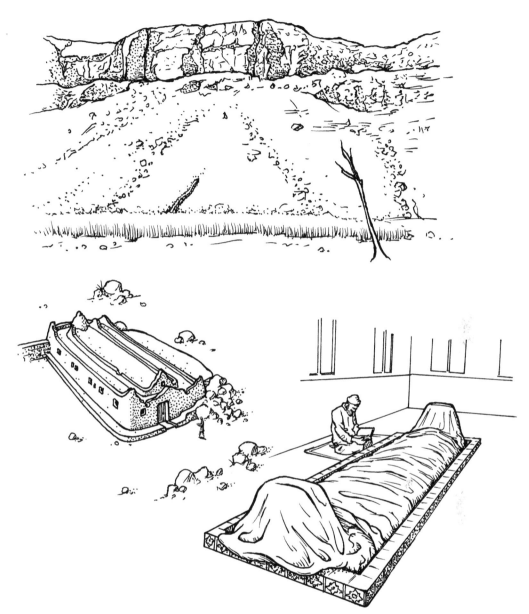

13. Pilgrimage places in Southern Arabia sometimes appropriate pre-Islamic prophets like Nabi Ayyūb (Job) whose shrine (bottom) in Dhufār is an elongated, plastered monument like that of Nabi Hūd or Mawlā Maṭar (left) in Hadramawt (adapted from Rodinov 1997: 111 Figure 2). These tombs in turn bear a striking locational and physical resemblance to likely Iron Age stone monuments whose original meaning is lost but which remain visible from the valley floor (top).

the *ziyārāt* (Knysh 1993). Finally, the pattern of a high-ranking religious family (Knysh 1993: 139, 145) controlling a *ḥāwṭah*, sponsoring pilgrimages (*ziyārāt*), pacifying local tribes, and controlling trade predates the contemporary *sāda* sociopolitical authority in Hadramawt (Sergeant 1954:

176–178) and, as we shall see in the next chapter, has long mediated the dynamic between tribe and state in Arabia. In this dynamic, pilgrimage is an integral and persistent practice, even as its meanings have changed.

Why Pilgrimage?

Why pilgrimage? Why does this particular practice, attendant with sanctuary, sacrifice, and feast, out of so many other Arabian cultural traits serve to distinguish and differentiate Arabian society? *Pilgrimage constitutes society, and it does so both during the actual season and action of pilgrimage and throughout individuals' lives, whether or not one actually ever makes a pilgrimage.* By belonging to a pilgrimage-making society – as a Muslim, as a bedouin tribes person, as the devotees of a particular saint – an individual is invested with the potential experience of a wider social body within which he or she experiences all the rights and obligations of participation. Haj is one of "five pillars" of Islam. Do these five things (witness Allah, pray, give alms, fast, go on Haj), and one is a Muslim: significantly, none but a Muslim may participate in Haj. In other examples and in other times, Arabian pilgrimage affirms a supraclan tribal identity (next chapter); in some cases it binds urban elite and desert-dwelling nomad in a socially mediated relationship (e.g., truces, fictive kinship as "children" of the god: see examples from pre-Islamic Mecca and Qabr Nabi Hūd). If one follows Durkheim's argument that pilgrimage (religious ritual) actually worships society itself, then the desire to experience the religious community of the shrine actually indicates a desire to uphold social ideals. This principle was articulated in Robertson-Smith's seminal early twentieth-century study on "The Religion of the Semites" (1907a: 80) in which he argued that pilgrimage was founded on the principles of hospitality and served to weaken the close link between man and the deity (first based on the metaphor of kinship), thereby establishing a wider community of believers linked through clientship and voluntary hospitality. A temporary society with injunctions on violence and a commonly held sacred center (Eliade [1949] 1954: 12–18, [1952] 1961: 39–41) implies belief in a greater social constitution beyond the segmented groups normally competing within a tribal culture (e.g., Dostal 1991: 216).

Of course such an ideal society is contested, both perpetually and historically. There are many concurrent facets of pilgrimage that contribute to its important role in social constitution. These aspects include the individual meanings and intentions of pilgrims (which differ), communal and agreed rites (a time for pilgrimage, acceptable sacrifice, apportionment of the feast), social discourse, and the formation, consolidation, or confederation of community in pilgrimage. Pilgrim rites offer a context for negotiation and expression of social status, and these rites may be appropriated and manipulated by one class for control over others, as occurred with the emergence of state societies in Southern Arabia (next chapter) (cf. Kertzer 1988). Modern ethnographic studies of pilgrimage capture a vignette, an ahistorical frame of a quintessentially temporal phenomenon in examples like Sallnow's (1981) study of identity politics in Andean pilgrimage or gender discourse in Naples (Lahti 1994). Archaeology and the long-term trajectory of ancient cultural studies in the Near East afforded through archaeology and texts offers an important diachronic perspective on social discourse and, most important, helps understand how that discourse and the terms of its expression changed through time.

There are essential attributes of pilgrimage, worth listing briefly (I leave exploring their roles in explaining pilgrimage as a central motif in Arabia for a later chapter). These attributes make pilgrimage a primary arena for wider social discourse and ultimately contribute in explaining why pilgrimage in Arabia persisted over long time frames and major cultural changes (Chapter 7).

1. Requires mobililty

   Pilgrimage requires a journey; regular pilgrimage requires regular mobility. In societies characterized by high mobility such as transhumant or nomadic pastoralists (i.e., Arabia's bedouin tribes people), the mobility of pilgrimage could articulate with seasonal rounds or with the congregation and dispersal of people annually or over greater periods of plenty and drought. Pilgrimage also reifies such mobility with ideological justification of economical practice.

2. Affirms social identity

   Social identity is of course highly contingent and contextual, and pilgrimage can play an important role in the constitution and dissolution of identity in a wider context, embracing social groups not otherwise linked through social relations. For example, segmentary tribal groups may affirm kinship at the supraclan level through common acknowledgment of supreme deity and practicing common tribal rites (including pilgrimage, contra Turner's dichotomy between pilgrimage and tribal rites).

3. Enables economic exchange

By bringing together groups otherwise feuding or unengaged, pilgrimage can promote otherwise unsanctioned or logistically impossible economic transactions. In this chapter the defining activities and pre-Islamic roots of Arabian pilgrimage clearly show that Haj (or Old South Arabic *hj* as we shall see for ancient Arabian civilizations in the next chapter) inimically facilitates economic exchange within and as part of wider social practice (Bourdieu [1980] 1990: 113–116) in the constitution of a temporary society of different ethnic or cultural groups (e.g., bedouin and urban dwellers, different tribes, multinational pilgrim assemblies).

4. Encounters temporal punctuation

Pilgrimage is enacted, but people (usually) return from pilgrimage. Impermanence serves both as incentive and barrier to wider (e.g., segmentary tribal) social formation: as incentive because the social bonds that form through temporary societies (requiring only temporary investment of time, energy, and resources) provide the benefits of widened access to resources such as pasture and food in times of famine or uncertainty and strength in numbers of "one's own" for protection against outsiders. On the other hand, impermanence also serves as barrier because the social bonds that form through temporary societies remain weaker than the social ties of daily practice. Therefore punctuation – especially in regular, predicted, and repetitive pilgrimages – serves to reinforce and renew wider social affinities. At the same time a paradox prevails – all in a pilgrimage-making society need not actually join pilgrimage and experience its punctuated tempo, provided that some members do, to experience at least some of its effects in sustaining wider communities.

5. Supports dramatic rites

These rites may be as simple as a prescribed bodily movement at the apogee of pilgrimage (e.g., *ṭawwāf*, ritual encircling, or falling to one's knees at the saint's tomb, or dance as shown on rock and plastic art (Khan 1993: 142, Wengrow 2001a)), but it is important that Arabian pilgrimage entails gathering, sacrifice, and feast. Their significance for Arabian cultural history will become clear later (Chapters 3 and 4). Sacrifice and feast dramatically transform material goods (cattle, incense) into what Bourdieu ([1980] 1990: 112–115, after Mauss) has identified as symbolic capital, that is, the recognition – whether gratitude, obligation, affinity, or status – that accrues to the sacrificer and host. Participation in sacrifice and feast at the heart of Arabian pilgrimage rites constitutes practitioners in a common social order.

Pilgrimage persisted across massive changes in society and political economy with the establishment of Islam (especially the inclusion of non-Arabs in the ninth century AD), yet we will see in the next chapters that this religious transformation pales in the context of preceding political, social, and economic transformations in Arabian historical and pre-historic pilgrimage societies. Persistence of pilgrimage as a religious ideology therefore requires some explanation if it is not to be relegated to the archives of epiphenomenal, relict cultural idiosyncrasy inexplicably retained through thousands of years of cultural change.

And why should it not be thus relegated? Other things, ideological even, persist and change. We still use cloth to make the man, eyes are a window to the soul, we bury the dead. Our question thus becomes not, how does pilgrimage function? – functioning presupposes an essentialism divorced from the actions and perceptions of individual pilgrims motivated to make a faith journey – but *how can pilgrimage continue to be a resonant and central cultural motif even as cultures change with the rise and fall of urban centers, the advent of monotheism, the "clash of civilizations" through which some Western observers would have one believe that contemporary Muslim identities are shaped?* In short, pilgrimage meets larger theoretical issues of explanation of cultural transmission and culture change.

Eickelman (1976: 5) grasped this when he approached Moroccan pilgrimage through Weberian analysis:

As Max Weber was concerned to demonstrate by his empirical studies of the major world religious traditions (e.g. Weber 1952), beliefs and ritual action are often invested with new meanings or change direction as they are introduced in novel situations and social frameworks different from those in which they were initially developed. For this reason, ideas and systems of ideas, especially those which fundamentally shape men's attitudes toward the world and their conduct in it, cannot be analytically construed as ahistorical Platonic entities, unaffected by the ravages of time. They are in a constant tension with social reality, shaping it and in turn being shaped.

Weber sought to recognize the shaping and being shaped between ideas and society, while seeking an analyst's perspective and overarching explanatory framework of ideas. A Weberian analytical framework has been similarly applied to Household societies by David Schloen (2001), who characterized the new power relations of state and class in the Near Eastern Bronze Age in terms of Weber's patrimonialism mode of production and argued that a native perception of father-son relationships structured all society from small households to the authority of the king. The universal metaphor for Bronze Age social and economic interactions was the "House of the Father" symbolically and dramatically reproduced in fractal hierarchy throughout a wide swath of the ancient world.

This book on Pilgrimage and Household takes a different approach to the relationships between ideas and social order. Weber's analysis is theoretically situated within a historical materialist dialectic within which historical modes of production give way to successive modes of production. The approach here emphasizes and explains the longevity of Pilgrimage as socially constituting framework outside and despite change. In understanding Pilgrimage and its longevity, it is critical to explore explanations for its continuity found in practice theory and structuration, although these approaches ultimately require an archaeological perspective on social constitution and the maintenance of symbolic repertoire across massive social change (Chapter 7).

Bourdieu's Theory of Practice and the Practice of Pilgrimage

French anthropologist Pierre Bourdieu ([1972] 1977, [1980] 1990) wrote about practice, its role in culture and cultural explanation, and how cultural practitioners situate practice in the context of decisions and logic of available options. Bourdieu sought a theoretical resolution to the tension between objective and subjective epistemologies (e.g., Lévi-Strauss 1963: 281) and argued that neither approach could fully satisfy the goals of theory. His work transcends "the limits of the objective and objectifying standpoint which grasps practices from outside" ([1972] 1977:3) by replacing a structuralist anthropological approach with a theory of practice. Primary experience of culture (by the native) gives rise to a set of dispositions that guide practice. Bourdieu's intent was to generate an abstract rendition – a scientific theory – of the dialectical relationship between objective frameworks drawn by the observer and the regular tendencies born out of native experience that shape what the observer calls culture. A paradox runs through his work – the closer one gets to native experience (one is born and educated within it), the further one is from an objectivist framework: this means that "participant observation is, in a sense, a contradiction in terms (as anyone who has tried to do it will have confirmed in practice)" (Bourdieu [1980] 1990: 34). To resolve this one must study not the outcome of practice – the frameworks objectively drawn, but the *habitus* that informs practice.

Decisions about practice, while inimical, highly contextual, and largely unconscious, are informed by the habitus, a historical product of culture. Habitus describes the temporally and perceptively fluid framework of cultural and natural dispositions that regulate the transmission and reproduction of culture through practice. Each individual has habitus acquired through education and conditioning in the practice of culture over a lifetime, but there also exists a collectivity, enough overlap among individual habitus to ensure that there are limits to practice and to the decisions individuals make in practicing culture (Bourdieu [1972] 1977: 82–86, [1980] 1990: 74–75). Bourdieu ([1972] 1977: 72) defined habitus as "systems of durable, transposable dispositions, structured structures predisposed to function as structuring structures," and he meant that practices are both generated by and reproduce the framework of tenden-cies that shape decisions about what people do. Pilgrimage exists in a logic of practice inimical/habitual to the practitioner (it is the done thing to do) but is still the objective of the objectifying observer (it shapes and perpetuates societies that do pilgrimage) (Bourdieu [1980] 1990). Through practice, people unconsciously reproduce the defining frameworks of culture, relying on bodily habituation rather than cognition (Connerton 1989: 22). Thus, Bourdieu would argue that Durkheim's observation that society worships itself through religious ritual (e.g., pilgrimage) objectifies society in a manner unrecognizable to participants. Instead, the logic of practice – deciding to practice pilgrimage – is inculcated through habitus.

The most famous example of the structuring structures that produce habitus (Bourdieu [1972] 1977: 72) is the Kabyle house, described by Bourdieu the ethnographer ([1972] 1977: 87–95) and cited by archaeologists studying houses, households, and social reproduction (e.g., Johnston and Gonlin 1998: 145, Hodder and Cessford 2004: 18, Hodder 1990, 2006, Gonzàles-Ruibal 2006). The house, a material condition of existence, is built according to learned custom and within its material structure (the way it is built) encodes notions about social relationships such as the membership (size, age classes) of households and gender separation and gendered labor roles. These are concepts that I will discuss further (Chapters 5 and 6), but for Arabian societies that eschewed permanent houses for most of Arabian history and pre-history, habitus was produced by and generated shrines (a ḥarām or a ḥāwṭah) to which people practiced pilgrimage. Spatial and temporal distribution of people going to shrines differs quite substantially from that of living in houses, a point to consider in greater detail in Chapter 7. Still, I argue that Arabian shrines are the outcome of habitus, just like the form of the Kabyle house. Practicing pilgrimage comes out of habitus and, at the same time, produces habitus (see also Lahti 1994: 31).

What makes people go on pilgrimage? It is certainly not a conscious desire to constitute and reconstitute an objectified social order through worshiping an essence reflecting that order. According to Bourdieu ([1980] 1990: 50), religious belief is acquired through "continuous, unconscious conditioning that is exerted through conditions of existence as much as through explicit encouragements or warnings." To the pilgrim, pilgrimage is neither rational nor rationalized, it is not economic: it is innate and follows a logic of practice whereby the pilgrimage is "justified by its very performance . . . done because it is 'the done thing,' the 'right thing to do'" (Bourdieu [1980] 1990: 18). So Muslims are born to Islam, not "initiated" (Grimes 2000: 102) and acquire a habitus that disposes them to perform Haj.

Through time habitus changes, and such change may occur within the lifetime of an individual or over generations of practice. Habitus not only explains short-term cultural action (practice) but also has embedded within its definition – transposable dispositions – an explanation for change. Now a once-in-a-lifetime event as seen in Haj, Arabian pilgrimage has a long tradition as a habitual, repetitive "codified aspect of social existence" (Bourdieu [1972] 1977: 97) much like the Kabyle calendar that Bourdieu as ethnographer used to demonstrate generative schemes that may be perceived and acted upon differently by different individuals in highly contextualized practice. Such generative schemes, like the calendar, are of such importance to a group's social and economic existence that they engender sayings, proverbs, taboos, injunctions, and other schemes that reinforce a collective perception and serve as a set of limits to the native practitioner. In our concern for the endurance of pilgrimage in Arabian culture history, it is important to remember that like the (temporally punctuated) Kabyle calendar of islands of time seen in the context of what one is doing (Bourdieu [1972] 1977: 105), pilgrimage is always related to something else, in the context of other practices that negotiate social order. It is these contexts that changed. Pilgrimage constituted society throughout Arabian culture history.

CHAPTER 3

PILGRIMAGE PRACTICE IN ARABIAN ANTIQUITY

> The culmination of Arab paganism was the tribal pilgrimage to a sacred stone at specific times, the worshipers being obliged to observe certain rules in respect of clothing, shaving the head, etc., and certain taboos, the whole ceremony ending with ritual processions round the shrine, the sacrifice of an animal or animals upon the sacred stone, and a communal sacrificial meal.
>
> H. A. R. Gibb 1948: 21–22

There are abundant references to pilgrimage in central Arabian practice during the *Jāhilīyah*, the time of pre-Islamic Arab society known through Qur'ān, poetry and early Islamic histories. These sources are sufficiently numerous and substantively in accord: it is uncontroversial to recognize that Islamic Haj grew out of pre-Islamic pilgrimage centered on Mecca. It was the Prophet Muhammad himself who recognized the supremacy of Mecca for Haj rites and discouraged pilgrimage and rites at other shrines. But the Meccan rites were linked to widespread Arabian practices with deep roots in Arabian antiquity. Following Wellhausen (1887), G. Ryckmans (1951) divided pre-Islamic Arabian religion into three geographic spheres – Southern, Central, and Northern. Of these, the Southern Arabian religious sphere has a historical record a thousand years before Islam and clear evidence of the socially constituting cultural practice of pilgrimage, and much of Central Arabia's pre-Islamic religious traditions stem from Southern Arabia. This chapter examines both the evidence for Old South Arabian pilgrimage and its role as a socially constituting practice in Southern Arabian civilization.

Moreover, pilgrimage underwent profound shifts in meaning and practice during the rise and constitution of Southern Arabia's historical states. Prior to the establishment of urban centers dependent on large-scale and complex irrigation works and caravan traffic in the desert margins of inland Southern Arabia around 1300 BC, Southern Arabian society had flourished as a network of small farming settlements, mobile pastoralists, and highland towns (e.g., Wilkinson, Edens and Barratt 2001, De Maigret 1990). Evidence for the preurban interdependency of these is scant (Edens 1999), but from later, urban contexts, their developmental coalescence into a cooperative Southern Arabian state is incontestable. Pilgrimage played a major role in this coalescence, a role made glaringly evident through the care with which pilgrimage rites were maintained by the Southern Arabian states. Even so, evidence for pilgrimage before states has hitherto been scant or lacking.

The ancient Arabian states were founded upon an agricultural base maintained through complex and large-scale irrigation works, but their flourishing owed much to the incense traffic they assiduously controlled. Competing lowland centers sought to draw to their coffers the wealth of aromatics traffic, but scholars have only begun to understand how this was achieved. To do so, urban elites had to depend upon highland tribal pastoralists for the production and safe transport of frankincense and myrrh, resins from trees that grew only in highland areas occupied by territorial tribes people. This was especially the case for Shabwa, capital of the Hadramawt, which was still a frankincense-producing region while the state was emerging. Southern Arabian polities achieved these goals by appropriating and manipulating existing tribal practices, especially pilgrimage rites, to the cult of newly paramount federal gods. By redefining existing practices of pilgrimage to facilitate social alliances among tribes (thereby pacifying and securing routes) and between tribal confederacies and the state (thereby accessing labor and tithes), Southern Arabian elites secured new economic and social networks that maintained new inequalities in the metaphor of traditional practices. As we will see in Chapter 4, large gatherings, sacrifice, and feasts already were part of the social landscape in ancient, prestate Southern Arabia, but the antiquity of these practices has not been previously recognized. From historical texts, inscriptions, and archaeological remains, we can appreciate how these practices were maintained and

Table 1. Chronological Schema of Southern Arabian Civilization.

Dates	Period	Economic Base	Social Networks	Political-Ideological	Material Culture
AD 525–621	Pre-Islamic	Pastoralism, agriculture, caravans	Migrations, collapse of Southern Arabian societies	Sanctuary and pilgrimage	Cities, *hjr*, crafted goods, exotics
280 BC–AD 525	Himyarite	Agriculture, pastoralism, caravans	Tribes and classes, nonkinship clans	Kings hold office of sacrificer	Fortresses, *hjr*, temples triliths, graffiti
900–280 BC	Old South Arabian	Agriculture, pastoralism, caravans	Clan bayts, qaylite bayts	Mukarribs, kings hold office of sacrificer	Writing, cities, *hjr*, temples, camels
1300–900 BC	Iron Age	Pastoralism, agriculture, incense production	Clan bayts, metaphorical kinship	Apotheosis? Appropriating ancestors through pilgrimage	Ceramics, irrigation, (emergent writing?)
1950–1300 BC	Bronze Age	Caprine pastoralism, agriculture in territories	Bayts as lineages	(record poor)	Stone houses, highland settlements
2200–1950 BC	Bronze Age	Caprine pastoralism, agriculture in territories	(record poor)	Wealth displays of prestige goods, visits to tombs?	Wall Tombs, tumuli, prestige metals, highland settlements
3300–2200 BC	Bronze Age	Caprine pastoralism, agriculture in territories	Lineages through tribal ancestors	Mortuary rites	High circular tombs, runoff farming, open-air sanctuaries
4400–3300 BC	Late Neolithic	Dispersed and mobile caprine and cattle pastoralism	(record poor)	(record poor)	Nonformalized lithics
5000–4400 BC	Middle Neolithic	Cattle-caprine pastoralism	Territorial supra-household groups	Gathering, collective sacrifice, feasts	Collective-built stone monuments, skull arrangements
6750–5000 BC	Early Neolithic	Hunting-herding	Households?	Individual hunting, magic?	Domesticated cattle and caprines, technically-fine stone points

fostered as integral ideological, social, and economic constructs of Old South Arabian civilization.

1. The Evidence – How We Know What We Know

Before we explore ancient Southern Arabian pilgrimage as a fundamental practice that constituted complex societies in ancient states, the evidence for ancient Arabian practices deserves brief review. There are four primary sources upon which all subsequent scholarship draws. These are (1) early and medieval Islamic texts (Arabic), (2) classical texts, (3) ancient Southern Arabian inscriptions (in Old South Arabian dialects), and (4) archaeological discoveries. They offer broadly differing but complementary information about ancient pilgrimage and related practices such as sacrifice and feast, truce and sanctuary, offerings, tithes, and their management.

Islamic sources: The greatest changes to Arab society appeared not with the initial emergence of Islam, but with Islam's spread and conquests, especially with the incorporation of non-Arab Muslims into state politics and function in the eighth-century Abbasid caliphate in Baghdad (Gibb 1948: 23–24). The introduction of the customs and traditions of non-Arab peoples into Muslim life and the circulation, dissent, and codification of sayings (*ḥadīth*) attributed to the Prophet fueled an urgent curiosity about the context in which the Prophet and early *ummah* (community of believers) had lived. In the centuries immediately after the Prophet's death, early Islamic writers produced biographies of the Prophet (*sīrah*) and histories, some of which exist today only as fragments cited in later works. Al-Ṭabarī (d. 923) (Goetje et al. 1879–1901) in his late ninth-century histories cited the earlier biographer Ibn Isḥāq, whose original work on Southern Arabian history has mostly been lost. The original "Book of Idols" about pre-Islamic religion written by Baghdadi historian Hishām Ibn al-Kalbī (d. 819) was known from sections reproduced by medieval geographer Yāqūt al-Ḥamawī (Wüstenfeld 1866–1873) until a 1920s Cairo discovery of an original stolen from a Damascus archive (Atallah 1969: XLIX). In his seminal study of ancient Arabian religion, Wellhausen (1887) relied heavily on Ibn al-Kalbī, as have many subsequent scholars (Henninger [1981] 1999: 109–110), despite the mythical quality of Ibn al-Kalbī's narrative (Peters 1994: 21–23) and its focus on bedouin rather than urban traditions.

Islamic sources of course include Qur'ān itself but also include early *tafsīr* (commentary on Qur'ān), and collected pre-Islamic poetry (El-Tayib 1983). Important early descriptions of ancient Southern Arabia are contained in Al-Himyari and in Ḥasan ibn Aḥmad Al-Hamdānī (d. 945), whose geographical work represents the oldest and most complete study of tribal relations of Arabia, and who provided an important topography of the Himyarite period (third to sixth century AD) (de Maigret [1996] 2003: 31). Careful scrutiny shows that these works are most reliable for later periods of Southern Arabian states, deriving (like Ibn al-Kalbī's religious practices) all chronological-historical figures from the Biblical patriarchs and entirely mythical (but including some historical resonance) for periods prior to the second century AD (J. Ryckmans 1975: 444). Finally, there are important clues to long-lived pilgrimage practices and pre-Islamic customs in the *riḥlah*, or travelogues of medieval hajjis like Ibn Al-Mujawir (d. 1291) ([1204/5–1291/2] 1986), whose circuitous route home from Mecca passed through Hadramawt, Mahra, and Dhufār.

Classical sources: Whereas Islamic sources all cast backward in time and derive historical information through a filter of previous works, myth, and polemic, classical sources have the advantage of being near contemporaneousness, with the disadvantage of considerable geographical and cultural distance. Most survey works of Southern Arabian civilization open with a discussion of classical sources, which include passages from the anonymous Greek "Periplus of the Erythraean Sea," Strabo's geography, Heroditus' history, Ptolemy's geography, and Pliny's "Natural History." With the possible exception of the author of the "Periplus," these writers drew on other's accounts, perhaps some eyewitnesses, with mixed result (Groom 1981). The accuracy and meaning of their accounts has been extensively examined, and the accounts range from the fantastical – flying snakes that Heroditus reported as guarding frankincense trees (Groom 1981: 59–60) – to mundane matters – such as Strabo's much discussed accounts of Sabaean marriage customs (Robertson-Smith [1885] 1907b: 270–272, cf. Korotayev 1995, Dostal 1989a). Classical writers viewed Arabia through a particular lens; they were interested in Arabia as a source for incense, and their accounts accordingly concern history, geography, economy, and trade.

Southern Arabian inscriptions: The best way to evaluate classical and Islamic texts is through critical study of the epigraphic evidence, which was produced by the literate elites in Southern Arabian states and is concentrated in and around urban centers. Scholarship of the past fifity years has dramatically changed our understanding of the ancient Southern Arabian religion and its significance for pre-Islamic religious practices of the sixth century AD. Unfortunately the corpus of ancient Southern Arabian texts is highly restricted, with fewer than 10,000 known, and consists mainly of dedicatory inscriptions in temples, on large-scale public works like the great dam at Ma'rib, and carved on rock faces. In content, these inscriptions typically contain petitions and dedications – of bleeding sacrifices and other offerings – and a few emphasize property and water management – mending dams, building, and petitioning for rain (Obermeyer 1999: 42, J. Ryckmans 1973a: 82). Although dedicatory inscriptions are most common and show conceptualization of the relationship between humans and divinity (e.g., Pirenne 1972, 1976: 183–186), inscriptions also provide significant insight into ancient religious practices such as ritual sacrifices, hunts, banquets, pilgrimage, and the consummation of tribal alliances. A small number of inscriptions placed by rulers or tribal assemblies codify rules for commerce, pilgrimage, land rights, and irrigation. Some inscriptions commemorate historical events like military campaigns and construction works (Robin 1984). Most surviving Southern Arabian inscriptions are highly refined, carved in stone or on bronze plaques, but some are rural inscriptions marked on rock faces. Only a few examples of cursive script attest to a lost corpus of letters, contracts, and other economic transactions recorded on the fragile stalks of palm leaves (Ryckmans, Müller and Abdulla 1994). There exist also a few words on pottery and graffiti carved on natural rock faces.

Archaeological evidence: Good overviews summarize the material culture of ancient Southern Arabian states (e.g., de Maigret [1996] 2003, Breton 1999, Doe 1971), of which there remain well-preserved cities with stone architecture, refined statuary, and relief arts (often as dedicated offerings and funerary contexts) in metal and stone, household debris as ceramics and food waste, irrigation works, coinage, and chipped stone. The archaeological evidence for religious practices is particularly well examined and understood through temple plans and their associated installations (Maraqten 1994) and buildings. For example, excavations by the Soviet Yemeni Expedition and recently the Russian Expedition at Raybun, a regional center in the Kingdom of Hadramawt between 1200 BC and AD 150, have uncovered the ruins of temple buildings still containing votive stelae, inscriptions, the altar table, gutters and pits for liquid (blood?) offerings, and the discarded remains from preparing ceremonial banquets in adjacent halls (Sedov 2000, 2005). Rural temples and sanctuaries also were maintained by settled elites (Breton 1979, Mouton et al. 2006: 235) and clearly were the focus of periodic pilgrimage and ritual practices by nomadic tribes people (Pirenne 1991, Robin and Breton 1982, Ghul 1984). Archaeologists can therefore identify in ancient Southern Arabian contexts the places of gathering, sacrifice, and feasts that served as the manifestation of an Arabian habitus of pilgrimage.

2. Southern Arabian Religion and Practice – What We Know

The basic pattern of ancient Southern Arabian religious practices engaged people of different social castes (defined in terms of tribal affinity) in common devotions to "federal gods" whose supremacy over lesser clan and lineage deities framed a political-religious geographic region claimed by the state. Pilgrimages to a god's sanctuary were a socially constituting practice, and the confluence of tribal groups at the federal god's sanctuary was accompanied by truce, dedication of tithes, sacrifices, and a feast, often sponsored or officiated by a political leader whose authority was manifested and consolidated in part by this performance. There were significant differences to this pattern both in space and time that interest us here. The current study will not detail the breadth of diversity in all Arabian religious practice prior to Islam and especially skirts the rich literature of Northern and Central-Western Arabian practices and the politico-religious relations between the *Quraysh* and various bedouin and tribal groups in the era of the Prophet Muhammad (e.g., Fabietti [1988] 1999, Lammens 1919, 1926, Chelhod 1958). Instead, it is important to recognize an uncontested continuity in the basic elements of Arabian religious practice (Korotayev 2003, Pirenne 1976, Robin 2000) and to recognize also that one's view of them depends in part on whether a classification or historical trajectory is emphasized.

a. Classification: Southern Arabian Religion and Regional Variation

Beyond geographic classification, with clear differences in the pantheon of different Arabian regions (G. Ryckmans 1951), there were also differences between the religious rites in urban-based, settled societies and the practices of nomadic or seminomadic tribes people ("pre-Islamic Arabs" or "bedouin") in the deserts and at the margins of settlement (Pirenne 1976: 12, Henninger 1948, [1981] 1999, Chelhod 1955). Some scholars have viewed these groups and their intertwined religious practices in the model of dynamic structural opposition familiar from Ibn Khaldūn's (1967) influential history, a view that emphasizes tensions between groups and the mediating role of practices that fulfill religious obligations of both groups and provide confluent contexts for the forging of new social identities. Anthropological views of the emergence of Islam have taken this approach (e.g., Wolf 1951, Eickelman 1967, Korotayev, Klimenko and Proussakov 1999), as has Obermeyer (1999) in describing the relationships between hinterland highlands and lowland oasis states in ancient Southern Arabia.

Bedouin-Arab practices have been described as a "cult of the betyls" (Lammens 1919) with reverence for a stone house of the god (Pirenne 1976), which may at various times and contexts been a standing stone (nuṣb, pl. anṣāb) (Atallah 1969: 27), a natural outcrop, or a mobile idol. By bedouin or pre-Islamic Arab, scholars implicitly recognize largely nomadic, pastoral peoples ethnically bound through a principle of consanguineous descent. Henninger ([1981] 1999: 110) argues that there is insufficient data to understand pre-Islamic bedouin religion (but the practice of pilgrimage to sanctuaries is well attested (Korotayev, Klimenko and Proussakov 1999)), and some of the rural sanctuaries at which tribes people gathered housed tribal gods that in deep antiquity could have originated as tribal ancestors in a long-forgotten ancestor cult (Henninger [1981] 1999: 116, Lammens 1919: 88–101, Chelhod 1955: 118–119, see also Kertzer 1988: 178). By the period of ancient Southern Arabian states, rural sanctuaries housing tribal gods existed throughout the highlands (Obermeyer 1999: 42) and rural hinterlands of the urban centers (Pirenne 1991) and to these gathered nomadic, semi-nomadic, and settled tribes people. Bleeding sacrifices, with blood poured over the betyl, were offered in expectation of the god's benefi-cence and reciprocal attention (Chelhod 1955, Pirenne 1976) in a cos-mology focused on the relationship between humans and their divinity (Robertson-Smith 1907a: 65, Chelhod 1955: 26, Pirenne 1976). And it seems that sacrifices were consumed (Chelhod 1955: 26), providing the means of feasts to a gathering in honor of a god, although archaeological evidence of the provisioning of a camel or horse in honor of the dead show that some sacrifices (those in honor of a deceased but not a god) were not consumed (Vogt 1994, Uerpmann 1999).

The practices of urban-dwelling, settled classes in ancient Southern Arabia were focused on temples, whose architecture and layout leave no doubt of the autochthonous origins of Southern Arabian temple wor-ship (Sedov 2000, Robin and Breton 1982, de Maigret [1996] 2003: 303). While early scholars suggested that Mesopotamian religions inspired Southern Arabian temples, suggesting astral deities derived from Mesopotamia, sacred prostitutes, and a dedicated priestly class (dis-cussed in Henninger [1981] 1999: 109–110, G. Ryckmans 1951, Beeston 1972: 264), Southern Arabian epigraphic evidence contradicts this view (especially Pirenne 1972, J. Ryckmans 1973a: 82, Jamme 1947, Robin 2000). Each state center maintained an important temple to a federal god to which allied tribes within the religio-political sphere of the state came for pilgrimage in a designated month. Rules of pilgrimage included injunctions on hunting in the sacred perimeter, bearing arms, disputes, shedding blood, sexual relations (Robin 2000: 158), menstru-ation (Maraqten 2008: 241), dress (Noja 1985), and cutting hair (Ghul 1984). Disputes were adjudicated, truces arranged, and pacts affirmed (G. Ryckmans 1951: 33–37). Temples were maintained by donations and taxes or tithes (Ghul 1984: 34–35, Korotayev 2003: 68–70, 1994a), which were paid to an administrator at the time of pilgrimage or as private dedications. Dedicatory statues, stelae, plaques, and inscriptions (e.g., Robin and Frantsouzoff 1999, Brown and Beeston 1954, Frantsouzoff 2001, Maraqten 2008: 240) incorporated into temple buildings amply attest the gifts by individual donors and supplication for the divinity's intercession – for favor of the king; fertility of women, fields, and animals; protection against disease and vermin; healing; personal

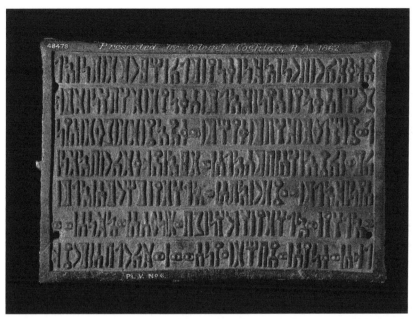

14. Bronze dedicatory plaque to Sayyin from Shabwa (Yemen). The Trustees of the British Museum.

protection against violence or humiliation; liberation if captured; travel; peace and protection in warfare (G. Ryckmans 1951: 34). From the placement of altars and drainage channels, benches, and halls, archaeologists can infer the practice of animal sacrifice and feasts in Arabian temples (Breton 1979, Robin and Breton 1982, Sedov 2005). Smaller temples were maintained at outlying sites and served lesser divinities as lesser sites for managing tribal affairs and invoking divine protection for individual supplicants (Breton 1979, Mouton et al. 2006). And it seems that there was a hierarchy of divinities: after the paramount federal god came lesser tribe and clan divinities, then minor divinities of institutions, family and personal gods, and perhaps a class of divinities intercessionary between humans and gods (Robin 2000: 130–137).

Much has been made of a famous passage in Pliny the Elder's *Natural History* that says a tithe was taken by the priests for the Hadramitic federal god called Sayyin to defray a public expense, namely the ritual banquet served to pilgrims at Shabwa, capital of the Hadramawt kingdom (Müller 1979: 82, J. Ryckmans 1973b, 1973c: 330). Epigraphic evidence from the Middle Sabaean kingdom (first to fourth century AD) also suggests that a tithe of first fruits was due to the deity but might be paid in various ways to various deities (Korotayev 1994a: 15, 1994b). While it seems clear that central taxation was lacking in the Middle Sabaean kingdom (Korotayev 2003: 68, 1994a), such may not always have been the case. Taxing a portion of incense traffic in Hadramawt may have provided incense for ritual uses (Müller 1976, Henninger [1946/47] 1981: 222, Maraqten 1994: 161) and could perhaps be one indication of the appropriation of wealth by urban elites (those managing the temple with access to temple gains). Although there does not appear to have been a priestly class that alone could perform sacrifice (Pirenne 1972, G. Ryckmans 1951: 29), there were clearly leaders per- forming public rituals and collection of tithes (Robin and Breton 1982, Ghul 1984: 34, Korotayev 1993a: 101, 1993b: 5, Loudine 1990: 96, Beeston 1972). Some urban temples have domestic dwellings thought to be "priests's houses" in Hadramawt (Sedov 2000: 24), and the massive temple complexes there must have required some specialized mainte- nance. To the extent that nomadic pastoral and rural tribes people engaged in producing frankincense and other aromatics and in ensuring the safe passage of caravans, the appropriation of a tithe in frankincense and the persuasive lure of pilgrimage to the sanctuaries of federal gods cloaked the extraction of labor and surplus to the service of elites and state power. And although at Shabwa itself, the best evidence for pilgrim- age comes from a late period (fifth century AD) graffiti (*hj*, that is, *hajj*) on an earlier limestone decoration (Brown and Beeston 1954:61), its con- text – and attested pilgrimage in Sabaean, Qatabanian, and Minaean contexts – has led scholars to infer that pilgrimage lay at the core of traditional Hadramawt practice.

Finally, the practice of ritual hunts, presided by political leaders and accompanied by sacrifice (ibex) and feast is attested in the Sabaean, Qatabanian, Minean, and Hadramitic kingdoms (Loudine 1990: 98, J. Ryckmans 1976). The ritual hunt apparently played a ceremonial role ensuring the fecundity of pasture animals or the prosperity of an under- taking or construction (J. Ryckmans 1976: 301–302). It was practiced on significant occasions like the succession of a king and also appears – through the engagement of political leaders and kings and the attendant feast and commemorative construction of an altar – to have played a ceremonial role integrating pastoral tribes people into a common society with the elites sponsoring the hunt.

By the time Southern Arabian societies were documenting their devotions in writing, they belonged to a class-based society in which the relations of class were expressed and masked in the metaphor of tribal social relations (segmentary kinship). Access to the primary means of production – land and water – was adjudicated by the elite through the metaphor of tribes people's obligations to a tribal divinity (Beeston 1972: 266). We have no means as yet of documenting in proto-state ancient Arabia the transformation of an ethnic tribal society linked through the metaphor of kinship – what Ibn Khaldūn (1967: 97–99) would call 'asabiya, or "group feeling" – to a society with classes based on access to wealth and the appropriation of surplus (tithes, first fruits, labor as military, construction, and other service). But we can be reasonably certain that the fundamental metaphors and motifs of social constitution in Arabian states reflect and manipulate shared habitus. The basic social roles and relationships in ancient Southern Arabian states, then, are transpositions of preexisting ethnic, territorial tribal social relations (e.g., Beeston 1979: 117).

The basic socioeconomic unit in ancient Southern Arabian states was the *byt* (*bayt*, or house). Beeston (1972) suggested that the bayt represented a community and its agricultural land and buildings, and embodied a village society defined in territorial but emphatically not in kinship terms. Other epigraphers, notably Korotayev (1993a, 1993b, Robin 1984), disagree with the territorial and agricultural identity of a bayt, arguing instead that a bayt indeed did represent a basic socioeconomic unit constituted through kinship terms, even though un-free *'dm* (*adam*, or client; Beeston 1979: 118) members of some Arabian bayts were linked neither by blood or marriage (Korotayev 1994c). An appropriate translation for *bayt*, then, is clan or lineage community, the two differentiated by descent from an eponymous, mythical ancestor (clan) or a progenitor (lineage) (Korotayev 1993b: 60–61). Sometimes entire bayts were clients of the powerful qaylite bayts (Beeston 1979: 120). Korotayev's (1994c) analysis of the Middle Sabaean (first to fourth centuries AD) bayt indicates a patrilineal, exogamous socioeconomic unit composed of a hierarchy of individuals. Most important in decision making and power were the leading group (male adults), which could be a father and sons or several brothers and their sons. Secondary members belonged to senior and junior generations ("brothers" and "sons") as close relatives of the leading group, and a third set (including born to, unmarried sisters and daughters) formed the clan nucleus of members not joined in by marriage. Other lesser members were wives (married in) and clients (*'dm*, also *'bd, 'abd*), who generally do not use epithets and often formed entirely autonomous bayts from the powerful bayts (of the elites).

This generalized structure of the Middle Sabaean (first to fourth centuries AD) bayt serves as an example but not a template for all time. Indeed, one of the long-standing scholarly discussions crossing over disciplinary boundaries of religious history, social history, ethnography, and anthropology concerns a purported shift in kinship systems in ancient Arabia and its putative association with the incursion of (patriarchal) bedouin Arabs and formation of Arabian states and Arabian religions (Robin 1982a, Höfner 1959, cf. Dostal 1989a, 1989b). From the time of Robertson-Smith ([1885] 1907b: xi, 142–143, Wilken 1884), argument has centered on a supposed coexistence and shift in matrilocal and patrilocal marriage practices that may have figured in Strabo's ancient accounts of Sabean society. The concept interested sociologists, ethnographers, and anthropologists influenced by Morgan's and Engels's theoretical models of social evolution with a universally experienced original matriarchal society (see Korotayev 1995: 83, Henninger 1943: 10–16). Epigraphic evidence from ancient Southern Arabia is equivocal on the subject of matriarchy, but at least one third century AD inscription from Ma'rib seems to suggest a prominence of sisters and daughters in the internal hierarchy of a client bayt (*'dm*) given by the king to another noble (*'mr*) 'amir bayt. Andrey Korotayev (1995) argues that this inscription provides clues for interpreting other, less clear evidence for matrilineal descent and matrilineal bayts in Middle Sabaean society (cf. Avanzini 1991).

Walter Dostal (1989a) has suggested an alternative interpretation, namely that a prestate Arabian practice was the bilateral ordering of descent as cognatic kinship. In this case, the epigraphic evidence would show not a transition from matriarchy to patriarchy but the emergence of strong patrilinearity as a unilateral kinship system (see also Avanzini 2006). Dostal suggests that the organizational requirements for oasis-scale irrigation and the political systems that resulted were responsible factors for the abandonment of bilateral kinship, an essentially endogenous event unrelated to hypothetical (patrilineal) bedouin-Arab incursions. Furthermore, he and other ethnographers detect the relict practices of bilateral kinship today in the distinctive customs and terminology of Mehri, Socotri, and Shehri groups (Dostal 1989a: 47, 1989b). Linguistic and ethnographic arguments offer little in prestate chronological depth and stem from a broad array of theoretical supports and disciplinary traditions. Kinship classifications have become so typologically unwieldy as to be largely abandoned by many anthropologists (Kuper 1982a). What we can safely assume is that there was, over time and through the dramatic social transformations that accompanied the emergence of class-based state societies from kin-based territorial tribes, variation in the social relationships that constituted the bayt.

It is significant that the term bayt means "house." The efforts to classify Southern Arabian kinship systems mirror larger struggles in social anthropology that Claude Lévi-Strauss ([1979] 1982: 174) sought to address with his concept of House Societies (*sociétés à maisons*) in which the House is "a corporate body holding an estate made up of both material and immaterial wealth, which perpetuates itself through the transmission of its name, its goods, and its titles down a real, or imaginary line, considered legitimate as long as this continuity can express itself in the language of kinship or of affinity and, most often, of both." Cross-cultural examinations of this concept have underscored its potential as a critique of existing kinship classifications rather than a new classificatory type (Carston and Hugh-Jones 1995: 18–19) and have emphasized the usefulness of the interwoven transgenerational biographies of place (houses) and residents as a means to understanding the social relationships, boundaries, enactments, symbols, transmission, and memories that guide social interaction and leave enduring material components as houses (Gillespie 2000). These themes will be taken up in later chapters (5 and 6) in societies for which permanent houses and the daily practices within them were the major constitutive force (Household). For ancient Southern Arabian states, we may surmise that physical houses did attach some bayts (clans, lineages) in urban contexts, but this differs from the concept of Household habitus, and it is highly significant that through much of Arabia's pre-history and for many of its historic occupants, no one lived in houses at all. Other dispositions and another set of social practices (Pilgrimage) constituted societies made up of social, but not physical, bayts.

Beyond membership in the bayt, we can identify a number of social roles in the ancient Southern Arabian state. Several bayts together constituted a territorial subtribe or third-order *sh'b* (*sha'b*) often with its own fortified center or *hjr* (*hajar*) and tribal god to which tithe and pilgrimage was due (Obermeyer 1999: 43). Second-order sha'bs were political tribal entities with leadership authority in the role of the *qyl* (qayl), whose bayts held large tracts of land and collected substantial revenue from land rent by clients. And these second-order sha'bs in turn could belong to or entirely constitute a first-order sha'b, an ethnic tribe with a common deity, eponymous ancestor (Banu X, or Sons of X), and a distinctive tribal calendar with pilgrimage months particular to the tribal god (Korotayev 1993a). Such sha'b were the Sabaic language speakers whose military campaigns and diplomacy (pilgrimage rites) confederated other first-order sha'bs through the performance of a *mkrb* (*mukarrib*) (Beeston 1972).

We turn later to mukarribs and sovereigns and the historical transformation of political authority, but other discernable social roles deserve brief mention. Some of these could be held concurrently and at times invested religious, political, and economic power in the hands of one individual, albeit always through the explicit assumption of differentiated offices. The office of *rshwt*, sometimes translated as priest (Henninger, Joseph [1946/47] 1981: 266), seems to have been that of sacrificer and officiator at sacrifices (Pirenne 1976: 183, 203, 1972). A *qzn* gathered the tithe, while a *qyn* was an administrator (Beeston 1972: 266). All three offices could be held conjointly as was the case for at least one Qatabanian sovereign, whose royal title was "*qzn qyn rshwt* [of the federal god] 'Amm" (Korotayev 1994b: 5). The office of eldest son, or *bkr* as the (class-based) sovereign's, might be best understood as primus inter pares with a kinship designation a continued metaphor for the tribal sons or *wld* (*wuld*) of a god (Beeston 1972).

The metaphor of obligations of tribes people to a divinity (masking appropriated wealth and labor in caste/class relations) is a politically integrating motif in ancient Southern Arabian states, and throughout the historical period it knit highland tribes and lowland states (Obermeyer 1999). Epigraphic texts were especially expressive on these points, for they represent social relations as documented by the literate, dominant elites in a discourse of social identity. Edicts and proclamations about tribal people's obligations to federal gods inscribed by elites at sacred sites are just such a discourse, and its efficacy in cloaking the appropriation of wealth depended upon its harmonic resonance with a social landscape of territorial tribes constituted through pilgrimage.

b. Historical Trajectory

The constituting practice of *hj* – pilgrimage – is evident throughout the religio-political areas of Saba, Qataban, and Hadramawt and, along with ritual hunts, ritual banquets, human relationships to divinities, and basic patterns of social identification and status (clans, patronage and clients, political tribes), marks a common cultural sphere, despite the uses of different dialects and scripts. That there existed cultural differences such as the names and identities of divinities seems clear. But the basic structural similarities across the Southern Arabian states point to common political-social constitutions and, most likely, similar origins and historical trajectories in the interactions of territorial tribes.

Therefore an approach to understanding the heuristic classification between bedouin and urban practices is to view them through the lens of history, in which common practices derive from deeply ancestral rites common to both – a substrate (Pirenne 1976: 213) or better, a landscape of pilgrimage. Scholars from the times of Wellhausen (1887) and Robertson Smith (1907a) have winnowed common underlying themes in Semitic religious practice through etymological and ethno-historical analyses and have often assumed that the religious ideologies of Semitic states had roots in pastoral nomadism. In Chapter 4, new archaeological evidence points to the antiquity of pilgrimage practice among Southern Arabian pastoral nomads long before the emergence of agriculture, class, and state. A diachronic approach, aided by the epigraphic and archaeological evidence from complex Southern Arabian societies, suggests that the appropriation of extant pilgrimage practices served the ancient Southern Arabian state.

i. From mkrb to mlk

Historical development and social change is best known, with all its attendant uncertainties, from the Sabaean area (see summaries in De

Maigret [1996] 2003, Korotayev 2003, Obermeyer 1999, Beeston 1972). Although the inscriptions are largely silent about many aspects of society and social groups, it is clear that early (800–400 BC) political authority resided with one leader – a *mlk*, or king of his own ethnic tribe (first-order sha'b Korotayev 1993a) – appointed as mukarrib of a council of tribal leaders. The mukarrib issued edicts that carried out decisions by the council and presided over building projects, ritual hunts, and sacrifices. Some of the most famous inscriptions record the military conquests of mukarribs, who were evidently quite successful in confederating tribal groups through the rites of pilgrimage (at Jabal al-Lawdh, for example) and then using such social cohesion to conscript military forces. Obviously, by the time inscriptions document the doings of mukarribs, political tribes had already developed with a commonwealth decision-making code very like other tribally constituted states elsewhere (e.g., Stein 2004, Fleming 2004, Archi 1985), but the epigraphic evidence is silent about state origins prior to 800 BC. In time, the role of mukarrib gave way to the exercise of sovereign power by a king. The kings of Saba and Dhū-Raydān were several parallel dynasties seated at Ma'rib and in the Yemen highlands who claimed sovereignty over a territory that included many tribes of differing ethnic constitution but all devoted to the federal god Almaqah.

About the sociopolitical history of other regions we know less. Hadramawt concerns us greatly because of its proximity to and eventual control of primary incense production, which must have played a critical economic role in the emergence of complex Southern Arabian societies. The kings of Saba and Dhū-Raydān and the Sabaean mukarribs merely facilitated caravans originating in Hadramawt, so for all that we do know of Sabaean sociopolitical development, it offers only partial insight into the emergence of the state, if one presumes that class-based societies emerged in response to an external (Mediterranean) demand for aromatics. In Hadramawt, kings also emerged (Sedov 1998) and performed rituals comparable to the Sabaean ones (Loudine 1990: 97). Archaeological excavations show that the earliest (albeit poorly defined) settlements at the sites of Shabwa and Raybun date to the second half of the second millennium BC (Badre 1991: 233, Sedov 2003). Like the early occupations at Ma'rib and Hajar Yahir, the capital of the kingdom of Awsān (Raunig 1997), these remains suggest settled groups maintaining complex agricultural systems long before they leave historical records of themselves (Brunner and Haefner 1986, Brunner 1997a, Francaviglia 2002). Sabaic inscriptions in Hadramawt and Sabaean claims of a vast commonwealth and military campaigns leave little doubt that the early Sabaean commonwealth had significant influence over the emergence of an (ultimately) independent state in Hadramawt (Beeston 1972, Frantsouzoff 2005).

What does appear to have occurred in Hadramawt and can be historically reconstructed from the inscriptions and temple development is the shift in status of various divinities. For example, at Raybun the Raḥbān temple, sacred to the goddess Dhāt Ṣahrān (second century BC), was later incorporated into a complex sacred to Dhāt Himyam. Nearby lies the Kafas/Naʿamān temple also sacred to Dhāt Himyam. An early inscription showed it was originally named Dhāt Himyam Dhāt Kafas and later changed to Dhāt Naʿamān (Sedov 2000). As each manifestation of a god corresponded to a region and identity of a territorial group or clan (e.g., Frantsouzoff 2001, Beeston 1984: 260), one might suppose that such changes in name, perhaps accompanied by rebuilding and restoration projects, correspond with the ascendancy of particular social groups associated with the divinity. Sayyin was worshiped everywhere in Hadramawt (e.g., Sedov 1996: 253–254, 261, 270), but at Shabwa, the temple of Sayyin Lord of the Feasts held ascendancy over the lesser Sayyin Dhū-Mayfaʿān temple at Raybun. In the middle first millennium BC, Sayyin and Ḥawl together were the paramount divinities of Hadramawt, but later in time only Sayyin appears as the federal deity. A similar situation appears to have occurred in ancient Qataban with the deities ʿAmm and Anbay (Sedov 2005: 22). And perhaps ancestral to them all, the paramount god ʿAthtar or ʿAttar ceded place over time in Hadramawt, Qataban, and Saba.

There is a documented shift from ʾAthtar to Almaqah as the paramount deity in the Sabaean kingdom. In the time of the mukarribs, it was ʾAthtar who was worshiped at Jabal al-Lawdh, but by the time of the Sabaean kings, Almaqah at Maʾrib had become the paramount god (Robin and Breton 1982), and a similar process can be documented in the Northern Yemen highlands (Robin 1982b: 66–67). If each tribe had a god, then it is possible through the dedicatory inscriptions to appreciate the ascendancy and political fortunes of various social groups by the chronological changes in the pantheon and hierarchy of divinities. This attests to an historical social dynamic even if in all cases we cannot name the actual clan, tribes, or social classes associated with a particular divinity.

ii. The Southern Arabian State Appropriates Pilgrimage

This book focuses on continuity and thus is not the place to detail an outline of state emergence in ancient Southern Arabia, although one is sorely needed. Alas, the epigraphic evidence does not cover the period in question and classical sources are little help. Archaeological evidence is still too scant, particularly in Hadramawt nearest the incense-producing areas. Several historical developments show that the core practice of pilgrimage existed throughout the sociopolitical development of Arabian states and continuously manifested a long-term, if subjectively and temporally variable, Arabian habitus. It is axiomatic, if as yet unproven, that ideologically engineered shifts in a social landscape of pilgrimage played a critical role in the transformation of tribal social relations to de facto relationships of class in the earliest Arabian states.

If the basic socioeconomic unit in Arabia was the bayt (clan or lineage), then the paramount question is the following: How did some bayts outstrip others in access to means of production? Two possible solutions come to mind, and they resonate with long-tested anthropological theories of state formation elsewhere (Haas 1982, Yoffee 1995). In brief, one might envision that (1) irrigation and social organization of irrigation labor invested some qayls with authority over land and water allocation (e.g., Wittfogel 1957, Liverani [1998] 2006: 70) and (2) that exchange systems serving to mitigate supply risks inherent in the unpredictable environment of spate-water farming resulted in growing wealth differentials between bayts poised to exploit different resources (e.g., Halstead 1989).

Access to the primary means of production included access to land and to powerful runoff water, which could rain down somewhere else, maybe once a year, and flow in the middle of the night for a few hours. People had to be organized and ready to manage the complex and large-scale irrigation works that inherently required social technologies (organized systems of labor and adjudication) to cope with unpredictable spate waters. Recent research shows that Arabian irrigation technologies are indigenous inventions and apparently originated in highlands catchments with gentler, more predictable flow (Harrower 2008, Wilkinson 1999). Significantly, agriculture and irrigation appeared late in Arabian culture history as an adjunct to mobile pastoralism, and its first practice was therefore fitted to the economic, social, and territorial frameworks of tribal pastoralists (McCorriston 2006, Cleuziou and Tosi 1997). The quantities of available water for irrigation even in the largest desert-margin oases was limited, limiting both the populations and agricultural surpluses (Cleuziou 1997, Brunner 1997b, Wilkinson 2003) that could be tapped by elites (D'Altroy and Earle 1985). Surpluses that could be tapped were pastoral – animals culled from herds for sacrifice and the labor and product of collecting and transporting aromatic resins from wild trees in the highland territories of pastoralists. Exchange doubtless took place; however, supplying pastoralists with foods like dates and with cloth, the taxation of caravans, and the maintenance of pilgrimage at the sanctuary of Sayyin at Shabwa points to an elite appropriation of the wealth and labor of pastoral highland tribes peoples.

c. Pilgrimage, Sacrifice, and Feast in Southern Arabian States

At the official times of pilgrimage, there were ritual banquets, sponsored by elites, and paid by the tithes rendered to the god. Northeast of the Sabaean capital at Ma'rib lies Jabal al-Lawdh, a rock promontory in the Jawf, which was an important passage from desert interior to the highlands of Yemen and home of tribes not sharing kin-based ethnicity with the Sabaeans. The Sabaean mukarribs and, after them, a series of Sabaean kings maintained a rural sanctuary to which tribes people came to honor the god 'Athtar Dhū-Dhibān. At Jabal al-Lawdh, inscriptions tell us that pilgrims participated in ritual banquets sponsored by the paramount Sabaean leader. The inscriptions and their context imply that banquets followed sacrifice and tithe offerings to 'Athtar Dhū-Dhibān, and the inscriptions also refer to the commemorative erection of stelae and the construction of benches. Archaeological studies of the sanctuary and the context of inscriptions have identified both the places and practices of banqueting and pilgrimage in this ancient Sabaean shrine (Robin and Breton 1982). Similar practices are attested for the

Samʿaī tribe who practiced pilgrimage to the god Taʾlab's sanctuary at Jabal Riyām and enjoyed a banquet organized using the tithes. The god Taʾlab nevertheless enjoined his tribe to visit Almaqah in Maʾrib in the pilgrimage month of *dh-'bhy* (Dhū-Abhay, no accepted transliteration) (J. Ryckmans 1973b: 37, Ghul 1984). Over time, priority of place in the Sabaean pantheon was ceded to the federal god Almaqah, whose sanctuary at the Awwam temple in Maʾrib was the focus of pilgrimage and the federation rituals of the Sabaean religio-political area. Modern visitors to Maʾrib's famous "Maḥrām Bilqīs" (Sanctuary of the Queen of Sheba) with its haunting sentinel pillars engulfed in dunes can hardly guess that the oval enclosure once held the unarmed, purified, supplicant pilgrims converging to Almaqah's temple from across the Sabaean kingdom in the *ḥj* month of *dh-'bhy*.

Qatabanian inscriptions may also mention banqueting halls (J. Ryckmans 1973b: 36), and the practice of pilgrimage, tithes, ritual banquets, and federation into a religio-political area seems amply attested in Hadramawt, where the temple of Sayyin Dhū-Alīm (Sayyin Lord of [the temple] *'lm*) in Shabwa overshadowed all others (Frantsouzoff 2001). In Hadramawt, the actual banqueting preparation halls adjoined to temples are readily identified in the archaeological record by their layouts and the long benches and ample faunal remains from sacrifices and feasts (Sedov 2005).

Let us suppose that the majority of highland tribes people who made the pilgrimage to Sayyin of the Ritual Feasts at Shabwa were nomadic or seminomadic pastoralists. Given the conspicuous lack of highland settlements contemporary with the ancient Hadramawt kingdom and the failure of multiple surveys in the southern and northern Jol regions to detect significant permanent settlement, tribal pastoral nomads are the only candidates against which caravan-route fortresses (of which there are a number) would have been constructed. Pilgrimage served to confederate these tribes and to implement truces and periods of safe conduct for the passage of incense and caravans. I have argued that the tithe, which supports sacrifice and feast, provided an institutional levy on labor if it was indeed pastoralists who collected incense.

Pastoralists would also have significant economic incentive to do so, for studies of specialized pastoral societies have shown that pastoralists can reduce the herd size they need to maintain if they trade with

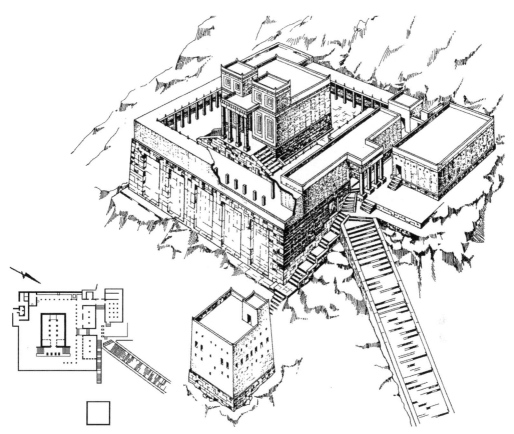

15. Temple of Sayyin Dhū Mayfaʿān at Raybun. Reconstruction by A. Sedov and E. Kurkina. Courtesy of Alexander Sedov.

agricultural societies (Dahl and Hjort 1976: 267). In this context, it is important to recall the economic transactions that pilgrimage supports in a time of truce when tribes people and caravans can safely travel, cross other tribes' territories, and meet in sanctuary. Incense collected and exchanged for grain and dates grown in the agricultural oases of the caravan kingdoms would help pastoralists to reduce herd populations, grazing pressure, and, ultimately, territorial behavior and tensions. Dates are particularly important in this context because they are less bulky (per calorie) than grain for transport and are easy to store. We know that dates were found as early as the sixth millennium BC in Arabia (Beech and Shepherd 2001) and that they were an important agricultural product in ancient Southern Arabian states (Levkovskya and Filatenko 1992).

16. Frankincense storage facility at Hānīn built ca. third century BC within the zone of maximum frankincense production in Dhufār (Oman). Hadramitic colonists constructed this outpost, which included what may have been a small shrine to Sayyin, federal god of Hadramawt. Author's photo.

Significantly, archaeologists have recovered some evidence for what must have been another (invisible) economic component linking agricultural bayts and pastoral nomads who came on pilgrimage – the production and dyeing of textiles. Linen can be produced from flax, which was introduced to Arabia (Reade and Potts 1993), but would not easily grow in ancient Arabia's irrigated oases, as could (summer) cotton (cf. Betts et al. 1994) when and if summer crops were adopted (Levkovskya and Filatenko 1992, Edens 2005, McCorriston 2006). The role of sheep in Southern Arabian pastoral economies at the time of urban oasis settlement is unclear: sheep were present but wool-bearing sheep were not the focus of pastoral economies. Pastoralists may have been wearing tanned hides (Noye 1985: 407), but they surely would esteem linen and cotton textiles if they could get them.

And perhaps they could. In 2000, Kenneth Cole (personal communication), a paleoecologist with the U.S. Geological Survey, reported linen scraps of textile sorted out of a 2,000-year-old hyrax midden he

17. Bar'ān temple at Ma'rib (Yemen) with stone monoliths typical of Southern Arabian temples. Deutsches Archäologisches Institut, Yemen/I. Wagner.

collected in the remote – always remote – Wadi Sana in the southern highlands of the ancient Hadramawt kingdom. Along with a few (Baltic?) amber beads, the linen scraps attest to the extraordinary reach of trade along the caravan routes during the time of the Roman Empire, but the find enigmatically raises the question of how linen and amber came to be available to a cave-dwelling hyrax about 2,000 years ago. The detection of a very small human phalange (finger bone) in the same midden, and recovery of another human phalange from another cave-sheltered midden several kilometers away provides a compelling clue – hyraxes were mining linen-wrapped corpses buried in caves along the Wadi Sana some 2,000 years ago. While these putative burials may have been unlucky caravaneers dying far from home, they may as plausibly have belonged to pastoralists who acquired linen and beads in their pilgrimages and exchanges with oasis centers like Shabwa and Raybun. At about the same time, linen-wrapped corpses were buried in caves in the Northern Yemen highlands: these "mummies" are on display at the Sana'a University Department of Archaeology and History Museum.

18. Hadramitic camel driver on the traditional road leading into Wadi Hadramawt from the southern Jol (Yemen). Note the tribal brands (*wusūm*) on the animal's necks. Author's photo.

While flax for linen could have been grown on a small scale in the highlands, it requires water, tending, and labor generally incompatible with pastoral tasks (McCorriston 1997) and is an unlikely crop for the small-scale, intermittent irrigation possible in Hadramawt's arid highlands (Harrower 2006, 2008). More likely as a crop would be small patches of grain or of indigo, a leguminous dye plant with several local wild varieties tended and set off-limits to grazing even today. Nomadic bedouin of the Al-'Alī clan (Humūm tribe) can remember when a herder would delimit a patch of wild indigo, harvest it, and bring it to town to the dyer along with (purchased) cotton cloth. Dyeing succeeds best with animal fibers, although cotton more readily accepts a dye than the bast fibers of flax. In living memory, tribes men in Hadramawt, Mahra, and Dhufār wore indigo-dyed cotton textiles (Stark 1953: 62, van der Meulen [1947] 1958: 21, 31, Thomas 1938: 53–54, Bent and Bent [1900] 1994: 78) and prized the effect of indigo, which turned

19. Resin oozes from a deliberate cut to the bark of *Boswellia sacra* Flueck. Harvesters will return within a few weeks for the hardened frankincense. Author's photo.

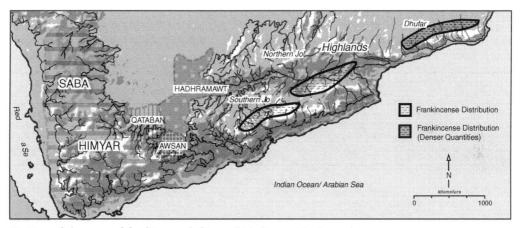

20. Map of the areas of frankincense habitat, which lie outside the settlement zones controlled by Southern Arabian kingdoms, which maintained routes to and through frankincense-producing regions.

their skin deep blue, keeping them warm at night, they said. By darkening and covering the skin, indigo may have mitigated sun exposure as a natural sunscreen, preventing the night chills that come with sunburn. In this capacity, it might be truly prized indeed, but the urban dyer's craft was needed to turn the plant into a (mostly) fast dye (Balfour-Paul

1997: 84–99). Did these economic interdependencies stretch far back in time so that nomadic tribal pastoralists were linked through pilgrimage practices to the markets and technologies of the ancient Hadramawt state?

Whatever role textiles played, texts and archaeology show that settled and mobile tribes people were linked through economic, social, and ideological practices in the ancient Arabian states. Pilgrimage bringing together all these elements was a common and constituting practice, and, as the next chapter demonstrates, its roots stretch deep into antiquity.

CHAPTER 4

THE CATTLE SHRINE AT KHESHIYA AND THE ORIGINS OF ARABIAN PILGRIMAGE SOCIETIES

A very important role in the integration of the religious-political area is played by the pilgrimage to the central sanctuary.

Korotayev 2003: 73

Introduction to Arabian Pre-history

Arabian pilgrimage stretches deep into the past. It finds its roots in rituals of preliterate, pre-historic tribal people. It has not always been easy to see this cultural continuity: indeed, to an earlier generation of archaeologists and epigraphers, the high Southern Arabian civilizations of Saba, Ma'in, Hadramawt, and Qataban seemed to have appeared without any local antecedents (cf. J. Ryckmans 1973a: 90). While this apparently abrupt emergence can be in part attributable to lacunae in the archaeological record that have been largely addressed since the 1980s (de Maigret [1996] 2003: 12–13, 1996: 335), Arabian pre-history and Arabian historiography draw upon different epistemologies, with the consequence that a structural break long perceived between pre-historic and literate societies of antiquity in reality reflects little more than disparities in research approaches of pre-historians and epigrapher-historians. *What* one knows is a function of *how* one knows. In the Arabian case, different epistemologies and an artificial boundary between pre-history and history have obscured a long-term cultural trajectory of social constitution through punctuated mobility and confluence, sacrifice, and shared feasts.

Whereas Arabian historiography, including our understanding of religious beliefs and practices, embraces a mix of archaeological and architectural studies, epigraphy of ancient Semitic inscriptions, and early Islamic commentary, our understandings of Arabian pre-history depend upon the intertwined approaches of archaeology and ethnography. The significance of ethnographic analogy in linking material remains from the archaeological record to human behaviors can hardly be overstated: as "Middle Range Theory," this approach lies at the methodological heart of most explicitly scientific archaeology since the 1960s (e.g., Binford 1967, Watson 1979, Stahl 1993). In the Near East, middle range theory and scientific archaeology were introduced largely as an outgrowth of Americanist anthropological archaeology and the epistemological-methodological debates prevalent in the social sciences through the 1960s and 1970s. Throughout this period, scientific archaeology maintained a dedicated emphasis on economic rationalism determining behavioral decision making, culture, and culture change (Leone 1982). Until recently, Near Eastern pre-history in the scientific tradition has focused on economy and been historically divorced from studies of ritual, ideology, belief, and the ways in which these cultural attributes link to societies, social formation, and social change. In following the cultural thread of pilgrimage practice deep into pre-history, one is therefore faced with a break between historical and scientific traditions. This structural break in the means of acquiring knowledge about the past has distorted the historical and cultural continuity in Arabian pilgrimage and distinctively Arabian society.

In Southern Arabia, there long persisted a precivilization gap (de Maigret [1996] 2003: 185, Tosi 1986a), now rapidly being filled by archaeological studies of highland planned towns (Edens, Wilkinson and Barratt 2000, Ekstrom and Edens 2003, Wilkinson 2003, Edens 1999), trading settlements on the coastal plain (Vogt and Sedov 1998, Phillips, 1988, 2005), and small villages based on mixed farming and pastoralism (de Maigret 1990, Fedele 2005) prior to the founding of cities in the desert margins. Systematic survey and excavation on a regional scale in highland Dhamār (Wilkinson 1997), the Tihamma coastal plain of Northern Yemen (Khalidi 2005, Tosi 1985, 1986b), the Jawf-Hadramawt fluvial system (Cleuziou, Inizan and Marcolongo 1992, Benoit et al. 2007, Mouton et al. 2006), interior wadi systems (Sedov 1988, 1996, 2003, Braemer et al. 2001, Braemer, Cleuziou and Steimer 2003), and Dhufār (Zarins 2001) all suggest

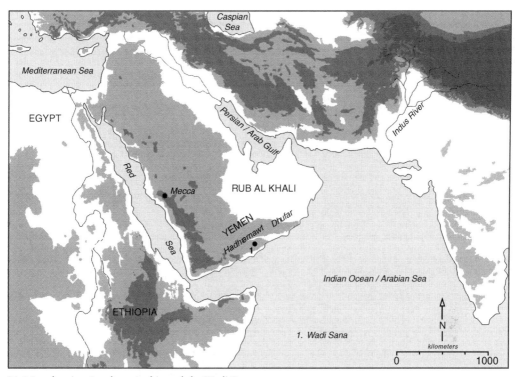

21. Map showing Southern Arabia and the Wadi Sana.

a gradual increase in regional economic specialization in the latter third and second millennium BC. During this time, for which there still is a frustrating dearth of archaeological or historical data, there coexisted pastoralists and agriculturalists with cattle and caprines across much of the arid highlands. (Recent excellent summaries of the Arabian cultural-historical sequences may be found in Cleuziou and Tosi (1997), Wilkinson (2003), and de Maigret (2003).) Importantly, the antecedents to the massive and carefully organized irrigation systems that supported later Iron Age Arabian polities and kingdoms appear about 3300 BC and suggest indigenous strategies to adopt agricultural crops, notably winter-grown cereals, from the Fertile Crescent (McCorriston 2006, Harrower 2006, 2008). With the institution of agricultural economies, highland terracing (Wilkinson 1999, Wilkinson, Edens and Barratt 2001), water management, and agricultural exchange with neighboring pastoralists, regionally integrated, specialized economies formed a ripe base for sociopolitical complexity and an essentially autochthonic state formation.

One of Arabia's many fascinating aspects is the early apparent emergence of independent pastoralism, based on cattle and initially unsupported, as far

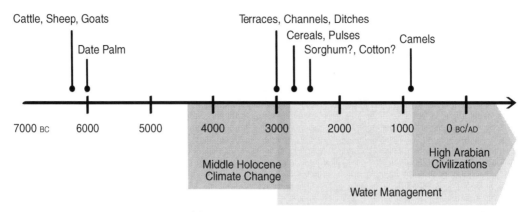

22. Appearance of domesticated animals and plants in Southern and Eastern Arabia.

as anyone can yet discern, by exchange for agricultural products (Cleuziou and Tosi 1997: 124, Martin, McCorriston and Crassard 2009, McCorriston and Martin 2009). Such a system is unknown ethnographically today, making it challenging to develop economic models for cattle pastoralism prior to agriculture (cf. Janzen 1986, Lancaster and Lancaster 1999a, Johnson 2002). Yet it was in such an economic context, before the major Middle Holocene aridification made agriculture attractive, that social and ideological practices shaping the landscape and habitus of historical tribal Southern Arabia emerged. Chapter 3 argued that Southern Arabian high civilizations appropriated tribal rituals to the cult of paramount federal gods, redefining the practice of pilgrimage so as to facilitate social alliances and appropriate the labor of highland agro-pastoralists to enrich the lowland polities. The antecedents of pilgrimage therefore lie in the tribal rites conducted by tribal pastoralists, for which this chapter will present new and dramatic evidence from Khuzmūm, long a place of ritual practices in middle Wadi Sana (Chapter 1). It is to the independent cattle pastoralists of the monsoon-drenched Early Holocene Southern Arabian highlands that one must turn for our earliest evidence of the punctuated mobility, confluence of people, cattle sacrifices, and great feasts that project pilgrimage practice deep into pre-history.

The Ring of Cattle Skulls at Kheshiya

Sometimes a small fieldwork moment can shift the course of archaeological research and interpretation: it happened to a survey team studying human

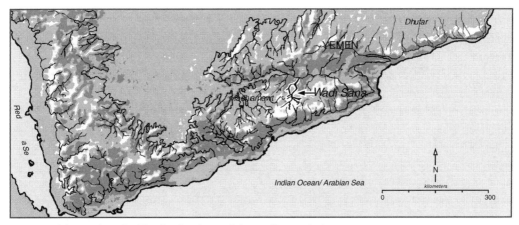

23. Map of the southern highlands of Arabia and the Wadi Sana drainage.

environments and responses to paleoclimate change in highland Southern Arabia. One too-long afternoon on the sun-baked banks of a long-dry wadi, RASA (Roots of Agriculture in Southern Arabia) team member Catherine Heyne called us over to look at several crumbling animal skulls. They were embedded nose-down in the natural section of a gully at Shiʻb Kheshiya. Northeastward across the main bed of Wadi Sana, one can easily see The Place of Khuzma, with which this book begins. Trusting local expertise, we asked Al-ʻAlī bedouin working with us if the skulls were camel or cattle, and we collected a few teeth for identification. These particular men keep goats, and they emphatically declared the skulls to be camel. Ironically, thus began a dramatic discovery of Neolithic cattle sacrifice, gathering, and feast.

Had the teeth indeed been from domesticated camels, they would have been the oldest in Arabia, for paleoecologists had established that the sediments formed around them had ceased to accumulate some 5,000 years ago. The bedouin can hardly be derided for misjudging cattle as camels, for these men had no more experience with cattle skulls than we archaeologists, with our comic deference to "native know-how" and no faunal analyst at hand. Amy Nicodemus and Louise Martin later identified the teeth, prompting further questions of how thirsty cattle came to be in this desert in antiquity. Cattle cannot today thrive in the arid wilderness of middle Wadi Sana, which has less than 100 millimeters of annual rainfall, insufficient grazing land, and no permanent water.

In 2005 the team returned with an excavation crew to probe the relationship between the cattle skulls – now more were showing in the

24. Discovery of the cattle ring at Kheshiya SU151–1, Wadi Sana. As soon as any one skull could be painstakingly salvaged from the crumbling gully edge, another appeared in section behind it. All skulls were planted nose-down on one ashy, lithic-strewn surface, and a later, higher ashy surface developed around the eye-sockets of standing skulls. Also visible in the higher ashy layer are thermally altered limestone clasts scattered from hearths in antiquity. Excavations proceeded northward from this natural gully edge and east of the stone structure. Author's photo.

gully section – and an adjacent tear-drop-shaped ring of upright stone slabs poking through the surface of the silt bed. The site at Shi'b Kheshiya proved extraordinary, with a ring of cattle skulls set in soft mud and later commemorated by a ring of stone slabs briefly occupied and then filled to make a solid platform. Details of the stratigraphy and remains will also appear elsewhere and therefore only a brief review follows. The site is dramatic for the use of cattle skulls as architectural elements in a deliberate emplacement unparalleled at any contemporary site. Burial of a chief at Kerma C (some 2,000 years later along the African Nile) used cattle skulls to ring a grave, but there is no human burial at Kheshiya. The best Arabian parallel, and one closer in time to Kheshiya, is a newly discovered Neolithic dugong bone mound on the Arabian Gulf (Méry et al. 2009).

Set against the local and regional pre-historic contexts of Southern Arabia's adoption of pastoralism and agriculture, the Kheshiya remains offer key insights to ritual, social constitution, and the emergence of territories held by tribes. Through the remainder of this chapter, analysis uses the parsimonious tests of economic rationalism and ecological constraints (human behavioral ecology) to eliminate and qualify alternative interpretations of the cattle ring, namely the implausibly rationalist hypothesis that it represented a range of economic activities somehow disembodied from rich social and ideological context. This approach draws upon the scientific rationalism that traditionally characterizes pre-historic archaeology (Leone 1982) while underscoring the limitations of strictly nutritional and reproductive currency in explaining the cattle ring. The approach seeks not to separate economic and social-ideological activities, but by refuting explanation in terms of only productive and reproductive energetics, it rejects economic explanation devoid of social-ideological cultural context. Overall, this approach aims to emphasize the integration of economic, social and ideological factors in the long-term cultural continuity of pilgrimage.

Environmental Contexts and Middle Wadi Sana

Near the end of the Pleistocene, about 15,000 calendar years ago, the southern portion of the Arabian Peninsula and much of Saharan Africa began to experience a gradual and initially unstable increase in annual precipitation. This rainfall, always occurring in summer, came from a strengthening of the Southwest Asian monsoon climate system largely in response to changes in the shape of the earth's orbit and tilt (Overpeck et al. 1996). Local effects in Southern Arabia included large bodies of permanent standing water – lakes, spring-fed pools, marshes – and flowing streams that seasonally expanded to fill ancient watercourses and drop deep deposits of sediment (Eric Oches personal communication, Cremaschi and Negrino 2005: 561, Figure 1). From the onset of the Holocene 10,000 years ago, global climate stabilized, and humans faced diminished inter-annual fluctuation (Richerson, Boyd and Bettinger 2001), making it easier to predict a range of resources, including water, and the extent to which annual flooding would extend and retreat. By the Middle Holocene (4000 BC), the monsoon wind belts (Intertropical Convergence

Zone, or ITCZ) began to weaken with the result that summer monsoons no longer pushed sea moisture across the inner Arabian Peninsula, and annual precipitation rates declined relatively rapidly (Sirocko et al. 1993, Sirocko 1996). Within about a thousand years, the inner Arabian parklands had become hyper-arid (like the Sahara), forcing humans to change their ancient survival strategies (Lezine et al. 1998). In Africa, it appears that people tended cattle as early as 7500 BC with certain domestication by 6,000 BC (Hassan 2000, Close and Wendorf 1992, cf. Grigson 2000). By 6000 BC there were domesticated cattle also in Southern Arabia (Fedele 1990: 38, 2005: 225, 2008: 166, Martin, McCorriston and Crassard 2009), and cattle herders there would have faced challenges in watering and grazing their stock in a steadily more arid environment.

The RASA project has been investigating the changes that occurred 5000–3000 BC both in environment and in human activities by focusing on one highland region, the Wadi Sana of southern Hadramawt. In this northward-draining wadi of the southern belt of uplifted limestone-and-shale mountains (southern Jol), an archaeological and palaeoecological team has developed a long-term sequence of human activities and environmental change (McCorriston et al. 2002, McCorriston 2006). This landscape history rests in part on paleoecological reconstructions led by RASA team member Eric Oches (personal communication) and on archaeological excavation of key sites for dating and recovery of economic and social indicators extensively discussed elsewhere. Survey data too have played a significant role in interpretation of human occupation and land use (McCorriston et al. 2005). From excavations and sampling the team has identified early encampments (McCorriston et al. 2002, Crassard et al. 2006) that, with analysis of dung-rich deposits and domesticated animal bone, provide insight into pastoral life-ways around 6000 BC (Martin, McCorriston and Crassard 2009). The opportunities and constraints presented by keeping domesticated animals probably sparked the emergence of tribal territories, setting the stage for rituals of confederation, affirmation of tribal identity, initiation, truce and treaty, and genealogical recollection and retelling. These rituals and the tribal confluences that characterize them in turn foreshadow pilgrimage practice in Arabia.

By the Middle Holocene period, cattle herders in the Middle Wadi Sana were periodically setting deliberate fires to clear dry and tough vegetation and maximize the new growth potential in what had come

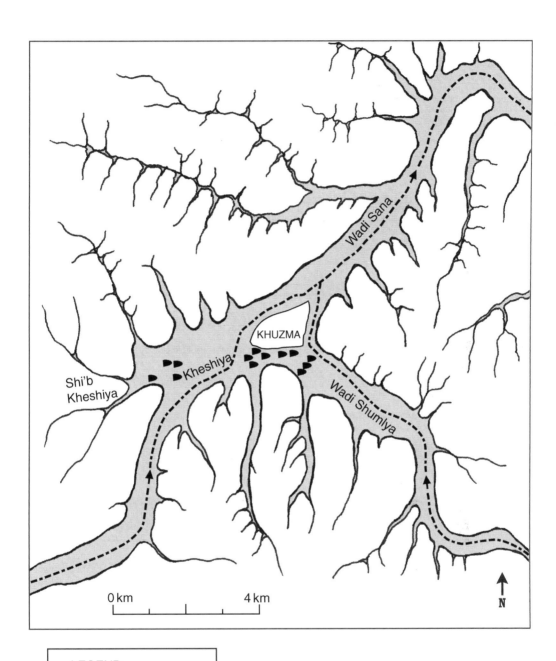

25. Map detail of the Middle Wadi Sana drainage showing locations of platformed structures, including the stone platform at Kheshiya.

26. Modern marshland at a semipermanent pipe leak protected from any grazing in the upper Wadi Ḥarū (Yemen) serves as an analog habitat for ancient vegetation in Wadi Sana. Note the dense cover of tamarix, acacia, perennial grasses, sedges, and leafy annuals. Author's photo.

to be limited territories. When the first evidence for tribal gatherings and rituals appears 4500 BC, such intensification strategies had already been in use for at least 500 years (McCorriston et al. 2005). In these circumstances, pastoralists built tear-drop and D-shaped stone pit-houses of upright slabs (as at Kheshiya 151-1, Khuzmūm 037-3, 054-6 and -8) that were briefly or seasonally occupied (with interior hearths, McCorriston et al. 2002: 76-77) and thereafter deliberately filled with tabular limestone slabs or large cobbles. Associated with many are finished limestone block betyls or *anṣāb* (Atallah [after Ibn al-Kalbī] 1969: 27, Scagliarini 2007: 256) as standing stones set up outside, possibly to house a god at a significant place (Pirenne 1991).

The receding margins of a seasonally flooded marsh zone in the Middle Holocene Wadi Sana were a highly seasonal resource that attracted herders or foragers in annual congregations around permanent water. In the wake of the monsoon rains, plants set out new foliage and seedlings, animals produced litters and milk, and cattle herders could disperse widely across the uplands to take advantage of seasonal water

27. Wadi Sana today in stark contrast with the vegetated marshy bottoms of the Middle Holocene. Author's photo.

and graze. Only when upland surface waters dried and the margins of marshy oxbows receded were the narrow confines of Wadi Sana opened to grazing. While rich and attractive, the area had spatially limited grazing resources because soils had long since disappeared from the plateaus. Limited graze land allowed only a few herding families to maintain residence throughout the dry season. There simply was not enough graze to support large herds, and the available supply was enhanced through careful landscape management by herders.

In another thousand years (around 3300 BC), tribes people would begin another activity designed to intensify their use of local resources when they began manipulating the flow of flood waters into rock-lined canals, perhaps to cultivate local forbs or fruit trees like dates and Christ's thorn (*Zizyphus* sp.) (Harrower 2008, McCorriston 2006). Such intensive cultivation and land management set the stage for adopting crop plants as the moist, Early Holocene monsoon weakened about 3000 BC. By the time crop agriculture and settled communities emerged in Southern Arabia, tribes people had already been practicing the rites of pilgrimage for at least 1,500 years.

Excavation and the Remains of Pre-historic Pilgrimage

Excavations at Kheshiya showed that the cattle skulls belonged to a 1.75-meter-wide oval ring of skulls placed with frontals facing in and horns interlocking. Mandibles had been removed from the skulls, and the maxillary teeth faced outward. A gap in the long western side appears deliberate, and the southernmost extent of the oval must be inferred (natural erosion that exposed bone in the gully also truncated that part of the ring). A central skull, the largest (Louise Martin, personal communication), faced westward (the western gap). When pressed into soft mud in antiquity, the skulls originally protruded about 30 to 40 centimeters, so that the horns once showed above the ground surface. Archaeologically this was a tough excavation assignment: the entire array – composed of fragile bone that crumbled with each sun-baked hour – needed to be quickly exposed in full so that its architectural plan and construction details could be fully documented along with its relationship to the adjacent stone structure.

28. Kheshiya Cattle Shrine under excavation. Neolithic cattle skulls and stone-platformed structure were buried in silt terraces cut by later Holocene erosion (gulleys, middle foreground and behind goats). February 2005. Author's photo.

29. Kheshiya Cattle Shrine overview showing partially excavated stone platform and skull ring. Photo by Michael J. Harrower.

A few meters to the west, the Kheshiya 151-1 stone structure was built afterward by sinking tabular limestone slabs against the edges of a shallow pit dug into moist sediments. A slight interlocking provided greater support for the slabs' (mostly) above-ground protrusion. Within the stone structure was slight evidence of occupational activities – several discrete baked, charcoal-flecked surfaces and scattered thermally altererd rocks indicated in-situ fires; there were a few flakes of chert and obsidian and a clear floor overlain by ashy debris. Subsequently, this structure was deliberately filled with limestone slabs and a few smaller cobbles to make a stone platform. A solitary slab, the only worked stone and carefully shaped on top by pecking, stood outside and to the southeast of both stone and skull rings. It was perhaps an associated betyl set into the basal ashy surface and predated both the stone platform and skull ring. Because today's gully profile reveals deeper slabs (and the gully bottom has slabs that had eroded from unknown positions), it is possible that

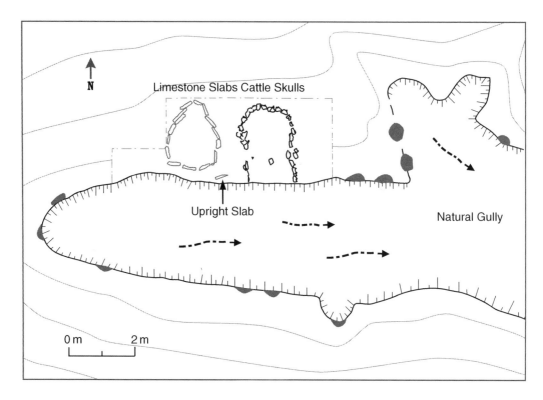

LEGEND

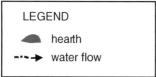

30. Plan of the Kheshiya 151-1 Cattle Ring and stone slab structure after removal of artificial stone fill that made up the stone platform. Excavations showed that the stone structure had been briefly occupied before being filled, so this plan shows a phase earlier than the artist's depiction. Hearths were not all contemporary.

earlier structures, perhaps even providing some stones for reuse in the later one, underlay the site. Whatever the sequence of stone structures, it is clear that like other stone platform sites, in Wadi Sana, Kheshiya 151–1 had a use cycle, the final stage of which consisted of a platform protruding above the surrounding alluvium next to a standing stone and a ring of half-buried cattle skulls.

Other features attest to an occupational history relatively dense for the Middle Wadi Sana. Over about 500 years, many nearby hearths with thermally altered rock and charcoal deposits were buried by flood waters, and more than a dozen of these can be traced in the modern gully profiles

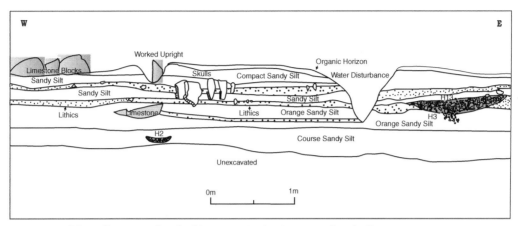

31. Section of the gully cutting the Kheshiya 151-1 Cattle Ring. Note that the limestone uprights of the stone structure have been included although they are not revealed in the gully cut but protrude from the modern ground surface. The lowest limestone block belongs to an earlier phase of the site.

extending to the south, east, and west of the stone platform and cattle skull ring. From stratigraphic context alone, it is clear that some hearths predate the construction of the cattle ring and that many can be associated with an upper ashy layer (AA66861 5514 ± 48 BP uncalibrated on charcoal) that developed within the year or two after the cattle skulls were placed. Overall, the sequence includes scattered hearths from the early fifth millennium BC and a cattle skull ring that immediately predates the formation of an upper ashy layer around 4400 BC. The hearth fires and ring were commemorated immediately thereafter by a stone platform built, occupied, and filled long before flooding and sediment accumulation ceased around 3000 BC. This stone monument was visible for thousands of years on the surface of a once marshy landscape.

From the manner in which they were sunk – probably rammed down by stomping on the occipitals – it is clear that the Kheshiya skulls were originally deposited virtually simultaneously in soft mud. Both stone platform and skull ring were set in an annually fluctuating flood zone at the margin of a marshy oxbow, and the people who built Kheshiya chose soft, water-laid sandy silts from which the flooding had just retreated, a perfect consistency to push in and support skulls and the adjacent stone slab ring. Such conditions would occur annually (December–January) after the end of the flood season. Today, hard silt banks forming the youngest terraces of the hyper-arid Middle Wadi Sana drainage are all that remain of the marshlands at Kheshiya.

32. Kheshiya Cattle Ring during excavation (detail). Taurine skulls were set nose down in winter mud after overbank flooding and physically pushed into the soft sediments. Horns were interlocking and frontals faced inward: the central skull faced a gap in the west. Photo by Michael J. Harrower.

Analytical Results

The cattle skull ring originally consisted of about forty-five to fifty crania, at least some of which were originally horned, and it is significant to their interpretation as sacrificial victims that they were slaughtered and deposited at one time. Several excavation details point to this conclusion, namely, the large number of skulls, their integral placement supporting one another with interlocking horns, the limited annual window for formation of the soft mud matrix into which they were pushed, the fleshed condition of some of the skulls at time of deposit, and the formation of a continuous ashy occupation surface around all the skulls' eye sockets. The rapid rate at which bone deteriorates on the surface makes it unlikely that previous years' skulls would be long visible for cumulative additions in a new season, and construction details indicate simultaneous burial.

This surface at the level of eye-sockets suggests that horns were exposed above the ground and weathered in antiquity. In most cases, neither horn cores nor occipital areas survived burial and excavation. In addition to the thirty-three specimens recovered sufficiently intact to take osteological measurements, three or four other individuals crumbled from the gully edge or broke apart when removed during the initial survey of the Kheshiya site. And the gully itself, which exposed the site through erosion, removed perhaps six or seven crania before the site was discovered. One can therefore consider the implications of this site based on a minimum estimate of forty-two slaughtered cattle.

According to Louise Martin of the Institute of Archaeology, London, the cattle skulls belong in all probability to domesticated cattle: the animals were small, definitely taurine (*Bos taurus*), and retained maxillary teeth that allow further study of diet through microwear and isotopic analyses, tooth eruption, and wear. From tooth eruption and wear patterns, Martin estimates that all animals, with the exception of one very juvenile and one very senior example, were culled in their prime, between one and four years of age. These age estimates are also supported by the unfused cranial and facial sutures, which typically fuse after four years of age. From clearly dimorphic traits in the palate area, it appears that there may be several populations or perhaps both males and females. Cut marks on the nasal bones and palate of only a few specimens may indicate skinning, but field observations of fine sediment traces next to the bone are characteristic of those found when fleshed bodies are buried. The cattle skulls represent a large kill and a simultaneous, very large amount of fresh meat.

The Cattle Shrine at Kheshiya and the Anthropology of Sacrifice

Economic Rationalism, Social Formation, and Ritual Sacrifice

Were the Kheshiya cattle sacrificed? One way to address this question is through economic rationalism as a constraining evolutionary factor in human behavioral ecology (Winterhalder and Kennett 2006: 11). This approach assumes that decision making in pastoralism (or foraging or cultivation) optimizes the energetic return for human labor investments

33. Zooarchaeologist Louise Martin analyzing cattle skulls in the Mukalla Museum, 2006. Author's photo.

(Russell 1988:1), recognizing that such returns may be delayed or offset against avoiding risk or impeded by historical contingencies (Winterhalder and Kennett 2006: 11). Under the optimization assumption, relative return rates (caloric yield/time invested) and the calculations of risk and discounting (immediate versus long-term benefit) can explain pastoral decision making (Russell 1988: 1, Alvard and Kuznar 2001) such as the simultaneous culling of prime animals at Kheshiya. Thus the kill-off and availability of cattle meat would have to have been energetically efficient – a proposition that can be tested (with considerable uncertainties) against existing ethnographic models and the ecological constraints of cattle pastoralism in Early Holocene Wadi Sana (e.g., Alvard and Kuznar 2001, Dyson-Hudson 1980, Johnson 2002, McCabe 2004).

Energetic efficiency as a tool of economic rationalism need not preclude sacrifice, but it offers a way of evaluating sustainability and therefore long-term practice of sacrifice. Existing ethnographic models resoundingly demonstrate that pastoralists' calculations for maintaining herd size, age and sex distributions, and willingness to sell or sacrifice animals cannot be entirely explained through the combined factors of economic rationalism and random variation (Dahl and Hjort 1976: 175,

Ryan et al. 2000: 471, Johnson 2002, McCabe 2004). In ethnographies of Eastern African and Dhufāri cattle pastoralists, who represent the closest analogies available for Wadi Sana's Middle Holocene Kheshiya pastoralists (because of environmental, ecological, and historical factors), there are clear indications of the immense social and symbolic roles cattle play in pastoral cultures and the influence of ideology, custom, history, and social expectations that affect economic decisions (e.g., Herskovits 1926, Kuper 1982b, McCabe 2004, Dyson-Hudson and Dyson-Hudson 1999). These cultural constraints on optimization should not be a rationale for rejecting the potentially informative insights of human behavioral ecology, but they serve as a severe impediment to quantitative assessment of cattle herding in antiquity. Also, and not insignificantly, ethnographic cases today probably do not encompass the full range of variation in pastoral adaptations, leaving us, in the case of Kheshiya cattle herders, to contemplate pastoralists independent of any agriculture or exchange with farmers and perhaps unlike any organizational state of pastoralism known today (cf. Johnson 2002: 169, Marx 1992, Sperling and Galaty 1990).

Notwithstanding the variability in cultural and historical contingencies in pastoral decision making, existing pastoral models and an assessment of the economic efficiency of kill-off point to some ecological parameters for sacrifice at Kheshiya. For example, if Wadi Sana's cattle herders in a strongly seasonal environment chose to reduce herd size during lean months so as to remain within the ecological limits of graze and population, it seems unlikely that they would eliminate prime animals rather than very old ones and very young males. But could the skulls have come from diseased animals or a wild herd that perished in a flood or hunt? Both latter possibilities seem unlikely precisely because the cattle apparently were in their prime, mostly between one and four years at age of death. The strongest animals are least likely either to succumb to disease or to be culled in a hunt or overwhelmed by spate waters. Possibly only the prime beasts were selected for skull placement from a larger range of dead animals, and many diseases often leave no indications on bones and teeth. But here too, the lack of other animals means no firm evidence is available to suggest either disease or a wild herd.

One of the major constraints on interpretation at Kheshiya is the lack of economic data on broader pastoralist herd structures and adaptations. Had the bone assemblage come from the discarded elements of

34. Cattle sacrifice at Kheshiya commemorated a gathering of herders in the Wadi Sana winter grazing lands by erecting a ring of skulls beside which was later built a stone structure filled to make a platform. Hearths throughout the archaeological section show that people returned to this place over at least 500 years. Reconstruction drawing by Matt Indrutz.

cattle in trash deposits, then postcranial elements, butchery marks, indication of a smokehouse, and butchery tools would yield important clues. But of the evidence available, the death assemblage and animal size suggests neither a wild herd that perished or was hunted nor the deliberate cull of the youngest, oldest, and weakest among domesticated animals. Associated hearths suggest grilling meat, as is practiced among contemporary bedouin using such hearths today, and grilling would imply immediate rather than delayed consumption of meat, as some burned cattle bone in hearths also attest (McCorriston et al. 2002, 2005). Furthermore, the practice of sacrifice and ritual offering nearly universally requires prime, healthy animals. These are animals most nearly like the qualities of the divinity for which they stand (Hubert and Mauss 1898: 125) and must be near perfect (Chelhod 1955: 75, 126, 151). Altogether the evidence seems to point to a sacrifice, gathering, and feast, attendant with mobility and social constitution (i.e., pilgrimage) that belongs to a long-term Arabian habitus and endured across many millennia and tremendous economic, social, and ideological changes.

Ecological Models and Constraints on Sacrificers and Feasters

The cattle skull ring at Kheshiya raises two major questions: how many people slaughtered these animals, and how many people ate them? Ecological models alone suggest that the number of sacrificers was moderate, at a minimum about sixty people, and that the number of participants was large, up to about 5,000 people, who converged briefly from a wide area beyond Wadi Sana.

In developing ecological models, two major impediments must be noted. On the one hand, an assemblage of about forty-two cattle skulls is an odd, nearly unprecedented zooarchaeological find and one not easily compared to typical zooarchaeological postcranial assemblages. Bones discarded after attached meat and marrow are consumed provide the standard zooarchaeological evidence, raising important methodological challenges for the interpretation of the Kheshiya faunal assemblage (Louise Martin personal communication). Without trash remains, it is also difficult to reconstruct herd composition – not only the population of cattle but also mixed sheep and goat herds (cf. Uerpmann and Uerpmann 2000) that would constitute alternative responses to the ecological parameters on cattle herding, including seasonality of milk production (Dahl and Hjort 1976: 210, 235, Lancaster and Lancaster 1999b) and lack of agricultural products.

A second related problem lies in the presumed pure pastoral status of Kheshiya's cattle herding tribes people, that is, an expectation that they preferred to subsist entirely on their herds (Sperling and Galaty 1990: 73). There is no definitive evidence for agriculture – the earliest Arabian remains of water management postdate Kheshiya by at least 1,000 years (Harrower 2006, 2008); there are no charred plant remains of domesticated plants, and mortars for plant processing have been found in surface context only and cannot be linked to the Kheshiya occupation of the fifth millennium BC. Changes in stone tool technology, especially the disappearance of balanced points made by technically skilled knappers perhaps suggest a diminished or vanished proportion of wild game in the diet (McCorriston and Martin 2009, Crassard 2008). Without agriculture or exchange for agricultural products (there was no Arabian agriculture at this date), pastoralists must practice strategies unattested in the ethnographic record, wherein every case from which we can potentially draw a model is one of interlinked pastoral-agricultural economies (Sperling and Galaty 1990, Johnson 2002). With these important caveats, we can turn to the ecological frameworks within which Kheshiya's herder-sacrificers lived.

How Many Sacrificers?

One can get a sense of the minimum number of sacrificers from a reconstruction of the herd size from which forty-two prime age animals might be sustainably culled. The following calculations assume that the herds were cattle only, the animals were healthy, and that the sacrificers intended to maintain a healthy, viable herd. If the animals indeed represent sacrifice, they were almost certainly in excellent physical condition, a near-universal requirement for sacrificial victims.

Using data compiled from the wide African ethnographic literature (of varying quality and detail) and from agro-economic studies, Dahl and Hjort (1976) developed a generalized model of African pastoralism and explored some of its implications. Although the model makes several critical assumptions (including exchange with agriculturalists), it is predicated on cattle pastoralism in African environments somewhat comparable to that of the ancient Wadi Sana. Dahl and Hjort's model relies on African zebu (*Bos indicus*) herding, while the Wadi Sana cattle are taurine (*Bos taurus*). With all its uncertainties, the Dahl and Hjort model nevertheless provides a valuable point of departure for understanding the ecological context of cattle slaughter in ancient highland Hadramawt.

Dahl and Hjort's model seeks to provide an ethnographically informed prediction of cattle herd dynamics under the ecological constraints of strong seasonality in rainfall and browse in the monsoonal tropics. As an ecological model, it largely ignores cultural variations (such as numbers of adult males kept to maturity (Dahl and Hjort 1976: 75)) and strong cultural ideas about herding cattle, including reluctance to sell or slaughter animals and their roles in negotiating social status (e.g., Ryan et al. 2000, Kuper 1982b, Herskovits 1926). The model recognizes both annual and interannual fluctuation in rainfall and in herd vitality, including milk production (Dahl and Hjort 1976: 115–118, 142, 158), and predicts the herd sizes required to maintain sustainable herds under normal conditions.

Using the ethnographic examples from African cattle pastoralism, it appears that approximately eight or nine households, some sixty to seventy people, would constitute the *minimum number* of sacrificers to have provided the forty-two head in the Kheshiya cattle ring. To do so, these herders would have relied on a combination of fresh milk, milk products, blood, and some meat off-take year-round, for although herders theoretically could live on a diet virtually entirely of fresh milk, such a case has never been documented (Dahl and Hjort 1976: 155, 158), and cattle milk is not available year-round in a sharply seasonal climate like Wadi Sana's. Instead, lactating female cattle that do produce an excess of milk from that required by nursing calves do so only three to four months per year, November to March in Wadi Sana (Dahl and Hjort 1976: 142, 235, Janzen 1986: 100–101, Evans-Pritchard 1940: 59–60). There were probably some plant food supplements, like the *Zizyphus* fruits found charred at the Kheshiya site, but there is no evidence for agriculture or for exchange with agriculturalists elsewhere – irrigation strategies essential for any local agriculture first appeared about a thousand years later (Harrower 2006, McCorriston and Oches 2001, McCorriston 2006). The calculation of

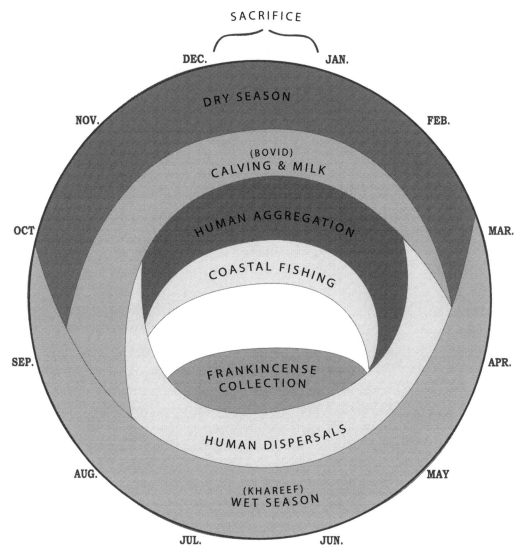

35. Annual cycle of pastoral economy in fifth-millennium BC Wadi Sana reconstructed from modern ethnographic and ecological analogs in East Africa and Dhufār, Oman, and from paleoecological data from Arabia.

sacrificers depends in large part on the sustainable dynamics of herds that could be maintained in the grazing available near Wadi Sana.

Dahl and Hjort's model shows that the number of cattle needed for a family of seven to subsist on milk alone surpasses the labor that family can provide to herding. For a milk-only diet, between 395 and 593 animals would be needed, more than half of them females (Dahl and

Hjort 1976: 158). (If sheep and goats were included in mixed herds, the number of cattle per household would have been smaller.) Given the impossibility of subsisting in a sharply seasonal climate on milk alone, the herd size per family would have been much smaller and in scale with the grazing resources locally available. Other food sources must have included wild plants and hunted game, including waterfowl and fish.

For a household of seven (including two children), Dahl and Hjort estimate a herd size of between fifty and sixty-four animals. There would be great interannual fluctuation and periodic drought and epidemic reductions, suggesting that the higher figure, sixty-four, is the more conservative for herd maintenance. The model herd size estimated through nutritional requirements and ecological constraints on milk production compares well with ethnographic data showing herd sizes between 50 and 100 animals (Dahl and Hjort 1976: 175–181, Janzen 1986: 101, Sperling and Galaty 1990: 76, Andom and Omer 2003: 549), and the higher end of the range may reflect conservative strategies intended to preserve the herd during drought. From these figures, it is relatively straightforward to estimate the grazing capacity of ancient Wadi Sana and thus the numbers of wet season human residents. Details of this analysis will appear elsewhere but are summarized below.

If at Kheshiya a single household maintained about sixty-four animals, then each herd needed a twelve-kilometer grazing radius around a permanent water source (Dahl and Hjort 1976: 238–240, Andom and Omer 2003: 550), which would have been the marshy oxbow pools during the dry season of December through February in ancient Wadi Sana. During this period, the shallow pools and temporary rain-fed basins up on the high plateau would disappear, and the marsh margins at Kheshiya would shrink. Spring rains in March would expand the grazing areas for cattle, with a July to October season of abundance during which herders could disperse across the uplands (Janzen 1986: 116–117) and would have been excluded from Wadi Sana by flooding.

Such herds could sustain an 8 percent off-take for meat or sacrifice, usually of bulls and bullocks, and another 8 percent would die natural deaths (Dahl and Hjort 1976: 265). Dahl and Hjort's (1976: 114–129) model cattle herd with an 8 percent cull takes no account of sustainability and disastrous die-off in interannual cycles of drought (Ellis and Galvin 1994: 346). Therefore, it is reasonable to suppose that conservative herders might sacrifice fewer animals or at least perform such sacrifice less than annually. An 8 percent off-take for sacrifice from a sixty-four-head cattle herd would be about five animals (fewer if there were fewer cattle in a mixed herd with goat and sheep). To generate forty-two sacrificed animals at Kheshiya through sustainable practice, a minimum of nine herds (5 animals × 9 = 45) belonging to nine house-holds, or about sixty-three people would have contributed victims. While this represents the *minimum* number of sacrificers, the calcula-tion does not preclude a larger number of people or households contributing animals, which would have to have been brought from some distance.

Eight or nine households would have been supported by and provided the labor for a cattle population of 400 to 576 head, including 42 sacrificial victims and assuming no mixed strategy with caprines. The latter would reduce the minimum number of cattle required to sustain humans while not requiring extra land: cattle and goats especially choose different graze and browse and do not compete (Dahl and Hjort 1976: 244, McCabe 2004: 80). If goats formed part of the herds, reducing the minimum numbers of cattle, then the number of sacrificers must have been greater and cattle off-taken from more than nine herds, assuming of course, that the sacri-ficers intended to maintain viable cattle herds into their futures.

Because one herd (sixty-four animals) uses a twelve-kilometer radius around a water source during the dry season, the local water restrictions meant that cattle herds were concentrated around the marshes in Wadi Sana from November to March. Cattle eat herbaceous forage and need to drink every other day, perhaps rarely every three or four days (McCabe 2004: 46, 75, Dahl and Hjort 1976: 238–239, Leslie and Dyson-Hudson 1999: 234), so their mobility would have been seasonally restricted (Janzen 1986: 100, Evans-Pritchard 1940: 59–60). The topography of Wadi Sana, with a substantial climb and major vegetation changes between its marshy bed and the soil-denuded uplands only a kilometer to the east and west, constrained wintering herds to a grazing area along the bed and lower slopes. Thus, the minimum number of sacrificers, eight households, probably represented all the territorial cattle-herding occupants of the Middle Wadi Sana region, strung in territories that included sections of the wadi bed and extended east and west into the uplands during summer (wet season) dispersal period (cf. Janzen 1986: 100–101).

36. Winter rangeland within 40 kilometers of Shiʻb Kheshiya modeled using ethnographic analogs, ecological constraints on cattle herds (Andom and Omer 2003, Dahl and Hjort 1976, Janzen 1986, Leslie and Dyson Hudson 1999, McCabe 2004, Sperling and Galaty 1990), and paleoecological studies of sediment histories (Eric Oches, personal communications) on MODIS (Moderate Resolution Imaging Spectroradiometer) satellite image. Upland areas of the southern Jol had no soil and supported insufficient grasses to graze cattle, which must have depended on the long and narrow dry-season ranges on the marshy wadi bottoms (shown to scale in white). Grazing areas were produced by stream-order buffering of areas where flow from more than 5,000 SRTM (Shuttle Radar Topography Mission) topographic grid cells accumulates. The area available for grazing accounts for all the Wadi Sana inhabitants as a minimum number of sacrificers at the Kheshiya Shrine. A larger number of consumers must have been drawn from groups grazing adjacent wadi systems. GIS analysis and figure by Michael J. Harrower.

The inclusion of smaller livestock in mixed herds or exchange with agriculturalists would reduce the minimum cattle numbers, while cultural factors and interannual herd depletion and recovery could have increased them, as could specialized pastoral production of surplus animals and animal products for exchange with complex societies (this latter is not a viable option for Neolithic Wadi Sana, which shows no evidence for direct contact with the Ubaid or Levantine Chalcolithic). Thus, it remains challenging further to refine an economic model that establishes a minimum population of about 400 to 575 cattle and between sixty and seventy herders in the Middle Wadi Sana during the latter Neolithic. Sixty people is a population roughly comparable with today's modest group of about ten or twelve pastoral households practicing primarily goat herding with a handful of camels and limited primarily by sources of drinking water. (Water is trucked in and deposited in barrels, and the marshes are gone.)

How Many Consumers?

Were the cattle killed off to store meat for a long-term supply of jerky or were they the basis of a gathering and great feast? Archaeological evidence (numerous hearths) points to grilling meat, and a calculation of consumers (minimum and maximum numbers presented) also suggests a gathering and feast.

At a minimum, perhaps sixty herders were killing cattle during the dry season to preserve dried meat rather than keeping meat on the hoof. The economic advantages for such a strategy are not obvious. They would include the portability and range of dried meat to supply hunting parties or raiders moving farther and faster than cattle tied to water and graze in the dry months. Another possibility is that available graze dwindled at the end of the dry season, making it somehow more attractive to store meat than to pasture all cattle. Graze can be restricting: modern Dhufāri pastoralists maintaining herds with thirty to fifty animals while enclosing agricultural land require supplemental fodder (Janzen 1986: 100). To counter the diminished quality of graze, the Nuer and other pastoralists deliberately set fire to dry pasture lands to stimulate new growth as soon after the rainy season as the grasslands have dried (Evans-Pritchard 1940: 59–60, 83). The likeliest explanation for the Middle Holocene episodic brush and grass fires, whose magnetic and charcoal signatures are retained in the sediment deposits of Wadi Sana today (McCorriston et al. 2002: 66, McCorriston 2006: 221), is human-set fires for landscape management. In Middle Wadi Sana, it would have been the high marsh reeds and tussock grasses that burned, much as they did in the periodic fires set by Sudanese cattle herders in historic times. It is significant that burning as a land management technique regularly appears as an intensification practice associated with territoriality and resource maximization strategies (Smith 2001: 30–31, Keeley 1995: 255).

37. Erosion that cut through the Middle Holocene silt terrace of Wadi Sana revealed three superimposed layers of anthropogenic burning. Radiocarbon dates on the middle layer and extensive magnetic testing showed that vegetation cover burned in place around 6000 BC (McCorriston et al. 2002: 66 Figure 2). Author's photo.

For sixty people in Wadi Sana, a kill-off of forty-two animals would provide about a three-month supply of dried meat if one assumes no supplement of other foods. The meat from forty-two cattle represents about 5,000 meals, which would provide adequate caloric value for sixty people for eighty-three days without appreciable other supplement (see following discussion). Perhaps it was more efficient to kill, strip, dry or smoke, and tan the hides of all animals at once, possibly with the combined labor of all available women. In Dhufār (Janzen 1986: 104) and culturally similar areas of cattle pastoralism in highland East Africa, women are tanners by tradition (Brandt and Weedman 2002) and perhaps also handled meat drying in antiquity. A communal butchery and jerky-making event would have gathered all the households of the Middle Wadi Sana and provided the mechanism for exchange of marriage partners and affirmation of group identity for a small tribal section. But the event took place during a season of plenty – milk was available in the winter months (Janzen 1986: 101, Dahl and Hjort 1976: 235, Evans-Pritchard 1940: 83, Galvin and Little 1999: 130), and the ethnographic record of East African and Arabian pastoralism suggests that dried meat is quickly consumed unless preserved as confit. Meat is most important for subsistence when milk is not available (Dyson-Hudson and Dyson-Hudson 1999: 72). At Kheshiya, milk would presumably have been available and diminishing in quantity when the cattle ring was constructed (during winter months). The use of dried meat almost exclusively for nearly three months is unattested ethnographically for cattle pastoralists in comparable environments and difficult to reconcile with local ecological conditions.

Wadi Sana was a tropical environment in 4500 BC, as it is today, with high daytime temperatures (25–35°C) even in the coolest winter months. Meat quickly spoils unless preserved through smoking or drying, practices theoretically feasible. Preservation of fresh seafood is known – herders in Oman and Yemen to this day spread fresh sardines on the beaches to dry and transport for cattle and camel feed (Janzen 1986: 101); furthermore, shellfish (El Mahi 2000) and fish are also dried for human consumption, as may be the case with wild game (Thomas 1938: 60). Dhufāri mountain pastoralists (using ceramics) used to render the fat of slaughtered animals and then pack wind-dried meat in jars or leather with liquid fat that would congeal against airborne microbes. Such practices require ceramics for the rendering of fat (these were not present at Kheshiya) and can preserve meat up to six months. African cattle pastoralists may employ smoking to preserve meat for at most a few weeks, although the practice can in theory provide stores edible for several months. In practice, those African herders that dry meat consume it within a few weeks (Dahl and Hjort 1976: 169, 192–193). Modern pastoral peoples may extol the ideal of subsistence only or predominantly on animal products – dried or not – but in practice none have been observed to forego plant foods, agricultural cereals, and fish, and meat is typically rare, expensive, and a small proportion of the diet (Marx 1992: 257) There is therefore good ecological and ethnographic reason to suppose that the Kheshiya cattle, or at least a good portion of them, were eaten fresh, and thus consumed by a large congregation of tribal pastoralists sharing the feast, and the archaeological record of grilling hearths is consistent with this interpretation.

The cattle sacrificed at Kheshiya were probably the basis for a great feast. If all the cattle skulls were buried at least partially fleshed and simultaneously, the slaughter of more than forty individuals represents an

Table 2. Econometrics of Cattle Pastoralism and Sacrifice in Fifth-Millennium BC Wadi Sana, Hadramawt.

	Econometric Estimates			Wadi Sana Capacity	
Number of Cattle Sacrificed	Meat Yield (kcal)	Person Meals (1,990 kcal/day)	Number of Herders for Sustainable Off-take	All Cattle	All Humans
1	236,000	119	(standard)	–	–
42	9,912,000	4,981	60	525	60–70
50	11,800,000	5,930	70	640	60–70

extremely large mass of fresh meat, available to a *maximum* of 5,000 people gathered for an extraordinary meal. Using the FAO/WHO estimate of 1990 kilocalorie minimum dietary requirement per person per day, the 9,912,000 kilocalories produced by forty-two cattle (= 236,000 kilocalories per head × 42 head; Applegate, Gautier and Duncan 2001:487) would provide 4,981 meat meals, each one equivalent to one day's energy requirement for an adult. The higher estimate of 5,000 assumes that some people need fewer calories and supplemented the feast with other foods such as seeds and fruits, dates, tubers, milk, and cheese. If fifty or more cattle skulls formed the original ring, these figures would be higher.

Or perhaps fewer than 5000 congregated in an encampment of, say, 700 to 1,500 people for three to seven days. As one great feast, or as several meaty meals, the sacrificed cattle and remains of associated cooking and rituals at Kheshiya are evidence of an uncommonly large, brief gathering whose purpose included social and ritual practices. The ecological constraints of cattle pastoralism in Middle Holocene Wadi Sana could only sustain such gatherings as temporary ones, from which mobile tribes people and their herds were quickly forced to disperse.

The Kheshiya cattle sacrifice revealed through excavations at SU151-1 was surely not a unique event. There may have been another cattle ring (unexcavated) where the gully face revealed a cattle skull west of the commemorative stone platform. There were meat-grilling hearths throughout the sequence of at least 500 years. Elsewhere in Wadi Sana, archaeological survey has revealed a bone-rich landscape with deposits of mixed carcasses and lenses of large mammal bone (e.g., SU 033 –15, 1998–x) clearly visible in natural sections and eroding from the surface, notably associated with other fifth millennium BC stone structures (e.g., SU 026–1,

037–4). Sacrifice, gathering, and feast at Kheshiya formed part of a repetitive series of pilgrimage practices that constituted a mobile society.

Territory, Convergence, and Tribal Identities

In the Middle East, mobile pastoralists along the arid margins of agricultural zones have long been economically linked to tribally defined territories that ensure grazing usage while excluding over-grazing (Lancaster and Lancaster 1999a, 1999b, Schoup 1990, see also, Stein 2004, Archi 1985, Fleming 2004). Adoption of domesticated animals in the Early Holocene brought with it deferred gains and the need for people to defend both labor investments (in tending animals) and pasturage needed to feed herds (Alvard and Kuznar 2001, Dyson-Hudson and Smith 1978, Hardin 1977) One expected outcome of the shift from hunting to herding is greater territoriality, which may be expressed in a variety of ways. Territory may be defended through social networks, in turn maintained through periodic gathering, sacrifice, and feast.

The notion of tribal identity now evokes so large a literature concerning the relative significance of social and political factors in tribal constitution that most researchers define "tribe" before using the term. Groups socially constituted as "tribes" generally maintain historical genealogical narratives of contingent and contextual kinship (segmentary lineages) that regulate their economic and political activities including membership as corporate groups, and they exist as political and loosely bounded entities. Tribal linkages to place are important: as environments and political circumstances change, so resource distributions and access also change, engendering shifts in tribal identities and territories.

In Arabia, the widespread presence of many different monument forms (e.g., Braemer et al. 2001, Braemer, Cleuziou and Steimer 2003, Bin 'Aqil and McCorriston 2009, Cleuziou and Vogt 1983, de Maigret 1996, Frifelt 1991, Méry et al. 2001, Steimer-Herbet 1999, 2004, Vogt and Velde 1987, Vogt 1985) signaled the presence and traditional access rights of tribes (Steimer-Herbet 2004, de Maigret 1996), as did perhaps the use of distinctive marks (*wusūm*) evident in rock art and brand marks for livestock (Khan 2000, 1993). Monuments have great antiquity and were constructed through the combined labor of small groups to mark significant sites – for example, the burying places of ancestors (whose lineages and recollection served as socially cohesive forces for tribes people). Firmly linked with mobile, pastoral people (Steimer-Herbet 2004: 29–31, De Maigret 2005), monuments commemorate the rites and rights of societies that rely upon (rite and right) practice to constitute themselves as tribes (Cleuziou 2001, 1997). Neither houses nor tombs, the upright slab stone rings at Kheshiya nevertheless belong to a wider Arabian tradition of stone monuments (sometimes called shrines). The Kheshiya monuments served a commemorative and evocative purpose in social constitution (and perhaps territorial usufruct) among usually dispersed mobile pastoralists.

Practice of Arabian Sacrifice

If the gathering at Kheshiya served ideological and social purposes, what might we discern of them, now nearly 7,000 years later? Possibly very little of their specific context, but by considering wider geographic context and anthropological theories of sacrifice, it is possible to recognize in the Kheshiya rites a faint refrain of the meta-structure that defines Arabian cultural history thereafter.

Ritual sacrifice – sometimes connected to pilgrimage – plays an important role in religions around the world, and like pilgrimage, sacrifice is a practice that constitutes social cohesion and identity. Hubert and Mauss built on the seminal studies of J. G. Frazer (1894) and W. Robertson Smith (d. 1894) (1907a, [1885] 1907b) to suggest that all sacrifice contains a foundation of reciprocity, thus "il n'y a pas de sacrifice où n'intervienne quelque idée de rachat" (Hubert and Mauss 1898: 135). A group collectivity can perform sacrifice and receive its benefits, and so a group can establish and affirm common identity through sacrifice. Others have emphasized the potential of sacrifice, like pilgrimage, to form a social bond among the participants through the shock and collective guilt of a grisly and violent death perpetrated upon a designated victim (Burkert [1972] 1983, Girard 1972). Many recognize in sacrifice a ritual cycle with sacralization and desacralization (Hubert and Mauss 1898: 132, cf. Eliade [1949] 1954), purification and new social form (Burkert [1972] 1983: 40, Durkheim 1915). Turner drew on this idea with the concept of liminality of pilgrimage and suspension of social rules in communitas, a framework nevertheless explicitly rejected here even as the socially constituting mechanism of pilgrimage remains an important theme.

Like pilgrimage, sacrifice as ritual practice has deep antiquity in the ancient Near East. Robertson Smith (1907a) suggested a primal origin for Semitic sacrifice (including Hebrew sacrifice), and others have argued for common Arabian roots to Biblical, Islamic, and other Arabian traditions (Ryckmans 1983: 14). All latter-day sacrifice would have devolved from this common origin, and according to nineteenth-century philosophies of social evolution, the progress of civilization led to the end of sacrifice as food production became a more distant struggle. Thus, ancient wild totems of clans (Robertson Smith 1907a: 290–294, 444, 448–449, Robertson Smith [1885] 1907b: 238–239) were substituted by domesticated animals in the cults of pastoral peoples, and as the sacrificial animal became increasingly sacred, it became at last taboo for profane people to touch, only available to the priests for eating. Finally, the sacred character of the animal turned it into an object of impurity (suggesting the origin of proscription of pork). In the meantime, human sacrifice came to be substituted but not actually practiced: societies practiced strong mechanisms for the protection of individual lives and prohibited anthropophagy. Even though Robertson Smith's scheme does not stand up against the more recently published evidence from epigraphic and archaeological sources, many have since agreed with him that "the origin and meaning of sacrifice constitute the central problem of ancient religion" (Robertson Smith 1907a: 28).

Humanists have approached this central problem from a variety of perspectives. Notably the recent theories of René Girard (1972), Walter Burkert ([1972] 1983), and Jonathan Z. Smith (1982) draw upon literature, anthropology, and critical theory to generate different theories of sacrifice and religion, each envisioning a schematic ritual sacrifice and a putative origin from which it is derived. Humans are the primal sacrifice, later substituted by animals, according to Girard; Burkert attributes the origin of sacrifice to Paleolithic hunting ritual; and J. Z. Smith argues for the function of sacrifice – and its origins – in resolving social conflict. Of these seminal and contemporary humanistic theories of sacrifice, Burkert's theory most explicitly draws upon anthropological approaches, including Hubert and Mauss's idea of reciprocity in sacrifice; Lévi-Strauss's structural opposition of death and life, group violence and society; Durkheim's view of religion as a justification of society itself; and Marett's (1914) concept of cathartic release of emotional tensions through ritual.

Ultimately, Girard, Burkert, and Smith provide functional arguments for the meaning of sacrifice (although Burkert ([1972] 1983: 27, 82) hints at the transformational role of habitus in changing meanings of sacrifice through time) with imagined origins ungrounded in pre-historic (or archaeological) data (Mack 1987).

Arabian sacrifice, understood from Islamic and pre-Islamic sources through historical and sociological approaches, offers an important context for the Kheshiya cattle ring and has the advantage of geographic and cultural proximity to these ancient herders. Although no direct observations of Arabian sacrifice trace as far into pre-history as the cattle ring and therefore can only provide a later transformation of its meaning, they nevertheless underscore the social significance of sacrifice and its close connections with pilgrimage in an Arabian meta-structural framework.

As discussed in Chapter 3, Gonzague Ryckmans's (1951) study of Arabian religion identified three regional traditions – northern, western, and southern (after Wellhausen 1887). These regions map significant differences in sacrifice, which like pilgrimage, is an inherited and syncretized component in all three traditions. Sacrifice lies at the heart of the old Southern Arabian pilgrimage tradition (Henniger [1946/1947] 1981: 225), closest to Kheshiya in time and space, and is attested through epigraphic inscriptions and the altar sites for bloody sacrifices (Maraqten 1994, Breton 1979:13). In drawing a contrast between northern and southern traditions, Henninger ([1946/47] 1981: 234–237) emphasizes the role of cattle offered as bloody sacrifice, pilgrimage, incense, tithes, temples, and organized priesthood in Southern Arabian antiquity. I have already argued that the emergence of complex Southern Arabian societies involved appropriating and reshaping the rites and practices of pastoral tribes people, including gatherings, sacrifice, and feasts, as a means of appropriating labor and resources to the maintenance of inequality. By the time states arose, domesticated camels were in use across Arabia. But whereas northerners preferred camels in sacrifice, the southern tradition was cattle (Henninger [1946/47] 1981: 234) and still is today (Dostal 1983), perhaps relict from the practice of cattle sacrifice by pre-historic tribes people, for which we now have solid archaeological evidence at Kheshiya.

Significant differences also appear between the bedouin sacrifices of Arabia's pre-Islamic nomads, known from Qur'ān and pre-Islamic poetry, and urban sacrificial rites in the centuries prior to Islam (Henninger [1981]

1999: 111). In the nomadic tradition, sacrifices were not always at fixed places but were practiced at sacred places – a sacred tree (Chelhod 1955: 104–105, Henninger [1948] 1981: 197), selected standing stones, or a tomb (Chelhod 1955: 116–119, Henninger [1948] 1981: 200, Lammens 1919: 91–93). Most such sacrifices were followed by a communal feast (Henninger [1948] 1981: 198, Chelhod 1955: 116–117), and only rarely, as in the case of mounts slaughtered for use by or out of obligation to a tomb's occupant, were the carcasses abandoned or interred intact, as may be inferred also in several archaeological cases (Henninger [1948] 1981: 199–200, Chelhod 1955: 116–117, Vogt 1994, Uerpmann 1999, Bin 'Aqil and McCorriston 2009). There is considerable significance to the sacrifices and communal feasts at a tomb, which may fill a social purpose in uniting clan members who might otherwise be dissipated by the death of a venerated member. Thus, a greater society is created through the symbolic unity of living and dead (Chelhod 1955: 116–117). For Chelhod, sacrifice among the Arabs prior to Islam fulfilled a role of both purification and gifting. As purification, sacrifice atoned for breaking rules, such as the sanctuary and abstinence proscriptions in pilgrimage. At the same time, sacrifice as gift anticipated a greater gift in return, such as the renewal of life force, a multiplied harvest or flock increase, free enjoyment of pasture, and fertility of young animals (including tribal youth).

There is wide dissent about the meanings of sacrifice and the identities and roles of divinities in nonliterate pre-Islamic society (Henninger [1981] 1999, Robertson Smith 1907a, Chelhod 1955, Atallah 1969). Just as sacrifice changed in meaning(s) from pre-Islamic to Islamic times (Chelhod 1955: 81–83), bedouin sacrifice of the *Jāhilīyah* is far removed from the cattle sacrifices at Kheshiya and offers only the faint echo of Kheshiya's tribal rites. To further probe the meaning of sacrifice at Kheshiya some 5,000 years earlier, we must turn to cattle herders in broader pre-historic context.

Cattle and Herders in Wider Regional Context

Although the Cattle Ring itself is unparalleled in the archaeological record, an ideological and economic focus on cattle in Wadi Sana has parallels and precedent elsewhere in Arabia and beyond. The 6,500-year-old Kheshiya

Cattle Ring represents neither the earliest indication of domesticated Arabian cattle, nor the earliest manipulation of cattle for symbolic and ideological purpose. What Kheshiya does offer is a crucial and vivid link between the earliest domesticated cattle, the significance of cattle for Arabia's earliest herders, and the later practices of pilgrimage, sacrifice, and feast that constituted and reaffirmed Arabian social order and social landscapes.

Domesticated Cattle in Ancient Arabia

With genetic and zooarchaeological evidence suggesting independent domestications of cattle in Africa and the Levant (Hanotte et al. 2002, Grigson 1991, 2000), the origins of cattle in Arabia, most particularly in Southern Arabia, are a critical and unresolved question in the spread of Neolithic economies and the Post-Pleistocene resettlement of Arabia. The Kheshiya cattle are among the earliest in Southern Arabia, but not the earliest, even in Wadi Sana. Their significance for the question of origins is of secondary concern here. In brief, they could have come from Africa or the Levant, perhaps as early as the seventh millennium BC, or they might have arrived via Mesopotamian traders in the Arabian Gulf in the sixth or fifth millennium BC. Cattle have a long significance for hunters and herders in Arabia.

It is clear that wild cattle existed in Post-Pleistocene Arabia, along with the wild buffalo (*Syncerus caffer*) present also in African fauna. Geologist Henry McClure (1984: 215) recovered remains of wild bovids associated with the early Holocene interior lakes of the Arabian desert, and wild buffalo appear as prey in early rock art, even as some pictoral indications suggest incipient control and domestication of *Bos taurus* (Garcia and Rachad 1997, Garcia et al. 1991, Anati 1972: 56–57, 67, 1974: 12, 30, 64, Rachad 2007: 84). In early rock art cattle depicted often have *wusūm*, or markings of ownership and tribal identity, on their shoulders, necks, or adjacent rock surfaces. (Today *wusūm* are used as camel brands distinctive to tribe and region, and about a hundred modern *wusūm* can be traced into antiquity through rock art (Khan 2000: 105).)

One claim for early domesticated cattle in Arabia comes from Ash-Shumah, a shell midden and human burial site on the African-facing Red Sea coast of Northern Yemen. By association with radiocarbon-dated brackish water shell, the animal bone has been linked to the seventh millennium BC (6684–6475 BC calibrated). Ash-Shumah provides an early but not entirely convincing date for domesticated cattle: the full faunal assemblage is small (1,013 identified specimens), dominated by equids (92 percent), and has never been fully published (Cattani and Bökönyi 2002: 44–50). Most important, only one specimen is of "undoubtedly domesticated" cattle – a horn core fragment that could not be measured but was judged sufficiently thin-walled to exclude aurochs (*Bos primigeneous*), which was nevertheless attested in other postcranial fragments (Cattani and Bökönyi 2002: 46). While suggestive, the evidence is slender, hampered as are all cattle measurements from Arabia, by the lack of a modern Arabian wild cattle reference assemblage. In its other characteristics, the faunal assemblage from Ash-Shumah reflects its African proximity and may be one indicator of early contact and cultural influences across the Red Sea. Other late seventh- and sixth-millennium BC *Bos taurus* have been recovered from the Northern Yemen highlands (Hadjouis 2007: 51, Fedele 2008), and Wadi Sana itself, alongside sheep that could only derive from the Levantine-Iranian arc of the Fertile Crescent (Martin, McCorriston and Crassard 2009).

By the fifth millennium BC, there are good archaeofaunal indicators elsewhere of domesticated cattle. In highland Northern Yemen, the Neolithic site of Ath-Thayyilah III has an assemblage with few but definitive bones from domesticated *Bos taurus* (Fedele 1990: 37–38, 1992: 72, 2005: 225). Along the Arabian Gulf shores and islands, there are a number of sites that show contact with the Ubaid culture in Southern Mesopotamia (summarized in Cleuziou and Tosi 1997: 124–125) and include the remains of domesticated cattle (e.g., Zeder in Masry 1974: 167, M. Uerpmann 1992: 101). A transhumant herding and fishing economy has been particularly well-documented at the inland cemetery site of Jebel Buhais, with a mixed caprine and cattle herd (Uerpmann and Uerpmann 2008, 2000, Uerpmann, Uerpmann and Jasim 2000). While it is certainly possible that cattle in Eastern Arabia were acquired from sea-going Mesopotamian traders, domesticated cattle appeared earlier in highland Yemen (both Southern and Northern).

Recent studies by Peter Bellwood (2005), Diamond and Bellwood (2003) and Colin Renfrew (Bellwood and Renfrew 2002) examine the global distribution of modern languages as a key to understanding processes of ancient agricultural dispersals. The modern geography of Semitic languages in Africa suggests to Bellwood (2005: 99–110) a dispersal of early farmers (Pre-Pottery Neolithic B) from the Levant. As others have noted, the persistence of non-Arabic languages (Johnstone 1975, Simeone-Senelle 1991) among small populations of modern Southern Arabian cattle herders may be a relict of an earlier, widespread cattle-herding ethnic group across Southern Arabia (Dostal 1967). This Modern Southern Arabian languages distribution might stem from a Neolithic substrate (fifth millennium BC) as Zarins argues (1992), or from later Himyarite/Old South Arabian dispersals (Holes 2006: 33). Some linguists emphasize that the origins of Afro-Asiatic languages was in Africa, and the early spread of Semitic language was into, not out of, the Levant (Ehret 1984, Zohar 1992: 170–171).

There are several other potential complications with the direct acquisition of cattle (and language) from Early Neolithic Levantine immigrant herders as envisioned by Bellwood's sweeping hypothesis (also Dreschler 2007). Late Neolithic Levantine peoples apparently did arrive in Lower Egypt around 6500 to 6000 BC (Shirai 2005), and probably brought cereals and caprines with them (Hassan 2002). Middle seventh-millennium BC domesticated caprines near the Red Sea coast may be introductions from across the Red Sea or along its coastal margins from the north (Vermeersch et al. 1994: 39), perhaps emphasizing the Red Sea littoral as a distinctive cultural area rather than a barrier or route to somewhere else. But if Early Neolithic Levantine herders brought cattle along with caprines directly to Southern Arabia, they passed through a peculiar geographic and cultural filter to do so. Domesticated taurine cattle were available in the Northern Levant from the seventh millennium BC, but peoples occupying the desert margins of the Southern and Eastern Levant near Northern Arabia favored a hunting lifestyle (Martin 1999, Rosen 2002, Avner 1998: 150). The Sinai was occupied by a separate population of hunting peoples, probably Arabian in origin, until the fifth millennium BC (Hershkovitz, Bar-Yosef and Arensburg 1994, Bar-Yosef and Bar-Yosef Mayer 2002: 361, Rosen et al. 2007). Where domesticated animals do appear in the fauna of desert margin sites with Levantine connections, caprines were clearly the favored species (Nowell in Henry et al. 2003, Martin 1999, Horowitz et al. 2000, cf. Twiss 2007: 136–137). Domesticated cattle, like agriculture, had to cross a "rainfall barrier" (McCorriston 2006) from the winter rainfall in the Northern Levant to the summer monsoonal rainfall (today in Southern Arabia, formerly perhaps across much of the peninsula; Zarins 1992, Avner

1988: 188). Crossing a rainfall barrier would have surely generated economic challenges as herders struggled to shift their expectations of seasonal milk and forage. As Ingold (1982) and Alvard and Kuznar (2001) point out, once hunters commit to herding, a behavioral and cultural threshold is crossed that makes it difficult to return to the open-access behaviors of hunting. Thus a movement across the Northern to Southern Levant of Early Neolithic (Middle Pre-Pottery Neolithic B, seventh millennium BC) farmers with cattle into the arid desert margins as foragers to then bring cattle pastoralism into Southern Arabia is implausible, even as other cultural traditions may have been transmitted (e.g., Byblos and Amuq points, Hershkovitz, Bar-Yosef and Arensburg 1994, cf. Crassard 2008). If Early Neolithic people did disperse into Arabia, they were more likely caprine herders who left domesticated cattle and plants behind (cf. Hassan 2002).

The more likely explanation for Southern Arabian domesticated cattle is a spread of African domesticated cattle across the Red Sea, which may more plausibly than a barrier be considered a circum-maris cultural area in which exchange relationships between socially related peoples were maintained. Zarins (1992) argues that cattle were an essential, if archaeologically scarcely visible, component of the Northern Arabian pastoral techno-complex and that early Holocene monsoon enhancement allowed Arabian (and African) cattle herders to occupy far north into the peninsula in the fifth millennium BC (cf. Fedele 2005: 239). Indeed, many of the early pastoral sites of the Sinai, Negev, and eastern margins of the Southern Levant include minor w? >components of cattle bone and clearly ritual use of cattle (Zarins 1992: 236-237, Eddy and Wendorf 1998), and Nilotic cultures of the Egyptian pre-Dynastic appear to be predicated on cattle pastoralism and attendant symbolism derived from African traditions (Wengrow 2006).

Cattle and Arabian Rock Art

Cattle clearly played important and symbolic roles in early Arabian societies occupying the wetter Early Holocene desert margins, oases, and highland basins where rock art attests to their significance. There have been a number of studies of Arabian rock art beginning with the Philby-Lippens-Ryckmans expedition of 1951 (Lippens 1956, Anati 1972, 1974). As with any history of rock art studies, the range of field and analytical approaches makes it challenging to integrate results, yet a broad chronological pattern seems clear enough (Khan 1993, Anati 1972, Garcia et al. 1991). The earliest Arabian rock art depicts cattle with high frequency (Khan 2000: 103, Garcia et al. 1991), indicates their ownership by specific groups, and often shows cattle as components of ritual scenes. Rock art of different eras may include scenes of hunts, ritual hunts ('Abdalrahman Bin 'Aqil 2004: 42), raiding parties, dances (Khan 1993: 142), clan or tribal marks (*wusūm*) (Khan 2000, Van Gennep 1902: 89), and regionally distinct stylistic conventions (Anati 1972, 1974), but the depictions include high frequencies of cattle, goats, ibex, and camels, all animals known to be preferred in later sacrifice and ritual (Henninger 1946–1947 cited in Vogt 1994: 284). Even the earliest cattle depictions seem to be of piebald – therefore domesticated – animals (Zarins 1992: 27). Some of the most systematic work comes from (Northern Arabian) sites in Wadi Daum, where in the earliest period, some of the cattle have forward-pointing horns, and some have horns that point backward. The difference in horn alignment could perhaps be a sign of domestication (wild type with horns pointing forward and domestic type with horns pointing backward), or it might reflect a difference between bulls and cows as is thought to be the case for early African cattle (Grigson 1991). Khan (1993: 51, 103) dates these depictions to a Neolithic phase antedating Middle Holocene climate shifts and aridification. By the subsequent period, very loosely dated to 5000–3500 BC, cattle usually appear beside or marked with *wusūm* (Khan 1993: 109) clearly indicating ownership of the cattle themselves (Khan 2000: 12) and also by inference, territorial claims to the grazing lands that support them (Alvard and Kuznar 2001: 303) marked out by regionally distinct *wusūm* in rock art.

Rock art demonstrates the deep antiquity of *wusūm* and of geographically distinct social groups (Khan 2000: x–xi, 9–12). The constellation of group social identities, territorial access, pastoralism, and marking (rocks, cattle, camels, persons) with *wusūm* has a long tradition in Arabia and appears in literary and Qur'ānic (Koranic) references to pre-Islamic sacred practices. In tracing the etymology of the noun *wusūm*, Joseph Chelhod (1955: 152–159) notes its links to concepts of pasturage and seasonal flush of available graze. The term has long indicated marked animals as belonging to particular pasturage, hence a concept of territory (also Van Gennep 1902: 89). But the term also was used in antiquity to designate animals marked for sacrifice (which in turn releases

38. Piebald (domesticated) cattle on rock faces near Bir Hima (Najrān, Saudi Arabia). Rock art from Southwestern Arabia include depictions of wild and domesticated cattle among the earliest dated examples. Courtesy of Lars Bjurstrom/Saudi Aramco World/ SAWDIA.

constraints on the free use of the rest of the herd, once herders have consecrated and offered to the divinity the first fruits or first-born animals). Other closely related terms include a verb with two meanings – one, to allow to go freely to pasture and the other, to mark.

Of this second meaning – to mark – there are further pre-Islamic social and religious connotations discussed by Chelhod and his predecessors. In brief, the term *wasm* can mean any mark – whether by red-hot iron or knife – that gives a ready symbol by which one can identify belonging to a group. Robertson Smith (1907a: 248–250) first suggested the study of *wasm* in rock art to delimit tribal territories and further argued that "in olden times the *wasm* was not placed on camels alone but was tattooed on the persons of tribesmen" called *shi'b* and that "there is an etymological link between such marks and a man's [tribal] name." Van Gennep (1902) disagrees with an inference of human tattooing, but emphasizes the social character of *wasm*. Chelhod links the one-time marking of young women to the same seasonal time as marking of animals (when breasts begin to produce milk). His analysis links the initiation of young

39. *Wusūm* marked into the ruins of a first-century AD temple at Palmyra (Syria). Author's photo.

women, celebrating rites of passage, and (by a practice parallel to first fruits sacrifice of prime animals) freeing most tribal youths and young women by offering a young girl to sacred prostitution in the temple (the latter without historical justification or evidence and certainly wrong, see also J. Ryckmans 1983: 17–18).

The symbolic meanings of cattle and sacrifice at (preliterary) Kheshiya lie well beyond the reach of such analysis. But the long rock-art tradition of depicting *wusūm*, cattle, and sacrifice (Khan 1993: 127, 137, 192) and the later significance of these elements to tribal social constitution suggest that cattle, sacrifice, and territorially delimited social groups belong to the habitus of pilgrimage in Arabia.

Cattle Cults in the Holocene Sahara and South Asia

There were cattle cults beyond Arabia, most notably in the Early Holocene Sahara and South Asia, and these attest to a broader, but equally enigmatic significance of cattle for early human societies. The intriguing interest Anatolian and eastern Mediterranean people had in

40. Arabian stone altar with bull horns (Yemen). Erich Lessing/Art Resource, New York.

wild cattle during the ninth and eighth millennia BC (Peters et al. 1999: 40, Russell, Martin and Buitenhuis 2005, Hodder 2006) seems too far afield to warrant more than mention here, but it has been frequently cited in the mythic origins of Eurasian religions (Cauvin 1994). In the Levant and Anatolia, recently excavated remains of aurochsen and their interpretations hint at feasting, perhaps also with sacrifice in the Pre-Pottery and Early Ceramic Neolithic of the seventh and sixth millennia BC (Goring Morris and Kolska Horowitz 2007, Khalaily et al. 2007, Bogaard et al. 2009, Peters and Schmidt 2004). Such interpretations suggest a tantalizing affinity between Levantine and Arabian Neolithic societies whose frameworks for social constitution otherwise show significant differences (Chapter 6). Closer both in time and space to the Kheshiya ritual were the ritual associations of cattle and humans in the early African pastoral communities (Di Lernia 2006). As in Arabia (Rachad 2007,

Hadjouis 2007), in Saharan Africa wild cattle may have been significant long before domestication. For example, at the Late Paleolithic site of Tushka, one grave was marked by the long horns of cattle (Wendorf 1968). For ritual use of domesticated cattle in the Sahara, the earliest dates come from the region of Nabta Playa. Excavators have claimed a presence of domesticated cattle as early as 9000 BC (Close and Wendorf 1992, 2001: 70, Gautier 1984, Wendorf, Close and Schild 1987, Gautier 2001: 631–632) despite criticism of the data set and underlying assumptions (Grigson 2000, Wengrow 2003: 200). Ritual use of cattle for periodic sacrifice may have provided an important context for desiring scheduled and predictable access and sparked cattle domestication itself (Marshall and Hildebrand 2002: 111, 113, Russell and Martin 2005: 55–56, see also Cauvin 2000, Bar-Yosef and Bar-Yosef Mayer 2002: 349). Archaeologists most comfortably accept a domesticated status for cattle around 6500 BC (Gifford-Gonzalez 2005: 196), not much earlier than the earliest Arabian domesticates (Martin, McCorriston and Crassard 2009). Archaeological evidence for ritual use of cattle first appears at Nabta Playa in the middle sixth millennium BC (Applegate, Gautier and Duncan 2001).

The most dramatic evidence comes from one of the North Tumuli of the Late Neolithic Nabta Playa Ceremonial Complex, Tumulus E-94–1N, in which an entire domesticated cow was deliberately interred (6480 ± 270 ^{14}C yr BP). Other nearby tumuli also contained cattle bones along with jackal, gazelle or caprine, sheep, and, in one case isolated from any fauna, human remains. The only other radiocarbon date serves as a terminus ante quem of 5500 ± 160 ^{14}C yr BP (contemporary with the Arabian Kheshiya cattle skull ring). Nabta Playa's cattle cult Tumuli date to the Late Neolithic phase, contemporary with other Saharan deliberate interments of cattle (Applegate, Gautier and Duncan 2001). Building on Wendorf and associates' hypothesis that "cattle symbolize status and power," Di Lernia (2006) suggests that social complexity and ranking in human societies can be traced through the substitution of human for cattle burials and related causally to an "abrupt dry crisis" at the end of the fifth millennium BC (cf. Panchur and Hoezlmann 1991).

Certainly by the fifth millennium BC, there had emerged along the Nile Valley indigenous cattle herder–forager societies who used ceramics in economic and ceremonial contexts, probably cultivated wild sorghum, and included cattle in the burial practices of chiefs. In the El-Geili

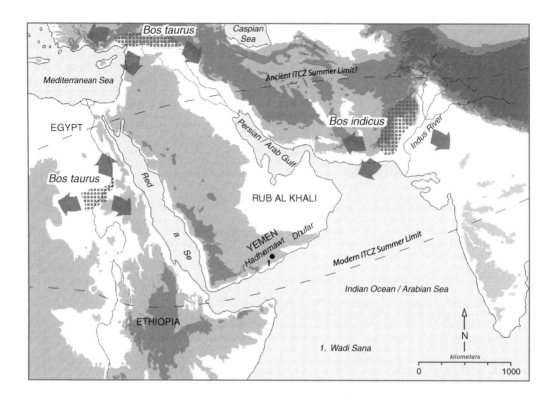

41. Map of cattle domestications in multiple locations across the Near East.

(Khartoum Neolithic) settlement dated to the middle fifth millennium BC (5570 ± 100 ^{14}C yr BP), excavators recovered signs of ephemeral occupations of herders with domesticated cattle, caprines, and ceramics who camped and fished periodically between episodes of flooding (Caneva 1998: 22–27, Gautier 1998: 59–61). At other sites, hearths, sandstone pavements, and postholes marked temporary occupations of the Khartoum Neolithic (Jesse 2004: 39–40). Most significant for comparisons with the contemporary (but unrelated and far distant) pastoralists of Hadramawt are the ritual uses of cattle, accompanied by ceramics, and cereals (Haaland 1992, Reinhold 2000: 58). Ceramics and cereals are unattested in any remains from contemporary Hadramawt and emphasize that these regions shared no direct cultural contacts. Indeed, the use of ceramics for food preparation and presentation (Haaland 2007) strikes a distinct contrast with the meat-grilling hearths used in Arabia.

In associations with human burials, the Saharan cattle rites also differed from those in Arabia, pointing to a very different cultural trajectory. There are a number of associations between humans, cattle, and high social rank in burial rites in the fifth-millennium BC Khartoum Neolithic. At the El-Kadaba cemetery, a central and distinctive tomb contained multiple burials, interpreted by the excavator as a high-status interment, covered in cattle hides, with several human sacrifices. Also included were several cattle bucrania (Reinhold 2000: 64, 1994: 95). At the Kadruka cemetery, the principal tomb (K1/131) contained two cattle bucrania with horns, a central "chief," and rich goods, including ceramics: elsewhere in the cemetery was an infant buried with bucrania (Reinhold 2000: 72–76). The Kadruka cemetery has been interpreted as the community burying ground of a lineage of related families (Reinhold 2000: 74), and the associations of cattle sacrifice with human social constitution – the so-called cattle cults of pre-history – have been implicated in the ideological foundations of later Nubian and Egyptian complex societies (Chaix 1988, Wengrow 2001a, 2006).

Cattle were also deeply significant in the Neolithic Ashmound Tradition dependent on monsoon seasons of Southern India (3000–1200 BC) (Boivin 2004). As in the Saharan and Arabian sequences, domesticated cattle, probably zebu, and a pastoral lifestyle preceded agricultural production and the use of domesticated plants for nearly a millennium (Fuller 2006: 52–54, Fuller and Madella 2001). The South Asian sequence considerably postdates Arabian and Saharan adoption of domesticated cattle and implies no broad cattle complex reaching across the Indian Ocean in pre-history. Instead, alongside African and Arabian examples, this third case of independent pastoralists transitioned from indigenous foraging groups in monsoon habitats suggests an important alternative to sedentism and agriculture for groups intensifying food production, delaying resource consumption, and using a resource surplus (cattle) to constitute social frameworks and develop territorial rights (Fuller 2006: 58, Garcea 2004, McCorriston and Martin 2009).

Table 3. Regional Traditions across the Near East, Northern Africa, Arabia, and Southern India All Show an Early Symbolic Focus on Cattle, but Various Authors Indicate Very Significant Differences in the Broader Social, Ritual, and Symbolic Aspects of Food Preparation, Deposition of Remains, and Commemoration of Ritual Events.

Regional Tradition	Relevant Dates	Symbolism	Monuments	Food Preparation Syndrome
Near Eastern Neolithic (Pre-Pottery Neolithic B)	8000–6800 BC	Wild cattle, feasting, skulls	Houses, shrines, community buildings within settlements	Oven baking, griddles
Saharan Neolithic	6000–5000 BC	Cattle, sacrifice, human bodies/ burials	Megalithic alignments, tombs, cemeteries	Cooking pot, boiling, brewing
Arabian Late Neolithic	5000–4000 BC	Cattle, sacrifice, skulls	Bone rings, stone platforms, standing stones	Grilling meat
South Indian Neolithic	3000–1200 BC	Cattle, fire, ash	Ash mounds	Boiling, grinding flour, dry roasting

Data drawn from Haaland 2007, Boivin 2004, Di Lernia 2006, Fuller 2006, Fuller and Madella 2001, Fuller, personal communication, RASA Project unpublished results, McCorriston et al. 2002, Méry et al. 2009, Uerpmann, Uerpmann and Jasim 2000, Atalay and Hastorf 2006, Wengrow 2005, Russell and Martin 2005, Goring-Morris and Kolska-Horwitz 2007, Khalaily et al. 2007, Applegate, Gautier and Duncan 2001.

Initiation and Pilgrimage at Kheshiya

The ritual at Kheshiya differed from its African Neolithic contemporaries, sharing only the common motifs of cattle sacrifice and the constitution of social order. In fifth-millennium BC Arabia, there appears no linkage between cattle sacrifice and human burial (Di Lernia 2006), nor between cattle and the meat-boiling food complex signaled with African pottery traditions (Haaland 2007). While the domesticated cattle themselves may – *may* – have had common origins in African stock, Nilotic and Southern Arabian societies had already constructed different social landscapes as the long-term habitus for widely differing social complexities.

The distinctly Arabian habitus of pilgrimage was already in place at Kheshiya. From 4500 BC, pastoralists traveled to a sacred site for ritual purposes, including cattle sacrifice, communal feast, and a seasonal, temporary community whose cosmic beliefs were constructed out of a system of structured and structuring dispositions. This system – the habitus of pilgrimage – was constituted in the practices we can discern in the archaeological record. Our struggle to understand its meaning dissolves in the twin mirages of history and native logic (Bourdieu [1980] 1990: 19); we can only grasp at a continuously shifting object. We will never know what Kheshiya's sacrifices meant, but we can argue that they were rites that constituted social landscapes of mobile peoples.

It is from the Kheshiya cattle sacrifices that we can discern the roots of pilgrimage in tribal rites, reframing in historical terms the structural juxtaposition between tribal rites and pilgrimage upon which Turner (1974b: 367) insisted. Instead of ahistorical, heuristic classificatory opposites, the relationship between tribal rites and pilgrimage is a developmental trajectory in Arabia. In discussing pilgrimage, Turner largely ignored the ritual of sacrifice that lies at the heart of pilgrimage practices in Arabia, allowing him to draw a spurious contrast between (African) tribal initiation ceremonies and (Christian) pilgrimage. As Chelhod's (1955: 137–138, 158–159, 165) and other studies have argued, sacrifice at the heart of pre-Islamic Arabian pilgrimage has clear historical and ontological links with sacrificial rites in other Arabian contexts, including the cutting of hair and tattooing as initiation of tribal youth (Robertson Smith 1907a: 330). In tribal initiations, sacrifice accompanies a rite of passage. General theories of sacrifice include the suggestion that the sacrificer through purification symbolically becomes divine, transitioning through the rite of sacrifice (Hubert and Mauss 1898: 50–51, 90, Van Gennep 1909). By participating as group sacrificers, a group assumes collective identity through sacrificial rites, just as individuals assume new identities or transition to a collective through initiation rites (Hubert and Mauss 1898: 38, Grimes 2000: 106). Pilgrimage, which is in Arabia tightly intertwined with sacrifice, offers a similar transition to or assumption of new identities as a social collective.

Quite simply, Turner was not thinking historically. But the Kheshiya Cattle Skull Ring and other Arabian monuments offer evidence for a historical view of tribal rites and pilgrimage. Monuments like the Cattle Skull Ring and adjacent stone platform play a mnemonic role in socially constructed landscape, which serves as long-term habitus. Monuments, erected through practice of rites of passage such as burial (tombs) or initiation (confluence, sacrifice, and feast) are the objectification of the structuring structures that generate practice (Bourdieu [1972] 1977: 72, 90). It is no longer (and never was for the objectifying observer) possible to identify the meanings of constitutive practice at these monuments, but such practices in antiquity gave rise to later pilgrimage rites. The monuments were themselves, through historical improvisations of symbol and meaning, predisposed to give rise to new principles for social construction in the practice of pilgrimage in a monumentally marked landscape. Socially constructed landscape as habitus suggests long-term change in the strategies of practice; in an Arabian case, pilgrimage began as temporary gathering – a component of tribal rites – but, through a history of practice, generated pilgrimage as both constituting collectivity in Islam (Hitti 1968: 41, Peters 1994) and transcending the tribal and other narrow social identities its earlier practice had served to accentuate.

CHAPTER 5

HOUSEHOLD PRACTICE IN MESOPOTAMIAN ANTIQUITY

> The reification of social relations, or the discursive "routinization" of the historically contingent circumstances and product of human action, is one of the main dimensions of ideology in social life.
>
> Giddens 1984: 25

Just as pilgrimage practice constituted ancient Southern Arabian societies as the manifestation of a long-term habitus, so belonging in households – what I shall call here household practice – constituted (Southern) Mesopotamia's urban social life and provided the enduring structure within which social transitions, transformations, and discourses were located. Households were kin-groups or metaphorical kin-groups who formed a basic socioeconomic unit of production and reproduction, often under one roof that physically represented the corporate group identity. Belonging in households as a key practice in belonging to social groups of various scales has both great antiquity and also was expressed across the rural – urban framework of Southern Mesopotamia. In earliest times households or groups of kin-related households held corporate lands, the primary means of production for the agrarian-based states (Gelb, Steinkeller, and Whiting 1991, Diakonoff 1975, Renger 1995: 276), although primordial corporate land-holding has also been criticized as a nineteenth-century theoretical construct (Bernbeck 1995, Van De Mieroop 1997: 103–104, 108–109, Yoffee 2005, Schloen 2001: 65, 239). In Mesopotamian states, temples to the gods functioned as super households (Pollock 1999, Postgate 1992, Renger 1994: 170), the state's core metaphor in maintaining the relations of class in the guise of kin-based systems. The state was literally held together as one household: each city-state had its city god with the largest and most important temple household dominating (literally, from atop a ziggurat) that city (Lamberg-Karlovsky 1989: 252–254, Stone 1999: 214). Assyriologists and archaeologists have long argued about the nature of this domination – to what degree was it an economic authority, that is, to what degree did the temple (or palace) control the primary means of production (land and labor)? (See Foster 1981, Diakonoff 1975, Gelb 1971, Renger 1994, 1995, Stone 1999, Seri 2005.) The answer changes through time and across the Mesopotamian landscape, but it is true that citizens could belong to private households, temples, and palace households in differing degrees, contexts, periods, and social roles (e.g., Gelb 1972, 1979, Diakonoff 1975: 126, Stone 1987: 74, Zettler 1992, Liverani [1998] 2006: 28, 61) and that they negotiated social networks through these affiliations. It is also uncontroversial to recognize that the appropriation and manipulation of kinship roles in households constituted the social identity of early Sumerian states (Diakonoff 1991: 73, Fox and Zagarell 1982, Foster 1982: 113, Gelb 1979: 5), later followed by appropriation of the divinity's role ensuring the reproduction of households by Akkadian rulers crowning themselves with the "horns of divinity" (Nissen 1988: 172–173, Michalowski 1987: 54). Even as the economic importance of various types of households (corporate, private, temple, palace) was in flux or contested, the social and ideological impact of belonging in households was undisputed (Schloen 2001). Household practice lay at the core of Mesopotamian states and underpinned the distinctive Mesopotamian phenomena of urban life. This chapter briefly summarizes the evidence and arguments advanced in detail elsewhere and contrasts the constitutive cultural elements of Household with Pilgrimage.

From the earliest Mesopotamian texts, super-household practice as a key organizing socioeconomic principle can be detected in the organization of the economic archives of the wealthy institutions (temples or palaces) in the Late Uruk (late fourth-millennium BC) levels of the Eanna precinct at the site of Warka (Nissen, Damerow and Englund 1993, cf. Liverani [1988] 2006: 30). But household practice as a socially constituting force extends deep into pre-history, the subject of the next chapter. Archaeologists are greatly hindered by the lack of earlier Uruk architecture and associated finds in Southern Mesopotamia (Yoffee 2005: 213, Pollock

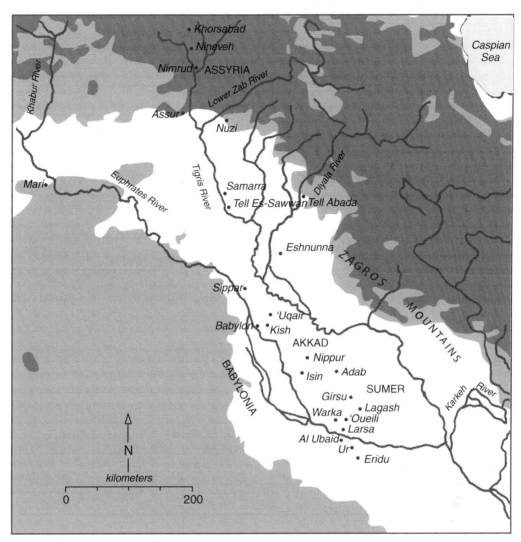

42. Map of Mesopotamian site locations.

2001: 185–187, Nissen 2001: 150–153) for it was surely in the earlier Uruk (ca. 3800–3500 BC) that important transpositions and restructuring of the dispositions or notions of "belonging in households" occurred. While this forms a real impediment to our understanding of state formation in Southern Mesopotamia (Algaze 2008, Yoffee 2005: 41, 55, Van De Mieroop 1997: 103–104), the concern here is not state formation itself and the details of how economic and social differentiation and integration occurred (e.g., McCorriston 1997, Algaze 2005, 2008) but the system of durable, transposable dispositions – the Mesopotamian habitus of house-hold – evident across the temporal trajectory of state formation and collapse (Yoffee 2005: 154–155, 1988).

The habitus of household differs widely from the habitus of pilgrim-age, and these differences frame this chapter. The evidence from Mesopotamia is well attested, more abundant, and in many respects better summarized and synthesized than evidence from Arabian civiliza-tions, so one need only briefly paraphrase the work elsewhere on the core constituting practice of household in Mesopotamian city-states (e.g., Diakonoff 1991, Pollock 1999: 117–148, Postgate 1992: 88–108, Schloen 2001, Stone 1987, 1997, Yoffee 1995, Zettler 1992). Where this chapter breaks new ground is the comparison of constituent elements of household practice and pilgrimage practice, emphasizing how very dif-ferent they are, even for complex societies like Mesopotamia and Southern Arabia in which elites maintained Houses as envisioned by Lévi-Strauss in House Societies (Gillespie 2000: 40–41, 47).

1. The Evidence – How We Know What We Know

As with our understanding of Southern Arabia's pilgrimage society, interpretation of Mesopotamian evidence rests upon particular and incomplete data. Furthermore much of the data can never be quantified: there is simply no way to ever know to what extent the conclusions drawn from particular cases and groups of finds represent greater Mesopotamian society. The nature and problems inherent in Mesopotamian textual and archaeological data have been reviewed before (e.g., Van De Mieroop 1997: 5–10, Pollock 1999, 2001: 185–187) and the best scholarship draws upon both data sets (e.g., Stone 1987, Zettler 1992, Keith 1999, Postgate 1992, Yoffee 2005). A cursory summa-tion of Mesopotamian sources is all that is required here.

Assyriological (Text) Sources

Insights from textual sources – cuneiform literary, religious, lexico-graphic, economic, historical and other documents on clay – are invalu-able for discerning various social identities of urban dwellers and their rural neighbors. Sumerians and Akkadians, Gutians, Amorites, Kassites, Aramaeans, Assyrians, Hurrians, and Chaldeans are apparent from texts, languages, and as coexisting ethnic and subgroups (Emberling and Yoffee 1999, van Soldt 2005) – groups with common professions formed in the metaphor of "families," using a common name that probably denoted a shared trade rather than shared genealogical kinship (Van De Mieroop 1997: 108–110, 221). Citizens and residents of an individual city had a common social bond based on the focal role of the city itself (Van De Mieroop 1997: 101). Cross-cutting wealth-based classes (Lamberg-Karlovsky 1989: 257), there may have been social identities associated with particular neighborhoods, although textual evidence for this is slim (Keith 2003, Seri 2005: 64–65). Sections of Old Babylonian cities such as Sippar are named after an Amorite subgroup (e.g., Charpin 2004: 92). As in all societies, social bonds formed by gender, age, and blood-kin (in nuclear families with dependent elders and siblings) remained significant components of social frameworks. But in Mesopotamian cities, large public institutions such as temples and palaces played an especially prominent and defining role as socially constituting organizations, of clear importance even as the written records coming from temple and palace archives may disproportionately inform us of their functioning and significance (Foster 1981, Renger 1995: 287, 299, 311–313, Seri 2005, Van De Mieroop 1997: 5–10).

Archaeological Evidence

The material culture of Mesopotamia and its archaeological recovery can be best summarized by referring to the environments in which Mesopotamian cities thrived (e.g., Ochsenchlager 2004, Algaze 2005, Potts 1997), present-day preservation conditions (e.g., Adams 1965, 1981: 37–43, Adams and Nissen 1972, Wilkinson 2000: 222, 230–232, 2003: 71–99), and the history of archaeological fieldwork (e.g., Larsen 1994, Banning 1996a, Fedele 1992). In Southern Mesopotamia, once extensive marshlands and combined sedimentation have either buried pre-Dynastic (pre-third millennium BC) sites below the floodplain, many beyond the detection and reach of archaeological investigation, or more than five millennia of deflation have eliminated stratigraphic deposits of once protrusive pre-historic sites, leaving behind a carpet of heavily abraded sherds (Huot 1989: 38, Stone 2000: 235, Wright and Pollock 1986: 328). Excavations have focused on Mesopotamia's great southern cities like Ur, Warka, Lagash, Girsu, and Larsa, or the Babylonian region's Nippur, Abu Salabikh, Shurrupak, and Mashkan shapir. Combined with the infrequency of surface remains from rural occupations and the historic inclination of archaeologists to excavate sites containing important temples, palaces, and rich tombs, the paucity of indigenous durable materials (baked clay, ceramic, and bitumen are significant exceptions) has made the archaeological record of Southern Mesopotamia a skewed one in which the massive remains of mudbrick city walls and ziggurats rise above a scoured and barren plain. This problem has been only partly addressed through survey and comparative studies of population (Adams 1981, 1972, 1965, Banning 1996a, Johnson 1988–1989, Pollock 1999, 2001, Wenke 1975-6, Wilkinson 2000, Wilkinson and Tucker 1995).

Northern Mesopotamia preserves a different record, due to different preservation conditions and a different history of research. Burial of early sites both by colluviation and subsequent occupation remains a problem and challenges quantitative approaches to the earlier periods (Wilkinson and Tucker 1995). In Northern Mesopotamia, rural communities and small-scale sites remained a significant feature of the agricultural landscape through Assyrian times (Renger 1995, Wilkinson 2000: 235, 241, 246), whereas some estimates put population residency at 80 percent in early-third-millennium BC cities in Southern Mesopotamia (Adams 1981: 138). In Northern Mesopotamia, a generally flat landscape is broken by rivers and tells, the man-made mounds left by multilayered remains of mudbrick ruins. Tell occupations and land-tenure systems stabilized during the Early Bronze Age (third millennium BC) and significantly shaped the historical geography of Northern Mesopotamia thereafter (Wilkinson 2003, Wilkinson, Ur and Casana 2004). Use of mudbrick has made rural settlements widely visible (e.g., Röllig and Kühne 1983, Monchambert 1994, Lyonnet 2001) in a sharp contrast to the effaced pisé-and-reed constructions of the (rural) south. Material traces of pastoral groups have been a recent subject of study (Geyer and Calvet 2001, Kouchoukos 1998), and some centers have proven surprisingly visible in the steppes (Castel and Peltenburg 2007, Orthmann 1995).

Tells are not unique to Northern Mesopotamia, of course, but they preserve there a range of materials that are badly abraded on Southern

Mesopotamia's desert surface (Stone 2000: 235). The range of material culture is comparable to that of Southern Mesopotamia. Even more significantly, the emphasis of the 1980s and 1990s on rural and non-elite contexts for understanding the development of complex societies (e.g., Wattenmaker 1998, McCorriston 1998, Schwartz and Falconer 1994) and the opportunities and mandates to excavate numerous small sites threatened by modern dam construction have led to systematic investigations into internal and intersite spatial patterns of artifact categories, architectural types, and the production and circulation of goods. Significantly, the recovery and analysis of food remains (charred plant remains and animal bone) has been much more successful and systematic in Northern Mesopotamia (e.g., Zeder 1994, 1998, Fedele 1992, Stein 1987, McCorriston and Weisberg 2002, Colledge 2003, Charles and Bogaard 2002, Miller 1997, Willcox 2002, Willcox, Fornite and Herveux 2008).

Synthetic studies show that Northern and Southern Mesopotamia had immense contacts and influence across culturally and ethnically distinct populations. From the proto-historical Uruk period, colonies of Southerners appeared in distinct enclaves (Stein 1999: 91–108, 138–158, Algaze 1993) in a Northern Mesopotamian social arena that, despite its many southern contacts, remained economically, socially, and politically distinct from Southern Mesopotamia throughout a long history (Stein 2004, Renger 1995, Wilkinson 2003). There are many excellent syntheses of these cultural trajectories (e.g., Nissen 1988, Postgate 1992, Pollock 1999, Akkermans and Schwartz 2003); therefore, the purpose of this chapter is to explore the ideological warp of household practice interwoven into Mesopotamian cultural discourse (Schloen 2001: 262–265).

Archaeological data for social identities has traditionally centered on two basic types of evidence - *architecture* (for household social groups and wealth-based differentiation of class (e.g., Johnston and Gonlin 1998, Wilk 1983, Smith 1987)) and *burials* (for bio-skeletal indicators of access to resources and labor histories, mortuary analysis of groupings, and associated grave goods (e.g., Campbell and Green 1995, Saxe 1970, Brown 1995, cf. Morris 1991)). In Mesopotamia, only architectural data are widely available for most periods. Burials are particularly scarce in the fourth millennium BC (maddening for those interested in the earlier

Uruk beginnings of state formation) but are in all periods very unevenly preserved and have seldom been the focus of systematic archaeological excavation and study. Even though the association of burials, burial practice, and monumental display has suggested important social identities and especially lineage and class statuses at a few notable sites, mostly Northern Mesopotamian (e.g., Porter 2002, Schwartz et al. 2003, Carter and Parker 1995, Pollock 1991, Peasnall 2002: 232), burials and burial practices do not appear to have been consistently manipulated to encode and signal social identities over the long trajectory of Mesopotamian history. Texts tell us that burial under the floor of houses was considered a normal way of affirming household identity in Old Babylonian Sumer (Charpin 2004: 58, Stol 2004: 81). In archaeological perspective, the treatment of the body and its (afterlife) abandonment as a feature of the urban social landscape stands in stunning contrast to Egypt, where Wengrow (2006) has made a compelling case for the long-term incorporation of "body politic" in the metaphor of body treatment. In Mesopotamia, society was constituted by household practice, the paramount material manifestation of which was the Mesopotamian house, private, public, and metaphoric/literary.

2. Mesopotamian Households, Private and Public

Although social frameworks and social conditions in Mesopotamia were fluid and dynamic both through time and across a physical terrain differentiated by topography, moisture regimes, agricultural practices, transport, and access, it is reasonable to emphasize the centrality of households (however variably expressed and experienced) not only as a basic economic unit but also in social and ideological terms. Household practice was a core constituting principle of Mesopotamian society throughout the social and cultural changes wrought with the rise, transformations, and collapses of economic strategies, states, dynasties, kingdoms, and empires (5000–500 BC).

Households are not the same as houses, which are but one physical manifestation of households. The archaeological record of houses – form, size, contents, context, construction – correlates, albeit not perfectly, to households (e.g., Bernbeck 1995, Yoffee 2005: 203, Wilk 1983), which are usually the smallest socioeconomic unit of production in agrarian societies (Sahlins 1972: 76, Wilk and Rathje 1982, Smith 1987: 297, Netting 1993: 58–62). From economic and other texts, we have a clear indication of the variability and importance of households in Mesopotamian society.

In Mesopotamian cities, there existed private and public households, so defined by social relationships that bound householders together. All households used the same terms of kinship, such as "father," "children," "spouse," to describe their membership, but one of the most significant differences lies between private households, in which such kinship was based on biological and marriage relationships and public ones in which kinship operated as a metaphor masking class relationships defined by wealth (Schloen 2001: 54–58). Wealth in ancient Mesopotamia was primarily measured by access to land and access to the labor of those without land.

The normal *private household* consisted of a nuclear family or sometimes several coresident nuclear families, at least in cities (Van De Mieroop 1997: 101, Stone 1987, Postgate 1992: 93–94, Gelb 1979), which is where the majority of Southern Mesopotamia's population dwelt from the third millennium BC. Alongside large public households, private households were largely self-sustaining and self-reproducing subsistence units with facilities for daily food preparation, basic provisioning, and manufacture (Keith 2003: 77, Pollock 2001: 207–208). Houses (and the households that occupied them) do not appear normally to have been segregated into different class or professional sectors within Southern Mesopotamian cities (Keith 2003: 75–77, Stone 2000: 241, Emberling 2003: 261), although a typical feature of Northern Mesopotamian cities did include a high acropolis area (over preexisting settlement) with elite residences and large public households overlooking a walled lower town of poorer residences (Stone 2000: 243–244). There existed social ties based on residential area (Stone 2000: 243) as well as ethnicity (Emberling and Yoffee 1999, Charpin 2004: 93), profession, city of residence, and public household membership (Van De Mieroop 1997: 110–111). But the household was always the basic social unit (Van De Mieroop 1997: 15) against which all other social affiliation was measured and in the practice of which other social affiliation was enacted. For example, social identification with city ("Children of the God") and affiliation with temple or palace ("House of the God") (Postgate 1992: 114, Groneberg 1986: 94) were manifestations of household practice, using the rhetoric of belonging in households to facilitate the socio-economic differentiation and integration of states.

Public households – temples and palaces – appeared early and were a persistent feature of Mesopotamian life. Because we understand poorly the preliterary societies of earlier Uruk, there remain significant uncertainties about how temples emerged, but it is clear that they did so in the metaphor of large households. Temples and palaces held land as households, and kin-groups held land and thereby assured temple household members access to land and food. It remains unclear how temples and palaces acquired the vast estates and labor forces they managed, but they did so under conditions of changing technology, labor requirements, and environmental conditions of production that accompanied the process of urbanization (Fox and Zagarell 1982, McCorriston 1997, Algaze 2005, 2008). Public households (temples and palaces) are not only indisputably evident from the third millennium BC, but they dominated the Mesopotamian social framework thereafter.

While it has proven impossible from the skewed and incomplete available archival records to quantify the significance of temple or palace in the economic functioning of Mesopotamian cities (Van De Mieroop 1997:14), it is certain that the significance of such institutions varied both temporally and spatially. Palaces and temples were major landholders, at brief times perhaps the only landholders (Renger 1994: 185–189), and over time the palace institution emerged as the more influential in Northern Mesopotamia (e.g., Schloen 2001: 283), while temples retained paramount significance in the constitution of Southern Mesopotamian city-states (Renger 1995: 306–313, Van De Mieroop 1997: 94, 111, Stone 2000). At times when extensive private landholding is clearly attested, large "*oikos*" households still maintained prominence (Stol 2004: 692–693, 495). The significance of temples in Babylonia, where by 500 BC "it seems quite evident that a large, if not the largest, portion of arable land around Warka was owned by the Eanna temple" (Renger 1995: 313), has led to considerable discussion of the role of temple not only in social and ritual life but as the artery of early urban economies.

The Mesopotamian Temple-State – Households, Land, and Rations

In the late nineteenth century and within the intellectual model of Marx's Orientalist mode of production with its despotic political authority and stagnant economy, scholars proposed that Mesopotamia's great temple households controlled and organized access to all economic resources, including, most importantly, land and labor (Deimel 1931, Falkenstein 1974, Gelb 1979, Foster 1981, Van De Mieroop 1997: 13–14). Such economic domination confers overwhelming political power. Given the nineteenth-century perception of ancient Mesopotamia as a static, nonentrepreneurial, and primitive political economy, the colliery view would then be; take away the temple stranglehold on resources, and the state itself would collapse. But as Yoffee (1993, Emberling and Yoffee 1999) has repeatedly emphasized, the defining characteristic of Mesopotamian civilization is a Great Tradition, repeatedly embraced and transmitted by new ethnic groups. This Great Tradition, whether it upholds Mesopotamian unity through "standard literary language, systematization of the gods and cosmos, and preservation, transmission and revision of bodies of texts" (Yoffee 1993: 302) or whether it is reflected by "the persistence of city-state organization in the face of repeated attempts at political unification" (Stone 2000: 26), endured even as temple control of economic resources waxed and waned over time and space.

The potent and enduring symbol of the Mesopotamian temple (as a super household) played a dramatic and contextual role in the symbolic and ritual construction and negotiation of power throughout history (cf. Kertzer 1988), even as its economic role varied (Foster 1981: 299–300, Stone 1987, Renger 1994, 1995, Maekawa 1980, Seri 2005: 127, McCorriston 1997). Gelb (1979: 139) has argued that the temple-state hypothesis was overstated, largely predicated on the reading of a single archive detailing landholdings of the É2-Bau (or house/temple of Bau, consort of the chief male god of the city) at Lagash. On the other hand, Renger (1994: 188, 1995: 278, 287) defends the notion of a temple-state – or at least temple control of agricultural land – for the end of the third millennium BC in the southernmost part of Mesopotamia. With particular emphasis on the exploitive and extractive nature of the temple economy and its supporting bureaucracy, Pollock (1999) summarized the workings of the *oikos*, or super-household, model of third-millennium BC temple-states. In Northern Mesopotamia, the economic power of the temple was largely attenuated by the influence of another super-household, the palace: indeed, by the fourteenth to eleventh centuries BC, wealthy families controlled vast economic resources (land) through their attachments to the palace (Renger 1995: 306–308, Schloen 2001: 283), another super-household.

Class in the Metaphor of Domestic Kin

Social identity was expressed in the metaphor of belonging to households, so emerging relations of class were expressed in the metaphor of domestic kinship relations as social differentiation and integration occurred in the fourth and third millennium. The argument has been made before that changes in household organization of labor with the emergence of specialized economic producers affected gender and kinship relations in Mesopotamian households (McCorriston 1997, Wengrow 1998) and that a lower-class workforce was ultimately attached as dependents to the super-household of the temple (Gelb 1972).

The enacted practice of belonging in temple and palace households entailed ritual and symbol, used to consolidate social solidarity through the potential tensions of class conflict. The reflexive nature of such symbolic action is well attested, for by use of symbols "ritual action becomes part of the universe [even as] it gives meaning to the universe" (Kertzer 1988: 9). By feeding the gods and kings and clothing them (e.g., Postgate 1992: 119, Waetzoldt 1972: xxii, 1980–1983: 592, Zettler 1992: 144), enacting sacred unions (e.g., Yoffee 2005: 116–130), registering the obligations of householder to household and vice versa through writing, and distributing food to members of the god's household (Postgate 1992: 120), the rituals of super-households reproduced the practices of private households, thereby "nurturing and expressing the people's belief in the legitimacy of the politically powerful and the system they represented" (Kertzer 1988: 38). Even as encumbered laborers in temples and the dependent retainers in palace households were bound to each other by conditions of wealth – access to land and rations – not birth and marriage, the practice of belonging in public households masked the transformation of social relations and connected disparate social (and ethnic) groups to a federal urban identity.

Ubaid Super-Households

Archaeological, pictographic, and Sumerian-Akkadian written records suggest that super-households emerged in the fourth and third millennia BC, and their precursors can be found in the household practices of Ubaid societies. Prior to the transpositions in meaning and structure that occurred with the development of Mesopotamian urban life, household practice was in the Ubaid (sixth and fifth millennia BC, a Late Neolithic period) a deeply embedded and constituent principle in agrarian social life. In the absence of written records, evidence for household practice in the Ubaid comes from the houses themselves, which present compelling data in form, context, and associated artifacts.

The oft-cited and direct link between Ubaid households and the emergence of Uruk super-households (temples) is the architectural plan of the lavish and expensive temples (or palaces or community meeting halls (Forest 1996: 113, 1999: 2–3)) of the Late Uruk period (late fourth millennium BC) at Warka (Nissen 1988, after Heinrich 1982: 7–14, 45–46), Eridu (Oates 1986: 382, Safar and Ali 1981), and Tell Uqair (Lloyd and Safar 1943: 136–137, Plate V). Several of the buildings follow the tripartite form of Ubaid houses, which consisted of a central hall flanked by two rows of apartment rooms presumed to serve two units of an extended family (Forest 1996: 40–41, Bernbeck 1995: 17–18). The same tripartite plan is reproduced in the largest buildings of the late Ubaid period, notably the "Temple VII" at Eridu (4300 BC) and the plan of the Late Ubaid building under the Anu precinct at Warka. Regardless of their functions (and great significance has been attributed to their locations and orientations on sites later occupied by temple and ziggurat), all agree that these buildings had a socially constituting purpose to which can be attributed their larger scales, elaborate furnishings, and critical locations (Forest 1996: 103–130).

The earliest Ubaid houses found in Southern Mesopotamia lie in the basal sequence in the sixth and early fifth millennium BC at Tell el-'Oueili. All three houses are so similar to the tripartite houses at Tell es-Sawwan "that we may speak of a common tradition, the origins of which are possibly to be found in the previous Hassuna culture" (Forest,

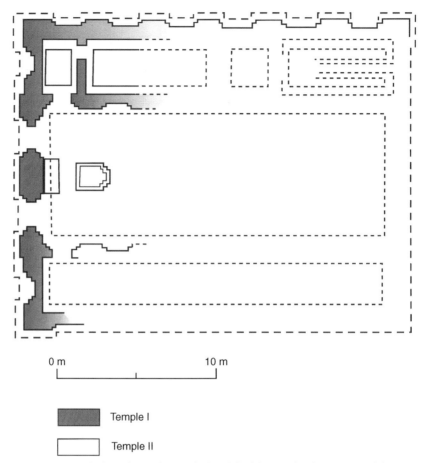

43. Reconstructed plan of two phases of a lavish building under the remains of the Anu Ziggurat at Warka. The plans of the earliest Uruk "temples" follow the tripartite plan of Ubaid 4 houses, here shown in gray as "Temple I." Redrawn after Forest 1996: 109 Figure 85.

Huot and Vallet 1991–1992: 276). Excavations at Tell es-Sawwan, located along the Tigris River at the northern margins of Southern Mesopotamia, have produced a relatively complete settlement plan, from which archaeologists can infer a shift over time in house form, household size, and community structure. In the transition from Sawwan I–II to Sawwan III levels, predominant house form shifted from the extended family (tripartite central hall type) to nuclear family (T-shaped) type (Forest 1996: 40–43, 57). The interpretation of household-family structure comes from traffic and access analysis (Forest 1996: 40–43), relative size (Bernbeck 1995), and ethnographic observations (Aurenche 1981: 223) and may be mitigated by the presences of additional stories not visible in

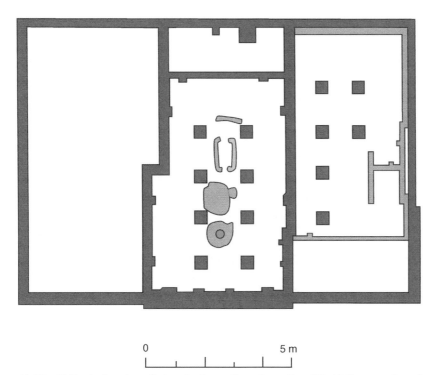

0   5 m

44. 'Oueili (Iraq) plan view of tripartite house from the earliest (Ubaid 0) occupation of Southern Mesopotamia. This plan is later reproduced in the platformed buildings that underlie sacred precincts of Mesopotamian cities where the household of the god was established in historic times. Redrawn after Huot 1992: 191.

archaeological house plans (Margueron 1986: 370, cf. Roaf 1986: 427). Elsewhere other fifth-millennium communities built either tripartite or T-shaped houses, but these forms appear to be mostly exclusive: at any given period most communities have either one or the other, reflecting different norms for domestic household groups.

Another significant insight into household practices comes from the form and context of granaries, which ceased to be large communal structures and were subsequently attached to particular compounds at the beginning of the Ubaid period (Forest 1996: 48, Bernbeck 1995: 16, Pfälzner 2002). Bernbeck (1995: 16) argues that as households depended less on communal storage within the community and more on household storage, so the social distance between households increased. This development would strengthen social identities of belonging to households, already well in evidence by the time a large, possibly communal granary appeared in the late Ubaid levels of Tell el-'Oueili (Huot 1989: 32, 39).

There persists a debate about the emergence of super-households. Yoffee (2005: 31) and Wright (Wright and Pollock 1986: 324–328) find little evidence in the Ubaid period for emerging inequality that would give members of one household access to greater power, while others (Bernbeck 1995: 20, Forest 1996: 105, Jasim 1985: 202–203, Margueron 1986: 376, Stein 1994: 38–39) cite some of the same evidence (Tell Abada, Tell es-Sawwan, and the Ubaid buildings at Eridu VII and Warka) to suggest greater authority and wealth in larger households. If one considers the changing technology and aesthetic investment in ceramic, textile, and basket production, it is clear that the control and manipulation of aesthetic production came under the control of super-households by the later Uruk period (Nissen 1988: 83–87, McCorriston 1997, Wengrow 2001b: 183). Appropriation of aesthetic production by some households materially tracks ascendant political power that the manipulation of symbols confers (Kertzer 1988), but these patterns are not evident through the Ubaid. This transformation may be linked to what Stein (1994: 42–43) has argued is a shift from staple to wealth finance in the Late Ubaid period (cf. D'Altroy and Earle 1985). Stein argues that in a system of chiefly staple finance, emerging elites used ritual behavior – I would insert "belonging in super-households through ritual mobilization of surplus cereals" here – to appropriate labor and agricultural staples like grain and dates for the maintenance and manipulation of elite power through redistribution rights. The model draws on large Late Ubaid (ritual) buildings at Warka and Eridu, a granary for large-scale storage at Late Ubaid 'Oueili (Huot 1989: 32), and strengthened group identity expressed in cemeteries (Hole 1989). A test of this model will be the recovery of earlier Uruk buildings to bridge the gap between large Ubaid buildings and the Late Uruk temples in Southern Mesopotamia.

Indeed, it seems likely that not only is the entire earlier Uruk absent (architecturally) from the archaeological record but also that there were entire categories of ephemeral architecture now missing from earlier and later periods. Modern use of reed construction in Southern Iraq's marshlands has been frequently documented, and pre-historic reed buildings have been noted at Ur, Tell Ubaid, and Warka (Aurenche 1981: 105–107). Reed-and-pisé construction can be quickly erected and relatively easily replaced, requiring no access to the more expensive straw (produced through agricultural labor) needed for mudbrick. Such straw had other

valuable uses, notably as fodder, so the mudbrick buildings that archaeologists most commonly recover represent the more wealthy and durable
investments. Labor and access to agricultural land and products (straw
in surplus of fodder needs) are displayed with the construction of
mudbrick houses. (But archaeologists cannot recover any aesthetic display or collective labor potentially invested in constructions of reed, and
Southern Mesopotamia's dramatic and collectively produced *maḍīf*
(community guesthouse) architecture serves as a sober reminder of the
unrecoverable archaeological record (Ochsenschlager 2004), as do the
reed boats that plied the Gulf waters (Vosmer 2003)). The archaeological
sequence at Tell el-'Oueili showed a transition from clay-loaf-and-pisé
construction to mudbrick about 6000 BC (Forest 1987: 25), but it is by no
means clear that simple reed constructions vanished: indeed their occasional discovery at pre-historic sites and the sometimes presence only of
sherd scatters to mark sites suggests that there long existed a widespread,
ephemeral landscape of reed houses with perhaps somewhat mobile and
flexible households that occupied them.

In this reconstructed countryside that includes ephemeral buildings,
consider not only the greater longevity of a mudbrick house but its
greater resistance to flooding. In the relatively flat and seasonally inun-
dated landscape of Southern Mesopotamia, the larger mudbrick buildings rising above the floodplain, constructed sometimes on massive
terraces as at Tell el-'Oueili (Forest 1987: 25 Figure 1b) and Warka
manifested longevity and endurance of the community itself (Forest
1996: 105, 110). Communities structure themselves and their identities
through creation of social memories, shared and enacted to provide a
sense of place (e.g., Tilley 1994, Feld and Basso 1996, Barrett 1988,
Cummings 2003, Cosgrove 1984). Practices that establish social cohesion may include ritual behavior, narrative, representations and objects,
and the transformation of space into a sense of place with a remembered
attachment (Van Dycke and Alcock 2003: 4–5). Participation in the
creation of a place like an artificial mound (Pauketat and Alt 2003:
160–163), a Great House (Van Dycke 2003), or, in Mesopotamia, a
large building or terrace, both enacted and inscribed community membership. Just as mudbrick houses conferred greater longevity to the
household than did simple reed-and-pisé, so also social memory of
house construction constructed the household itself.

45. *Maḍīf* (guesthouse) from the marshlands of Southern Iraq. These impressive guest houses and community gathering places built of reed bundles have also been depicted on Mesopotamian cylinder seals from the third millennium BC. Photo courtesy of H. E. Wright, Jr.

With the passage of time, those houses that stood above the floodplain most visibly manifested social memory and became significant places in the landscape. As such, they may have provoked practices such as their upkeep and periodic reconstruction by successive generations who thereby commemorated their belonging to place through the renewal of household practice. As the physical manifestation of habitus, the significance of such houses demanded their upkeep with household labor: as terraces and scale increased, this labor would have engaged a larger part of the community. Eridu's successive phases of buildings culminating in historic temple households need not have begun as a house of the god, but as a mudbrick house more visible than neighboring reed-and-pisé structures. I am suggesting a process similar to that proposed for earlier Neolithic sites where building continuity seemingly played a significant role in the differentiation of buildings and the constitution of societies. In some cases, "ordinary domestic structures could gradually acquire ritual significance and become central to a larger group of households" (Düring 2005: 24). In early Southern Mesopotamia, the actual economic and social events that allowed a few households to build in mudbrick spared by floods may have been as

46. Making mudbrick in Northern Mesopotamia today (Syria). Author's photo.

episodic and historically contingent as the events of evolution itself (Gould 1986) and equally lost in time.

In the Ubaid period, belonging in households, of which large buildings are a manifestation, was the paramount socially constituting practice, a metaphor for belonging in communities. David Schloen (2001) has made a persuasive argument that the metaphor of patriarchal family was the core organizing principle of societies across the Near East in the Bronze Age. In Mesopotamia the large buildings constructed in the plan of houses suggest that communities constructed their corporate identities in the practice of household, at least as early as the Late Ubaid period. Whatever the "function" of the late Ubaid and Late Uruk great buildings, they manifested the practice of belonging in households, which served as a structuring metaphor for any ritual – religious rites (temple), administration (chief's house, palace), assembly (hall of elders), and we do not know which or what combination of these served – that constituted a common social identity.

Households and Ethnicity in Early Mesopotamia

Different ethnic groups may also have had different practices. Mesopotamia was always a multiethnic landscape (van Soldt 2005,

47. Reconstructed view of Ubaid memory house in mudbrick. Drawn by Matt Indrutz.

Kamp and Yoffee 1980), even given the challenge to differentiate ethnic groups in the archaeological record (Emberling and Yoffee 1999) or to understand the implications of different social identities ethnic in origin. The earliest direct evidence for ethnicity comes from language, which only becomes apparent to history as texts were written in the last centuries of the fourth millennium BC. Although language is often one of the distinguishing criteria of distinct ethnic groups, there remains some doubt as to the origins and status of Sumerian, language of the archaic texts (Rubio 2005: 330–331, cf. Englund 1988: 81, Whittaker 2005: 447). Sumerian may not have been spoken at all; rather, it may have emerged as an artificial construction of elites incorporating many dialects (including some Akkadian) (Yoffee 1993: 303). Rubio ([1990] 1999: 11, 2005: 331) likens the "linguistic picture of early Mesopotamia" to a "fluid and variegated canvas of words traveling together with the objects and techniques they designate" in a visual imagery that implies many languages and dialects contributing to the symbolic repertoire from which emergent elites crafted ritual enactment of household obligations through writing. This would seem to be the beginnings of Mesopotamia's "Great Tradition" (Yoffee 1993, Beld 2002: 227) differentiating elites from non-elites.

With the persistence of multiple ethnic groups and historical introductions of new ones, one may wonder whether different house forms such as tripartite and smaller T-shaped houses that sheltered very different forms of households were linked with distinct ethnic and cultural groups with greater or less social emphasis on the practice of belonging in households. I doubt this was so simple. Family form has been shown to change as the labor needs, technologies, and environmental constraints of production change (Mitterauer 1992, Rudolph 1992, Netting 1993: 88–100). The introduction of irrigation and its labor and water-sharing networks in the Late Neolithic surely had an effect on family form (Liverani [1998] 2006: 28). Different house forms are also linked with changing household size and configuration to accommodate different conditions of production. Different house forms need not imply ethnic and language differences but are just as likely to be also constrained by differences in economic and environmental conditions (Aurenche 1981). That the practices of belonging in households continued into the Late Uruk and beyond implies their enduring successes in perpetuating agrarian production and household reproduction in a changing society.

Household practice was a discourse and the locus of contested and negotiated symbolic action (Bourdieu [1972] 1977, Giddens 1984). Elites set an agenda for social participation, manipulating and enacting cultural practices through ritual behaviors, including writing, drama, and narrative. Household practice provided a context for the legitimation of power (for example, exclusive banquets (Garfinkel 2003a: 83, Pollock 1991: 379-382)), just as it also provided a framework for resistance to emergent elites. In this exchange, the participation of multiple ethnic groups in Southern Mesopotamia's changing fifth- and fourth-millennium political economy was interwoven with a paradigm of household practice. The social identities of community groups (clans, tribes, assemblies) that persisted throughout Southern Mesopotamian history (e.g., Yoffee 2005: 110-111) may as readily be seen as subversive and contesting political enactment (cf. Beld 2002: 38-44) as relicts of an utopian pre-state communal form (Liverani [1998] 2006: 31-32, Schloen 2001: 65, 189, 239) or the social practice of distinct ethnic groups. Into this contestation may also be read the enactment of Mesopotamian pilgrimage rites to temples, for which there is no archaeological or textual evidence of widespread (i.e., non-elite) participation and the purported significance of which can be traced to sociologists' theoretical speculations on the origins of cities (Wheatley 1971, Eliade [1949] 1954: 12-18).

3. Cultural Elements of the Habitus of Pilgrimage and of Household

Households are important in most agrarian societies as the basic socio-economic unit of production (Sahlins 1972, Le Roy Ladurie [1975] 1979: 24-52, Duby [1962] 1968: 28-47, 213-214, Netting 1981, Lévi-Strauss [1979] 1982), but Mesopotamian and other Near Eastern Bronze Age societies (Schloen 2001) were distinctive in their use of household practice as the metaphor for wider social order. Belonging in households, with its reflexive and recursive practices (Kertzer 1988: 76, 79-81, Inomata 2006) and long-term manifestations in houses, temples,

Table 4. Cultural Elements in Mesopotamia and Arabia.

Cultural Elements	Pilgrimage Southern Arabia	Household Mesopotamia
Ritual observance	Temporary, punctuated, brings together temporarily a social group: gathering, sacrifice, feast	Regular, steady, knits a permanent community: feeding and clothing the god, observing household obligations of production and reproduction
Redistribution of offerings	Intermittent, feasts	Regular, rations
Social structure	(*Bayts*) clans, lineage group (genealogy)	Nuclear and extended families (lineal, agnatic descent)
Group residence and social cohesion	Mobile, fluid, segmented	Fixed by central place
Physical manifestation of habitus	Monuments, shrines, tombs, *hjr*	Houses, temples, palaces, city
Social memory (mostly)	Incorporated	Inscribed
Social identity affirmed by	Time (*hj* season, individual journeys, genealogical time = social distance)	Place (houses, temple and palace institutions, city)
Class in the idiom of	Clans, tribes	Household
Primary means of agricultural production	Water (most is intermittent through sayl)	Land (stable, most water is also stable through canal system)
Economic framework (the state)	Caravans (with agriculture, pastoralism, incense collection)	Agriculture (with trade and animal husbandry, textile production)
Settlement patterns	Territories, oasis centers	Site hierarchies

palaces, and individual cities, gave structure to Mesopotamian cultural life just as practicing pilgrimage gave structure to Arabian societies.

Table 4 provides a summary comparison of the cultural institutions of Pilgrimage and Household. Although cultural elements are dynamic over time, reflexively interrelated, and subjective in experience, the table here offers a simplified, comparative, and static model that describes and, most significantly, contrasts prevalent and recurrent characteristics of Southern Arabian and Mesopotamian civilizations. Some cultural elements have already been extensively discussed, but others require elaboration. In both Southern Arabia and Mesopotamia, the social construction of space to form remembered places where social participation may be narrated and enacted plays an important role in the constitution of social groups – indeed, social construction of place is common to all societies (Cosgrove 1984, Tilley 1994, Van Dycke and Alcock 2003). The economic practice of mobility (caravans, pastoralism) in Southern Arabia accompanied a flexibility and fluidity in social groupings and their construction around temporally punctuated events – a visit to a particular monument or place where a particular and contextual identity could be temporarily affirmed. This offers an important contrast to Mesopotamian identity around households and their embedded daily economic and social reproduction with continuously negotiated and contextualized social identity. Rowlands (1993: 142) after Connerton (1989) usefully draws a distinction between *inscribed memory* – formed through practice that relies on frequent repetition and ritual discourse to integrate knowledge into daily life and inculcate membership in a social group – and *incorporated memory* – formed by practices that use secrecy, exclusion, avoidance of analytical (exegetical) commentary, iconic symbolism, and infrequency to generate stunning experience with persuasive and enduring impact. Monuments, shrines, or tombs are places that commemorate such incorporated memories and can be used in a temporary drama of reenactment for social constitution such as pilgrimage. They differ from houses, whether palaces or temples or domiciles, in which routine practices that ensure the production and reproduction of the household take place.

Some cultic journeys in Southern Mesopotamia entailed punctuated visits (by ruling elites) to the temple of a distant god or goddess. Such journeys likely coincided with agricultural and astronomical cycles and served to reinforce the authority vested in rulers through their close affinities with gods receiving offerings (Beld 2002, Hall 1985). Mesopotamian cultic journeys entailed a small entourage of elites and served "as a mechanism for integrating . . . heads of other cultic institutions with the ruling family" (Beld 2002: 107). Mesopotamian cultic journeys practiced by elite few, sometimes accompanying the image of the deity, differ sharply from Arabian Pilgrimage, in which participation and the expectation of participation served to integrate a common social identity across social classes. And Mesopotamian cultic journeys synchronized to significant festivals were always set against the daily backdrop of the routine care and feeding of the gods (Hall 1985: 259). Significance of pilgrimage centers in Mesopotamia can otherwise be traced only to broader sociological theories on the origins of cities, unfounded in Mesopotamian literary and archaeological data.

The differences between Pilgrimage and Household institutions cannot be ascribed simply to different memory practice but instead spring

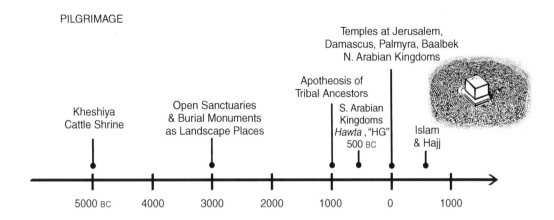

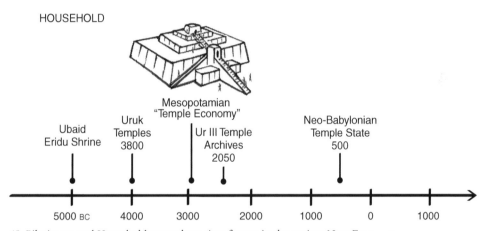

48. Pilgrimage and Household across long time frames in the ancient Near East.

from a long-term set of dispositions that endured throughout culture change. Over time cultural transmission may shift from greater reliance on the practices that generate incorporated to inscribed memory or vice versa (Bradley 1985), although both forms may be in use (Rowlands 1993: 149). Arabian pilgrimage, originating in pre-history from the (perhaps infrequent) rituals of gathering, sacrifice, and feast, may in time have attached to the singular burial or commemorative rites of a leader or tribal initiations (incorporated memory), whose resting place eventually became a shrine and the habitual gathering place where inscribed memory was inculcated through punctual pilgrimage. Perhaps in ancient Mesopotamia, incorporated memory built the communities who constructed the enduring houses at sites like Eridu and

Warka, but later in time social memories were primarily inscribed by the repetitive household practices in super-household institutions.

4. Just Two Near Eastern Meta-Structures?

Just how many meta-structures were there in the ancient Near East? The ancient Bronze Age world system (Frank 1993, Ratnagar 2001, 2003, Kardulias 1999) offers a useful geographic and cultural set of boundaries in which to consider this question as this period saw the emergence of states in many distinct regions. During the third millennium BC and perhaps also during the pre- and proto-historic period of the fourth millennium BC (Algaze 1993), exchange systems and cultural contacts were at a historic apogee. Much of the cultural interconnectivity of geographic regions from the Eastern Mediterranean through Central Asia, South Asia, and the northern margins of the Indian Ocean centered on economic exchange (Edens 1992, Ratnagar 2003, Potts 1994: 250–269, Weisgerber 1983, Cleuziou and Tosi 1994, Algaze 1993, Stein 1999), which occurred not in our modern context of economic rationalism but through social networks predicated on recognized social relationships (Schloen 2001: 86–89, 189). By the third millennium, a common cuneiform writing system and symbolic constructs linked the elite urban dwellers across Northern and Southern Mesopotamia in a greater "Kish civilization" (Gelb 1992) and facilitated exchanges of textiles, metals, and dyestuffs, among other raw and finished products. Throughout this broad interconnectivity, the parallel temporal strands of Household and Pilgrimage practice persisted even as their practitioners transmitted and transformed cultural schemes across time and space.

The intercultural exchange between Household and Pilgrimage societies deserves further study on its own merit, but the research of Serge Cleuziou and Maurizio Tosi (1994, 2000, Cleuziou 2003) along the Magan coast of Bronze Age Oman sheds some important insight into the role that exchange plays in the integral maintenance of distinct meta-structures. Contacts between Household and Pilgrimage societies are reminiscent of Marshall Sahlins's (1981, 1995) brilliant study of "Historical Metaphors and Mythical Realities" played out in the exchanges between Hawai'ian Islanders and Captain Cook's crew on his third deadly voyage. In Hawai'i, the natives perceived Cook as the returning god Lono due offerings for a limited season; for Europeans, the natives were inferiors whose largesse was to be appropriated to the service of Britain as needed. (Hawai'ians killed Cook/Lono when his crippled ship sailed back to Kealakekua Bay after Lono was supposed to have left Hawai'i for the year.) In the case of Mesopotamians arriving in Magan, captains and crews would have perceived exchanges of material goods (grain, beer, flax and woolen textiles, finished metals, ceramics, transshipped soapstone vessels and beads for provisions of meat, dates, milk, fish, raw metals, worked marine shells, leather, horn, indigo and madder dyes, and incense) within the context of Household practices. Mesopotamians could only sail down the Gulf seasonally, arriving predictably during winter when the mobile pastoralists of the Ja'alān were seasonally on the beaches. To Mesopotamians the food supplies looked like predictable rations provided in the patrimonial household model (Schloen 2001); to Arabian pastoralists, commodity flows took place in the social context of forging a common bond through gathering and feasting with Mesopotamians at a seasonal time. The outline of this exchange is here speculative (based on solid archaeological data from Ra's al Jinz and the Arabian Gulf) but suggests a case study for the maintenance of distinct cultural meta-structures through sustained cultural contact.

Within the cultural spheres of an interconnected Bronze Age world system, across the Levantine-Mesopotamian arc of the Fertile Crescent and Arabia (excluding Egypt and the Indus), I find just two meta-structures – Household and Pilgrimage. The differences between them are so profound and their practical enactments so antithetic one to another that they constituted two very different kinds of societies and explain two distinct culture histories. Others have tried to explain the broad differences in social form by drawing a contrast between Desert and Sown (Bell [1907] 2001, see also Parker 1987, Banning 1996b, Wiseman 2000), Nomadism and Sedentism (LaBianca 1990, Rowton 1973, 1975, 1976), Pastoralism and Agriculture (Stein 2004), and Irrigation and Dry-Farming (Weiss 1986, Renger 1995). These are essentially economic foundations for social differences, and it is unsurprising that where the environmental and technical conditions of production differ, social relations of production also differ. But ethnographic studies repeatedly show that people who practice different and sometimes mixed economic strategies may identify themselves as one ethnic or social group (e.g., Lancaster and Lancaster 1999a, 1999b, Fleming 2004, Tapper 1990, Cleuziou 1997), often alongside other groups practicing similar and similarly mixed socioeconomic strategies. This is only surprising if one believes that environmental and technical factors (completely) determine cultural strategies and social identities. However they arose, practices of Pilgrimage and Household significantly shaped and recursively were shaped by the societies that constituted themselves through their enactment. It seems that the historical contingencies provided the anchor for enduring cultural meta-structures that transcended not only the socioeconomic interactions of different cultural groups but also the temporal drift of social memories and changing political economies.

Conclusions

The differences in Pilgrimage and Household point to different long-term core elements – what Giddens (1984: 17) calls "structural principles" – of different culture histories in the Near East. From at least as early as the fifth millennium BC, some mudbrick houses surviving inundations on the southern floodplain inscribed a sense of community among Ubaid villagers, whose practices of belonging in households were transcribed and enshrined in the emergence of super-households. These became the house of the god, a transformation that confederated individual households into an urban matrix, also through the inscribed memory transmitted through daily and public practice. Pilgrimage practice in Southern Arabia was very different, relying on incorporated memory through intermittent gathering, sacrifice, and feast, even during the *bayt* societies and the urban experiences of the ancient Southern Arabia states.

Viewed in these terms, it is unsurprising that epigraphic South Arabian evidence finally demonstrated to scholars the autochthonic nature of Southern Arabian religion after nearly a century of futile speculation that Mesopotamian religion must have inspired that of Southern Arabia (Pirenne 1990: 129–130). In a Durkheimian framework, it would be impossible to construe Southern Arabian religious practices as being derived from Mesopotamia's, for if religion truly functions as the mirror of society (cf. Boyer 2001: 26–27), then the religions of ancient Mesopotamia and Southern Arabia mirror antithetically different societies springing from two of a very few Near Eastern meta-structures, the manifestations of cultures sharing virtually no common structured structures, no systems of durable, transposable dispositions, and no social institutions. Therefore, the one (Southern Arabia) is fundamentally undisposed to constitute itself in the metaphor of another's (Mesopotamia's) religious practice.

Finally, it is apparent that just as Neolithic cattle herders practicing gatherings, sacrifices, and feasts in Southern Arabia instituted Pilgrimage (Chapter 4), so Household practice and the meta-structure of Household in the Near East is apparently an historical outcome of Neolithic life, reinforced in Mesopotamia through the growing importance of certain Ubaid households. The next chapter examines the Levantine Neolithic and explores how Neolithic practices – storage and allocation of intra-annual food surpluses – provided clues to the longevity of social constitution.

CHAPTER 6

NEOLITHIC HOUSES AND SOCIAL PRACTICE IN SPACE

There is a small revolution underway in Near Eastern Neolithic archaeology. Not so very long ago, most archaeologists considered the Neolithic an *economic* revolution, following the lead of Gordon Childe. After Childe, virtually everyone defined Neolithic cultures by domestication and food production (cf. Hodder 1990), until French archaeologist Jacques Cauvin (1994, 2000) set the field of Near Eastern pre-history on its ear with the assertion that the Neolithic was extraordinary not for economic transformations but for symbolic and mental constructs that radically changed the social and ideological frameworks of human existence. Domestication and food production – the mere mechanics of getting a living to support newly settled communities – simply followed unremarkably. Following Cauvin, many now argue that Neolithic communities took up new practices generated by and reproducing new habitus, which was the truly revolutionary aspect of the Neolithic (e.g., Hodder 1990, 2006: 240-245, Hodder and Cessford 2004, Kuijt 2000a: 96-97, Watkins 2004, 2006). It seems that Household practice emerged during the Neolithic experience of living in houses, and supra-household communities thereafter adopted Household as a highly effective idiom for the constitution of social life.

This chapter both investigates the historical contingency of the habitus of Household and, at its end, reviews the question of its origins. It addresses neither plant and animal domestication issues more pertinent to the Neolithic economic revolution (e.g., Zeder et al. 2006, Zohary and Hopf 1988) nor economic and environmental processes underway at the end of the Pleistocene period and the beginning of the more stable, warm, and seasonally demarcated climate of the Holocene period. Extensive summaries and expanded scholarship on these issues may be found elsewhere (e.g., Bar-Yosef 1995, Bar-Yosef and Meadow 1995, McCorriston and Hole 1991, Richerson, Boyd and Bettinger 2001, Simmons 2007: 10–43, Lev-Yadun, Gopher and Abbo 2000, Zeder 2009). While these economic and environmental issues are pertinent to the development of populations, adaptations to environmental diversity across the Near East, and the bio-evolutionary successes of food-producing societies, they are not the focus of this book. Nor will this study consider prime movers, external causes, and strictly rational economic decision making favored in evolutionary and functional explanations of Neolithic origins (cf. Asouti 2006, Giddens 1984: 14, Ingold 1996). In conclusions only will I consider just why the revolutionary Neolithic social experiments of household practice were so successful in agricultural communities.

At the outset, I am more concerned with the long, culturally distinct drama of how Household practice persisted. Just as human evolution is ultimately historical narrative within the parameters of evolutionary processes (Gould 1986, Landau 1984), so too the story of long-term habitus of Household begs no cause or explanation beyond historical contingency and the entwined agency and structure of practice theory (Bourdieu [1972] 1977: 78–87, Giddens 1984: 244). What this means is that one need not seek an external mover – climate change or ecological circumstance – to explain how the idiom of Household became and remained a powerful structuring principle for human society. Contingency, actors, and structuring principles (or structuring structures) are the elements of the drama that privileged Household over other socially constituting practices in the northern Near East. It happened, apparently in different regions and different circumstances, that household practice "won out" over other social constructs of the revolutionary Neolithic. This chapter reviews the evidence for how that happened. Household practice is rendered no less interesting for the specific and historic Neolithic circumstances that gave rise to broad and enduring patterns of cultural behavior than is the excitement of human evolution dulled by the historical details of placement of the larynx or the first upright steps on the savanna. But analogy with evolutionary theory ends with the similitude of history within process. In short, this chapter will not explain the origins of Household practice by addressing its Why (indeed the recursive practices arising from habitus contains both its past and its future (Giddens 1984: 14, Hodder and Cessford 2004: 18–19)). But it will review Household practice in Neolithic societies and explore strong tensions between Household and other practices of social constitution (here called Community practices). These tensions were manifested in elaborate and durable Neolithic material culture and so are evident to archaeologists. The goal is to position Household broadly within the Neolithic social institutions and ideological changes evident from the archaeological record in the ancient Near East.

The Neolithic of the Near East: The Nature of the Evidence

Material Manifestations of Neolithic Societies

The Pre-Pottery Neolithic cultures of the Eastern Mediterranean first appeared about 12,500 calendar years ago as hunting and foraging groups who elected to settle year-round in areas of supplemental water or high water tables where they could practice intensive cultivation of cereals and other plants, especially flax. For all the fanfare that archaeologists have made about domestication and food production as prime movers for village life, it is now clear that sedentism preceded domestication in the Near East (Garrard 1999, Simmons 2007: 47, Byrd 2005a) and therefore that plant domestication does not explain the emergence of sedentary societies. Although there are significant regional differences, a pan–Near Eastern Neolithic cultural chronology begins with the Pre-Pottery Neolithic A (PPNA, 12,500–11,200 calendar years ago). During this time people constructed buildings and settlements with manifestly greater material and labor investment and broader variation in architectural form than any encampment that had preceded them, and the elaboration of these differences and investments continued through the Pre-Pottery Neolithic B period (PPNB, 11,200–8,000 calendar years ago). The construction of houses in pisé, stone, and timber, and later (PPNB) mudbrick, involved more labor and generated more archaeological debris than had any earlier shelters of the Epi-Palaeolithic and marks profound changes in peoples' social lives and identities (Wilson 1988). Furthermore, architecture in PPNA communities was newly

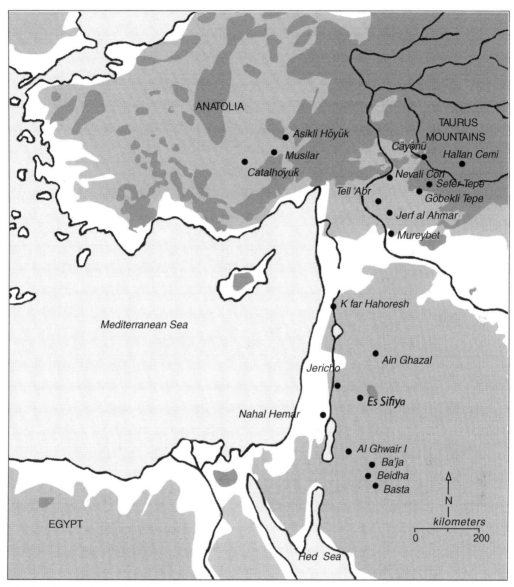

49. Map of Levantine site locations.

differentiated. For example, in addition to houses, at PPNA Jericho, a single tower and settlement boundary wall involved communal labor (Naveh 2003, Bar-Yosef 1986, Kenyon 1981), as did the contemporary construction at Göbekli Tepe of large circular stone buildings with monolithic anthropomorphic stone pillars weighing up to 50 tons each and decorated with wild animals in bas-relief (Schmidt 2001: 46).

A suite of new material culture accompanied the first (at least the unequivocally first) permanent settlements in the Near East. New tool forms and technologies appeared along with the use of plaster, clay, paints, and dyes in noncorporeal decorative and symbolic contexts; an emphasis on human form as a symbolic motif alongside wild animals, especially bulls (Cauvin 1994, 2000); socially strategic and mnemonic burial practices (Kuijt 2001, 2008); and new socially meaningful exchange networks transporting raw obsidian, shells, and salt (Asouti 2006: 90). Ian Hodder (2006: 248–249) has emphasized the "entanglement" of materiality and societies with "social relations necessary to obtain material and goods, and material goods . . . necessary to provide the materials and media for increasingly complex social interactions."

What makes the Levantine and Anatolian Neolithic so startling in current research is the significance of new structural principles for social constitution and the new symbolic frameworks used to communicate meaning and memory. New social arrangements and their maintenance are increasingly recognized as being equal to or surpassing food production in human adaptation and developmental narratives (Asouti 2006: 118, Atalay and Hastorf 2006: 283–285, Byrd 2005a :232, Watkins 2004, Gebel 2004: 31). Buildings played a symbolic and structuring role in these social arrangements, and houses, the dominant feature of almost all settlements, were indisputably central to the process (Watkins 2004).

From the sixth millennium BC, villagers produced ceramics, which have provided archaeologists with one convenient marker to differentiate societies and regional networks of socially charged economic exchange. The pan–Near Eastern Pottery Neolithic (PN) lasted about 1,500 years and was marked at its beginning by substantive changes in settlement sizes (generally smaller) and configurations, mobility, and changes in architectural forms and in architectural differentiation. Ceramics were available for new food preparation techniques and presentation that manifested new household practices and routines (Wright 2000: 117, Hodder 2006: 248–256). Eventually ceramics were decorated as the primary medium for encoding community practices (Verhoeven 2002a: 9–10, Garfinkel 2003a: 63, 2003b: 84), as Household practice (including the production within households of ceramics symbolically conveying community ideals) became and remained the primary socially constituting mechanism for communities.

Cultural Contexts of the Neolithic

It is remarkable how poorly we understand the interactions and intergroup dynamics of the earliest Neolithic communities (Peltenburg 2004, Peltenburg et al. 2001, Schmidt 2005a with comments by Belfer-Cohen and Goring Morris 2005: 23, by Hole 2005: 31, and by Kuijt 2005: 35). The earliest PPN (Pre-Pottery Neolithic) communities sought common ground (literally and socially) but regionally manifested different strategies to mediate emergent tensions between social ties to the larger community and immediate households. Even though the earliest (PPNA) villages chose settings that were environmentally much more similar one to another than were PPNB village settings, there existed strong regional differences in cultural approaches to the same emergent problem of sedentism. From the outset, that problem was the tensions between social identities of belonging in households and belonging in larger communities. Some have commented on the regionally distinctive solutions (e.g., Kafafi 2006: 34, Bar Yosef 2002, Asouti 2006: 118, Kuijt 2008: 180) by arguing that commonly held strategies of mediating these tensions through community practice show regional patterning and therefore can be equated with intersite social identities – what Bar-Yosef and Bar-Yosef Mayer (2002) call "tribes" by the Middle PPNB. The term "tribe" is confusing both because it is difficult to apply either its political or social sense (Tapper 1990: 50–51) to what we can infer about Early Neolithic societies and territories, and because classificatory cross-cultural neo-evolutionary social types have so demonstrably constrained and muddled archaeological analyses of social development and change (e.g., Giddens 1984: 228–243, Yoffee 2005: 15–21). Regional differences (and site by site differences) in the rituals that new PPNA communities employed to emphasize community social identities included the shared labor and shared symbolic meanings invested in erecting Göbekli's massive pillars (Schmidt 2001: 48, 2005) or Jericho's wall and tower (Naveh 2003), belonging to hierarchical regional site clusters (Naveh 2003: 93, Simmons 2007: 106–107, cf. Hole 2000), and the practices of mortuary rituals to reinforce community social ties (Kuijt 1994, 1996, cf. Kuijt 2002, 2008, Testart 2008).

Cauvin (1994, 2000, 2001) has argued that Neolithic cultures expressed new ideological and symbolic conventions that led them to settle and develop agriculture. Why there should be new symbolic behaviors in the Neolithic remains a matter of conjecture: some argue for human biological evolution of new cognitive function (Lewis-Williams and Pearce 2005) followed by new cultural innovation (Watkins 2004, 2006, cf. Donald 1991, 2001). Other adaptationist-evolutionary explanations look to the greater stability afforded by global climate changes (Richerson, Boyd and Bettinger 2001, Byrd 2005a) as a cause for sedentism, and there is still debate about whether the symbolic innovations of the Neolithic can be traced to the latter Paleolithic period (e.g., Nadel 2006, Schmidt 2005a: 18, Belfer-Cohen and Goring-Morris 2005: 22).

The PPNB period lasted longer and marks the appearance of Neolithic life-ways, including new experiences and mixes of sedentism, agriculture, and pastoralism in a wider diversity of environmental and cultural settings. It must no longer be supposed that the history of the PPNB charts a successful demographic and adaptational spread of farmers from a single point of origin (Asouti 2006, cf. Kozlowski and Aurenche 2005: 46, 83). As Asouti (2006: 90) has recently argued, evolutionary and demographic emphasis on diffusion (e.g., Ammerman and Cavalli-Sforza 1984, Cavalli-Sforza and Cavalli-Sforza 1995: 130–136, Bellwood 2005) has tended to overplay the significance of single-point origin, especially in the face of archaeobotanical and archaeozoological evidence of multiple domestications and the merging of regionally distinct domesticates into an agrarian package over time. The great historical phenomenon of the PPNB includes the elaboration and maintenance of social alliances, community identities, and social constitutions through cultural practices and cultural innovations shared and transformed in meaning across ever wider divergences of resource availability, environmental settings, and adaptation strategies across the Mediterranean and arid lands of the Near East (Asouti 2006).

Much of the elaborate symbolism and ritual activities in PPNB villages seems to have engaged the negotiation of social identities and the reflexive structuring of societies. The institutions through which societies were maintained varied not only temporally, but across the vast region of the PPNB "koine" or interaction sphere (Cauvin 1994). Regional differences (discussed later) suggest that PPNB people did not recognize or share a common ideology in the conventional sense – an abstract speculation of ideas – and indeed the cultural-historical evidence for polycentric origins of PPNB cultures leaves little theoretical explanation for a widespread convergence of human perception and dispositions (Asouti 2006: 90, Gebel 2004: 31–32, cf. Boyer 2001: 80–90, 133–135). What Asouti (2006: 90) has called "the operation of exchange as a socially situated process" is the manifestation of contextually situated practices to meet a common set of challenges across PPNB regionalism and cultural diversity. That set of challenges arrived with the expanding of populations and crowding in sedentary conditions where social identities embraced and negotiated with greater frequency a broader spectrum of household, kin-group, community, and alliances to associate communities. This was an utterly new social life in a hundred thousand years of human experience. PPNB villagers needed to negotiate their ties to the productive unit of the household, to the common cause of village life, and to the broader alliances possible with other villages needing to share and allocate regional resources and the networks to secure them. PPNB villagers relied on different practices and rituals to situate themselves in different social contexts and to habituate the tensions of community life. Mortuary rituals were practiced across the PPNB cultural world, but differently so, in different contexts. For example, Ian Kuijt (2004: 191, 2002: 83, 2008) has argued that an ideology of egalitarian ethos was manifested through mortuary practices (skull removal and treatment) in some regions of the Levantine PPNB, even as specialists may have accrued and practiced authority through their special knowledge of skull treatments. In seeming contrast, similar Neolithic mortuary practices (burial of individuals under house floors) in Central Anatolia seem to have strengthened intracommunity social groups otherwise differentiated one from another (lineages, clans) (Düring 2005: 21, Hodder 2006: 147, Pillaud 2009).

By the Pottery Neolithic the tensions between household and community identity became unbearable for many. In the case of the Southern Levantine Middle to Late PPNB "mega-centers," group living itself broke down, and smaller units of one or a few families characterized many sites of the succeeding early Pottery Neolithic period (Banning 1998: 218). There may have been significant climatic and environmental changes, including aridification and anthropogenic degradation of local resources and consequent competition for scarce agricultural lands, grazing, and construction materials, that precipitated shifts in settlement (Simmons 2007: 43–45, 185–188, Rollefson and Rollefson 1992) and in mobility (Akkermans and Schwartz 2003: 124). Whether attributable to changing resource availability or more to social dynamics within large communities (Kuijt 2000a: 96–97, Gebel 2004: 30), many households groups chose to mitigate the tensions of household and community identity through practices and rituals that emphasized household identities. In some cases in the early Pottery Neolithic, this meant moving away, with families or groups of families physically separating themselves but retaining some social ties to groups at nearby sites. Many communities were entirely abandoned by the Pottery Neolithic, even as others showed a continuity of occupation with radical changes in ritual and symbolism (Akkermans and Schwartz 2003: 110–112, Verhoeven 2002).

Where large communities were still inhabited, there were substantial architectural changes that reflected new daily practice in new spatial patterns. House plans changed to better accommodate households of larger, extended families linked by shared activities such as food preparation in courtyards (Garfinkel 2006: 109–110, Wright 2000: 114, Kafafi 2006). In the Pottery Neolithic cultures of Northern Mesopotamia, communities developed elaborate ceramic decoration (with prominent motifs of dancing, a ritual practice that strengthens community identity (Garfinkel 2003a: 77–981, 2003b) to signal community group membership. Significantly, these ceramics were probably produced at the household level (Verhoeven 2002: 9–10) and were used in food presentation and consumption, a daily practice in households that could be adopted as the basis for infrequent rituals of community practice such as feasting and feeding the elders/gods.

Where people invested substantial labor, skill, and symbolic messages in food presentation technology (e.g., ceramics), their investments may indicate that food presentation played an important role in social constitution and social identities (Dietler 1990, Hodder 1982). In addition to decorated ceramics, the Pottery Neolithic period has the first evidence for wine (McGovern et al. 1996), an alcoholic beverage consumed as much for its social significance as for nutritious value (Joffe 1998). Garfinkel (2003a: 82–83) has argued that ceremonial banquets later became the distinguishing practice of elite classes, who appropriated these from feasting practices (that constituted societies or social groups) of the ceramic Neolithic period (cf. Helwing 2003). The process of excluding lower classes from banquets may well have accompanied the already mentioned (Chapter 5) control and manipulation of aesthetic production (e.g., decorated ceramics) by super-households by the later Uruk period (Wengrow 2001b: 183). In the Pottery Neolithic, the development of highly elaborate ceramics and of community-wide storage (Banning 2003: 15, Akkermans and Schwartz 2005: 117) may point to an increasing reliance on the practices of belonging in households as the basis for rituals and activities that bound communities – the beginnings of communities constituted in the idiom of households. The mortuary rituals – practices of life cycle or "life-finality" (Giddens 1984: 35) that had enstructured communities of the PPNB – were generally abandoned across the Levant (Rollefson 1997: 304, Kuijt 2004, Verhoeven 2002). Household practice won out.

Regional Expressions

Throughout the Neolithic period there existed discernable regionalism. A recent cartographic survey of multiple categories of material culture suggests that there are three major divisions – Eastern Wing, Western Wing, and High Valleys – of the Fertile Crescent and that the Neolithic lifestyle emanated out of a "Golden Triangle" that encompassed the intersection of these geographical and ethnic boundaries (Kozlowski and Aurenche 2005: 46, 80, 83). Substantial evidence for a polymorphic origin (see Asouti 2006, Gebel 2004) and the evidence for independent experiences of sedentism in the Northern Levant (Moore, Hillman and Legge 2000), the Taurus region (Rosenberg et al. 1995, 1998), the Southern Levant (Byrd 2005a, Bar-Yosef and Belfer-Cohen 1989, 1992), and Central Anatolia (Düring 2005, Düring and Marciniak 2006) suggest that these regions at least developed Neolithic traditions from disparate existing hunter-forager lifestyles, a point recognized also in the point-of-origin perspective (Kozlowski and Aurenche 2005: 65).

Regionalism was expressed not only in economic activities, material cultures, and ethnicity (Kozlowski and Aurenche 2005) but also in social life, ritual activities, and symbolic references to ideological concepts. In the Early Neolithic, architecture everywhere manifestly encoded ideas about the world and people's places within it (Watkins 2006). In permanent settlements, houses made up most of the architecture – with a few exceptions – and therefore it is likely that living in houses played a highly significant role in structuring the way that people lived in and built societies (Hodder and Cessford 2004, Watkins 2004). But the physical houses differed from region to region, as did other architecture and [the physical remains of] other practices – burials, feasts, sacrifices, communal hunts. Although the prevalence of houses and the limited size of all "public" buildings (Hodder and Cessford 2004, Hermanson 2005) would seem to suggest that most social identities were formed and expressed through practice in small groups, and especially families in households, the specific practices and uses of symbols differed between communities and regions (Hodder 2001). Details have been extensively discussed elsewhere (e.g., Simmons 2007, Özdoğan and Başgelen 1999, Bar-Yosef and Bar-Yosef Mayer 2002, Cauvin 1994, 2000, Kozlowski and Aurenche 2005, Watkins 2006), so this brief review will only introduce and highlight regional expressions of ritual activity as a basis for examining the tensions between Neolithic Community and Household identities.

Northern Levant and the Euphrates

Excavations at Tell Mureybet (Cauvin 1979), Jerf al-Ahmar (Stordeur 2000), and Tell 'Abr (Yartah 2004) along the Middle Euphrates river have revealed large (6–12 meter diameter) circular-eliptical subterranean buildings among the familiar rectilinear houses of the early settlements. These round buildings have interesting "biographies" (Düring 2005: 10, Waterson 2000: 187) with a foundation deposit of human skulls in one, a use-cycle that emphasized storage and meetings (bins and benches), elaborate symbolism in limestone slabs with relief carvings of pendant triangles, vulture-like birds, headless bodies, limestone stelae that may represent combined anthropomorphic and animistic concepts, and, at Tell 'Abr, animal designs and clay-"plastered" cattle bucrania (Yartah 2005: 5). The final and deliberate closing of structure EA 30 at Jerf al-Ahmar entailed placing a spread-eagled human corpse in the central area with a human head, intentional burning and refilling (Stordeur 2000, Watkins 2006: 17, Testart 2008).

Perhaps as interesting are the contemporary houses of the Middle Euphrates communities with oval and rectangular houses often deliberately fired and in-filled and containing the domestic equipment of daily living (Stordeur 2000: 1–2). Such houses also contained caches including knapped blades (Astruc et al. 2003), plaques, and aurochs skulls that hung on the walls. Symbolism and labor investment in houses and their demise signal importance of the house as a place where social relationships were formed, enacted, and perpetuated through daily practice and long-term memory (Joyce 2000).

The Urfa/Taurus Sites

To the north, the earliest settlement known in Eastern Anatolia at (PPNA) Hallan Çemi had structures built in stone and timber, with less substantial wattle-and-daub buildings over plaster floors (for storage). Size alone (5–6 meter diameter) led the excavators to question whether circular semi-subterranean buildings were houses sheltering nuclear families or served some larger group purpose (Rosenberg 1999: 27). Houses appear to have been arranged around a central activity area littered with the remains of animal carcasses one typically finds associated with feasting (Rosenberg 1999: 26), suggesting perhaps that intermittent community-wide rituals played a role in the social constitution of sedentary communities from their earliest inception (Rosenberg and Redding 2000: 57–58).

The apparent symbolic and cultural links with Middle Euphrates sites are more pronounced with the appearance of later sites (end of PPNA, Early PPNB) at Nevalı Çori, Çäyönü Tepesı, Göbekli Tepe, and Sefer Tepe (Watkins 2006: 16, Kozlowski and Aurenche 2005: 262–263, maps 12.3 and 12.4). New ideas about community identity were literally built into – or "incorporated" by (see Rowlands 1993: 142 after Connerton 1989, Carsten and Hugh-Jones 1995: 40–46) – group building projects. Archaeologists have labeled these projects "cult buildings" (Hauptman 1999), "ritual architecture" (Rollefson 2005), or "community buildings" (Kozlowski and Aurenche 2005: 263). While not all of these would necessarily require the combined labor of entire communities, the most spectacular (Göbekli Tepe) clearly was a large-group project. Besides the similar construction style and details of community buildings, there clearly existed a similar repertoire of symbols, perhaps with some similar meanings across sites (Stordeur 2004: 49).

Mortuary rituals associated with some community buildings (e.g., the Skull Building with several hundred cached skulls at Çäyönü (Özdoğan 1999)) were perhaps practices that reinforced the social identities of communities or supra-household groups (cf. Bradley 1985, Bloch 1971,

Cherry 1978, Méry et al. 2001, 2004, Renfrew 1973, 1976, Parker-Pearson and Ramilisonina 1998, Testart 2008).

The highly prominent mound of Göbekli Tepe deserves special description, as perhaps the epicenter of regional participation in ritual practices that linked multiple communities and was spectacularly constructed (Schmidt 2005a, 2005b). Göbekli Tepe was constructed through the deliberate in-filling of about twenty very large subterranean stone structures containing sometimes huge (up to 5 m tall) monolithic stelae. The stone circles (9 meter across) are dominated by an opposing central pair of T-shaped (anthropomorphic) stelae: other stelae are set within the perimeter walls, and most are decorated with bas-relief sculpting of wild animals. Some of the relief was hidden when the stelae were set in the walls, suggesting that they have been discovered in a context of re-use (Schmidt 2001, 2005a). The extraordinary structures and lack of domestic features suggest to the excavator that the site was unoccupied except by periodic visits of labor parties from settlements in a 200-kilometer radius and that the site served as a cult center that united a very dispersed set of communities into a common political and social framework prior to the establishment of sedentary life (Schmidt 2005a, 2005b); in short, a pilgrimage center. Others are less convinced that no one lived at Göbekli Tepe (Banning in press, Bar-Yosef and Bar-Yosef Mayer 2002: 351, Kuijt 2005: 35), or that Göbekli Tepe could be the only such center in such a large region (Hole 2005: 31, Belfer-Cohen and Goring-Morris 2005: 23, Çelik 2006).

Other settlements with houses had some but not all of the features of Göbekli (Schmidt 2005a: 15, Çelik 2006). At settlements such as Nevalı Çori and Çäyönü, houses also were invested with significant labor and symbolism, notably built of stone, through the careful treatment of floors and burial of individuals and "gifts" under the floors (Özdoğan 1999, Hauptmann 1999). Houses were carefully rebuilt on existing foundations and axes. At abandonment, they were deliberately buried with distinctive layers of pebbles (Özdoğan 1999: 46). It is important to recognize that alongside the visually imposing symbolism and cult in community buildings, Neolithic settlers performed burial rites within the physical context of houses, placing their dead under floors and in walls. Household and other community practices side by side are evident in the earliest settlements of the Taurus.

Southern Levant

The extent of research and availability of data from the Southern Levant surpasses other regions, allowing a detailed regional view of the early transition to village life and its attendant challenges in a regionally distinct cultural setting. It is from a sequence at Jericho that the terms PPNA and PPNB were first coined, and their use beyond the Levantine region can feel clumsy and misleading, implicating ethnic and social groups who actually shared few or no beliefs or common identity with the villagers of the Southern Levant. In villages, and especially by the Middle PPNB, houses were built as constituent parts to build communities in which people apparently used mortuary rituals to maintain supra-household communities (Kuijt 2000b, Goring-Morris 2000). In striking contrast to the spectacular community buildings of the Middle Euphrates and Urfa/Taurus regions, settlements of the Southern Levant had few and isolated examples of community buildings, the most impressive of which is the Jericho wall and tower of the PPNA (Kenyon 1981).

Jericho's unique stone wall, tower, and hand-dug ditch involved an impressive input of communal labor and set a striking contrast with the modest pisé houses of the settlement. Recent interpretations of the Jericho wall and tower reflect a growing emphasis on social and ideological explanations of Neolithic material culture. Ronen and Adler (2001) argue that the walls were magical since their physical efficacy in defense (Kenyon 1957: 75) and as flood barrier (Bar-Yosef 1986) can be called into question. Naveh (2003) links the permanency of wall and tower built (unlike other settlement architecture) in stone to a symbolic realm in which a message of staying put and stability was intended. The construction contributed both to intragroup social differences (those who had built and those who had not) and intergroup social differences (Jericho territorial claimants and others). As a visible claim on the spring (which the wall may have enclosed) and adjacent spring-and-flood-watered lands, the stone community buildings may have functioned to unify the Jericho community at a supra-household level. If storage was indeed communal or organized above the household level, the permanency and solidity of the tower and wall may have "functioned as a metaphor for that stability" that reassured depositor of a delayed return (Naveh 2003: 91).

Other examples of community buildings in the Southern Levantine PPN are less easy to identify. The largest buildings at Beidha (Byrd 2005b: 118) have been cited and disputed (Kozlowski and Aurenche 2005: 263 map 12.4, Coupland and Banning 1996) as candidates for community buildings. Other sites are even less clear. Rollefson's (2000) suggestion that community buildings existed at Ain Ghazal points to architecture that lacks the scale, degree of distinctive decoration, and differentiation from houses that characterize community buildings elsewhere and appeared only in the Late PPNB period. Special buildings have also been noted at other PPNB sites – Jericho, al-Ghwair I, and es-Sifiya (Bienert et al. 2004: 157).

In the Southern Levant, the architectural evidence strongly suggests that houses played a major role in structuring social life. Each house – and by the Middle PPNB they were very tightly packed in dense settlements (e.g., Kafafi 2006: 87, Byrd 2005b, Gebel 2006) – was its own productive and reproductive unit with internal storage and food consumption. Over time changes in the placement of equipment, hearths, pits, bins, benches, platforms, activity areas, and caches suggest that PPNA villagers had little interest in preparing and sharing food in visible areas, but in the PPNB, "food preparation was an arena for social interaction between households whilst meal consumption [was] about privacy, the residential group, and enculturation within the household" (Wright 2000: 101, 110–111). The care and labor in building and renewing PPNB houses reflects significant investment. New and costlier materials were used – mudbrick with straw additives, stone walls of greater scale than any precedent, and lime plaster. Lime plaster was important for interiors, especially floors, symbolically separating "the quick and the dead" (Goring-Morris 2000) while linking them. Lime plaster links the living and the dead by allowing subfloor burial of rotting corpses in lived-in houses and by its use in modeling on skulls and statues that keep representations of the dead in living memory (Goring-Morris 2000: 126, Rollefson 1990, 2000: 170).

Subfloor burial of a limited number of the dead and skull retrieval linked (presumed) ancestors to households. The physical presence of dead links living householders' social identities as members of a corporate body that, in the terms of Lévi-Strauss ([1979] 1982: 174), "perpetuates itself … down a real or imaginary line considered legitimate as long as this continuity can express itself in the language of kinship or affinity." House as shelter for dead and living blurs the distinction between houses and people (Carsten and Hugh Jones 1995: 41) so that the house both stands for society and at the same times enstructures the actions of its occupants. Mortuary practices asserted and affirmed the long-term continuity of Houses (in the sense of Lévi-Strauss), a continuity that could be and was expressed through multiple renewals of interiors and rebuildings along the same plan and same locations. At Ba'ja, ground plans were raised by multiple rebuildings and deliberate in-filling of earlier rooms and stone-built houses were so tightly packed that the community could only grow upward (Bienert and Gebel 2004: 123, Gebel 2006, Gebel et al. 2006: 14–15).

In such tightly packed communities, the occupants developed mechanisms other than ritual activities in community structures for moderating the tensions between household and community. Kuijt (2002: 83, 2004: 191) has argued that in the Southern Levant region, an "egalitarian ethos" was maintained through mortuary rituals, most especially the practices of skull removal, caching, and decoration. Skull plastering developed into elaborate rites that may have required specialists (Kuijt 2002: 85, Goring-Morris 2000: 128). There thus potentially existed a nascent tension between the practice of mortuary rituals used "to maintain or increase solidarity between individuals and households by stressing shared egalitarian themes" (Kuijt 2000b: 137–138) and the emergence of specialists (Kuijt 2002: 83). If one accepts that mortuary rituals in the PPNB played a significant role in moderating the competition that arose among different households and indeed Houses (perhaps multiple households) (Kuijt 2000b: 141), then the selection of few ancestors for special treatment and perhaps communal burial of skulls at an annual ceremony (Kuijt 2000a: 95, 2000b: 155–156, 2008) represented community practice based on life-cycle time (Giddens 1984: 35) in a punctuated practice. Dead ancestors (buried under the floors of houses) strengthened the lineage claims of Houses while their skull treatments integrated the wider community.

Some PPNB cult centers were situated off-site. Kfar HaHoresh – thus far unique in the Southern Levant – was a place of select human interment with wild animals, under plastered surfaces and containing animal symbolism but no domestic architecture (Goring-Morris 2000,

Goring-Morris and Horwitz 2007). A cave at Nahal Hemar was used to stash objects used in rituals, presumably performed nearby but far from any known PPNB settlement (Bar Yosef and Alon 1988, Bar-Yosef and Bar-Yosef Mayer 2002: 353). The excavators at Ba'ja suggest that the village itself (containing only domestic architecture) was in its entirety a site with ritual significance (Gebel 2002: 126, Bienert and Gebel 2004: 119), but it is also clear that people living at Ba'ja developed social interactions and identities based on the encounter patterns of living in houses.

But the suggestion that entire sites may have held ideological significance and that they manifested a supra-household social identity is entirely my point. In the Southern Levant community buildings were generally not evident in the PPNA and were relatively small, undistinguished, and few in the PPNB. They could hold few people (Hermanson 2005: 29); therefore, putative rituals performed in them to develop community identities did so with limited or differential participation by community members, limiting the enactment of community practice and its routinization for community constitution. By the Late PPNB, there existed "megasites" of sudden large size with dense settlement, elements of settlement planning, and indications of diversification of labor roles. It is still a challenge to understand or explain in purely economic-demographic terms the crowding of people into these large sites, especially since they are not central to or supplanting smaller ones – what was the attraction? (Hole 2000, Gebel 2004, Kuijt 2000a). Archaeologists still have very limited knowledge of the biggest PPN sites where impressive community buildings might yet be found. But it seems that instead of community buildings, PPNB people built entire settlements as a community-building corporate of houses, communities in which people incorporated themselves, family and all, in an impressive symbolic display of social identity as belonging in community.

Central Anatolia

The corporate collectivity of entire villages (or at least neighborhoods) as community structures finds its apogee in Central Anatolia. What the Middle PPNB and Late PPNB mega-centers of the Southern Levant do seem to share with other Neolithic regions is that the settlement itself was the community building, manifesting a supra-household commitment to living in relatively large social groups, with all the attendant tensions of household and community social identities that followed. Yet even as the architects of this collective status, over several thousand years people in Central Anatolia came to identify themselves most strongly as groups belonging in households.

The crown jewel of the Central Anatolian Neolithic is Çatalhöyük (7400–6000 BC), an extraordinary site for its elaborately decorated house interiors and densely packed settlement without streets or doors over a 13-hectare mound in the middle of a marsh. When one shifts focus from the site of Çatalhöyük to a broader region, the evidence plausibly suggests that important in-situ Neolithicization occurred in Central Anatolia in a distinct pattern affected by socially situated exchanges (especially obsidian and food) with a broader Near Eastern set of Neolithic settlements. The symbolism evident at Çatalhöyük finds parallels in the Urfa/Taurus region and the Middle Euphrates, possibly through common mythology (Cauvin 1994, Hodder 2006: 163, Belfer-Cohen and Goring Morris 2005: 22). Nevertheless, the experience of living in settlements over 2,500 years in Central Anatolia took its own distinct regional course.

Çatalhöyük was the only settlement in the Konya Basin throughout its occupation, during which up to 8,000 people at a time were deeply committed to the community life that living in Çatalhöyük represented (Hodder 2006: 73–90). The houses were so tightly packed that people stepped over each other's roofs to reach their own roof entryways. For antecedents to Çatalhöyük's unprecedented growth and scale, archaeologists have looked to the earlier settlements of Asıklı Höyük (8500 BC) and Musilar about 100 kilometers away. Living in communities larger than a few households was clearly important from the very founding of Asıklı Höyük (Düring and Marciniak 2006).

Asıklı Höyük had a "large monumental complex around a large courtyard" where a significant portion of the community could gather for ritual practices, including feasting. By contrast, the houses at Asıklı were small, one-story buildings built independent one from another and from their predecessors, entered by the roof, and arranged in neighborhoods of about sixty houses (Düring and Marciniak 2006: 174, Düring 2005: 18, Esin and Harmankaya 1999). Neighborhoods of repetitive houses were the defining intrasettlement architecture and persisted through the settlement's life; households were not the initial building blocks of Neolithic society. Düring and Marciniak (2006: 167) argue that households were "embedded in larger social institutions" manifested as neighborhoods and the collectivity of the site itself. Frequent encounters of many people made possible, facilitated even, by physical crowding would strengthen such larger institutions as the primary institutions of social life.

Later Çatalhöyük lacks any special community buildings like those at Asıklı, PPNA sites, and the more modest PPNB examples in the Southern Levant. Despite original excavator James Mellaart's (1967) famous identification of elaborately decorated rooms as "shrines," recent excavations have shown that all the buildings on the mound were used for domestic activities like food preparation, sleeping, and food storage; at the same time, houses manifested an elaborate, mythologically grounded set of beliefs about society and social rules (Hodder 2006). In an eloquent and fascinating argument, Hodder reconstructs the emergence of real history – remembered ancestors, (commemorative?) feasts, and other events – that is symbolically hidden and periodically revealed in the walls and floors of houses, appropriating the symbolism of collective mythology for the strategic positioning of individuals in social groups in houses. House structures played an essential role. Over the life of the settlement "building biographies" accrued and served as an increasingly important context for people to acquire a sense of what was done, not done, and had been done in social life while participating in socially and architecturally constituting practices (Düring 2005, Hodder 2006). It seems that individuals were buried beneath house floors, but some houses over time accumulated a greater number of dead than can be supposed actually lived in that house (Düring 2005: 18), suggesting that such houses were preferred because they provided access to previous lineage members (Hodder and Cessford 2004: 30–31). These "dominant" houses may have been the focus of social identity (as in House Societies) or at least played a significant and competing role with larger community ethos and smaller households in individual houses. Groups of houses clustered around these high-status buildings formed neighborhoods, which eventually broke down (Levels V–I) to be replaced by autonomous and individuated households practicing craft specialization and independent production (Hodder 2006:

254–256, Düring and Marciniak 2006: 181). At Çatalhöyük, house-holds emerged as the "primary component of society" after 2,000 years of embedding in larger community institutions like neighbor-hoods and Houses (Düring and Marciniak 2006: 180–181).

Underpinning all of the reconstruction of building biographies, the bodily identification with houses, and the role of the physical house in socialization at Çatalhöyük are theoretical assumptions of practice theory. Like Bourdieu, Hodder has particularly emphasized the signi-ficance of daily practice for socialization, but it is clear that other tempos of practice (Giddens 1984: xxiv–xxv, 35, Connerton 1989: 65–66, 100–104, Kertzer 1988, Adams 2005) play an important role in habituat-ing social rules and codes. With the extraordinary archaeological record and cooperative research at Çatalhöyük, we are afforded rather detailed access to the daily and life-cycle practices that enstructured social life and even to some of the actors and strategies (Twiss et al. 2008) that trans-formed its social institutions in the Central Anatolian Neolithic.

Ritual Behaviors

Another way of looking at scale and tempo of habituation in social constitution is through ritual behavior. Ritual – "symbolic behavior that is socially standardized and repetitive" (Kertzer 1988: 8–9) – is performed: there is no such thing as a ritual house or ritual landscape (Boyd 2005, Bell 1993). Ritual connects past, present, and future: it has a temporal as well as a social dimension (Kertzer 1988: 10, Connerton 1989). The social dimension of ritual behavior, that is, its recognized effect in constituting society (see Chapter 4 on "sacrifice," Chapter 2 on "pilgrimage") does not provide in itself sufficient explanation for why humans engage in ritual behavior (Boyer 2001: 26–27, Connerton 1989: 49–51, Verhoeven 2002b). Humans share beliefs that stem from basic human cognition (inference systems, schemas) activated by a stimulating combination of violated and preserved expectations (Boyer 2001, Fiske and Kinder 1981). What that combination of expectations actually is (for example, dead who talk, animals who turn into humans) varies culturally, which is to say, such beliefs are among the durable, trans-posable dispositions predisposed to function as principles that generate and organize practices and representations that appear to conform to rules (because of their collectivity) but are not organized by rules (Bourdieu [1980] 1990: 53, Kertzer 1988: 79–80). So beliefs are shared and passed along as part of habitus, bringing us to ritual, or the practices of belief. If "solidarity is produced by people acting together not by people thinking together" (Kertzer 1988: 76), then repetition and inclusiveness of ritual will affect the solidarity of people.

This is where scale as number of performers and tempo of recurrence becomes significant, and it is spatial scale of practice rather than tempo that will concern the rest of this chapter. (We will consider the tempo of habituation in Chapter 7.) Neolithic rituals may be heuristically considered in categories – individual, household, and public (Verhoeven 2002c: 252), and the performance of such rituals in an expanding circle of social alliances would constitute ever-widening social groups around each participant (cf. Giddens 1984: 79–143). To individual rituals can be attributed figurines, and the contexts of their deposition suggests that in the Neolithic period, individual rituals were performed within houses and households (Voigt 2000, Banning 2003: 19). Household rituals engaged multiple members of households who by their participation associated themselves more clearly with the household social group. In the Early Neolithic, such rituals included burial of household members including infants under house floors, the renewal and elaboration of interior spaces using different materials, caching and retrieving objects in walls and under floors, and food consumption and sharing among household members on a daily basis. Public rituals, such as large animal sacrifice and feasting, were enacted in open spaces or large communal structures and probably used masks, horns, plastered skulls, and large stelae. According to Marc Verhoeven (2002a: 8), public rituals in the Pre-Pottery Neolithic exhibited the principles of communality (suprahousehold social identity), dominant symbolism (derived from common mythical roots), people-animal linkage, and vitality. Public rituals constituted societies in what I have termed community practice.

Tension between Household and Community

There was tension inherent between belonging in households and belonging in communities. Although it is important to recognize variability and integration among the three classes of ritual discussed earlier, they heuristically separate multiple and contemporaneous arenas of social identity and social practice. Our interest lies in documenting how the social identity of the household and its symbolic referent, the house, emerged as a powerful theme in social life, for it continued to be so for thousands of years thereafter. As we have seen in Mesopotamian states, ritual enactment of household practices – such as feeding the gods, clothing them, enacting sacred unions, registering obligations of house-holders and households, and distributing food and access to the land to produce it – became the constituting dramas of supra-household societies. In Central Anatolia and arguably in other regions, household social identities as a dominant theme in social life emerged during the Neolithic as the outcome of 2,000 years of sedentism but apparently not as its cause. The growing importance of a strong social identity of belong-ing in households introduced conflicting allegiances for individual mem-bers of communities (Kuijt 2002, Düring 2005, Düring and Marciniak 2006), even as people's senses of selfhood and individuality may also have been increasing (Hodder 2006: 219–232). Some of the same PPNB rituals performed to reinforce egalitarian ethos and supra-household identity with community were perhaps performed by and with a select few. Under such circumstances, these rituals were ironically effective in the differentiation of select groups such as ritual practitioners and the house-hold/lineage members privileged (through skull deformation) for special treatment (Kuijt 2002, 2004). In House Societies (if these truly emerged in the Neolithic), lineage groups adopt houses as symbols to knit multi-generational, intracommunity social groups invested in heritable wealth of material and immaterial (e.g., title, status, totem) kind. By the Late Neolithic, after 2,000 years of gradual change, households and commu-nities were experiencing social tension. The locus of conflict in social identities and the medium for its negotiation proved to be the house.

The House: Spatial Manifestation of Habitus

If people build houses, houses also build people. Houses are artifacts "encoded with generative meaning" (Johnston and Gonlin 1998: 143). Houses may be consciously constructed to convey symbolic messages about the occupants' social status with displays of wealth and labor invested in construction and furnishings (e.g., Smith 1987, Earle 1997, Moore 1986, Lyons 1996), or to display a commonly held social ideal (Rapoport 1969: 46–47, Wilk 1983). Wilson (1988) argued that domestication of people is tied to houses: permanent architecture organized space with confines that visually and physically reproduced new social boundaries in sedentary communities.

Building houses is recursive (e.g., Heidegger 1971: 147–148, Rapoport 1982: 80–86 Figure 11). Bourdieu ([1972] 1977: 89–91) argued that in nonliterate societies, "inhabited space – and above all the house – is the principal locus for the objectification of the generative schemes," meaning that through the physical medium of constructed house space, underlying cultural codes are unconsciously patterned so that a person bodily enacts and habituates him/herself to his or her perception of cultural norms through "the earliest learning processes." Giddens (1984: 68–145) also emphasizes houses as important "locales" for enstructuration. Inside houses as places that shelter and include the same small groups of householders, small gatherings recur frequently (daily) that routinize the mutual monitoring and positioning that persons engage in at every social gathering. By virtue of the frequency and restricted range of persons, these gatherings "constrain" bodily engagements to promote repeated contextualized enactment of social rules (as individuals perceive them) that make such rules second nature. The small group size of households and repetitive time-space framework of daily practice underscores Hodder's insistence on living in houses as an explanation for social formation and the creation of social memories in the Neolithic (at Çatalhöyük) (e.g., Hodder and Cessford 2004: 22). Practice makes perfect, or if not perfect, at least perfects bodily automatism as learned social behavior (Connerton 1989: 95). Therefore daily activities and daily social gatherings play the greatest role in shaping and perpetuating social systems. In sedentary societies, the majority of these activities and gatherings take place in houses, so houses were and are hugely important.

Transformations of Society between PPN and PN: Household Practice Wins Out

Daily practice proved to be a powerful socializing mechanism, more compelling for house dwellers than intermittent rites that had initially enacted community practice. Gatherings and rites in community buildings, occasional feasts, and the ritual practices surrounding death, burial, and ancestors simply disappeared as belonging in households became a more important practice of community membership. It was not that belonging in communities ceased to be important. It remained so, and people continued to live in supra-household-sized communities. Once the practices of belonging in households had emerged as a strong socially constituting force, then the rites of belonging in households proved a most effective idiom for binding communities of households. These rites included frequent preparation and sharing of food and the use of common storage and distribution. Rituals were adopted and syncretized from the daily practices of belonging in households to commemorate and practice the identity of entire (multiple household) communities. Over the Late Neolithic and into the Ubaid period, such rituals included food presentation and sharing in ceramic vessels that embodied through painted symbolism community ritual (dance), community storage of agricultural produce, and, ultimately, community identity in the metaphor of household.

We can explore how this happened in both a theoretical sense and through the archaeological data set. In theoretical terms, household practice was adapted to commemorative ceremony (ritual behavior) in which Household came to substitute the master narrative of collective identity (Connerton 1989: 70). If we accept that community practices in community buildings and open spaces involved many people and were intermittent (as surely were the feasts of large, fierce wild animals at Hallan Çemi, Göbekli Tepe, Çatalhöyük, and Kfar HaHoresh (Goring-Morris and Kolska Horwitz 2007), the burial of structures with sterile fill, or the erection of stone pillars), then there existed a social memory that links the many participants across the time between performances. Connerton (1989: 22) described the components of social memory as including personal memory (history of self), cognitive memory (recognition of the object of memory, even if not from personal encounter or history), and habitual memory (which must develop from bodily practices). Commemoration and commemorative ceremonies depend upon personal and cognitive memory for a master narrative of community identity, but this narrative is "more than a story told and reflected on; it is a cult enacted." Cult is persuasive because it is habitually practiced

NORTHERN LEVANT and EUPHRATES

COMMUNITY STRUCTURES

HOUSES

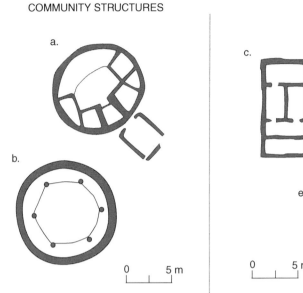

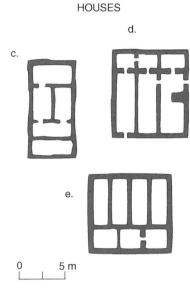

TAURUS REGION

COMMUNITY STRUCTURES HOUSES

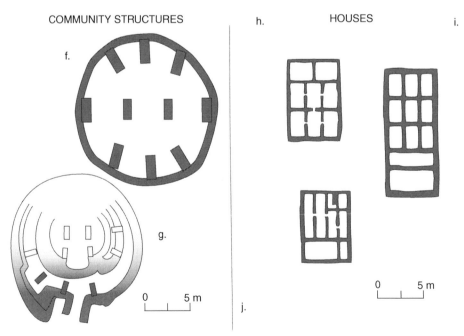

50. Community structures and houses compared: (a, b) Jerf al-Ahmar, (c) Abu Hureyra, (d, e) Bouqras, (f, g) Göbekli Tepe, (h, i) Çäyönü, (j) Nevalı Çori.

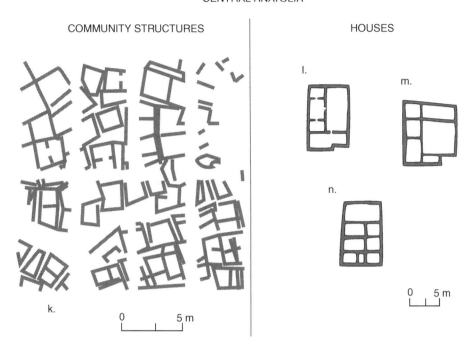

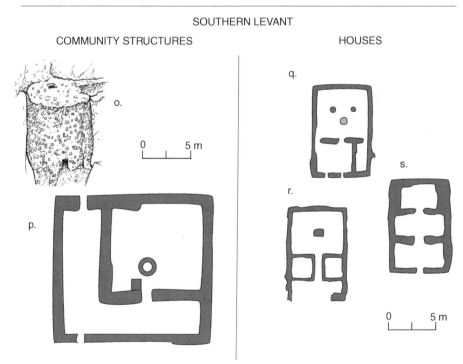

51. Community structures and houses compared: (k) Asiklı Höyük, (l–n) Çätalhöyük, (o, q, s) Jericho, (p, r) Beidha.

(Bell 1993: 197–204), and habitus is critical to cult enactment. Community buildings built to symbolically represent and constrain performed narrative gave to commemoration ceremonies the same syntax-like framework that houses gave to bodily behavioral learning, with significant differences – exclusion of community members and tempo of repetition.

Houses (we may presume) were open to all household members, although there may have existed intrahousehold differentiation of knowledge and tasks that were enacted through differential access and bodily practices (e.g., Hodder 2006: 207–218). Houses were (we presume) shut, or at least less accessible to nonmembers. Likewise, community buildings were often too small, particularly at the end of the Early Neolithic period, to provide access to all community members. Even though Jericho's wall and tower could be seen by all, access to the structure on top was a narrow stair, eventually deliberately blocked by burials of a select few. Few could crowd into the community buildings at Beidha, and the large structures at Göbekli were numerous, suggesting that with inclusivity came separation from other groups in other similar buildings. Community buildings included and excluded as houses do, so the inclusive practices of both became a powerful way of practicing community life. But not everyone could fit into community buildings (at the same time), yet all fit into houses. The tempo of household practice is more routinizing than the wider encounters with larger groups of people visually encountering community buildings even on a daily basis (surely the more common experience of most members of a community than commemorative ceremonies within community buildings). Even living in megasites could not provide the routinization that living in houses within those megasites provided. The spatial experience of household practice simply swamped other ritual enactments as a powerful symbolic framework and habituation of belonging in social groups.

The demise of non-Household community practices can be seen in the abandonment of community buildings at the end of the PPNB along with the cessation of Early Neolithic mortuary rituals like skull removal, skull plastering, and skull caching (Kuijt 2004, 2008, Rollefson 1997: 304, Verhoeven 2002a: 8). There were significant changes in house architecture that reflected changes in household form, access, and tasks. During the LPPNB/PPNC (Late PPNB to Pre-Pottery Neolithic C) period there were increases in spatial differentiation and internal storage capacity, and a decrease in asymmetry in house form of the Southern Levant, from which one may infer that household size and labor pool and internal storage grew as a function of growing social and economic autonomy of households (Banning 2003: 18, 2004, Banning and Byrd 1987). Karen Wright's (2000) spatial analysis of cooking and dining suggests that in the LPPNB there occurred important shifts with task separation and internal storage to intensify food production for larger groups of people. This may have accompanied household tenure of parcels of agricultural land and expanding family size to ensure an adequate household labor pool for harvest and processing. At the same time, spatial arrangements of artifacts and installations indicate greater emphasis on privacy and property in households (Wright 2000: 114). By the PN in the Southern Levant, megasites had ceased altogether and new, small settlements consisted often of only a few households. Something of an exception is the PN site of Sha'ar Hagolan, which contained relatively large houses, built around courtyards. Access patterns and ethnographic parallels suggest that such use of common space (courtyard) would suit extended families composed of multiple nuclear families cooperating in a relatively autonomous socioeconomic unit. Houses were separated by planned streets and alleys, further emphasizing their autonomy through spatial separation (Garfinkel 2006, Rollefson 1997). In the upper levels of Çatalhöyük, clustered neighborhoods around high-status buildings were abandoned with increasingly self-sufficient households making their own ceramics, other special crafts, and expressing new household form and householder roles through bigger and more widely spaced houses with new internal arrangements of cooking and other facilities (Hodder 2006: 249–256, Düring and Marciniak 2006: 181). Households, both physically and metaphorically, emerged as the basic building blocks of society.

What Are the Origins of Household Practice?

Not the Right Question to Ask about Time!

The term "Neolithic" has always tagged something temporally new in human development, whether stone tools and technologies, economic reliance on domesticates, or sociobehavioral evolution in the ways that humans transmit culture (Watkins 2004, Donald 1991, 2001, Renfrew 1998). In the latter case, few are prepared to address why this occurred when it did (Cauvin 1994, 2000, Hodder and Cessford 2004: 19), but the evidence is fairly clear that in the Near East, dramatic cultural evolution occurred about 12,500 years ago (cf. Nadel 2006, Belfer-Cohen and Goring-Morris 2005, Byrd 2005a). So it is tempting to ask why people began building houses.

Origins are tempting, if ever elusive. The answer to why people began building houses lies in the recursive interplay of agency and structure. To pinpoint a historical event in the space-time modes of practice forces genesis on the ontogeny of social constitution (Giddens 1984: 3, 244–246) by stripping the routinization of gatherings and repetition from social life. Social life without temporality and position-ing leaves only the objectified class of social form (or call it social type, a bounded society) that requires outside mechanisms or intervention (climate change, technological shift, resource availability) for change (the "Why?" question). Social constitution carries within it the expla-nation of social change ("How?") through practice and the positioned agency of social actors, and the interesting loci of change are at the intersections, boundaries, or overlap of social types (Giddens 1984: 244). One needs no *deus ex machina* in the performance of social life. So the answer to why people began building houses lies in habitus as process – due to historical contingency, people were culturally disposed to build houses.

Dispositions in Biological and Cultural Historical Context

But people were not *always* culturally disposed to build houses. Although this book is about continuities in the face of change – the persistence of Household and Pilgrimage – and not about change itself, or origins, the question lingers. Why did the habitus of household practice emerge?

Perhaps one may link the seeds of household social identity to the economic strategies of household division of labor, an approach with a long history in anthropological theory (Engels 1978, Marx [1964] 1989, Sahlins 1972, Terray 1972, Godelier [1975] 1984). It is certainly demon-strable that as household labor tasks and scheduling needs change, household form (family form) also changes (Rudolph 1992, Mitterauer 1992). Biological study of human ancestors and other primate groups shows that humans did not always divide labor tasks within a corporate group that worked cooperatively as a productive and reproductive unit. The first modern humans differed greatly from Neanderthals in musculature and hunting-foraging strategies and, unlike Neanderthals, divided labor across sex and age so that biological family members practiced different strategies (Kuhn and Stiner 2006). In the first sedentary societies of the Natufian, sexual division of labor is very pronounced, suggesting that families may have operated as households, producing and sharing food cooperatively (Peterson 2002: 112, 128). There has long been an idea that nuclear families (Byrd 1994: 642–643) or extended families (Flannery 1972) living in households appeared with sedentism. On a temporal scale, the sexual division of labor (which may have narrowed considerably in the Early Neolithic (Peterson 2002: 112, 128, cf. Eshed et al. 2004)), construction of permanent dwellings, and the emergence of Household habitus spread across more than 50,000 years. This surely does not constitute quick change and begs an analytical attention to conservative cultural dispositions equally comparable to the attentive efforts by archaeologists to document and explain origins and change.

Other biological and cultural shifts, especially those in human cognitive function, probably also played a role in the emergence of architecture. One of the salient points of evolutionary psychology is the understanding that human inference systems have been shaped as evolved responses to recurrent problems in ancestral conditions, problems such as overcoming lack of bodily hunting equipment with cunning, information, and information transmission across generations and groups, and cooperating in groups through developing information about others' mental states (Boyer 2001: 118–128). Citing Merlin Donald (1991, 2001), Watkins (2004: 13–15) argues that three major adaptations characterize the evolution of the human mind from the primate mind, and in each of these, the capacity for storage and transmission of information has been enhanced. Two are biological capacities – mimetic culture and language. The third adaptation or transition is theoretic culture supported by "external symbolic storage," which archaeologists have argued links language and visuo-symbolic imagery so that information can be stored and accessed outside the mind of one indi-vidual (Watkins 2004: 15). The use of visuo-symbolic imagery exploded during the Early Neolithic, suggesting that Neolithic people were the first to be truly like ourselves (Watkins 2004: 20, 2006: 16, Lewis-Williams and Pearce 2005: 59). If architecture stores information by encoding social practice, then its appearance in the Neolithic archaeo-logical record, along with a rich panoply of symbolic images, tracks a major cultural shift in human cognition.

Storage and Agriculture

If one steps away from evolutionary psychology to look at the archaeo-logical data, the chronological and regional patterns suggest that com-munities symbolically referenced social memory through regionally distinct community practices in and around architectural community buildings. As buildings differed at Göbekli, Jerf al-Ahmar, Jericho, Asikli, Beidha, and Ain Ghazal, so did each community practice – one could not perform precisely the same bodily actions in differently shaped and configured spaces. Yet all these buildings stored knowledge that could be accessed through social memory, which relies upon perfor-mance and ritual practice to link oral tradition (language) to visuo-symbolic imagery.

Stored knowledge in buildings was a new thing in the Neolithic and everywhere a little different. From the storage of knowledge came the "binding of time and space to make history" (Giddens 1984: 258–262, Hodder 2006: 141–168) and the containment of authoritative resources that predicate power. Giddens usefully distinguishes between author-itative resources (e.g., knowledge) and allocative resources (e.g., materi-als, crops, land, tools) while emphasizing that it is the availability of both that ensures the continuity of societies across time and space. Retention and control of both types of resources constitute power, which is merely the capacity to achieve outcomes. Storage of both knowledge and crops in buildings meant that recall depending on human memory of how the done thing was done could be drawn out. The media of buildings stored resources over longer time frames than individual memory and could allow retrieval by persons not engaged in production – that is, anyone absent at the time of deposition, construction, decoration, commemoration, or storage. In the (final phase) of the Jerf al-Ahmar and Mureybet community structures, the interiors were partitioned into bins, presumably for storing crops (Stordeur 2000: 2), which are allocative resources incorporated into the building that already stored knowledge. In retrieval of resources, whether allocative or authoritative, skilled interpreters might be called upon perhaps as ritual practitioner specialists who could recite and enact dramas of community practice, including possibly partition and distribution of stored crops to households or wild animals sacrificed for feast.

But the medium of architecture led no more inevitably to a social hierarchy of specialists in interpretation than did communal storage of crops inevitably lead to a social hierarchy of specialists in allocation. Storage of allocative resources as a medium in the expansion of domination is well understood in historical context, and there are numerous examples from around the world (e.g., D'Altroy and Earle 1985, Halstead 1989, Pfälzner 2002), but not all communal storage leads to social hierarchy. In Early Neolithic societies, tensions between community and household identities may have been expressed not only as we have seen with authoritative resources – the storage of knowledge and the investment of social memory in architecture – but with allocative resources and where each of these resources were stored in buildings. Thus, shifts documented in different regions and along differing chronologies in the storage of allocative resources are significant components of the historical emergence and trajectory of Household practice.

The new Neolithic social practices of Household were particularly successful in agricultural communities where crops and other allocative resources could be stored in permanent buildings. Sedentism, delayed returns of crop storage, and buildings provided a new and unparalleled constellation for telescoping time and space to ensure the continuity of societies through new cognitive devices for storing authoritative and allocative resources. Household emerged over 2,000 years in tandem with the slow adoption of full agriculture (Balter 2007, Garrard 1999), contributed to the demise of alternate community practices in agricultural villages, and gained preeminence as the paradigmatic metaphor for later community social constitution.

The Right Question to Ask about Time: Is the Cycle and Recurrence of Daily Practice Paramount in Constituting Societies?

Houses provide spatial constraints so that daily practice is repetitive. How important is it that people living in houses not only encounter each other more frequently than they encounter dwellers in other houses but also (through repetition) have greater experience of the practices within households than the rituals and daily practices that incorporate other social groupings in a sedentary society? Does the frequent tempo of recurrence – daily practice – of people living in houses constitute society more effectively than other social institutions? Geographers have developed space-time "maps" to chart the possibilities of and constraints on social life through the patterning of human physical occupation of space in time. Since humans cannot be in two places at once (a physical constraint) and also observe institutional constraints, their paths through daily activities in space can be schematized. "Bundles" appear where human paths converge, and these are the locales in which social life takes place and where institutional constraints are learned. Analytical models of time-geography identify "home base" as an important institutional constraint, so that "the daily round is organized on the assumption that there is a home base which must be returned to every night" (Gell 1992: 191–195, Hägerstrand 1975, Giddens 1984: 110–118). It is important to recognize that time-space geography analytically charts what is, but does not try to explain it: in other words, it is a methodological tool rather than a theoretical perspective and the technique is not aimed at demonstrating that what is empirically the case must be rationally so.

The tempo of repetition and construction of cultural landscapes by societies living in houses and those that do not build them is a topic to discuss in the next chapter. But the short answer is that repetition, not houses, is key to habitus. Elsewhere houses are important in supra-household societies, as in the widespread occurrence of House Societies (Lévi-Strauss [1979] 1982, Joyce and Gillespie 2000, Carsten and Hugh-Jones 1995). Yet such social constitutions (corporate groups transmitting estates through name, goods, and titles down a real or imaginary lineage) are by no means inevitable. While the example of the Near Eastern Neolithic underscores the importance of living in houses for sedentary, agricultural communities, it is *bodily repetition* and *structuring structures*, agency and structure – not the constraint of houses – that preserve and carry forward social memory. David Wengrow (2006) has argued that for Egyptians, a habitus of "body politic" can be traced back to mobile Neolithic cattle herders, and Egyptians lived in houses without developing an overarching paradigm of social constitution in the metaphor of Household. In sum, Mesopotamian Household was not inevitable but the historical and cultural outcome of Neolithic social institutions.

CHAPTER 7

LANDSCAPE AND THE TEMPO OF SOCIAL PRACTICE: EXPANDING THE SCALE OF HABITAS

On a high promontory overlooking the Jarzīz road up from Ṣalālah's sea breezes sits the tomb of Nabi Ayyūb (Prophet Job). Surrounded by quiet gardens and the gentle attentions of an elderly caretaker, Job's final resting place is marked by an extra-long plaster casing like those of Nabi Hūd, Mawlā Maṭar, and Aḥmad bin 'Isā Al-Muhājir. How Job came to rest in Dhufār, Oman, is a story for theologians, but his presence knits communities today, and all are welcome at the domed enclosure that shelters a prophet to Jews, Christians, and Muslims alike. Pilgrimage at Qabr Nabi Ayyūb enacts and constitutes the tolerance and acceptance of difference found throughout contemporary Omani society. Resident Kerala Christians in Ṣalālah proudly offer a visiting Christian their church, said to be built with the permission of the Sultan. Ṣalālah's beaches in Friday leisure are shared by families fully dressed, sport-clad soccer youths, equestrians in breeches, Bangladeshis line-fishing in kurtas, and the occasional European wearing too little. However Job's long grave came to play a role in the constitution of common cause, Job's well-attended presence today reflects and structures a detribalized identity consistent with Oman's modern national character. I cannot say exactly who goes to Job's tomb or whether separate groups integrate at the shrine, but the grave itself is surely pre-Islamic, like its parallels elsewhere (Bin 'Aqil and McCorriston 2009). I went twice as tourist, removing only shoes, covering hair, and offering money in token respect for others motivated by faiths more literalist than mine. The visits fascinate me as a window onto ritual practice and Pilgrimage meta-structure. At Qabr Nabi Ayyūb, as elsewhere, one is left with the task of explaining long-term continuities despite the massive changes inherent in the emergence of complex societies, the imposition in the case of Dhufār of colonizing groups, and the dramatic shifts in economic and social lifeways over historic and pre-historic time-scales. This chapter addresses and explains such continuity in the long-term context of archaeological time.

In so doing, this chapter addresses three other major implications of Pilgrimage and Household as meta-structure. First, it must reconcile the daily tempo of Household practice with the less frequent practices of Pilgrimage and, in so doing, return to earlier themes of ritual practice as manifestation of meta-structure (Chapters 1, 2). Second, this chapter highlights the significant role of archaeology in building social theory; and, finally, it provides an updated perspective on Turner's liminality with the concept of time islands and ethnoepochal time referenced through ritual. Chapter 6 was about house space; this chapter is about time.

The Problem of Tempo

For all that poststructuralist approaches provide in understanding how culture is transmitted and reproduced, there exists a pronounced emphasis on the iterative role of daily bodily practice within the short time span of human lives. Pilgrimage and household practice present a conundrum: whereas Household as meta-structure conforms to the theoretical expectations of practice theory, Pilgrimage seemingly does not. Practice theory privileges repetition and bodily habituation in the maintenance and transformation of culture and society (Giddens 1984: 64). Household fits this expectation because dwelling in houses enstructures the most frequent encounters of small groups. But Pilgrimage suggests that meta-structure, its persistence, and its ritual and symbolic manifestations require theoretical explanation beyond practical maintenance of social structure. This chapter attempts to reconcile the staccato of pilgrimage by stretching out the tempo of habitus through a longer time-space continuum – that of landscape. Pilgrimage takes place with the bodily practices of mobility, participation, economic exchange, and choreography of mobility and dramatic rites (Chapter 2), but it is the situation of these practices within landscape that explains robusticity of Pilgrimage meta-structure.

Pilgrimage is infrequent and provides sometimes distant and only temporarily activated locales of interaction for social construction. It is tempting to rely, as Victor Turner did, on the powerful and disruptive experience of place and ritual – the shock effect incorporating the individual into a greater social order (Rowlands 1993: 142, Whitehouse 1992: 794). But ultimately a theoretical emphasis on the influence of such events to construct and transform social communities is incompatible with the very precepts of habituation in practice theory (e.g., Bell 1992, Connerton 1989). Furthermore, this approach has been tried in the study of Pilgrimage: as discussed in Chapter 2, liminality and communitas are not entirely satisfying theoretical constructs to explain pilgrimage's significance in the constitution of Arabian societies. First, the objectified division between social time and liminal time ill-fits the stated reasons people give for going on pilgrimage (Morinis 1992a): liminality is a classificatory and functional conceptualization of social order and time by the objectifying anthropologist and neither mutable nor intertwined with the actions of pilgrims and the discourses they dramatize. Second, perceptions of time and event sequences vary among societies (Gell 1992: 84–92) so that the social time/liminal time opposition is as inappropriate a descriptor for all pilgrimage societies (contra Turner) as is a linear-historical construct of time for all non-Western societies (Eliade [1949] 1954, Lévi Strauss 1966, Evans-Pritchard 1939, Geertz 1973, cf. Bloch 1977, Gell 1992, Mytum 2007).

Practice theory provides some resolution for these problems (Chapter 2) but nonetheless brings a prediction that it should be the most frequent social encounters – what Giddens (1984: 71 after Goffman) calls "routine gatherings" – that by their very repetition offer the dominant stage for the enactment of habitus, including the improvisations that contribute to social change. With its punctuated practice, Pilgrimage ill-fits this expectation.

Pilgrimage practice, at least as I have emphasized its observance at specified intervals during which pilgrims engage in nonhabitual activities – enter a state of purity, wear specified dress, do not carry weapons, travel to a nondomestic location, engage in sacrifice, and share a communal feast – differs in tempo and boundaries from household practice. Pilgrimage practice relies on a "larger time-space stretch" (Giddens 1984: 143) than does Household. This in itself may not present an ultimate conundrum, especially if one relies on explanations of cultural transmission beyond bodily practice. For example, the challenges of a greater time-space distanciation can be overcome by cities and the centralization of administrative resources that play important roles in the maintenance and transmission of society (Giddens 1984: 143, Inomata 2006). Such administrative resources can include not only the fruits of production and technologies of the body but also authoritative knowledge. Chapter 3 offered an example of Pilgrimage practice (certainly a powerful binding connection between nomadic pastoralists and urban dwellers in the ancient Arabian high civilizations) that was authoritatively oriented toward federal gods and centralizing temples. But Pilgrimage practice also bound prestate societies unreliant on central authority for perpetuation, and its practical tempo raises interesting questions about social consensus and time.

The long trajectory afforded by culture history and archaeology shows that while Household practice did emerge from Near Eastern Neolithic house dwelling, it did not everywhere provide a long-term constituting metaphor for societies. Historically, the two long-term habituses I have described in this book did come into contact, with interesting results. Famously, Israel (a Pilgrimage society) was in captivity in Babylon ("If I forget you, O Jerusalem, let my right hand forget its skill," Psalm 137) and, while still remembering Jerusalem in song and prayer, brought into Judaism some of the religious beliefs of their captors (such as horned divinity (Satan) and the Flood story) and many practical routines. Likewise, the Palmyrenes had noble Houses and yet built a Bel temple in their "caravan city" (Rostovtseff 1932: 21, 134) to rival the pilgrimage attractions of contemporary Baalbek, Damascus, and Jerusalem. Of course the contacts between societies constituting themselves in the metaphors of Household and Pilgrimage appeared much earlier (one might look at the Chalcolithic Southern Levant here), and interesting tomes could be written about the historical trajectories of what Giddens (1984: 164) calls "intersocietal systems," that is, the forms of relations between societies of differing types:

> All societies both are social systems and at the same time are constituted by the intersection of multiple social systems. Such multiple systems may be wholly "internal" to societies, or they may cross-cut the "inside" and the "outside," forming a diversity of possible modes of

> connection between societal totalities and intersocietal systems. ...
> "Time-space edges" refer to inter-connections, and differentials of
> power, found between different societal types comprising intersocietal
> systems. (Giddens 1984: 164)

This endeavor should draw upon the work of anthropologists studying a
post-colonial "global cultural ecumene" (Gupta and Ferguson 1997: 3,
Urban 2001) and the connectivity of global "ethnoscapes" (Appadurai
1991). A project of culture history exploring much earlier contacts
between Neolithic Arabian herders and Ubaid Mesopotamian seafarers,
or between third-millennium monument-building pastoralists along the
arid margins and the Bronze Age farmers of the Levant has yet to be
written from the perspective of agency, enstructuration, and meta-
structure of Pilgrimage and Household. But that is not the concern of
this book.

Here I am trying to resolve the conundrum of how Pilgrimage practice
persisted as meta-structure while temporally punctuated and infrequent,
and at times seemingly at risk of being swamped by the daily habituation
of Household. There are two paths to this argument, neither entirely
exclusive of the other. In the first and easier approach, one might assume
that Pilgrimage practice also had mnemonic bodily, daily repetitions.
Bodily repetition can take many forms, some of which, as in tattoos and
ritual observance, may recall infrequent events. Tattoo can commemorate life histories, literally incorporating births, deaths, and social alliances into bodily, daily practice. These were among the practices in
Polynesia, where status and bravery were also displayed in tattoo (Ivory
2005: 28–35, Kaeppler 1988). Bodily repetition turns Muslims toward
Mecca in daily prayers, even though Muslims perform Haj annually at
best but, more usually, once in a lifetime. Modern-day Muslims are
enjoined to pray three to five times daily; in Muslim-majority cities,
this bodily repetition may also involve physical travel to a mosque multiple times a day. The ritual turning toward Mecca reminds Muslims
of Haj much as the presence of thirteenth- and fourteenth-century
Languedoc Cathar Perfects reminded Cathars of their once-a-lifetime
consolamentum or entrance to a permanent state of purity (usually just
before death). So might we hypothesize that in pre-history, Pilgrimage
events were openly commemorated through routine bodily practices at
nearby highly visible sites like stone monuments constructed to mark

a feast place, presence of a god, or the burial place of an ancestor, placing additional stones or building fires at such shrines, cutting or binding or loosing hair, turnings and prayer movement (perhaps daily circling), tattoo, or any combination of these. Unlike the secrecy of houses and the inclusiveness that also excludes, such routines would openly commemorate the infrequent gatherings, sacrifice, and feasts that constituted broader society through Pilgrimage. Unfortunately, we have no conclusive evidence that these were a part of daily life in pre-history – all that remains are the stone monuments (and bone placements) themselves.

The other approach is more difficult and requires some theoretical scaffolding to reconcile the long endurance of Pilgrimage and Household, especially in "intersocietal systems" (Giddens 1984: 164) where they persisted side by side for millennia. The example of the Levantine-Taurus-Anatolian Neolithic would predict that Household as a socially constituting metaphor should replace Pilgrimage as the interconnections and contacts among Near Eastern societies intensified from the third millennium BC. Evidently this was not so, since gathering, sacrifice, and feast remained important socially constituting metaphors through the experience of Israel and surrounding Iron Age (and later) societies. The question to address is how did Pilgrimage endure even when Pilgrims started living in houses?

Pilgrimage and Place

To address this question, we must return to the contrast between the secrecy (inclusive-exclusive) of houses and the open visibility of commemorative sites in the Arabian expression of Pilgrimage habitus. Archaeologists have long noted that most of the stone monuments and tombs were constructed above ground and, whether solitary or clustered, were very visible markers of socially organized territories (Cleuziou 1997, 2001, De Maigret 1996). In the case of ancestral tombs, they probably linked living kin-groups through lineal descent from a real or mythic ancestor and were sited to proclaim a descent group's claim to land or resources (Braemer, Cleuziou and Steimer 2003, Lammens 1919: 60). Such phenomena and the manipulation of ancestral tombs and markers for social and territorial identities have also been documented outside of Arabia (e.g., Holl 1998, Kuznar 2003, Bloch 1971, Parker-Pearson 2000:

52. Bronze Age (3000–2000 BC) High Circular Tombs with "tails" of small stone cairns against the Wadi 'Idim skyline, Hadramawt (Yemen). These monuments were built to be visible from wadis and routes and like this one, were revisited with new rites in the Iron Age. Photo by Tara Steimer.

124–141, Parker-Pearson and Ramilisonina 1998, Bradley 1985). Not only were the rural monuments and tombs openly visible and accessible to passersby, but Arabian temples in urban contexts had a notably open access, lacking outer compound walls, often with an open-air altar in a hypostyle hall surrounded by benches, interior spaces with benches to accommodate large numbers of people, banqueting areas, and votive stelae placed by worshipers in the temple interiors (Sedov 2000, 2005). The community structures – to return to that term – of Southern Arabia were built to include through rituals of gathering, sacrifice, and feast. Exclusion is not a noticeable feature of Pilgrimage practice.

In this inclusive and accessible nature, the places of Pilgrimage practice in Southern Arabia were as houses to Household practice, even though we recognize that all areas in houses may not have been uniformly accessible to all household members. Likewise, the narratives and myths of place may not have been uniformly accessible to all pilgrimage members and thereby may have constituted, in Giddens's (1984: 258) term, "authoritative resources." Pilgrimage structures – whether rude cairns on the heights around a part-year grazing site or elaborate temples in agriculturally based settlements – formed place from space and enstructured a socially constructed landscape into which people bodily incorporated themselves through Pilgrimage practice. Like houses, monuments have building biographies and may be used and re-used by many generations who reinterpret and reinvent their significance (Jones 2003: 65, Bradley 1993); excavations at Kheshiya revealed deeper, earlier placements of stones that may once have been an earlier monument dismantled and remodeled to form the stone ring. The difference between Household habitus and Pilgrimage landscape can be resolved by expanding the temporal and spatial scale of habitus itself. Landscape approaches provide some of the theoretical ground for an argument that the apparent contrasts between Household and Pilgrimage (Chapter 5) are actually different dimensions of the same socially constructed phenomena that use "technologies of remembrance" (Jones 2003, Renfrew 1998: 5, also Van Dyke and Alcock 2003: 4–5) and ritual practice to incorporate social identities.

Landscape and Archaeology's Role in Building Theory

Landscape approaches contest metaphysical space as a universally perceived reality and advocate the culturally relative locality of place (Harvey 1969, Meinig 1979, Cosgrove 1984, Schama 1995, Tilley 1994). The term "landscape" is ultimately derived from the "landschap" school of seventeenth-century Dutch painters who both projected and constructed a visual scheme of social order through depictions of idyllic countryside framed by prosperous industry and a righteous burgher class (Duncan 2000: 429). Just as one looks at Versailles down a long park vista where untrimmed chestnuts and planes grade imperceptibly into clipped poplars and box hedges lining the paths and aligning the eye to the symmetrical order of the palace itself, so "Landschap" painting sought to align nature to a cultural sense of place and social order.

But landscape approaches encompasses more than the visual world-views of seventeenth- through nineteenth-century European painters and their patrons. Landscape is a physical manifestation of the conflation of time and space and social existence so that landscape encodes and represents particular social frameworks and serves in turn as the mnemonic device for social storage, constituting thereby an authoritative resource. Such approaches rely upon an ideational rather than material basis for landscape (e.g., Bender 1993, Tilley 1994). Narrative, which may telescope past and present into a continuous now that binds ancestors and mythic time to place and society, may be closely tied to locality and the maintenance of place (e.g., Basso 1996: 54, Howey and O'Shea 2006, Wagner 2001). Landscape, continuously recreated, reinterpreted, and contested in the intertwined drama of agency and structure, serves to symbolize and at the same time structure social constitution. With this definition, landscape approaches, whether in geography, arts, anthropology, or history, can be used to understand social construction of space into place attendant with temporal and social positioning and the manipulation of authoritative resources for power (Leone 1984, Hastorf 2009, Panja 2003, Ashmore 1989).

The concept of landscape, usually with materialist assumptions of physical and environmental constraints on spatio-temporal constructs, has long been used as a methodological tool or analytical approach in archaeological circles, but archaeological data sets have not been widely used to advance theoretical perspectives on landscape. The growing applications of Geographic Information Systems (GIS) and geodetic sciences (remote sensing, global positioning, GIS) offer tools for data organization and pattern searching in data sets and provide powerful methodological frameworks for archaeological survey. In such approaches, landscape is more space than place (Tilley 1994: 3) and serves as a convenient container for the encapsulation and description of archaeological data. This is not to demean the usefulness of such tools, nor to suggest that archaeologists remain impervious to temporal (and cultural) aspects of landscape structure. Indeed, several archaeological schools have grappled with theoretical concepts of landscape history, including Annales (e.g., Barker 1991, Knapp 1992) and Historical Ecology (e.g., Crumley and Marquardt 1987, Kirch 1994, Kirch and Hunt 1997, Deetz 1990). These approaches, borrowing from allied disciplines in history and social thought (especially Marxist historical materialism), recognize a fundamentally material base (e.g., environment, ecological resources) to historical trajectories (e.g., Stone 1996, Jordan 2001). But they have not independently sought to develop a theory of landscape beyond applications of existing theoretical frameworks (from other disciplines) to archaeological data sets. So also are the new methodological approaches to landscape history also grappling with time but not generally developing new theory (cf. Llobera 2005). Increasingly, archaeologists accommodate geomorphological and human histories as dimensions of present-day physical survey conditions (e.g., Terrenato and Ammerman 1996, Alcock, Cherry and Davis 1994, Given 2004, Cherry et al. 1988, Cherry, Davis and Mantzourani 1991) while still maintaining a methodological and analytical focus and building no new landscape theory.

Building Landscape Theory

I suggest that the archaeological record of Pilgrimage and Household societies has an important role in *building landscape theory*. In this I have been inspired by the temporal and cultural aspects of landscape construction emphasized by poststructural theory, while yet hewing (Chapter 8) to a materialist base rather than an ideational and phenomenological one (Tilley 1994). Physical landscapes, like houses – the built environment in which people dwell (Heidegger 1971: 147–148) – encode and reproduce social and cultural frameworks (structures, institutions) through the practical agency (perception and behavior) of human beings. Habitus is a short-term phenomenon as the dispositions of human agents; habitus is individually conceived and intersects in society with other agents in collectively shared dispositions (Bourdieu [1980] 1990: 59–61). Thus, individual habitus spans (at most) the life of a human being, and collective habitus is (perhaps subtly) in constant flux with changes in group membership and the consensual dispositions of individuals. All this offers persuasive theory for conservative behavior, social production and reproduction, and change, but the drift of collectively shared and individually perceived dispositions in generational time cannot fully explain the long-term persistence – over thousands of years – of socially constituting behaviors despite other immense social changes, which are also transmitted through practice (e.g., Beck et al. 2007). Landscape with its physical and narrative dimensions (places) is the medium through which habitus is expressed and learned over multi-generational time and serves as the mnemonic device for society that bodily habit serves the individual. In this it is served by the technologies of remembrance, the ellipsis of social storage, and the bodily practices that reinterpret them.

Chapters 2–6 reviewed two archaeological data sets, the Fertile Crescent and the Arabian, and emphasized the significance of cultural continuities using terminology that emphasizes behavior and transmission of culture through practice, introducing the "habitus of Pilgrimage" and "habitus of Household" to identify long-term habitus. But there remain several problems, namely that (1) Pilgrimage seemingly defies the expectations of tempo in practice theory and (2) Household would, given those same expectations, seem to be inevitable where people lived in houses. Pilgrims have returned to Qabr Nabi Hūd for at least 1,500 years, and their forefathers were gathering for sacrifices upstream at Kheshiya 6,500 years ago, practically constructing habitus over 300 generations. Clearly there is other cultural transmission of knowledge besides bodily practice at work in the long-term persistence of mechanisms for social constitution.

Connerton (1989: 22, 72–23) argued as much in identifying personal, cognitive, and habit memory and identifying the combination of cognitive and habit memory in the storage and retrieval of social knowledge. Storage and retrieval are practices separated in time, and the tempo of their practice may vary across different instances. Tempo is a key issue here, and it is therefore incumbent that we examine more closely the intersection of practice theory and time. Landscape offers the storage device for cultural knowledge – place is the repository of stories, memories, lineage, and kin – that stretches out the memory of practice and habituation over long time frames.

Landscape Tempo – Time Islands, Time Maps, and Consensual Time

How is memory of practice "stretched" over long time frames? This is not a new idea (e.g., Rowlands 1993), but the archaeological evidence for

Pilgrimage and Household demonstrates a tempo only previously imagined by anthropologists and historians pondering the cultural construction of time. Anthropologists have long grappled with issues of temporal relativity. Evans-Pritchard (1939) among the Nuer argued that the mundane practices of daily life tuned to an ecological pace were encapsulated within structural time that does not pass, so that the intervening generations in a lineage that extend that lineage more than eight generations beyond ancestors are dropped or forgotten ("silently revised") (Wagner 1986: 82, Gell 1992: 16–21). An often-cited example is the case of Australian aboriginal groups, whose notion of being in the same time as mythic ancestors led Lévi Strauss (1966) to differentiate "synchronic" and "diachronic" time and, in the case of New World ethnographies, to link synchronic time with narrative (Lévi Strauss [1964] 1969: 15–16). Synchronic time refers to a timeless order of things so that "ancestors are still considered to be engaging, invisibly, in [the daily activities of traditional life] at all the relevant sacred sites specified in the myths" (Gell 1992: 27). In Lévi-Strauss's (1966: 236) words,

> Mythic history thus presents the paradox of being both disjoined from and conjoined to the present ... It is conjoined with it because nothing has been going on since the appearance of the ancestors, except events whose recurrence periodically effaces their particularity.

Through much of the anthropological discussion of time runs the question of whether there exists a real, objective, and metaphysical time or whether all time is culturally moderated perception. A powerful critique from cognitive psychology suggests that humans cognitively experience metaphysical time in universal fashion (Piaget 1970, Gell 1992: 97–103). There is but one time, so that the "life of any individual thing is embedded in four dimension space-time, forever there, linked to the rest of the universe by a web of converging and diverging causal relationships. ... Events happen only because we 'encounter' them in a particular causal order" (Gell 1992: 155). But it also is the case that there are profound cultural differences (and individual ones) in the perception of time. Although we may all experience time in one way, humans perceive time as "a thin screen of events in continuously changing and moving present ... presentness alone confers reality, but present bears the residual effect of the whole of the past, and prefigures the whole of the future ... thus the past changes in true present, past and future." In short, looking forward and back are inimical and highly variable components of time perception (Wagner 1986: 81, 89, Gell 1992: 156, Hägerstrand 1975: 5–6).

And these components are used to different vantage. This human way of perceiving time – reconfiguring history as new events occur or should occur – has very large implications for social constitution. The flexibility and contingency of relative time implies that for any event there will be opportunity costs assessed according to retrospection and prospection (inherent features in cognition of time), that is, every event is perceived in relationship to past and future. Furthermore, practice and practical tempo are socially constructed, so the perception of practical time is thereby consensual. Gell (1992: 280–284) uses the famous example of the Kula ring to argue that codified knowledge (i.e., an authoritative resource) can transcend practice, that is, a calculated tempo of Kula shell exchange can play as great a role in the configuring of social status as the rhythm of collective habitus. The Kula operator judges the opportunity costs of holding and trading shells from a vantage of deliberate intent to manipulate socially consensual perceived time (the proper delay required in exchange) by strategizing in an entirely different time framework – a representable totality comprised of many possible exchanges with computable outcomes (see also Hägerstrand's time-geography). This "representable totality" is best understood through the analogy of maps, a pseudo-objective (but still subjective) authoritative view of space.

The Foucaultan link between knowledge and authority is also implied since that codified knowledge, that is, the grasp of a time framework outside of the rhythm of practice, is none other than an authoritative resource (Giddens 1984: 258) that may be manipulated for the operator's own temporal and social transcendence (fame and status). Authoritative knowledge is knowledge *that* – a knowledge of "possession" ("like owning a sum of money") embedded in recognizing and organizing multiple time-space paths and the life chances that they imply (Giddens 1984: 258, Gell 1992: 274). The opportunity costs assessed by each Kula ring operator reflect a super-ordinate control over time (Gell 1992: 284) so that agents, while bound in the human cognitive experience of perceiving time, do so with the intent to stretch out a long present of temporal cognition against the tempo of habitus.

What the Kula operator's strategies and the relativity of perceived time in human cognition demonstrate is that for humans, the *perception* of continuity and habituation (an event series, each event with its retrospect and prospect) is as important as the *reality* or measure of habituation. Thus, Pilgrimage can be understood to achieve a perceived habituation – to stretch out (bodily) practice through codified knowledge (authoritative storage in monuments) even as the tempo of Pilgrimage in real time (i.e., relativity) is staccato. All this depends upon extending the retrospect-prospect that each present, now-moment embraces, through social consensus. For Pilgrimage and Household, the time has come to provide new definition to these larger cycles of habituation – Bourdieu's habitus, grounded in the expectations of daily bodily practice will no longer fully serve. Gell (1992: 326) uses the term "aberrant time" to describe "ritual practices that calendrically show and symbolically moderate collective representations of time in a dialectical relationship to mundane temporality." I prefer another term for this time (*ethnoepoch*), for reasons I will expand later and in recognition of the contributions archaeological data are making to ethnographic and anthropological understandings of habitus, tempo, and landscape.

How is this time-focused discussion related to space, and how does such theoretical contortion of tempo contribute to landscape theory? Time and space are difficult to disentangle: the body can be in but one place at one time, and throughout philosophy and sociology, the one (time or space) is explained in the metaphor of the other. Bourdieu ([1972] 1977: 103, 106–107) described practical time as time "made up of incommensurable islands of duration, each with its own rhythm . . . depending on what one is doing." In this he explicitly rejected a linear continuity to time while retaining a spatial metaphor so that islands of time are enclosed units within space and recognizing that the present retains the past and anticipates the future. Temporal maps and the representable totality of time in a spatial metaphor infuses Gell's description of the Kula ring operator and indeed, permeates much of anthropological representation of human temporal perception. Just as landscape has landmarks (localities, places) linked to time, so time has markers linked to space ("islands," "maps," "trajectories"), an idiom so habitual that one scarcely pauses to note the implied metaphor. Wagner (1986: 91–92) argues that Western science and the anthropological tradition it influenced has so thoroughly accepted this metaphor that the markers (measurements) and their structure in time (tempo) have come to stand for time itself. In other words, time (e.g., either the long present of temporal cognition or the practical time of daily life) is an integral (organic) interval between markers, not the structure or pattern (tempo) of the markers themselves. This is the root problem of tempo (see earlier) and is an important distinction as we consider next the interconnection of space and time in landscape.

Landscape as socially constructed space integrates time through the historical process of its construction; in other words, people acquire common perspectives of places through social experiences, events that draw upon a residual past and projected future (e.g., Bender 1993, Küchler 1993, Duncan and Duncan 1988, Duncan and Ley 1993, Schama 1995). Time, that is, its essence not its measurement, is embedded in place and is socially shared through narrative (Lévi-Strauss [1964] 1969) and through technologies of remembrance (e.g., monuments that evoke narrative). In his studies of American mythology, Lévi-Strauss ([1964] 1969: 15–16) recognized the essential nature of narrative (as myth) which, like music, is "an instrument for the obliteration of time." If time is an essence (a present now that includes both retrospection and prospection in human time cognition), not the daily, weekly, or interannual measurement of that essence, then place, often marked with technologies of remembrance, effectively inscribes time as essence, not just the tempo or interval measurement of daily practice. This means that monuments will be as effective in the commemoration of "aberrant time" as of "practical time." It means that the socially consensual perception of habituation in Pilgrimage practice is as effective as the temporally frequent habituation of Household practice. And this encapsulation of essential time in landscape balances the bodily habituation of daily practice. The archaeological record of Pilgrimage demonstrates this point.

Furthermore, the lowest denominator unit of "practical time" (daily) has garnered some critical scrutiny as the natural basis and building block of human experience. In his studies of Aboriginal myth and dreamtime, Roy Wagner (2001: 77) refers to landscape as an in-elective dimension of temporal perception, arguing that physical landscape and the way of seeing it comes after the narrative that structures cosmos, so that there is an intertwining of narrative, cosmos, and landscape vision (cf. Jordan 2001 for a contrasting view embedding landscape perception in materiality and praxis). Similarly, Gupta and Ferguson (1997: 7–9) challenge the notion of local and narrow locality as the original, centered, natural, authentic seat of culture opposed to the new, external, artificially imposed global world, arguing that locality and community are historically constructed from a wider narrative, a theme echoed by Appadurai's (1991: 199) discussion of "ethnoscapes." In these perspectives, narrative and immeasurable time are organic essences out of which social landscapes are derived in an inversion of historical materialism. In these arguments, ideology precedes materiality in social construction of landscape. Put differently, structure preempts practice (Sahlins 1976).

Although the precedence ceded to ideational constructs like cosmos, narrative, and essential time is extreme and indeed runs counter to a materialist base, few would argue that the dialectic between materiality (the physical landscape), social history, and narrative/essential time is necessary to understanding social landscape. This dialectic is difficult to study in short-term view, particularly in cases like pilgrimage where essential time eclipses the life span of the observer. Archaeological data sets like the long-term Arabian record of pilgrimage allow us to recognize and conceptualize the role of essential time in the building and maintaining of social landscapes and to construe the roles of materiality and cosmos in landscape construction.

Ethnoepochs and Liminal Time

With a supra-ordination similar to the notion of ethnoscape, coined to describe the maintenance of social identities without place (Appadurai 1991, Gupta and Ferguson 1992), an *ethnoepoch* henceforth refers to the maintenance of social identities using a culturally constructed long present of time cognition, the "larger cycles of habituation" referred to previously. I have adapted the term from Roy Wagner's (1986: 85–92) use of epoch to invoke the Greek sense of "stoppage or cessation" in time as a means to convey the integrity of time without flow or measure. If an epoch is "happening as one and the same as the frame within which it is perceived," then it can only be realized as a condition, not as the content or pattern – daily, weekly, or otherwise measured practice.

Pilgrimage and Household refer to *ethnoepochs*, culturally distinct time perceptions that transcend long chronological frameworks of social change rather than being described (and measured) by them. They exist essentially and organically, that is, without reference to the practical changes refracting transposable dispositions of individual and collective habitus. By this I mean that the memory of practice stretched over long time frames admits change simply by not recognizing change and flow as mechanistic components of social identity – the past changes in true present and prefigures the future. Ethnoepoch is an integral time island recognized through social consensus that explains the longevity of a socially constituting metaphor, that is, continuity in the face of change. Storage and retrieval of narrative ensures that individual agents of social constitution at once experience and conceive ethnoepochs as present-time islands (Bourdieu [1972] 1977: 103, 106–107) co-temporous with daily habit and repetitious bodily practice. In this sense, infrequent ritual contributes to habituation (consensually perceived) without being habitual (i.e., frequent practice in real time).

Ironically, Victor Turner's limen (Latin for threshold, a spatial referent) as the basis of liminality may have been closer to ethnoepoch that at first appears. Turner's liminal state of communitas describes a state of suspension of social rules (collective habitas), and liminality is clearly situated in a Western linear model of time unlike ethnoepoch. Turner envisioned communitas as transitional, but ethnoepoch is meta-structural, existing permanently outside the dialectics of change. It is the unchanging quality of ethnoepoch that liminality shares and the practical referent of ritual that accesses the long-term cultural meta-structure.

Gell (1992: 326) prefers the term "aberrant time" and advances the idea that calendrical rituals and festivals show and symbolically moderate collective representations of aberrant time in a dialectical relation to mundane temporality, not unlike Turner's liminality. My distinction rests on the real-time measure of the ethnoepoch. Pilgrimage and Household outstrip the ethnographer's toolkit: ethnoepochs are to the modern ethnographer's time chart what globalization is to his/her field site. It is archaeological data sets - from Arabia, the Fertile Crescent, and beyond - that have pointed toward a new theoretical construction of social landscape with ethnoepochs pinioned at its places through

53. Monolithic column exposed by quarrying a tableland of rock at Nabataean Petra's High Place (Jordon). Northern Arabian Nabataeans may have also constituted their society through pilgrimage as did other Arabian civilizations. Author's photo.

narrative, ritual, and the technologies of remembrance. As ethnoepochs, Pilgrimage and Household are essential (i.e., they are not constructed of a mechanistic tempo of the patterned intervals of daily practice but of a socially-consensual perception of habituation, existing beside and despite the daily practices of habitus).

Social Landscape and Habitus

People practiced gathering, sacrifice, and feast at places where the retrospective-prospective Now of doing pilgrimage stretched out a collectively consensual essential time through narrative. These were places of *that* – places in which the authoritative resources (the orchestration of people gathering here in Pilgrimage) were stored and retrieved and in which the agents of pilgrimage consciously sought to position themselves in supra-ordinate time (ethnoepoch). And in retrieval and retelling, narrative was revised in a long temporal Now that admits no change, even across changing mundane practice. At some times in the past, places were marked by monuments; at some times but not necessarily all, such monuments were tombs of ancestors. In the latter case, genealogies probably played a significant role in narrative.

Pilgrimage practice endured as the structuring metaphor for social constitution throughout the radical economic and social transformations of state formation precisely because socially constructed landscape is as influential in the transmission and continuity of culture through ethnoepoch as is habitus through the more constrained mode of daily practice. It is precisely the example of Arabian Pilgrimage, violating as it does the assumptions of daily bodily practice and its paramount importance for enstructuring society, that points us toward new theoretical alignment of the narrow (measured in daily time and bodily space) scope of habitus with the broad social landscape infused with ethnoepoch. Social landscape and habitus are moreover indivisible – one grades into the other, not as a set of separable modes of regionalization (Giddens 1984: 120–126) or inarticulately conjoined envelopes (Braudel [1966] 1972, Knapp 1992: 10) but as inversions one of the other, playing significant roles in social constitution and cultural transmission.

Social landscape therefore encodes the knowledge that Pilgrimage and Household societies are societies exclusive of all others while the practices of Pilgrimage and Household enstructure societies in social landscapes. Peoples socially constituting themselves through these different meta-structural referents could live in proximity, trade, and enter and dissolve economic interdependencies with frequent practical contacts. The flow of third-millennium trade goods and accompanying processes of commodification whereby material value changes with its transfer to new social actors helps define meta-structural social boundaries. Physical landscape served as the medium through which social frameworks were negotiated and contested through time. Understanding how this process took place is critical to understanding the success of Pilgrimage as an ethnoepoch for social constitution, even when houses, Houses, and households (but not Household as ethnoepoch) with their spatial exclusivity and repetitive social gatherings were present.

Landscapes without Houses

A key aspect of the process of social landscape formation is the transcription of social identity (usually via kinship, ancestors, clan gods) via narrative onto place (Tilley 1994). Ethnographic literature provides a number of examples even as it springs from a diversity of social theory approaches. Perhaps one of the most famous such ethnographies is Evans Pritchard's (1940) studies of the Nuer, for whom kinship defined all else, including small place units and people's positioning in them in ecological scales (Gell 1992: 16–21). Lancaster and Lancaster (1999a: 68–71) echo this theme in wide-ranging discussions of Arab tribal groups and territorial groups in the modern Bilād as-Shām (arid lands of geographic Syria, which includes portions of the nation-states of Syria, Jordan, Iraq, and Saudi Arabia). In a brief summary of pastoral "nomads," Brian Spooner (1973: 41) argued for a material base and ecological constraints to small group size and cohesion but also that "the native model of social organization" (i.e., kinship narratives) mitigates small group flux with a larger social group stability. Richard Tapper's (1990) important review and synthesis of tribal entities in the Middle East recognizes the importance of territory for the definition of some (but not all) groups but more significantly emphasizes the role of narrative (genealogy) in maintenance of tribal social identity. Such narrative loops the ethnographer back to the technologies of remembrance (making places) that enable narrative storage and retrieval as authoritative knowledge: here space and time are intertwined in landscape formation.

Whereas this book has made a case for the ethnoepochal essence of Pilgrimage (Chapters 2 and 3), it remains difficult to document the transcription of social identity via narrative to place in ancient Arabia. For historic Arabia, sources are significantly augmented by epigraphic geography – toponyms and territories generated through the historical record (e.g., Al-Hamdānī [d. 945 AD] 1986, Al-Tabarī (d. 819) 1879–1901, Smith 1954) and referenced to spatial-temporal distributions of inscriptions and graffiti found today (e.g., Robin 1982a, 1982b). Through such records, epigraphers have been able to reconstruct tribal territories in the centuries prior to and during the life of Muhammad and to trace territorial social groupings further back in history contemporary with the first-millennium AD Sabaean kingdom (e.g., Ghul 1984, Pirenne 1991, Sergeant 1971). In pre-historic Arabia, archaeological geographies of place are weak, due particularly to lack of spatial data sets from limited archaeological survey and uneven synthesis of the distributions of monuments and tombs. Nevertheless, it is possible at this time to construct models of long-term tribal dynamics in Southern Arabia interwoven with ethnoepochal Pilgrimage.

If landscape is the physical manifestation of socially constructed tribal identities, then landscape places physically constructed with monuments and tombs mark and store narratives of social construction retrieved through the practices of pilgrimage. Therefore, a study of monuments in space and time offers some powerful insights into social constitution and dynamics. "New British prehistory" (Renfrew 1998: 5) has been grappling with just such issues and applying landscape approaches to archaeological remains. Research into pre-historic Hadramawt and Dhufār, areas long occupied by mobile pastoral groups, has also generated chronological vistas that serve as testable models for long-term social dynamics.

In brief (and incorporating data and assumptions from earlier chapters), a short set of models for the Southern Arabian highlands can be outlined. These models should have distinct signatures of monuments and monument distributions ultimately generated through different time-geographies of social groupings (Pred 1977: 213–213). By this I mean that the places in which people built monuments were those in which concentrations of people practiced gathering, sacrifice, and feast (pilgrimage) as determined by space-time constraints, including "the fact that every situation is inevitably rooted in past situations" (Hägerstrand 1975: 12). There is both material and historical basis to such time-geography, and the historical basis is imbued with ethnoepochal perspective.

9,000 years ago – Highland Southern Arabia

Conditions were much moister than today under summer rainfall climate regime. The highland major north-flowing drainages were largely flooded and marshy during a portion of the year, and springs supplied scattered water in the dry season. Pastoralists camped by these springs in concentrated groups during the winter months (October–March), but needed to move animals away from flooding in the deepest canyons during rainy months (July–September). Domesticated cattle, sheep, and goats were herded. Alternate graze for cattle during rainy months could be found by dispersing into broader highland basins where seasonal standing water (pools) could be found. The demographic constraints (population densities, raiding, and violence) on dispersal are unknown. There are no known rainy season camps of this period (but the small size of the groups and short, dispersed occupations make these difficult to see archaeologically). The model site for this pattern is Manayzah (Wadi Sana) (Crassard et al. 2006), where bones from domesticated cattle, sheep, and goats appear from 8,000 years ago (Martin et al. 2009). Projectiles emphasized in tool technologies (Crassard 2008) may have been for hunting and for human violence. No monument building is known from this period, but there existed broad socioeconomic networks that facilitated the transfer of non-local marine shell and obsidian into the highland areas and maintained the widespread use of similar lithic production techniques across much of Southern and Eastern Arabia.

6500 BP – The Beginnings of Pilgrimage

Conditions were still more moist than today under a summer rainfall climate regime. By this time, there existed visible stone monuments – like the stone platform and cattle ring at Kheshiya – in many locations. Visible monuments attest most probably to increased population densities. This is because territorial social behavior (a demonstrated outcome of people packing, e.g., Rosenberg 1998) is implicit in monument construction (Cleuziou 1997, 2001). Furthermore, the visibility and increase in archaeological remains suggest that more people were around to build them. Some landscape places are always invisible to archaeologists regardless of population density (e.g., Jordan 2001, Shutova 2006), so it may be that monument construction and Pilgrimage commemoration began earlier and was more widespread than archaeological evidence can show. Ecological patterns of annual vegetation flush and withering were still determined by seasonal rainfall and strongly affected the gatherings and dispersals of people dependent on pastoralism. Aesthetic skill in making projectile points notably declined, suggesting a diminished emphasis on hunting, hunting magic in tool making, hunting prowess (with projectiles), or a shift to other tools (e.g., nets, fire drives).

Pastoralists camped in marshy oxbow areas like the Middle Wadi Sana for winter months (October–March) and dispersed during rainy season (April–September). Available rainy season graze and mobility was probably constrained by the lack of upland soils supporting grasses for cattle.

Pastoralists would have dispersed from the narrow marsh and spring reserves of winter to uplands where natural and tended reservoirs held ephemeral surface water in small basins that had also trapped sediments. Pastoralists were largely confined to north–south migratory patterns by the presence of other similar groups in adjacent northward-flowing wadis and the lack of soils on the uplands between them.

5000 BP – Pilgrimage and Tribes

Major climate change (aridification) occurred, possibly with greater inter-annual variability or more frequent droughts. Pastoralists needed to adapt to such conditions, and cattle largely disappeared from arid areas like Wadi Sana, leaving sheep and/or goats as the principal herded animals. These have a wider range with less frequent access to water, so that potential mobility was increased across larger territories, with a lower biomass supported per unit area. Social (tribal) confederations grew larger, ensuring individuals a wider social network, wider territorial range, and more options in conditions of greater variability. Interdependence/exchange networks were primarily within a tribal framework (narratives of kinship and genealogy) instead of between social groups. This situation implies stronger tribal social identities, maintained through pilgrimage at ancestor-linked places (tombs). Supplemental watering technologies (run-on irrigation) were introduced and with them presumably new land-tenure conventions, which entailed new social arrangements to ensure access to an array of resources and exchange between specialized producers (Harrower 2008).

4500–2800 BP – Tribal Gods and Pilgrimage

Southern Arabia continued to have an arid climate, including a phase of greater aridity than today and culminating in a shift to a bimodal rainfall pattern, with a short rain and a long rain in the rainy spring-summer season. Some zones formerly in (dry) seasonal use for grazing and browsing were used less frequently, and higher population pressure (people and animals) appeared at permanent water sources, which now were shrinking. Although archaeological data are not yet conclusive, it seems that some monument styles took on a distinctly regional character, reflecting the separation of tribal groups. Toward the end of this period, it is likely that localized tribal deities emerged as a focus of pilgrimage practices. Tribal deities, possibly originating as apotheosized ancestors, provided a non-kin-based focus for territorially defined social groups. Concurrently, social status may have been increasingly expressed with non-kinship criteria. People from a region practiced pilgrimage to tribal gods and thereby inscribed themselves in tribes that took on an increasingly territorial framework. Commitments to pastoral lifestyle diversified with the introduction of new farming technologies and investments (*āflaj*, or underground-to-surface conduits, and *ghayl*, or spring-fed canals) now that many people were increasingly constrained to permanent water sources and (some peoples') mobility was diminished. Exchange included metals, albeit not many – along with hides, frankincense, shells, honey, obsidian, textiles, beeswax, agricultural products – and specialization and surplus production accompanied exchange patterns that reached across tribal territorial boundaries. In wider context, a Bronze Age world system encouraged local groups' entry into far-reaching exchange networks (Frank 1993, Ratnager 2003), while the commodification of exotics emphasized social boundaries between producer and consumer.

2800–1500 B P *– Pilgrimage and Arabian States*

Climate was more or less as today, including a change around 3000 B P to the current bimodal pattern in summer rainfall, which favors pastoral rather than mixed pastoral-farming choices (Ellis and Galvin 1994: 346). Exchange networks among specialized producers flourished. Camels were certainly in use as transport animals, and the growing role of the state in long-distance exchange syncretized existing practices to incense extraction and mapped caravan passage onto extant pastoral routes. Territorial tribal pastoralists in the highlands were incorporated into state religious-ideological systems and into the political economies of Southern Arabian kingdoms through pilgrimage. States instituted federal gods, tithes, and centrally controlled tribal gatherings, sacrifices, and feasts. "Pacification" of tribal areas through state federation means zones of risk avoidance could be used in times of drought or by poorer tribes people. Tribal political entities emerged with leadership based on heritable wealth (the bayt system) and state offices (qayls).

Monuments marking place and ethnoepochal pilgrimage were now situated at the nexus of state narratives and authoritative resource storage – federal temples in cities, smaller temples in ancillary communities (e.g.,

Jabal al-Lawdh, Āmm of Labakh, Sayyin Dhū-Hlsm at Bā-Quṭfah), highland *ḥjr* essential to tribal territorial identities (Obermeyer 1999: 43), and at the interface of state and tribal confederates – that is, along caravan routes.

Post 1300 BP – *Islamic Pilgrimage as Ethnoepoch*

Islamic influences meant that in some cases Islamic saints were mapped onto existing monuments such as the tomb of Nabi Hūd at Qabr Hūd. Islamic burial practices shifted burials from high and middle ground and from monumental tombs to cemeteries close by agricultural land and accessible to lowland settlements (Bin 'Aqil and McCorriston 2009). In narrative alignment with Islam and, by extension, the Islamic state, tribes people rejected antecedent monuments as burying grounds while ethnoepochal pilgrimage continued to constitute Islamic societies in places that brought tribe-people together with other Muslims and social groups (Ho 2006). Tribal law (*'urf*), including socially mediated access to resources (i.e., tribal territories) continues to be practiced, sometimes with Islamic law (Sharia) taking precedent (Harrower 2008), but often with the latter interpreted in the framework of the former. There appear to be deep historical continuities for tribal territories in Southern Arabia. For example, the Humūm and Saybānī groups occupying Hadramawt territories today (and in recent history) exhibit distinct material culture (including monument types, architectural form, farming technologies) that mirror differences in the pre-Islamic eras.

Landscapes with Houses

Like Pilgrimage, ethnoepochal Household is one of a series of possible outcomes in consensual construction of time-space as place using technologies of remembrance. As Pilgrimage is ethnoepoch, so is Household ethnoepoch, that is, the stretching out of shared habitus over long time frames through storage and retrieval of authoritative knowledge as perceptively essentialized present that incorporates retrospect and prospect. Thus people from the Levant to Mesopotamia socially constituted themselves in the metaphor of Household across thousands of years and major social changes.

In Chapter 6, I suggested that Neolithic Household "won out" over other community practices through the physics of time-space geography (cf. Giddens 1984) so that the frequency of bodily habituation explains the eventual dominance of Household. By this logic, Pilgrimage should also disappear in Arabia with the appearance of sedentism and houses. But it does not. A missing piece in explanation of the perpetuity of ethnoepoch (e.g., Pilgrimage) is the role of history in shaping "authority constraints" within time-geographies (Hägerstrand 1975: 12, Pred 1977: 208), interwoven with material factors. (These material factors, which Pred calls "capability constraints" and "coupling constraints," are none other than environmental and economic factors familiar in materialist theory). History, with its potential for different agency (Sahlins 1985), intrinsically means that there were always different outcomes possible in the tensions between different socially constituting practices. Social integration requires the interaction of individuals and institutions (meaning the structural properties of social systems that stretch across time and space) outliving the individual (Giddens 1984).

In other words, Household ethnoepoch was not inevitable, and its culture history cannot be traced mechanistically to the routinization of bodily practice without reference to ethnoepochal authoritative knowledge. Household as the structuring metaphor of social constitution did not prevail everywhere there were houses, and Pilgrimage shows that this was so.

By the first millennium BC in Arabia, when agriculturally supported states were present, there existed plenty of houses and territorial, corporate groups (Beeston 1972: 257–258) who called themselves "House" (*bayt*). But these groups did not socially define themselves principally in the metaphor of a household within a house (Korotayev 1993b) but by using the metaphor of pilgrimage through tribal gods, gatherings, sacrifices, and communal feasts to constitute and reconstitute social networks linked to land tenure (Brown and Beeston 1954: 52). "Lord of the Bayt" referred to the tribal god to whom first fruits were offered, likely represented by a standing stone or betyl (Pirenne 1976: 191–192). It is significant also that the term "*bayt*" can mean the tomb of an ancestor (Pirenne 1976: 204, Lammens 1919: 88–93), an ancestor that may indeed have been apotheosized into tribal god.

So a House society, such as we may infer the wealthy qaylite bayts of the Middle Sabaean state to have been (and, by inference, also the Hadramitic kingdom), actually was socially constituted and perpetuated itself through

Pilgrimage (gathering, sacrifice, and feast). These were the most important ritual practices – they certainly left the biggest traces in the archaeological record – as people inscribed themselves visibly into pilgrimage societies through monument building, and later temple building, thereby constituting a state. Among the heritable offices of wealthy Houses were surely the offices of pilgrimage, such as the heritable role of sacrificer, or of feast distributer, or of water supplier to pilgrims, as we know to have been the strategic offices of pre-Islamic central Arabia (Mecca). In ancient Southern Arabia, the office of tithe or first fruits collector would presumably have strengthened and enhanced House and State economies. Such cultic offices could be consolidated through strategic leadership and partible through inheritance, as an anthropological analysis of *Quraysh* genealogical history suggests (Dostal 1991).

Conclusions

The two Near Eastern ethnoepochs recognizable from archaeological data point to fundamental and theoretically significant new insights into the "modes of regionalization" critical to bodily habituation and enstructuration of society (Giddens 1984: 121–126). Whereas the repetitions of time-geographical bodily practice are important in the expression and (re)formulation of social identities, unconscious bodily knowledge shares with authoritative knowledge the native maintenance of routine in essentialized time. In other words, just as the practitioner need not and indeed does not have an objective view of how well his or her bodily practices conform to those of others, so the subject's perception of time is a holistic ever Now that revises retro and prospect to align subject with social group through knowledge that the subject participates in community. Unconscious bodily knowledge is not the only habituation constraining social agents. Not all ritual is practice in practical time (Bell 1992). There exist also social landscapes embedded with consensual human perceptions of habituation (ethnoepochs) that play an equal role in social constitution with mundane practice. These ethnoepochs are maintained through authoritative knowledge – stored and retrieved with technologies, narrative (essentialized time), and, secondarily, bodily (if infrequent) practice. Ritual practice is none other than the retrieval of authoritative resources. Thus are ethnoepochs culturally distinct time perceptions (not liminal pauses in habituation, Chapter 2) that transcend long chronological frameworks of social change and mundane practice rather than being described (and measured) by them.

Furthermore, archaeological data pointing to the long-term persistence of ethnoepochs contribute to the development of landscape theory. In recognizing Pilgrimage and Household ethnoepochs in the ancient Near East, we have been pressed to address their significance and explain that persistence through millennia of social change. Ethnoepoch is a temporal essence stored in social landscapes and retrieved through technologies of remembrance. While the mechanisms of storage and retrieval of authoritative knowledge have long played an important role in archaeological landscape theory (e.g., Renfrew 1998: 5, 1976, 1973, Rowlands 1993, Jones 2003, Tilley 1994, Van Dycke and Alcock 1993, Parker-Pearson 2000, Cummings 2003), archaeologists have until now been largely inattentive to the longevity of such authoritative knowledge and inexplicit about its transmission across social and cultural change.

Social landscapes are constructed and maintained through an interplay of history and materiality, through the retrieval of ethnoepoch with mnemonic devices such as tomb and house places. The significance of social landscape in cultural continuity is consistent with a materialist approach to cultural and social dynamics (an entirely different affair!), and a materialist base underpins (but is not ultimately determinative of) social change and practice, a point for elaboration in the next chapter.

CHAPTER 8

CONCLUSIONS

> Historically grounded huge comparisons of big structures and large
> processes help establish what must be explained, attach the possible
> explanations to their context in time and space, and sometimes actually
> improve our understanding of those structures and processes.
>
> Tilly 1984: 145

On Meta-Structure and Anthropology

This book has referred throughout to meta-structure, a concept as
difficult to define in abstract as culture itself. It is easier to know it
when you see it. It is there in the cases of Pilgrimage and Household
in ancient Arabia and the Fertile Crescent of the ancient Near East. The
notion of meta-structure as ethnoepochal essence, persistent apart
from change, is no quaint structuralist archaism in a field charged
with theories of cultural change. To be sure, historical-materialist, or
biological-evolutionary, or combined theories are the approaches that
have driven recent archaeological fieldwork and interpretations. In
archaeology at least, structuralism has had its day and has been largely
abandoned for its chronological shortcomings (Leone 1982). But with
case studies in regions like Arabia and Mesopotamia, it is archaeology
itself that affords a perspective on culture not available to ethnographers,
sociologists, or even those historians who remain concerned with
structure and its constraining influence on practice and practical rationalism (Sahlins 1976, 1985, Bourdieu [1980] 1990, Braudel [1966] 1972).

Archaeology's long temporal frame reveals the existence of meta-structure, a phenomenon that, once exposed, has begged for greater anthropological explanation.

Archaeology reveals an unrecognized longevity of structure as meta-structure that endured across the development of complex societies from their simpler beginnings. Explaining this longevity and persistence has required recalibrating existing theory on culture and cultural transmission. Is meta-structure just a longer persistence of structure? There are significant theoretical approaches that identify long-term patterns that frame shorter events. In Bourdieu's "structuring structures," in Giddens' "institutions," in Radcliffe-Brown's (1940: 36) "social institutions," and in Braudel's and Sahlins's "structures" in history are valuable road markers to explain meta-structural persistence. In each case, persistence of structure is the outcome of myriad actions and the consensual rules of ritual. If ritual is simply group performance, then it helps to slow change in structural frameworks through the rules of socially condoned bodily practice. But the study of Pilgrimage and Household shows that practice and frequency of practical repetition alone do not sufficiently explain meta-structure and persistence of meta-structure even as practice changes. I have argued that ethnoepochal meta-structure exists and is a valid object of anthropological inquiry for which archaeology provides a unique view. There are some significant conclusions to be drawn from this argument and new directions for future research.

Meta-Structures and the Archaeological Record

Long-term persistence of meta-structure has been the focus of the most chapters. Chapters 2–4 have employed a combined (what some would call "triangulated" (Kirch and Green 2001: 42)) approach using ethnography, history, ethno-history, archaeology, and language. This multistranded approach shows that the socially constituting metaphor and linked practices of Pilgrimage endured from at least the middle Holocene Arabian Neolithic through the development of complex Arabian kingdoms and the emergence of Islam, a chronological span of at least 5,000 years. Likewise Chapters 5 and 6 demonstrated that Household enjoyed a similarly persistent socially constituting role across the so-called Fertile Crescent of Levantine-Taurus-Mesopotamian agricultural lands. The existence of such long-term continuities pointed to the need to amend existing theories of change, which do not adequately account for, and indeed do not recognize at all, such long-term phenomena.

One outcome of these arguments is to expand and perhaps somewhat shift the focus of culture history away from episodes of great change such as the Neolithic Revolution, the Origins of the State, and the Collapse of Societies. Of course much archaeology in a culture-history tradition already does probe other regional and historical phenomena, largely from a descriptive vantage, with some remarkable exceptions (e.g., Kirch and Green 2001). But anthropological archaeology in the Anglo-American tradition has favored episodes of change rather than long-term structure. This has been the case because materialist and evolutionary approaches view structure (sometimes called "culture") as the consequence and outcome of the forces that drive society (Sahlins 1976) rather than as determinative variables for social change.

The empirical existence of Pilgrimage and Household in early antiquity and the inadequacy of materialist and evolutionary theory to explain meta-structure lay out rich new territory and rationale for new theoretical and practical archaeological research. Patrimonialism as a mode of production in a Webberian historical-materialist sense appeared in the Bronze Age across wide sectors of the Near East and cross-cut pastoral and agricultural societies and numerous cultural and linguistic groups (Schloen 2001: 58). There may indeed be rich clues to changing economic and social conditions in early states through tracking patrimonialism, a distinctive new socioeconomic pattern that enacted a structuring cultural framework of Household. But Household is far older and unchanged: Household as ethnoepoch is archaeologically evident from the Neolithic. Its endurance across change should focus archaeological and anthropological attention on the processes of practice, storage, and retrieval of authoritative resources, and the rituals that bind them together as patterns of continuity. Pilgrimage and Household are not ideologies, a lexical term eschewed here and already deeply embedded in materialist theory with its emphasis on dialectically driven change in economic base and ideological superstructure. Nor are Pilgrimage and Household aptly described by Turner's short-term, processual focus on liminal stages with reversion to normative social order or progress to new society. Instead, the ethnoepochal integrity of Pilgrimage and Household lies outside of change, accessible through practices that can change, and ethnoepoch therefore cannot be subsumed within the plasticity of ideologies. Theories of change simply fail to provide the tools needed to explain meta-structures in the archaeological record

Two Near Eastern Meta-Structures or Many?

What may be needed instead are archaeological data sets that better document meta-structure as prelude to better explanation. How many other Near Eastern meta-structures are there? One must establish what is meant by Near Eastern, for the geographical boundaries of meta-structures are a second challenge for future research. A compelling definition for the ancient Near Eastern region may be drawn from the largely heuristic application of world system theory, the overall merits of which are not to be debated here. Trading relationships between core states and peripheral groups emerged in the Bronze Age to connect cultural groups across Eastern Mediterranean Europe, Western Asia, Northeastern Africa, and the Northwestern portion of the Indian sub-continent (Frank 1993). Because of its connectivity and synchronous declines in complex societies over long temporal cycles, the broader regional scope of the Near East (to include the preceding areas) embraced by world system theory has gained traction as an appropriate regional unit for explaining large processes and structures (Tilly 1984: 60ff., Algaze 1993). Comparable argument has been made for understanding migration and culture history in the Western Pacific, where the inter-connections between islands and island cultural groups play an important role in understanding long-term historical processes within islands (e.g., Kirch and Green 2001, Terrell 1986). Indeed, the widespread Pacific islander notion of an axial *mana* ("power"), *tapu* ("taboo"), and *noa* ("permitted") (Kirch and Green 2001: 239–241) might be usefully explored as meta-structure and could provide an interesting comparative case from an external area. Another might be the Andean *Heads of State* (Arnold and Hastorf 2008). Within the Near Eastern region, other ethno-epochal frameworks for social constitution appear in the archaeological records of Egypt and perhaps also of the Indus Valley.

Aptly called *Body Politic* by David Wengrow (2006: 258), meta-structure in Egypt persisted through the storage and retrieval of authoritative knowledge using bodily treatment, including funerary practice. Social identity and constitution in ancient Egypt was expressed in the metaphor of body, bodily unity, and bodily longevity. In studying the Indus civilizations, archaeologists have suggested an obsession with water, cleansing, and purification in culturally distinct *Wasserluxus* that links the monumental baths and hydraulic public works of Mohenjo-Daro and Harappa with persistent traditions of bathing and purification in contemporary India (Urban and Jansen 1984, Morinis 1984). Without access to a sufficient and decipherable corpus of Indus writings, it may prove impossible to trace or describe Wasserluxus as thoroughly as Pilgrimage and Household: this is certainly a challenge for specialists in the archaeological, literary, and ethnographic traditions of the Asian subcontinent.

The existence of multiple long-lived cultural metaphors for social identity and constitution raises another interesting problem. Giddens (1984: 164) suggests that the interconnections and time-space edges between different societal types are an important arena for new sociological research. Archaeology has much to offer here with long historical dimensions of the interface and encounters between societies socially constituting themselves in the metaphors of Pilgrimage and Household. These too are topics for a future study.

Disciplinarians outside anthropology and social sciences should engage here. The study of time-space edges of Pilgrimage and Household at Nabataean or Palmyrene sites or the archaeologically rich Latin Kingdoms of the medieval era has great potential to shape new field and analytical research orientations. These cultures and periods have long been the near exclusive concern of historians and classicists in culture history, with virtually no attention from anthropological archaeologists. Yet it is the dynamics of Nabataean sedentarization in urban populations along Arabia's western trade routes, or the banqueting Palmyrene Houses around their oasis Bel temple, or the now discredited infamous "clash of civilizations" between Franks and Muslims that furnish appropriate contexts for better understanding meta-structural continuities. In the early centuries before and after the Common Era, some of the mobile (pastoral) groups at the arid margins of farming states settled and expanded oasis life, adopting and adapting material cultural attributes from their neighbors. Nabataean groups strategically improved runoff farming and built urban complexes with religious and social practices resonant of both Household and Pilgrimage. As Arabist Michael Zwettler was fond of saying, "Anthropology is too important to be left to anthropologists."

Nabataeans were not the first groups to experience the interstices of concurrent and confluent ethnoepochs, for the Levantine Eastern Mediterranean lies at the geographical intersection of Egypt, Mesopotamia, and Arabia, and offers richly complex histories for sociological analysis. That these are histories difficult and diffuse to analyze, and which require dedicated studies of their own, should not unduly deter us from the significance of Pilgrimage and Household, nor from the potential of archaeology to grasp cases of ethnoepochal continuity in social constitution.

Meta-Structure and the Neolithic Revolution

The archaeological record first shows us evidence of Pilgrimage and Household in the Neolithic, that is, in the greatly expanded material records of growing populations in the first half of the Holocene. The appearance of meta-structure in the archaeological record raises interesting questions about its origins. Do Pilgrimage and Household really begin when archaeologists can first detect material evidence for them such as monuments, tombs, and house places? How long term are Pilgrimage and Household as socially constituting metaphors? Are they really Neolithic phenomena, and if so, to what new conditions can we attribute their constitution? These are questions that will inevitably re-engage theories of change, but they also are at present without answer and deserve greater attention.

Researchers in cognitive archaeology have argued that there was truly new Neolithic brain function that allowed humans for the first time to engage in symbolic storage and authoritative recall (e.g., Lewis-Williams and Pearce 2005, Renfrew 1998). Certainly we see the earliest material evidence for Pilgrimage and Household with the appearance of Neolithic period commemorative stone monuments and houses. But the archaeological record preserves only a tiny portion even of material culture, leaving us to speculate about more ephemeral aspects of landscape and the interplay of history and materiality using mnemonic devices that may not be preserved. Perhaps Pilgrimage and Household are older than Neolithic, but we cannot as yet tell. As emphasized in Chapters 6 and 7 this project has been primarily concerned with demonstrating meta-structural phenomena and building theoretical explanation for their persistence, not for their origins.

It would be fallacious to fall back reflexively on environmental determinism – pastoralists practice Pilgrimage, sedentary farmers incline to Household. The Levantine Neolithic appears to have been a time of new experimentation in social practice (not all of which persisted), such as the building of wall and tower at Jericho, the cemetery at Kfar HaHoresh, and gatherings at Göbekli Tepe. I have argued throughout that materialism provides no explanation for why meta-structure endures across change in material conditions. It makes no sense to derive meta-structure (as if it were merely a concept consonant with ideology) from changing conditions in a materialist base, such as a Neolithic economic shift from foraging to pastoralism and agriculture, thereafter only to exclude meta-structure from the dynamics of dialectic historical materialism. The problem of ethnoepochal origins seems to me a large one, engaging not only the economic roots of Neolithic societies but also new biological-cognitive processes arising perhaps 10,000 years ago and explaining the subsequent successes of societies constituted with new meta-structural frameworks. There lies ahead an immense challenge in collecting appropriate data to track these new processes and to detect ethnoepochal referents among the impoverished material records of ancient foraging societies.

Meta-Structure and Culture Contact

There are challenges also in understanding the intersocietal contexts in which practical habituation is oriented along new time-space paths. As archaeological and historical evidence unequivocally show, contact between Pilgrimage and Household societies was common, persistent, and patterned, leaving indisputable traces especially in economic traffic of oil and metals, aromatics, dyestuffs, shell, obsidian, ceramics, textiles, bitumen, wood, and stone. Exchange in the ancient world and particularly the notion of cross-cultural exchange has provided an important lens into the ancient relationships and contexts through which goods and materials passed from hand to hand and from one social context to the next. If one accepts from Webber and Polanyi that all exchange prior to market economies was predicated on social relationships (Schloen 2001: 79–80), exchanges imply habituation to Other, whether between Palestinian householders in Canaan and Egyptians extracting olive oil surpluses to Egypt or between Arabian pastoralists and hungry seafaring householders of Ur at Gulf coast winter shanties. In conceptualizing encounters between Pilgrimage and Household societies in the context of exchange, one risks overreliance on a geographical concept that reduces spatio-temporal dynamics to a friction zone between two monolithic physical entities, Arabian Pilgrimage and Northern Household. Such characterization cannot aid in understanding ethnoepoch, its persistence and resilient reformulation as an outcome of practical action and archived authoritative resources embedded in landscape places.

Instead it is the relationships of exchange itself that require further study. Chapter 5 suggests that a rich case study may be found in exchanges between Mesopotamians and Arabians in a Bronze Age world system. These have been richly documented archaeologically throughout the Arabian-Persian Gulf, but discussions have been limited to economic and political contexts without adequately considering the potential of this archaeological record for understanding how social relationships with the Other reinforced ethnoepochal meta-structures of social constitution.

Like Orientalism itself (Said 1979), the process of defining oneself socially in relationships with Other is a discursive one, empowering the Pilgrim through greater authoritative knowledge of Pilgrimage and correct practical enactment of socially sanctioned ritual. The more that Mesopotamians got it wrong, the more it empowered Arabian herder-fishers as the arbiters and negotiators of the social relations along which economic exchanges took place, among Pilgrimage people. From Mesopotamians' perspective, discourse worked in the opposite sense, with Mesopotamians empowered through categorizing Arabians as householders contributing labor and produce to the head of household.

From such a model of the social frameworks of culture contact, one might usefully generate archaeologically testable hypotheses that draw upon material remains of the places of exchange and the commoditization of goods, a project beyond the scope of this book.

Discursive self-definition through the categorization and objectification of Other catches all cross-cultural contact, including the scholarship of anthropologists, historians, classicists, and archaeologists (Said 1979). One of the salient characteristics of scholarship on the Orient has been the intertwining of political agendas of control with knowing the East, an agenda well-served through a pervasive emphasis on stasis. A look at Orientalist art of the nineteenth century provides rich visualization of this heuristic stasis. Biblical Judah (in the painting, "Judah and Tamar" Horace Vernet 1840) is a (modern Muslim) bedouin sheikh; Tamar veils herself in a modern fashion (inherited from Greek-Byzantine dress). "Hagar Banished by Abraham" (Horace Vernet 1837) wears nineteenth-century Palestinian embroidery and carries a Gazan amphora. "The Journey of the Magi" (James Tissot, 1894) shows the wise men on camels decorated with Arabian bedouin silver jewelry. *National Geographic* ran pictures of early twentieth-century Palestinian villages captioned with references to Biblical events, flattening the elapsed twenty centuries as if nothing had changed (even with the introduction of Islam!). Ethnoarchaeologists have struggled to emerge from the shadow of Orientalizing static models of village life and pastoralism and have endured criticism that their approaches cast modern peoples in a backward light. Anthropological archaeology focused on change has made its own Orientalizing contribution. By defining three great changes of relevance to the West (Chapter 1), Childe relegated intervening and especially subsequent periods as less significant local chronicles irrelevant to the larger picture of how Man Makes Himself. Anthropological archaeology has followed a Childean agenda for nearly a century.

Against this backdrop focused on change, orientation toward meta-structure and long-term continuities supplies a new focus on periods and cultural histories ill-served by social sciences. Meta-structure appropriately integrates long periods of Near and Middle Eastern history and pre-history without focus on change. Ethnoepochal continuity makes no comment on stasis as antithesis to change (or discursive backwardness to modernity) but merely points to distinctive and enduring cultural identities meta-structural outside and enveloping materialist categorizations of change and stasis. Far from being another Orientalist essentializing, the definition of meta-structure in the Near East holds a reflective mirror to other regions and civilizations. What are ethnoepochal frameworks for social constitution elsewhere and how are they referenced? What is meta-structural in today's world?

Pilgrimage and the People of 'Ād

Mobile people leave few material traces behind them, but the stories they tell endure for many generations. Not far from the Kheshiya Cattle Skull Ring are a series of linear monuments arranged on low terraces overlooking the (once) waters around Khuzmūm. Long an enigma to archaeologists, these distinctive "trilith" monuments (De Cardi, Doe and Roskams 1977) consist of repetitions of three uprights arranged in tripods along low gravel platforms parallel to a row of meat-grilling hearths. The curious have asked the locals for centuries about the function of these highly patterned monuments, and for the past 800 years, the answer has been pretty much the same.

To Yūsuf Ibn al-Mujawir detouring from Meccan pilgrimage in the late 1200s, local people explained that God had sent plagues of biting ants upon the (pre-Islamic) people of 'Ād, who had built the monuments so that they could sit off the ground and built fires to keep away the ants (Ibn Al-Mujawir [1204/5–1291/2] 1986: 258–260). The answer resonates with Qur'ānic stories of the Prophet Hūd, who enjoined the people of 'Ād to recognize one true God and whose tomb lies in the region. Illiterate bedouin today, who neither recite nor read Qur'ān nor Ibn al-Mujawir's medieval travelogue, tell pretty much the same story, as do literate residents of nearby Dhufār province (Oman).

Eight hundred years is a long time to tell the same story about a people long gone and their ways antithetical to modern Islam. It is surely possible that the recitation of Qur'ānic stories reinforces the account. But there is another explanation, equally embedded in oral tradition. The linguistic terms for components of triliths point to an even older practice of social constitution through Pilgrimage – gathering, sacrifice, and feast,

54. Trilith or *āthāfī* monument in Wadi Sana constructed by Iron Age people to commemorate a social gathering. The remains of hearths (foreground, right) often yield datable charcoal fragments. Uprights set into low gravel platforms occur in sets of 1 and 3. Author's photo.

commemorative monument-building, and authoritative memory. In an analysis of the archaeological, ethnographic, and linguistic evidence, 'Abdalazīz Bin 'Aqīl and I found a correspondence between the physical elements of triliths and traditional linguistic terms for components of non-kin-based groupings of people whose social constitution has not caught the attention of anthropologists focused on tribes (segmentary lineage systems). We concluded that

> symbolic and semantic conflation of terminology for cooking fire, three stones, gathering of people, a group section, and permanent occupation suggests a connotation of territorial rights. Building a trilith monument may have symbolically built a social identity for people who came together to do so, an identity not specifically linked to kinship ties but to territory and community. The construction of and additions to triliths, or reuse of the associated hearths may have both constructed a group identity and served as symbols of communal territorial rights that could be read by mobile pastoralists and caravaneers moving through an area only seasonally occupied. (Bin 'Aqil and McCorriston 2009: 609)

55. Detail of a trilith-*āthāfī* showing ubiquitous arrangement of hearths (foreground), four stone blocks (middle), and uprights (rear) repeated in parallel alignments. Photo by ʿAbdalazīz Bin ʿAqīl.

Gathering, sacrifice, and feast, the elements of Pilgrimage, are all present in trilith building.

Pilgrimage has lasted a long time in Southern Arabia, oriented upon the commemorative monuments of communal gatherings and sustained through practical and authoritative knowledge. From Kheshiya's Cattle Skull Ring and commemorative stone monument through the tombs of eponymous and ultimately mythic ancestors, the signaling of territorial rights through trilith building, the appropriation of tribal pilgrimages to the federal gods of Iron Age kingdoms, and at today's Islamic shrines, Pilgrimage has been persistently pivotal. As one of many ethnoepochal meta-structures for social constitution, it has endured across long time frames and across tremendous social, economic, and ideological changes in the ancient Near East.

REFERENCES

Adams, Robert McC. 1981 *Heartland of Cities: Surveys of Ancient Settlement and Land Use on the Central Floodplain of the Euphrates*. Chicago: University of Chicago Press.

1965 *Land Behind Baghdad: A History of Settlement on the Diyala Plains*. Chicago: University of Chicago Press.

Adams, Robert McC. and Hans J. Nissen 1972 *The Uruk Countryside*. Chicago: University of Chicago Press.

Adams, Ron L. 2005 Ethnoarchaeology in Indonesia Illuminating the Ancient Past at Çatalhöyük? *American Antiquity* 70: 181–188.

Akkermans, Peter P. M. G. and Glenn M. Schwartz 2003 *The Archaeology of Syria*. Cambridge: Cambridge University Press.

Alatas, Syed Farid 1997. Hadramaut and the Hadhrami Diaspora. Pp. 19–34 in Ulrike Freitag and W. Clarence-Smith, eds., *Hadhrami Traders, Scholars, and Statesmen in the Indian Ocean, 1750s–1960s*. London: E. J. Brill.

Alcock, Susan E., John F. Cherry and Jack L. Davis. 1994 Intensive Survey, Agricultural Practice and the Classical Landscape of Greece. Pp. 137–170 in Ian Morris, ed., *Classical Greece: Ancient Histories and Modern Archaeologies*. Cambridge: Cambridge University Press.

Algaze, Guillermo 2008 *Ancient Mesopotamia at the Dawn of Civilization: The Evolution of an Urban Landscape*. Chicago: University of Chicago Press.

2005 The Sumerian Takeoff. Structure and Dynamics 1: http://repositories. cdlib.org/imbs/socdyn/sdeas/vol1/iss1/art2/.

1993 *The Uruk World System*. Chicago: University of Chicago Press.

Al-Hamdānī, Ḥasan ibn Aḥmad (d. 945) 1989 *Ṣifat Jazīrat al-ʿArab / taʾlīf al-Ḥasan ibn Aḥmad ibn Yaʿqūb al-Hamdānī; taḥqīq Muḥammad ibn ʿAlī al-Akwaʿ*. Baghdād: Ministry of Culture and Sciences, Dār al-Shuʾūn al-Thaqāfīyah al-ʿĀmmah "Āfāq ʿArabīyah" (in Arabic).

1986 *Kitab Al-Iklil*. (1st and 2nd parts). Beirut. (in Arabic).

Al-Masʿūdī, Abī al-Ḥasan ʿAlī ibn al-Ḥusayn ibn ʿAlī (d. 956?) 1965 *Kitāb al-tanbīh wa-al-ishrāf, li-Abī al-Ḥasan ʿAlī ibn al-Ḥusayn ibn ʿAlī al-Masʿūdī*. Beirut: Maktabat Khayyāt.

Al-Ṣabbān, 'Abd al-Qādir Muḥammad 1998 *Visits and Customs: The Visit to the Tomb of the Prophet Hud* [trans. Linda Boxberger and Awad Abdelrahim Abu Hulayqa]. Ardmore, PA: American Institute for Yemeni Studies.

Al-Ṭabarī, Abu Ja'far Muhammad bin Jarir (d. 819) 1987 *The Commentary on the Qur'an (Jāmi' al-bayān 'an ta'wīl āy al-Qur'ān)* [trans. J. Cooper]. Oxford: Oxford University Press.

1879–1901 *Tā'rīkh al-rusul wa al-mulūk.* M. J. de Goetje et al., eds., Leiden: E. J. Brill.

Al-Ṭabarī, Aḥmad ibn 'Abd Allāh (1218–1295) 1970 *Al-Qirā li-qāsid Umm al-Qurā.* Muṣṭafā al-Saqqā, ed., Cairo: Muṣṭafā al-Bābī al-Ḥalabī.

Alvard, M. S. and L. Kuznar 2001 Deferred Harvests: The Transition from Hunting to Animal Husbandry. *American Anthropologist* 103: 295–311.

Ammerman, Albert J. and L. Luca Cavalli-Sforza 1984 *The Neolithic Transition and the Genetics of Populations in Europe.* Princeton, NJ: Princeton University Press.

Anati, Emmanuel 1974 *Rock-Art in Central Arabia. Volume 4. Corpus of the Rock Engravings III and IV.* Publications de l'Institut Orientaliste de Louvain 6, Expédition Philby-Ryckmans-Lippens en Arabie. Louvain-la-Neuve: Université Catholique de Louvain.

1972 *Rock-Art in Central Arabia. Volume 3. Corpus of the Rock Engravings I and II.* Publications de l'Institut Orientaliste de Louvain 4, Expédition Philby-Ryckmans-Lippens en Arabie. Louvain-la-Neuve: Université Catholique de Louvain.

Andom, G. and M. K. Omer 2003 Traditional Cattle-Husbandry Systems in Eritrea: Cattle-Man Relationships. *Journal of Arid Environments* 53: 545–556.

Anschuetz, Kurt F., Richard H. Wilshusen and Cherie Scheick 2001 An Archaeology of Landscapes: Perspectives and Directions. *Journal of Archaeological Research* 9: 157–211.

Appadurai, Arjun 1991 Global Ethnoscapes: Notes and Queries for Transnational Anthropology. Pp. 191–210 in Richard Fox, ed., *Recapturing Anthropology: Working in the Present.* Santa Fe: School of American Research Press.

Applegate, Alex, Achilles Gautier and Steven Duncan 2001 The North Tumuli of the Nabta Late Neolithic Ceremonial Complex. Pp. 468–488 in Fred Wendorf, Romuald Schild and Associates, *Holocene Settlement of the Egyptian Sahara. Volume 1. The Archaeology of Nabta Playa.* New York: Kluwer Academic/Plenum Publishers.

Archi, A. 1985 The Archives of Palace G. Pp. 187–204 in H. Weiss, ed., *Ebla to Damascus: Art and Archaeology of Ancient Syria: An Exhibition from the Directorate General of Antiquities and Museums, Syrian Arab Republic.* Washington, DC: Smithsonian Institution Traveling Exhibition Service.

Arnold, Denise Y. and Christine A. Hastorf 2008 *Heads of State: Icons, Power and Politics in the Ancient and Modern Andes.* Walnut Creek, CA: Walnut Press.

Aschmann, Homer and Ernst Bahre 1977 Man's Impact on the Wild Landscape. Pp. 78–86 in Harold A. Mooney, ed., *Convergent Evolution in Chile and California: Mediterranean Climate Ecosystems.* Stroudsburg, PA: Dowden, Hutchinson and Ross.

Ashmore, Wendy 1989 Construction and Cosmology: Politics and Ideology in Lowland Maya Setlement Patterns. Pp. 272–286 in W. F. Hanks and D. S. Rice, eds., *Word and Image in Maya Culture: Explorations in Language, Writing, and Representation*. Salt Lake City: University of Utah Press.

Asouti, Eleni 2006 Beyond the Pre-Pottery Neolithic B Interaction Sphere. *Journal of World Prehistory* 20: 87–126.

Astruc, Laurence, Frédéric Abbès, Juan Jose Ibáñez Estévez and Jesús González Urquijo 2003 "Dépots," "réserves" et "caches" de materiel lithique taillé au Néolithique précéramique au Proche-Orient: quelle gestion de l'outillage? *Paléorient* 29(1): 59–78.

Atalay, Sonya and Christine A. Hastorf 2006 Food, Meals, and Daily Activities: Food Habitus at Neolithic Çatalhöyük. *American Antiquity* 71 (2): 283–319.

Atallah, Wahib 1969 *Les Idoles de Hicham Ibn Al-Kalbi [d. 819]*. Paris: Librairie C. Klincksieck.

Aurenche, Olivier 1981 *La Maison Orientale. L'Architecture du Proche Orient Ancien des Origines au Milieu du Quatrième Millénaire*. Paris: Librarien Orientaliste Paul Geuthner.

Avanzini, Alessandra 2006 Ancient South Arabian Anthroponomastics: Historical Remarks. *Proceedings of the Seminar for Arabian Studies* 36: 70–85.

1991 Remarques sur le "matriarcat" en Arabie du Sud. Pp. 157–166 in Christian Robin, ed., *L'Arabie antique de Karib'îl à Mahomet*. La Revue du Monde Musulman et de la Méditerranée 61. Aix-en-Provence: Éditions Édisud.

Avner, Uzi 1998 Settlement, Agriculture, and Paleoclimate in 'Uvda Valley, Southern Negev Desert, 6th–3rd Millennia BC. Pp. 147–202 in Arie S. Issar and Neville Brown, eds., *Water Environment and Society in Times of Climate Change*. Dordrecht: Kluwer Academic.

Badre, Leila 1991 Le Sondage stratigraphique de Shabwa 1976–1981. *Syria* 68: 229–314.

Bagby, Philip 1959 *Culture and History*. Berkeley: University of California Press.

Balfour-Paul, Jenny 1997 *Indigo in the Arab World*. London: Curzon Press.

Balter, Michael 2007 Seeking Agriculture's Ancient Roots. *Science* 316: 1830–1835.

Banning, Edward B. in press So Fair a House: Göbekli Tepe and the Identification of Temples in the Pre-Pottery Neolithic of the Near East. *Current Anthropology* 52.

2003 Housing Neolithic Farmers. *Near Eastern Archaeology* 66 (1–2): 4–21.

1998 The Neolithic Period: Triumphs of Architecture, Agriculture, and Art. *Near Eastern Archaeology* 61: 188–217.

1996a Highlands and Lowlands: Problems and Survey Frameworks for Rural Archaeology in the Near East. *Bulletin of the American Schools of Oriental Research* 301: 25–46.

1996b Peasants, Pastoralists, and Pax Romana: Mutualism in the Southern Highlands of Jordan. *Bulletin of the American Schools of Oriental Research* 261: 25–50.

Banning, Edward B. and Brian Byrd 1987 Houses and the Changing Residential Unit: Domestic Architecture at PPNB 'Ain Ghazal, Jordan. *Proceedings of the Prehistoric Society* 53: 309–325.

Barbir, K. 1980 *Ottoman Rule in Damascus, 1708–1758*. Princeton, NJ: Princeton University Press.

Barker, Graeme 1991 Two Italys, One Valley: An Annaliste Perspective. Pp. 34–56. In J. Bintliff, ed., *The Annales School and Archaeology*. New York: New York University Press.

Barrett, J. C. 1988 The Living, the Dead, and the Ancestors: Neolithic and Early Bronze Age Mortuary Practices. Pp. 30–41 in J. C. Barrett and I. A. Kinnes, eds., *The Archaeology of Context in the Neolithic and Bronze Age*. Sheffield: Department of Archaeology and Prehistory, University of Sheffield.

Basso, Keith H. 1996 Wisdom Sits in Places. Pp. 53–79 in S. Feld and Keith H. Basso, eds., *Senses of Place*. Santa Fe: School of American Research Press.

Bar-Yosef, Ofer 2002 The Natufian Culture and the Early Neolithic: Social and Economic Trends in Southwest Asia. Pp. 113–126 in Peter Bellwood and Colin Renfrew, eds., *Examining the Farming/Language Dispersal Hypothesis*. Cambridge: McDonald Institute for Archaeological Research.

1995 The Role of Climate in the Interpretations of Human Movements and Cultural Transformations in Western Asia. Pp. 507–523 in Elisabeth S. Vrba, George H. Denton, Timothy C. Partridge and Lloyd H. Burckle, eds., *Paleoclimate and Evolution, with Emphasis on Human Origins*. New Haven, CT: Yale University Press.

1986 The Walls of Jericho: An Alternative Interpretation. *Current Anthropology* 27: 157–162.

Bar-Yosef, Ofer and D. Alon 1988 Excavations in the Nahal Hemar Cave. *Atiqot* 18: 1–30.

Bar-Yosef, Ofer and Daniella E. Bar-Yosef Mayer 2002 Early Neolithic Tribes in the Levant. Pp. 340–371 in William A. Parkinson, ed., *The Archaeology of Tribal Societies*. Ann Arbor: International Monographs in Prehistory.

Bar-Yosef, Ofer and Anna Belfer-Cohen 1992 From Foraging to Farming in the Mediterranean Levant. Pp. 21–48 in Anne B. Gebauer and T. Douglas Price, eds., *Transitions to Agriculture in Prehistory*. Monographs in World Archaeology 4. Madison: Prehistory Press.

1989 The Origins of Sedentism and Farming Communities in the Levant. *Journal of World Prehistory* 3: 447–498.

Bar-Yosef, Ofer and Richard Meadow 1995 The Origins of Agriculture in the Near East. Pp. 39–94 in T. Douglas Price and Anne Gebauer, eds., *Last Hunters First Farmers*. Santa Fe: School of American Research Press.

Beck, Robin A. Jr., Douglas J. Bolender, James A. Brown and Timothy K. Earle 2007 Eventful Archaeology: The Place of Space in Structural Transformation. *Current Anthropology* 48: 833–860.

Beech, Mark and Elizabeth Shepherd 2001 Archaeobotanical Evidence for Early Date Consumption on Dalma Island, United Arab Emirates. *Antiquity* 75: 83–89.

Beeston, A. F. L. 1984 The Religions of Pre-Islamic Yemen. Pp. 260–261 in Joseph Chelhod, ed., *L'Arabie du Sud: histoire et civilization: I. Le people Yemenite et ses racines*. Paris: G-P Maisonneuve et Larose.

1979 Some Features of Social Structure in Saba. Pp. 115–123 in Abdelgadir Mahmoud Abdalla, Sami Al- Sakkar and Richard T. Mortel, eds., *Studies in the History of Arabia. Volume 1, Part 1*. Riyadh: University of Riyadh.

1972 Kingship in Ancient South Arabia. *Journal of the Economic and Social History of the Orient* 15: 256–268.

Beld, Scott 2002 *The Queen of Lagash: Ritual Economy in a Sumerian State*. Ph.D. dissertation, University of Michigan. Ann Arbor: University Microfilms.

Belfer-Cohen, Anna and Nigel Goring-Morris 2005 Comment: Which Way to Look: Conceptual Frameworks for Understanding Neolithic Processes. *Neolithics* 2(5): 22–24.

Bell, Catherine 1992 *Ritual Theory, Ritual Practice*. Oxford: Oxford University Press.

Bell, Gertrude 2001 [1907] *The Desert and the Sown*. New York: Cooper Square Press.

Bell, Richard 1926 *The Origins of Islam in Its Christian Environment*. London: Macmillan.

Bellwood, Peter 2005 *First Farmers: The Origins of Agricultural Societies*. Malden, MA: Blackwell.

Bellwood, Peter and Colin Renfrew, eds. 2002 *Examining the Farming/Language Dispersal Hypothesis*. Cambridge: McDonald Institute Monographs.

Bender, Barbara, ed. 1993 *Landscape: Politics and Perspectives*. Oxford: Berg.

Benoit, Anne, Olivier Lavigne, Michel Mouton and Jeremy Schiettecatte 2007 Chronologie et evolution de l'architecture à Makaynūn: la formation d'un centre urbain à l'époque sudarabique dans le Hadramawt. *Proceedings of the Seminar for Arabian Studies* 37: 17–35.

Bent, Theodore and Mrs. Theodore Bent [1990] 1994 *Southern Arabia*. London: Smith, Elder and Co. (republished by Garnet Press).

Bernbeck, Reinhard 1995 Lasting Alliances and Emerging Competition: Economic Developments in Early Mesopotamia. *Journal of Anthropological Archaeology* 14: 1–25.

Betts, Alison, K. van der Borg, A. de Jong, C. McClintock and M. van Strydonck 1994 Early Cotton in North Arabia. *Journal of Archaeological Science* 21: 489–499.

Bhardwaj, Surinder 1973 *Hindu Places of Pilgrimage in India: A Study in Cultural Geography*. Berkeley: University of California Press.

Bienert, Hans-Dieter and Hans Georg K. Gebel 2004 Summary on Ba'ja 1997, and Insights from the Later Seasons. Pp. 119–144 in Hans-Dieter Bienert and Hans Georg K. Gebel, eds., *Central Settlements in Neolithic Jordan. Studies in Early Near Eastern Production, Subsistence, and Environment 5*. Berlin: ex oriente.

Bienert, Hans-Dieter, Michele Bonogofsky, Hans Georg K. Gebel, Ian Kuijt and Gary Rollefson 2004 Where Are the Dead? Pp. 157–175 in Hans-Dieter Bienert and Hans Georg K. Gebel, eds., *Central Settlements in Neolithic Jordan*.

Studies in Early Near Eastern Production, Subsistence, and Environment 5. Berlin: ex oriente.

Bin ʿAqīl, ʿAbdalaziz Jaʿfar [no date] Report to the World Bank on Social Stratification in Hadramawt. Working papers for the World Bank Social Project in Hadramawt.

Bin ʿAqīl, ʿAbdalaziz Jaʿfar and Joy McCorriston 2009 Convergences in the Ethnography, Semantics, and Archaeology of Prehistoric Small Scale Monument Types in Hadramawt (Southern Arabia). *Antiquity* 83: 602–618.

Bin ʿAqīl, ʿAbdalrahman Jaʿfar 2004 *Qanīsun al-Waclun fī Ḥaḍramawt*. Ṣanāʾa: ʿĀṣmah al-Thaqāfih al-ʿArabiyah.

Binford, Lewis R. 1967 Smudge Pits and Hide Smoking: The Use of Analogy in Archaeological Reasoning. *American Antiquity* 32: 1–12.

Bittel, Kurt 1980 The German Perspective and the German Archaeological Institute. *American Journal of Archaeology* 84: 271–277.

Bloch, Maurice 1989 *Ritual, History and Power: Selected Papers in Anthropology*. London: Aldine.

   1977 The Past in the Present and the Past. *Man* (n.s.) 12: 278–292.

   1971 *Placing the Dead: Tombs, Ancestral Villages and Kinship Organisation in Madagascar*. London: Seminar Press.

Bogaard, Amy, Michael Charles, Katheryn C. Twiss, Andrew Fairbairn, Nurcan Yalman, Dragana Filipović, G. Atzu Demirergi, Fürsun Ertuğ, Nerissa Russell and Jennifer Nenecke 2009 Private Pantries and Celebrated Surplus: Storing and Sharing Food at Neolithic Çatalhöyük, Central Anatolia. *Antiquity* 83: 649–668.

Boivin, Nicole 2004 Landscape and Cosmology in the South Indian Neolithic: New Perspectives on the Deccan Ashmounds. *Cambridge Archaeological Journal* 14: 235–257.

Bourdieu, Pierre [1980] 1990 *The Logic of Practice* [trans. Richard Nice]. Stanford, CA: Stanford University Press.

   [1972] 1977 *Outline of a Theory of Practice* [trans. Richard Nice]. Cambridge: Cambridge University Press.

Bowman, Glenn 1992 Pilgrim Narratives of Jerusalem and the Holy Land: A Study in Ideological Distortion. Pp. 149–163 in Alan Morinis, ed., *Sacred Journeys. The Anthropology of Pilgrimage*. Westport, CT: Greenwood Press.

Boyd, Brian 2005 Comment: Some Comments on Archaeology and Ritual. *Neolithics* 2(5): 25–27.

Boyd, Robert and Peter J. Richerson 1985 *Culture and the Evolutionary Process*. Chicago: University of Chicago Press.

Boyer, Pascal 2001 *Religion Explained: The Evolutionary Origins of Religious Thought*. New York: Basic Books.

Bradley, Richard 2006 Danish Razors and Swedish Rocks: Cosmology and the Bronze Age Landscape. *Antiquity* 80: 372–389.

   1993 *Altering the Earth*. Edinburgh: Society of Antiquaries of Scotland Monograph series no. 8.

   1985 Consumption, Change, and the Archaeological Record. The Archaeology of Monuments and The Archaeology of Deliberate Deposits. Two Munro

Lectures given in the University of Edinburgh. University of Edinburgh Department of Archaeology Occasional Paper 13.

Braemer, F., S. Cleuziou and T. Steimer 2003 Dolmen-like Structures: Some Unusual Funerary Monuments in Yemen. *Proceedings of the Seminar for Arabian Studies* 33: 169–182.

Braemer, F., Steimer-Herbet, T., L. Buchet, J. F. Saliege and H. Guy 2001 Le Bronze ancien du Ramlat as Sabatayn (Yémen): Deux nécropoles de la première moitié du IIIème millénaire à la bordure du désert: Jebel Jidran et Jebel Ruwiq. *Paléorient* 27(1): 21–44.

Brandt, Steven A. and Kathryn Weedman 2002 Woman the Toolmaker. *Archaeology* 55(5): 50–53.

Braudel, Ferdinand [1966] 1972 *The Mediterranean and the Mediterranean World in the Age of Philip II*. New York: Harper Collins [English translation of second revised edition].

Breton, J. F. 1999 *Arabia Felix from the Time of the Queen of Sheba, Eighth Century BC to First Century AD*. Notre Dame IN: University of Notre Dame Press.

1979 Le Temple de Syn D-Hlsm a Ba-Qutfah. *Raydan* 2: 1–18.

Brown, James 1995 On mortuary analysis – with special reference to the Saxe-Binford research program. Pp. 3–26 in Lane Beck, ed., *Regional Approaches to Mortuary Analysis*. New York: Plenum Press.

Brown, W. L. and A. F. L. Beeston 1954 Sculptures and Inscriptions from Shabwa. *Journal of the Royal Asiatic Society of Great Britain and Ireland* 1954: 43–62.

Brunner, Ueli 1997a The History of Irrigation in the Wadi Marhah. *Proceedings of the Seminar for Arabian Studies* 27: 75–86.

1997b Geography and Human Settlements in Ancient Southern Arabia. *Arabian Archaeology and Epigraphy* 8: 190–202.

Brunner, Ueli and H. Haefner 1986 The Successful Floodwater Farming System of the Sabaeans: Yemen Arab Republic. *Applied Geography* 6: 77–86.

Bujra, Abdulla S. 1971 The Politics of Stratification. *A Study of Political Change in a South Arabian Town*. Oxford: Clarendon Press.

Burkert, Walter [1972] 1983 Homo necans. *The Anthropology of Ancient Greek Sacrificial Ritual and Myth* [trans. Peter Bing]. Berkeley: University of California Press.

Burns, Ross 2005 *Damascus: A History*. London: Routledge.

Burton, Richard F. 1964 *Personal Narrative of a Pilgrimage to al-Madinah and Meccah, by Sir Richard F. Burton* [edited by his wife, Isabel Burton]. New York: Dover Publications.

Butzer, Karl A. 1996 Ecology in the Long View: Settlement Histories, Agrosystemic Strategies, and Ecological Performance. *Journal of Field Archaeology* 23: 141–150.

1982 *Archaeology as Human Ecology*. Cambridge: Cambridge University Press.

Byrd, Brian F. 2005a Reassessing the Emergence of Village Life in the Near East. *Journal of Archaeological Research* 13(3): 231–290.

2005b *Early Village Life at Beidha, Jordan: Neolithic Spatial Organization and Vernacular Architecture*. Oxford: British Academy Monographs in Archaeology published by Oxford University Press.

1994 Public and Private, Domestic and Corporate: The Emergence of the Southwest Asian Village. *American Antiquity* 59: 639–666.

Campbell, Stuart and Anthony Green, eds., 1995 *The Archaeology of Death in the Ancient Near East*. Oxford: Oxbow Books.

Caneva, Isabelle, ed., 1998 *El Geili. The History of a Middle Nile Environment*. 7000 BC–AD 1500. Oxford: British Archaeological Reports: International Series 424.

Carsten, Janet and Stephen Hugh-Jones, ed., 1995 About the House. *Lévi-Strauss and Beyond*. Cambridge: Cambridge University Press.

Carter, Elizabeth and Andrea Parker, 1995 Pots, People and the Archaeology of Death in Northern Syria and Southern Anatolia in the Latter Half of the Third Millennium BC. Pp. 96–116 in Stuart Campbell and Anthony Green, eds., *The Archaeology of Death in the Ancient Near East*. Oxford: Oxbow Books.

Caskel, Werner [1954] 1998 The Bedouinization of Arabia. Pp. 34–44 in F. E. Peters, ed., *The Arabs and Arabia on the Eve of Islam*. Aldershot, UK: Ashgate. [Reprinted from *American Anthropologist* 56(2), Pt. 2, Memoir no. 76: 36–46.]

Castel, Corinne and Edgar Peltenburg 2007 Urbanism on the Margins: Third Millennium BC al-Rawda in the Arid Zone of Syria. *Antiquity* 81: 601–616.

Caton, Steven 1990 Anthropological Theories of Tribe and State Formation in the Middle East: Ideology and the Semiotics of Power. Pp. 74–108 in Philip S. Khoury and Joseph Kostiner, eds., *Tribes and State Formation in the Middle East*. Berkeley: University of California Press.

Cattani, Maurizio and Sandor Bökönyi 2002 Ash-Shumah. An Early Holocene Settlement of Desert Hunters and Mangrove Foragers in the Yemen Tihama. Pp. 31–54 in Serge Cleuziou, Maurizio Tosi and Juris Zarins, eds., *Essays on the Late Prehistory of the Arabian Peninsula*. Roma: Serie Orientale Roma 93, Istituto Italiano per L'Africa e L'Oriente.

Cauvin, Jacques 2001 Ideology before Economy. Review Feature: The Birth of the Gods and the Origins of Agriculture by Jacques Cauvin [trans. Trevor Watkins]. *Cambridge Archaeological Journal* 11(1): 106–107.

2000 *The Birth of the Gods and the Origins of Agriculture* [trans. Trevor Watkins]. Cambridge: Cambridge University Press.

1994 *Naissance des divinités, naissance de l'agriculture: la revolution des symboles au Néolithique*. Paris: CNRS publications.

1979 Les fouilles de Mureybet (1971–1974) et leur signification pour les origines de la sedentarisation au Proche-Orient. Pp. 19–48 in Noel Freedman, ed., *Archaeological Reports from the Tabqa Dam Project Euphrates Valley, Syria*. Boston: Annual of the American Schools of Oriental Research, 44.

Cavalli-Sforza, L. Luca and Francesco Cavalli-Sforza 1995 *The Great Human Diasporas: The History of Diversity and Evolution* [trans. Sarah Thorne]. Reading, MA: Addison Wesley.

Çelik, Bahattin 2006 A New Pre-Pottery Neolithic Site in Southeastern Turkey: Sefer Tepe. *Neolithics* 1(6): 23–25.

Chaix, Louis 1988 Le monde animal à Kerma (Soudan). *Sahara* 1: 77–84.

Charles, M. and A. Bogaard 2002 Chapter 12. Third Millennium BC Charred Plant Remains from Tell Brak. Pp. 301–326 in D. Oates, J. Oates and H. McDonald, eds., *Excavations at Tell Brak. Volume 2. Nagar in the Third Millennium BC*. McDonald Institute Monographs and British School of Archaeology in Iraq. Cambridge: McDonald Institute of Archaeology.

Charpin, Dominique 2004 Teil 1. Histoire Politique du Proche-Orient Amorrite (2002–1595). Pp. 25–484 in Dominique Charpin, Dietz Otto Edzard and Marten Stol, eds., *Mesopotamien: Die altbabylonische Zeit. Orbis Biblicus et Orientalis 160/4*. Fribourg and Göttingen: Academic Press Fribourg/ Vandenhoeck and Ruprecht Göttingen.

Chaucer, Geoffrey [1340–1400] 1977 *The Canterbury Tales* [trans. Nevill Coghill]. London: Alan Lane.

Chelhod, Joseph, ed., 1984 Problemes d'anthropologie culturelle sud-arabe. Pp. 21–54 in Joseph Chelhod, ed., *L'Arabie du Sud: histoire et civilization: I. Le people Yémenite et ses racines*. Paris: G-P Maisonneuve et Larose.

1958 *Introduction à la sociologie de l'Islam*. Paris: G-P Maisonneuve.

1955 *Le Sacrifice Chez les Arabes*. Paris: Presses Universitaires de France.

Cherry, John 1978 Generalisation and the Archaeology of the State. Pp. 411–437 in D. Green, C. Haselgrove and M. Spriggs, eds., *Social Organisation and Settlement*. Oxford: British Archaeological Reports International Series 47.

Cherry, John F., Jack L. Davis and E. Mantzourani 1991 *Landscape Archaeology as Long-Term History: Northern Keos in the Cycladic Islands from Earliest Settlement until Modern Times*. Monumenta Archaeologica 16. Los Angeles: UCLA Institute of Archaeology.

Cherry, John F., Jack L. Davis, A. Demitrack, E. Mantzourani, T. F. Strasser and L. E. Talalay 1988 Archaeological Survey in an Artifact-rich Landscape: A Middle Neolithic Example from Nemea, Greece. *American Journal of Archaeology* 92: 159–176.

Childe, V. Gordon [1942] 1950 *What Happened in History*. Hammondsworth: Penguin Books.

[1936] 1951 *Man Makes Himself*. New York: Mentor Books.

Cleuziou, Serge 2003 Early Bronze Age Trade in the Gulf and the Arabian Sea: The Society behind the Boats. Pp. 13–33 in D. T. Potts, H. Al-Haboodah and P. Hellyer, eds. *Archaeology of the United Arab Emirates*. London: Trident Press.

2001 Presence et mise en scene des morts a l'usage des vivants dans les communautes protohistoriques: L'example de la péninsule d'Oman à l'âge du bronze ancien. Pp. 11–30 in M. Molines and A. Zifferno, eds., *I primi popoli d'Europa*. Forli: Abaco.

1997 Construire et proteger son terroir: Les oasis d'Oman à l'âge du bronze. Pp. 389–412 in J. P. Bravard, T. Bernouf and C. Chouquer, eds., *La Dynamiqe des Paysages Protohistoriques, Antiques, Médiévaux et Modernes*. Antibes: ADPCA.

Cleuziou, Serge and Maurizio Tosi 2000 Ra's al–Jinz and the Prehistoric Coastal Cultures of the Ja'alan. *Journal of Oman Studies* 11: 19–73.

1997 Hommes, climates, et environments de la Péninsule arabique à l'Holocène. *Paléorient* 23: 121–136.

1994 Black Boats of Magan: Some Thoughts on Bronze Age Water Transport in Oman and Beyond from the Impressed Bitumen Slabs from Ra's al Junayz. Pp. 745–760 in A. Parpola and P. Koskikallio, eds., *South Asian Archaeology 1993. Volume 2.* Helsinki: AASF Series B 271.

Cleuziou, Serge, Marie-Louise Inizan and Bruno Marcolongo 1992 Le Peuplement pré et protohistorique du système fluviatile fossile du Jawf-Hadramaut au Yémen. *Paléorient* 18: 5–29.

Close, Angela and Fred Wendorf 2001 Site E-77-7 Revisited: The Early Neolithic of El Adam Type at El Gebel El Beid Playa. Pp 57–70 in Fred Wendorf, Romuald Schild and Associates, eds., *Holocene Settlement of the Egyptian Sahara. Volume 1. The Archaeology of Nabta Playa.* New York: Kluwer Academic/Plenum Publishers.

1992 The Beginnings of Food Production in the Eastern Sahara. Pp. 63–72 in Anne B. Gebauer and Douglas T. Price, eds., *Transitions to Agriculture in Prehistory.* Madison, WI: Prehistory Press.

Cohen, Erik 1992 Pilgrimage and Tourism: Convergence and Divergence. Pp. 47–61 in Alan Morinis, ed., *Sacred Journeys. The Anthropology of Pilgrimage.* Westport, CT: Greenwood Press.

Coleman, Simon and John Eade 2004 Introduction. Pp. 1–25 in Simon Coleman and John Eade, eds., *Reframing Pilgrimage: Cultures in Motion.* London: Routledge.

Colledge, Susan 2003 Chapter 11. Plants and People. Pp. 389–416 in R. Matthews, ed., *Excavations at Tell Brak. Volume 4. Exploring an Upper Mesopotamian Regional Centre, 1994–1996,* McDonald Institute Monographs and British School of Archaeology in Iraq. Cambridge: McDonald Institute of Archaeology.

Connerton, Paul 1989 *How Societies Remember.* Cambridge: Cambridge University Press.

Cosgrove, D. E. 1984 *Social Formation and Symbolic Landscape.* London: Croon Helm.

Coupland, Gary and Edward B. Banning 1996 *People Who Lived in Big Houses: Archaeological Perspective on Large Domestic Structures.* Madison, WI: Prehistory Press.

Crassard, Rémy 2008 La préhistoire du Yémen. *Diffusions et diversités locales, á travers l'étude d'industries lithiques du Hadramawt.* BAR International Series 1842. Oxford: Archaeopress.

Crassard, Rémy, Joy McCorriston, Eric Oches, 'Abdalaziz Bin 'Aqil, Julien Espagne and Mohammed Sinnah 2006 Manayzah, early to mid-Holocene Occupations in Wadi Sana (Hadramawt, Yemen). *Proceedings of the Seminar for Arabian Studies* 36: 151–173.

Cremaschi, Mauro and Fabio Negrino 2005 Evidence for an Abrupt Climatic Change at 8700 14C yr B.P. in Rockshelters and Caves of Gebel Qara (Dhofar-Oman): Palaeoenvironmental Implications. *Geoarchaeology* 20: 559–579.

Crone, Patricia 1987 *Meccan Trade and the Rise of Islam.* Princeton, NJ: Princeton University Press.

Crumley, Carole 1994 Historical Ecology: A Multidimensional Ecological Orientation. Pp. 1-16 in Carole L. Crumley, ed., *Historical Ecology: Cultural Knowledge and Changing Landscapes*. Santa Fe: School of American Research Press.

Crumley, Carole and William H. Marquardt 1987 *Regional Dynamics: Burgundian Landscapes in Historical Perspective*. San Diego: Academic Press.

Cummings, Valerie 2003 Building from Memory: Remembering the Past at Neolithic Monuments in Western Britain. Pp. 25-44 in Howard Williams, ed., *Archaeologies of Remembrance: Death and Memory in Past Societies*. New York: Kluwer Academic Publishers.

Dahl, Gudrun and Anders Hjort 1976 Having Herds: Pastoral Herd Growth and Household Economy. *Stockholm Studies in Social Anthropology 2*. Stockholm: Department of Social Anthropology, University of Stockholm.

Darwish, Mahmoud [2003] 2007 In Jerusalem. *The Butterfly's Burden* [trans. Fady Joudah]. Townsend: Copper Canyon Press.

D'Altroy, Terrence and Timothy Earle 1985 Staple Finance, Wealth Finance, and Storage in the Inka Political Economy. *Current Anthropology* 26: 187-206.

De Cardi, Beatrice, Brian Doe and S. P. Roskams. 1977. Excavation and Survey in the Sharqiyah, Oman 1976. *Journal of Oman Studies* 3: 17-33.

Deetz, James 1990 Landscapes as Cultural Statements. Pp. 2-4 in W. M. Kelso and R. Most, eds., *Earth Patterns: Essays in Landscape Archaeology*. Charlottesville & London: University Press of Virginia.

Deffontaines, Pierre 1948 Géographie des Pélérinages. Pp. 295-338 in *Géographie et Réligions*. Paris: Gallimard.

Deimel, Anna 1931 Sumerische Tempelwirtschaft zur Zeit Urukaginas und Seiner Vorganger. *Analecta Orientalia* 2: 71-113.

De Maigret, Alessandro, ed., 1990 *The Bronze Age Cultures of Ḥawlān at-Ṭiyyāl and al-Ḥada (Republic of Yemen): A First General Report*. 2 vols. Rome: Istituto per il Medio e Estreme Oriente.

   [1996] 1996 New evidence from the Yemenite "Turret graves" for the problem of the emergence of the South Arabian States. Pp. 321-337 in J. Reade, ed., *The Indian Ocean in Antiquity*. London: Kegan Paul International.

   [1996] 2003 Arabia Felix. *An Exploration of the Archaeological History of Yemen* [trans. Rebecca Thompson]. London: Stacey International.

De Maigret, Alessandro 2005 Excavations of the Turret Tombs of Jabal al-Makhdarah. Pp. 11-40 in Alessandro De Maigret and Sabina Antonini, eds., *South Arabian Necropolises: Italian Excavations at Al-Makhdarah and Kharibat al-Ahjur (Republic of Yemen)*. Reports and Memoirs, New Series IV. Roma: Istituto Italiano per L'Africa e L'Oriente.

Dever, William G. 1990 *Recent Archaeological Discoveries and Biblical Research*. Seattle: University of Washington Press.

Diakonoff, Igor M. 1991 *Early Antiquity*. Chicago: University of Chicago Press.

   1975 The Rural Community in the Ancient Near East. *Journal of the Economic and Social History of the Orient* 18: 121-133.

Diamond, Jared and Peter Bellwood 2003 Farmers and Their Languages: The First Expansions. *Science* 300: 597-603.

Dietler, Michael 1990 Driven by Drink: The Role of Drinking in the Political Economy of and the Case of Early Iron Age France. *Journal of Anthropological Archaeology* 9(4): 352–406.

Di Lernia, Savino 2006 Building Monuments, Creating Identity: Cattle Cult as Social Response to Rapid Environmental Changes in the Holocene Sahara. *Quaternary International* 151: 50–62.

Din, Abdul Kadir and Abdul Samad Hadi 1997 Muslim Pilgrimage from Malaysia. Pp. 161–192 in Robert H. Stoddard and Alan Morinis, eds., *Sacred Places, Sacred Spaces: The Geography of Pilgrimage. Geoscience and Man 34*. Baton Rouge: Louisiana State University.

Doe, Brian 1971 *South Arabian Antiquities*. London: Thames and Hudson.

Donald, Merlin 2001 *A Mind So Rare: The Evolution of Human Consciousness*. New York: Norton.

1991 *Origins of the Human Mind: Three Stages in the Evolution of Culture and Cognition*. Cambridge, MA: Harvard University Press.

Dostal, Walter 1991 Mecca before the Time of the Prophet – Attempt of an Anthropological Interpretation. *Der Islam* 68: 193–231.

1989a The Transition from Cognatic to Unilinear Descent Systems in South Arabia. Pp. 47–62 in Andre Gingrich, Siegfried Haas, Sylvia Haas and Gabriele Paleczek, eds., *Kinship, Social Change, and Evolution. Proceedings of a Symposium in Honor of Walter Dostal. Wiener Beiträge zur Ethnologie und Anthropologie 5*. Horn-Vienna: Ferdinand Berger and Söhne.

1989b Mahra and Arabs in South Arabia: A Study in Inter-ethnical Relations. Pp. 27–36 in Moawiyah M. Ibrahim, ed., *Arabian Studies in Honor of Mahmoud Ghul: Symposium at Yarmouk University December 8–11, 1984*. Weisbaden: Otto Harrassowitz.

1983 Some Remarks on the Ritual Significance of the Bull in Pre-Islamic South Arabia. Pp. 196–213 in Robin L. Bidwell and G. Rex Smith, eds., *Arabian and Islamic Studies. Articles presented to R.B. Sergeant*. London: Longman.

1967 *Die Beduinen in Sudarabien Eine ethnologische Studie zur Entwicklung der Kamelhirten-Kultur in Arabien*. Vienna: Berger and Horn.

Doughty, Charles M. [1936] 1979 *Travels in Arabia Deserta*. New York: Dover Publications.

Dreschler, Phillip 2007. The Neolithic Dispersal into Arabia. *Proceedings of the Seminar for Arabian Studies* 37: 93–109.

Dubisch, Jill 2004 "Heartland of America": Memory, Motion, and the (Re-)construction of History on a Motorcycle Pilgrimage. Pp. 105–132 in Simon Coleman and John Eade, eds., *Reframing Pilgrimage: Cultures in Motion*. London: Routledge.

Dubisch, Jill and Michael Winkelman, eds., 2005 *Pilgrimage and Healing*. Tucson: University of Arizona Press.

Duby, Georges 1968 [1962] *Rural Economy and Country Life* [trans. Cynthia Postan]. Columbia: University of South Carolina Press.

Duncan, J. 2000 Landscape. Pp. 429–431 in R. J. Johnston, Derek Gregory, Geraldine Pratt and Michael Watts, eds., *The Dictionary of Human Geography*, 4th ed. Oxford: Blackwell.

Duncan, J. and N. Duncan 1988 (Re)reading the Landscape. *Environment and Planning D: Society and Space* 6: 117–126.

Duncan, J. and D. Ley 1993. *Place/Culture/Representation*. London: Routledge.

Düring, Bleda S. 2005 Building Continuity in the Central Anatolian Neolithic: Exploring the Meaning of Buildings at Aşıklı Höyük and Çatalhöyük. *Journal of Mediterranean Archaeology* 18(1): 3–29.

Düring, Bleda S. and Arkadiusz Marciniak 2006 Households and Communities in the Central Anatolian Neolithic. *Archaeological Dialogues* 12(2): 165–187.

Durkheim, Émile 1915 *Elementary Forms of the Religious Life*. New York: The Free Press.

Dyson-Hudson, Neville. 1980 Strategies of Resource Exploitation among East African Savanna Pastoralists. Pp. 171–184 in David Harris, ed., *Human Ecology in Savanna Environments*. London: Academic Press.

Dyson-Hudson, Neville and Rada Dyson-Hudson 1999 The Social Organization of Resource Exploitation. Pp. 68–86 in Michael A. Little and Paul W. Leslie, eds., *Turkana Herders of the Dry Savanna*. Oxford: Oxford University Press.

Dyson-Hudson, Rada and E. A. Smith 1978 Human Territoriality: An Ecological Re-assessment. *American Anthropologist* 80: 21–41.

Eade, John and Michael J. Sallnow 1991 *Contesting the Sacred: The Anthropology of Christian Pilgrimage*. London: Routledge.

Earle, Timothy 1977 *How Chiefs Came to Power: The Political Economy in Prehistory*. Palo Alto, CA: Stanford University Press.

Edbury, Peter W. and John Gordon Rowe 1988 *William of Tyre: Historian of the Latin East*. Cambridge: Cambridge University Press.

Eddy, Frank W. and Fred Wendorf 1998 Prehistoric Pastoral Nomads in the Sinai. *Sahara* 10: 7–20.

Edens, Christopher 2005 Exploring Early Agriculture in the Highlands of Yemen. Pp. 185–211 in Amida M. Sholan, Sabina Antonini and Mounir Arbach, eds., *Festschrift for Alessandro de Maigret, Christian Robin and Yusuf Abdalla on the Occasion of Their 60th Birthdays*. Naples – Sana'a: Università degli Studi di Napoli "L'Orientale."

1999 The Bronze Age of Highland Yemen: Chronological and Spatial Variability of Pottery and Settlement. *Paléorient* 25(2): 105–128.

1992 Dynamics of Trade in the Ancient Mesopotamian "World System." *American Anthropologist* 94: 118–139.

Edens, Christopher, Tony J. Wilkinson and Glynn Barratt 2000 Hammat al-Qa and the Roots of Urbanism in Southwest Asia. *Antiquity* 74: 854–862.

Ehret, Christopher 1984 Historical/Linguistic Evidence for Early African Food Production. Pp. 22–35 in J. Desmond Clark and Steven A. Brandt, eds., *From Hunters to Farmers: The Causes and Consequences of Food Production in Africa*. Berkeley: University of California Press.

Eickelman, Dale 1982 The Study of Islam in Local Contexts. *Contributions to Asian Studies* 17: 1–16.

1976 *Moroccan Islam*. Austin: University of Texas Press.

1967 Musaylima. An Approach to the Social Anthropology of Seventh Century Arabia. *Journal of the Economic and Social History of the Orient* 10: 17–52.

Eickelman, Dale F. and James Piscatori 1990 Social Theory in the Study of Muslim Societies. Pp. 3–28 in Dale F. Eickelman and James Piscatori, eds., *Muslim Travellers. Pilgrimage, Migration, and the Religious Imagination.* London: Routledge.

Ekstrom, Heidi and Chris Edens 2003 Prehistoric Agriculture in Highland Yemen: New Results from Dhamar. *Bulletin of the American Institute for Yemeni Studies* 45: 23–35.

Eliade, Mircea [1949] 1954 *The Myth of the Eternal Return* [trans. William R. Trask]. New York: Pantheon Books, Bollingen Series 46.

Ellis, Jim and Kathleen Galvin 1994 Climate Patterns and Land-Use Practices in the Dry Zones of Africa. *Bioscience* 44: 340–349.

El Mahi, Ali Tigani 2000 Traditional Fish Preservation in Oman: The Seasonality of a Subsistence Strategy. *Proceedings of the Seminar for Arabian Studies* 30: 99–114.

Elsner, Jaś and Ian Rutherford, eds. 2005 *Pilgrimage in Graeco-Roman and Early Christian Antiquity: Seeing the Gods.* Oxford: Oxford University Press.

El Tayib, Abdulla 1983 Pre-Islamic Poetry. Pp. 27–113 in A. F. L. Beeston, T. M. Johnstone, R. B. Serjeant and G. R. Smith, eds., *Arabic Literature to the End of the Umayyad Period. Cambridge History of Arabic Literature.* London: Cambridge University Press.

Emberling, Geoff 2003 Urban Social Transformations and the Problem of the "First City." Pp. 254–268 in Monica L. Smith, ed., *The Social Construction of Ancient Cities.* Washington, DC: Smithsonian Press.

Emberling, Geoff and Norman Yoffee 1999 Thinking about Ethnicity in Mesopotamian Archaeology and History. Pp. 272–281 in Hartmut Kühne, Reinhard Bernbeck and Karin Bartl, eds., *Fluchtpunkt Uruk. Archäologische Einheit aus Methodischer Vielfalt. Schriften für Hans Jörg Nissen.* Rahden/Westf.: Verlag Marie Leidorf.

Engels, Frederick 1978 *The Origin of the Family, Private Property and the State* [trans. Alex West]. New York: International Publications.

Englund, R. K. 1988 *Texts from the Late Uruk Period. Mesopotamien 1: Späturuk-Zeit und Frühdynastiche Zeit (Orbis biblicus et orientalis 160–1).* Freiburg Schweiz: Universitätsverlag; Göttingen: Vandenhoeck & Ruprecht.

Eshed, V., Avi Gopher, E. Galili and Israel Hershkovitz 2004 Musculoskeletal Stress Markers in Natufian Hunter-Gatherers and Neolithic Farmers in the Levant: The Upper Limb. *American Journal of Physical Anthropology* 123: 303–315.

Esin, Ufuk and Savaş Harmankaya 1999 Aşıklı. Pp. 115–132 in Mehmet Özdoğan and Nezih Başgelen, eds., *Neolithic in Turkey. The Cradle of Civilization: New Discoveries.* Istanbul: Arkeoloji ve Sanat Yayinlari.

Evans-Pritchard, E. E. 1940 *The Nuer.* Oxford: Oxford University Press.
    1939 Nuer Time Reckoning. *Africa* 12: 189–216.

Fabietti, Ugo [1988] 1999 The Role Played by the Organization of the 'Hums in the Evolution of Political Ideas in Pre-Islamic Mecca. Pp. 348–356 in F. E. Peters, ed., *The Arabs and Arabia on the Eve of Islam*. Aldershot, UK: Ashgate. [Reprinted from *Proceedings of the Seminar for Arabian Studies* 18: 25–33.]

Falkenstein, A. 1974 *The Sumerian Temple City*. Malibu: Undena Publications.

Fedele, Francisco 2008 Wadi at-Ṭayyilah 3, a Neolithic and Pre-Neolithic Occupation on the Eastern Yemen Plateau, and Its Archaeofaunal Information. *Proceedings of the Seminar for Arabian Studies* 38: 153–172.

     2005 Wadi al-Ṭayyila 3: A Mid-Holocene Site on the Yemen Plateau and its Lithic Collection. Pp. 214–145 in A. M. Sholan, S. Antonini and M. Arbach, eds., *Sabaean Studies. Archaeological, Epigraphical and Historical Studies in Honour of Yusuf M. Abdallah, Alessandro de Maigret and Christian J. Robin*. Naples-Sana'a: Universita degli Studi di Napoli "L'Orientale."

     1992 Zooarchaeology in Mesopotamia and Yemen: A Comparative History. *Origini* 16: 49–93.

     1990 Man, Land, and Climate: Emerging Interactions from the Holocene of the Yemen Highlands. Pp. 31–42 in S. Bottema, G. Entjes-Nieborg and W. Van Zeist, eds., *Man's Role in the Shaping of the Eastern Mediterranean Landscape*. Rotterdam: A. A. Balkema.

Feld, S. and Keith H. Basso 1996 Introduction. Pp. 3–11 in S. Feld and K. H. Basso, eds., *Senses of Place*. Santa Fe: School of American Research Press.

Finkelstein, Israel and Neil Ascher Silberman 2001 *The Bible Unearthed. Archaeology's New Vision of Ancient Israel and the Origin of Its Sacred Texts*. New York: The Free Press.

Fiske, Susan T. and Donald P. Kinder 1981 Involvement, Expertise, and Schema Use: Evidence from Political Cognition. Pp. 171–190 in Nancy Cantor and John F. Kihstorm, eds., *Personality, Cognition, and Social Interaction*. Hillsdale, NJ: Erlbaum.

Flannery, Kent 1972 The Origin of the Village as a Settlement Type in Mesoamerica and the Near East: A Comparative Study. Pp. 23–53 in Peter Ucko, Ruth Tringham and Geoffrey Dimbleby, eds., *Man, Settlement and Urbanism*. London: Duckworth.

Fleming, D. E. 2004 *Democracy's Ancient Ancestors: Mari and Early Collective Governance*. Cambridge: Cambridge University Press.

Forest, Jean-Daniel 1996 *Mesopotamie: L'Apparition de l'Etat*. Paris: Méditerranée.

     1987 Tell el-'Oueili, Quatrième Campagne (1983). Stratigraphie et architecture. Pp. 17–32 in Jean-Louis Huot, ed., *Larsa (10e campagne, 1983) et 'Oueili (4e campagne 1983). Rapport Préliminaire*. Paris: Éditions Recherche sur les Civilisations.

Forest, Jean-Daniel, Jean-Louis Huot and R. Vallet 1991–1992 Tell el-'Oueili, 1987 and 1988. *Archiv für Orientforschung* 38–39: 274–276.

Foster, Benjamin J. 1981 A New Look at the Sumerian Temple State. *Journal of the Economic and Social History of the Orient* 24: 227–241.

Fox, Richard G. and Alan Zagarell 1982 The Political Economy of Mesopotamian and South Indian Temples: The Formation and Reproduction of Urban Society. *Comparative Urban Research* 9: 8–27.

Francaviglia, V. M. 2002 Some Remarks on the Irrigation Systems of Ancient Yemen. Pp. 111–144 in Serge Cleuziou, Maurizio Tosi and Juris Zarins, eds.,

Essays on the Late Prehistory of the Arabian Peninsula. Rome: Istituto Italiano per l'Africa e l'Oriente.

Frank, Andre Gunnar 1993 The Bronze Age World System and Its Cycles. *Current Anthropology* 34: 383–430.

Frantsouzoff, Serguei A. 2005 Ancient Hadramawt and the Rise of South Arabian Civilization: Formulating a Problem. *Vestnik drevnej istorii* 2005, 4: 3–23. [English abstract]

2001 Epigraphic Evidence for the Cult of the God Sin at Raybun and Shabwa. *Proceedings of the Seminar for Arabian Studies* 31: 59–67.

Frazer, James G. 1894 *The Golden Bough: A Study in Comparative Religion.* New York: Macmillan and Co.

Frifelt, K. 1991 *The Island of Umm an-Nar 1. Third Millennium Graves.* Arhus: Jutland Archaeological Society Publications 26/1.

Fuller, Dorian Q. 2006 Agricultural Origins and Frontiers in South Asia: A Working Synthesis. *Journal of World Prehistory* 20: 1–86.

Fuller, Dorian Q. and M. Madella 2001 Issues in Harappan Archaeobotany: Retrospect and Prospect. Pp. 317–390 in S. Settar and R. Korisettar, eds., *Indian Archaeology in Retrospect. Protohistory. Volume II.* New Delhi: Manohar.

Galvin, Kathleen and Michael A. Little 1999 Dietary Intake and Nutritional Status. Pp. 124–145 in Michael A. Little and Paul W. Leslie, eds., *Turkana Herders of the Dry Savanna.* Oxford: Oxford University Press.

Garcea, E. A. A., 2004. An Alternative Way Towards Food Production: The Perspective from the Libyan Sahara. *Journal of World Prehistory* 18: 107–153.

Garcia, M., M. Rachad, D. Hadiouis, M.-L. Inizan and M. Fontugnes 1991 Découvertes préhistoriques au Yémen. Le contexte archéologique de l'art rupestre de la region de Saada. *Compets Rendus de l'Académie des Sciences de Paris 313, série II.* 1201–1206.

Garcia, M. A. and M. Rachad 1997 *L'art des origins au Yémen.* Paris: Editions du Seuil.

Garfinkel, Yosef 2006 The Social Organization at Neolithic Sha'ar Hagolan. The Nuclear Family, the Extended Family and the Community. Pp. 103–111 in Edward B. Banning and Michael Chazan, eds., *Domesticating Space: Construction, Community, and Cosmology in the Late Prehistoric Near East.* Studies in Early Near Eastern Production, Subsistence, and Environment 12. Berlin: Ex Oriente.

2003a *Dancing at the Dawn of Agriculture.* Austin: University of Texas Press.

2003b The Earliest Dancing Scenes in the Near East. *Near Eastern Archaeology* 66(3): 84–95.

Garrard, Andrew 1999 Charting the Emergence of Cereal and Pulse Domestication in Southwest Asia. *Environmental Archaeology* 4: 47–62.

Gautier, Achilles 2001 The Early to Late Neolithic Archeofaunas from Nabta and Bir Kiseiba. Pp. 609–635 in Fred Wendorf, Romuald Schild and Associates, eds., *Holocene Settlement of the Egyptian Sahara. Volume 1. The Archaeology of Nabta Playa.* New York: Kluwer Academic/Plenum Publishers.

1998 Notes on the Animal Bone Assemblage from the Early Neolithic at Geili. Pp. 57–64 in Isabelle Caneva, ed., *El Geili. The History of a Middle Nile*

Environment. 7000 BC–AD 1500. Oxford: British Archaeological Reports International Series 424.

1984 Archaeozoology of the Bir Kiseiba Region, Eastern Sahara. Pp. 49–72 in Fred Wendorf, Romuald Schild and Angela E. Close, eds., *Cattle-Keepers of the Eastern Sahara.* Dallas: Southern Methodist University Press.

Gebel, Hans Georg K. 2006 The Domestication of Vertical Space: The Case of Steep-Slope LPPNB Architecture in Southern Jordan. Pp. 65–74 in Edward B. Banning and Michael Chazan, eds., *Domesticating Space: Construction, Community, and Cosmology in the Late Prehistoric Near East.* Studies in Early Near Eastern Productions, Subsistence, and Environment 12. Berlin: Ex Oriente.

2004 There Was No Center: The Polycenteric Evolution of the Near Eastern Neolithic. *Neolithics* 1(4): 28–32.

2002 Walls. Loci of Forces. Pp. 119–132 in Hans Georg Gebel, Bo Dahl Hermansen and Charlotte Hoffman Jensen, eds., *Magic Practices and Ritual in the Near Eastern Neolithic.* Studies in Early Near Eastern Production, Subsistence, and Environment 8. Berlin: Ex Oriente.

Gebel, Hans-Georg K., Bo Dahl Hermansen and Moritz Kinzel 2006 Ba'ja 2005: A Two-storied Building and Collective Burials. Results of the 6th Season of Excavation. *Neolithics* 1/06: 12–19.

Geertz, Clifford 1973 *The Interpretation of Culture.* New York: Basic Books.

1968 *Islam Observed. Religious Developments in Morocco and Indonesia.* Chicago: University of Chicago Press.

Gelb, Ignace J. 1992 Mari and the Kish Civilization. Pp. 121–202 in Gordon D. Young, ed. *Mari in Retrospect.* Winona Lake, WI: Eisenbrauns.

1979 Household and Family in Early Mesopotamia. Pp 1–97 in Edward Lipinski, ed., *State and Temple Economy in the Ancient Near East.* Orientalia Lovaniensia Analecta 5. Leuven: Leuven University Press.

1972 The Arua Institution. *Revue d'Assyriologie et d'Archéologie Orientale* 66: 1–32.

1971 On the Alleged Temple and State Economies in Ancient Mesopotamia. Pp. 137–154 in *Studi in Onore di Edoardo Volterra. Volume 6.* Rome: Publicazioni della Facoltà di Giurisprudenza del l'Università di Roma.

Gelb, Ignace J., Piotr Steinkeller and Robert Whiting 1991 *Earliest Land Tenure Systems in the Near East: Ancient Kudurrus.* Chicago: Oriental Institute.

Gell, Alfred 1992 *The Anthropology of Time.* Oxford: Berg.

Gellner, Ernest 1969 *Saints of the Atlas.* Chicago.

Geyer, Bernard and Yves Calvet 2001 Les steppes arides de la Syrie du Nord au Bronze ancien ou la première conquete de l'est. Pp. 55–68 in B. Geyer, ed., *Conquete de la Steppe, Travaux Maison de l'Orient Mediterranéen 36.* Lyon: Maison de l'Orient Mediterranéen.

Ghul, M. A. 1984 The Pilgrimage at Itwat. *Proceedings of the Seminar for Arabian Studies* 14: 33–41.

Gibb, H. A. R. 1948 Religious Thought in Islam. *The Muslim World* 38: 17–28.

Gibbon, Guy 1984 *Anthropological Archaeology.* New York: Columbia University Press.

Giddens, Anthony 1984 *The Constitution of Society: Outline of a Theory of Structuration*. Cambridge: Cambridge University Press.

1979 *Central Problems in Social Theory: Action, Structure, and Contradiction in Social Analysis*. London: Macmillan.

Gifford-Gonzalez, Diane 2005 Pastoralism and Its Consequences. Pp. 187–224 in Ann Brower Stahl, ed., *African Archaeology*. Oxford: Basil Blackwell.

Gillespie, Susan D. 2000 Lévi-Strauss, Maison and Société à Maisons. Pp. 22–52 in Rosemary A. Joyce and Susan D. Gillespie, eds., *Beyond Kinship: Society and Material Reproduction in House Societies*. Philadelphia: University of Pennsylvania Press.

Girard, René 1972 *La violence et le sacré*. Paris: B. Grasset.

Given, Michael 2004 Mapping and Manuring: Can We Compare Sherd Density Figures? Pp. 13–21 in Susan E. Alcock and John F. Cherry, eds., *Side by Side Survey: Comparative Studies in the Mediterranean World*. Oxford: Oxbow Books.

Godelier, Maurice [1975] 1984 Modes of Production, Kinship, and Demographic Structures. Pp. 3–28 in Maurice Bloch, ed., *Marxist Analyses and Social Anthropology*. London: Tavistock Publications.

Gonzáles-Ruibal, Alfredo 2006 House Societies vs. Kinship-Based Societies: An Archaeological Case from Iron Age Europe. *Journal of Anthropological Archaeology* 25: 144–173.

Goring-Morris, Nigel 2000 The Quick and the Dead: The Social Context of Aceramic Neolithic Mortuary Practices as Seen from Kfar HaHoresh. Pp. 103–136 in Ian Kuijt, ed., *Life in Neolithic Farming Communities: Social Organization, Identity, and Differentiation*. New York: Kluwer Academic/ Plenum Press.

Goring-Morris, Nigel and Liora Kolska Horwitz 2007 Funerals and Feasts during the Pre-Pottery Neolithic B of the Near East. *Antiquity* 81: 902–919.

Gosden, Chris and Lesley Head 1994 Landscape: A Usefully Ambiguous Concept. *Archaeology in Oceania* 29: 113–116.

Gould, Stephen J. 1986 Evolution and the Triumph of Homology, or Why History Matters. *American Scientist* 74: 60–69.

Grigson, Caroline 2000 *Bos africanus* (Brehem)? Notes on the Archaeozoology of the Native Cattle of Africa. Pp. 38–60 in Roger M. Blench and Kevin C. MacDonald, eds., *The Origins and Development of African Livestock. Archaeology, Genetics, Linguistics, and Ethnography*. London: UCL Press.

1991 African Origin for African Cattle? Some Archaeological Evidence. *The African Archaeological Review* 9: 119–144.

Grimes, Ronald L. 2000 *Deeply into the Bone: Re-inventing Rites of Passage*. Berkeley: University of California Press.

Groneberg, Brigitte 1986 Eine Einführungsszene in der altbabylonischen Literatur: Bemerkungen zum persönlichen Gott. Pp. 93–108 in Karl Hecker and Walter Sommerfeld, eds., *Keilschriftliche Literaturen: Ausgewählte Vorträge der 32 Rencontre Assyriologique Internationale*. Berliner Beiträge zum Vorderen Orient Band 6. Berlin: Dietrich Reimer Verlag.

Groom, Nigel 1981 *Frankincense and Myrrh*. London: Longman.

Gupta, Akhil and James Ferguson 1997 Culture, Power, Place: Ethnography at the End of an Era. Pp. 1–29 in Akhil Gupta and James Ferguson, eds., *Culture, Power, Place: Explorations in Critical Anthropology*. Durham, NC: Duke University Press.

    1992 Beyond "Culture": Space, Identity, and the Politics of Difference. *Cultural Anthropology* 7(1): 6–23.

Haaland, Randi 2007 Porridge and Pot, Bread and Oven, Food Ways and Symbolism in Africa and the Near East from the Neolithic to the Present. *Cambridge Archaeological Journal* 17: 165–182.

    1992 Fish, Pots and Grain: Early and Mid-Holocene Adaptations in the Central Sudan. *African Archaeological Review* 10: 43–64.

Haas, Jonathan 1982 *The Evolution of the Prehistoric State*. New York: Columbia University Press.

Hadjouis, Djillali 2007 Chapitre V La faune des grands mammifères. Pp. 51–60 in Marie-Louise Inizan and Madiha Rachad, eds., *Art rupestre et peuplements préhistoriques au Yémen*. Sana'a: CEFAS.

Hägerstrand, Torsten 1975 Space, Time and Human Conditions. Pp. 3–13 in A. Kalqvist, L. Lundqvist and F. Snickars, eds., *Dynamic Allocation of Urban Space*. Farnborough, Hants.: Saxon House.

Hall, Mark Glenn 1985 *A Study of the Sumerian Moon God, Nanna/Suen*. Ph.D. dissertation. University of Pennsylvania. Ann Arbor: University Microfilms.

Halstead, Paul 1989 The Economy Has a Normal Surplus: Economic Stability and Social Change among Early Farming Communities of Thessaly, Greece. Pp. 68–80 in Paul Halstead and John O'Shea, eds., *Bad Year Economics: Cultural Responses to Risk and Uncertainty*. Cambridge: Cambridge University Press.

Hanotte, O., D. Bradley, J. W. Ochieng, Y. Verjee, E. W. Hill, J. Edward and O. Rege 2002 African Pastoralism: Genetic Imprints of Origins and Migrations. *Science* 296: 336.

Hardin, G. 1977 The Tragedy of the Commons. Pp. 16–30 in G. Harden and J. Baden, eds., *Managing the Commons*. San Francisco: Freeman.

Harrower, Michael J. 2008 Hydrology, Ideology and the Origins of Irrigation in Ancient Southwest Arabia. *Current Anthropology* 49: 497–510.

    2006 *Environmental versus Social Parameters, Landscape, and the Origins of Irrigation in Southwest Arabia (Yemen)*. Ph.D. dissertation, The Ohio State University. Ann Arbor: University Microfilms.

Hartley, John G. 1961 *The Political Organization of an Arab Tribe of the Hadhramaut*. Ph.D. thesis, London School of Economics, University of London.

Harvey, David 1969 *Explanation in Geography*. London: E. Arnold.

Hassan, Fekri 2002 Holocene Environmental Change and the Transition to Agriculture in South-west Asia and North-east Africa. Pp. 55–68 in Y. Yasuda, ed., *The Origins of Pottery and Agriculture*. New Delhi: Roli Books.

    2000 Climate and Cattle in North Africa: A First Approximation. Pp. 61–86 in Roger M. Blench and Kevin C. MacDonald, eds., *The Origins and Development* of African Livestock. Archaeology, Genetics, Linguistics, and Ethnography. London: UCL Press.

Hastorf, Christine A. 2009 Agriculture as Metaphor of the State in the Andes. Pp. 52–72 in Steven E. Falconer and Charles Redman, eds., Politics and Power: Archaeological Perspectives on the Landscapes of Early States. Tucson: University of Arizona Press.

Hauptmann, Harald 1999 The Urfa Region. Pp. 65–86 in Mehmet Özdoğan and Nezih Başgelen, eds., Neolithic in Turkey. The Cradle of Civilization: New Discoveries. Istanbul: Arkeoloji ve Sanat Yayinlari.

Hawting, Gerald R. [1990] 1999 The "Sacred Offices" of Mecca from Jāhiliyya to Islam. Pp. 244–266 in F. E. Peters, ed., The Arabs and Arabia on the Eve of Islam. Aldershot, UK: Ashgate. [Reprinted from Jerusalem Studies in Arabic and Islam 13: 62–84. Max Schloessinger Memorial Foundation, Institute of Asian and African Studies, the Hebrew University of Jerusalem.]

Hecht, Richard and Roger Friedland 1996 The Power of Place: The Nebi Musa Pilgrimage and the Origins of Palestinian Nationalism. Pp. 337–360 in Sara J. Denning-Bolle and Edwin Gerow, eds., The Persistence of Religions. Essays in Honor of Kees W. Bolle. Malibu: Undena Publications.

Heidegger, Martin 1971 Poetry, Language, Thought [trans. Albert Hofstadter]. New York: Harper Row.

Heinrich, E. 1982 Die Tempel und Heiligtümer im Alten Mesopotamien. Berlin: Walter de Gruyter.

Helwing, Barbara 2003 Feasts as a Social Dynamic in Prehistoric Western Asia – Three Case Studies from Syria and Anatolia. Paléorient 29(2): 63–86.

Henninger, Joseph [1981] 1999 Pre-Islamic Religion. Pp. 109–128 in F. E. Peters, ed., The Arabs and Arabia on the Eve of Islam. Aldershot, UK: Ashgate. [Reprinted from Merlin Schwarz, ed. and trans., Studies on Islam. New York: Oxford University Press. pp. 3–22.]

1951 Spuren christlicher Glaugenswahrheiten im Koran. Schöneck/Beckenried: Admin. Der Neuen Zeitschrifts für Missionswissenschaft.

1948 Le sacrifice chez les arabes. Ethnos 13: 1–16. [Reprinted in Arabica Sacra: Orbis Biblicus et Orientalis 40, Freiburg/Göttingen 1981: 189–203.]

1946/47 Das Opfer in den altsüdarabischen Hochkulturen. [Reprinted in Arabica Sacra: Orbis Biblicus et Orientalis 40, Freiburg/Göttingen 1981: 204–253.]

1943 Die Familie bei den heutigen Arabern und seiner Randgebiete. Ein Beitrag zur frage der ursprünglichen Familienform der Semiten. Internationales Archiv für Ethnographie, Band 42. Leiden: P. M. W. Trap.

Henry, Donald O., J. J. White, J. E. Beaver, S. Kadowaki, A. Nowell, C. Cordova, R. M. Dean, H. Ekstrom, J. McCorriston and L. Scott-Cummings 2003 The Early Neolithic Site of Ayn Abu Nukhayla, Southern Jordan. Bulletin of the American Schools of Oriental Research 330: 1–30.

Hermanson, Bo Dahl 2005 Comment: Ritual as Function, Ritual as Social Practice? Neolithics 2(5): 29.

Hershkovitz, Israel, Ofer Bar-Yosef and Beno Arensburg 1994 The Pre-Pottery Neolithic Populations of South Sinai and Their Relations to Other Circum-Mediterranean Groups: An Anthropological Study. Paléorient 20(2): 59–84.

Herskovits, Melville J. 1926 The Cattle Complex in East Africa. *American Anthropologist, New Series,* 28: 230–272.

Higgs, Eric S. and Claudio Vita-Finzi 1972 Prehistoric Economies: A Territorial Approach. Pp. 27–36 in E. S. Higgs, ed., *Papers in Economic Prehistory.* Cambridge: Cambridge University Press.

Hirschberg, H. Z. 1939 Jüdische und Christliche Lehren im vor- und frühislamischen Arabien. *Polska Akademia Umiejetności, Komisja Orientalistyczna Prace. Volume 32.* Kraków: Polskiej Akademii Umiejetności.

Hitti, Philip K. 1968 *The Arabs: A Short History.* New York: St. Martin's Press.

Ho, Enseng 2006 *The Graves of Tarim: Geneology and Mobility across the Indian Ocean.* Berkeley: University of California Press.

Hodder Ian 2006 *The Leopard's Tale.* London: Thames and Hudson.

    2001 Symbolism and the Origins of Agriculture in the Near East. Review Feature: The Birth of the Gods and the Origins of Agriculture by Jacques Cauvin [trans. Trevor Watkins]. *Cambridge Archaeological Journal* 11(1): 107–112.

    1990 *The Domestication of Europe.* Oxford: Blackwell.

    1982 *Symbols in Action.* Cambridge: Cambridge University Press.

Hodder, Ian and Craig Cessford 2004 Daily Practice and Social Memory at Çatalhöyük. *American Antiquity* 69: 17–40.

Höfner, Maria 1959 Die Beduinen in den vorislamischen Inschriften. Pp. 53–68 in F. Gabrieli, ed., *L'Antica societa Beduina. Studi Semitici 2.* Rome: Centro di studi semitici, Istituto di studi del vicino oriente, Università.

Hole, Frank 2005 Comment: Arguments for Broadly Contextualizing Ritual. *Neolithics* 2(5): 30–31.

    2000 Is Size Important? Function and Hierarchy in Neolithic Settlements. Pp. 191–210 in Ian Kuijt, ed., *Life in Neolithic Farming Communities.* New York: Kluwer Academic/Plenum Press.

    1989 Patterns of Burial in the Fifth Millennium. Pp. 149–180 in Elizabeth Henrickson and Ingolf Thuesen, eds., *Upon This Foundation: The Ubaid Reconsidered.* Copenhagen: Carston Niebuhr Institute Publication 10.

Holes, Clive 2006 The Arabic Dialects of Arabia. *Proceedings of the Seminar for Arabian Studies* 36: 25–34.

Holl, Augustin F. C. 1998 Livestock Husbandry, Pastoralism, and Territoriality: The West African Record. *Journal of Anthropological Archaeology* 17: 143–165.

Horowitz, Liora K., Eitan Tchernov, Pierre Ducos, Cornelius Becker, Angela von den Dreisch, Louise Martin and Andrew Garrard 2000 Animal Domestication in the Southern Levant. *Paléorient* 25(2): 63–80.

Howey, Meghan C. and John M. O'Shea 2006 Bear's Journey and the Study of Ritual in Archaeology. *American Antiquity* 71(2): 261–282.

Hubert, M. M. Henri and Marcel Mauss 1898 Essai sur la nature et la function du sacrifice. *L'Année Sociologique* 2: 29–138.

Huot, Jean-Louis 1989 'Ubaidian Villages of Lower Mesopotamia. Pp. 18–42 in Elizabeth F. Henrickson and Ingolf Thuesen, eds., *Upon This Foundation: The Ubaid Reconsidered.* Carston Niebuhr Institute Publications 10. Copenhagen: Museum Tusculanum Press.

Ibn al-Mujawir, Yūsuf ibn Yuqūb [1204/5–1291/2] 1986 *Sifat Bilād al-Yemen wa Makka wa ba'ad al-Hijaz al-musamman Tarikh al-Mustabasira*. Beirut: Oskar Lufgren. [in Arabic]

Ibn Baṭūṭah, Muḥammad [d. 1354] 1971 *The Travels of Ibn Battūta*, A.D. 1325–1354 [trans. H. A. R. Gibb; eds., C. Defrémery and B. R. Sanguinetti]. Cambridge: Published for the Hakluyt Society at the University Press.

Ibn Khaldūn, 'Abd-ar-Raḥman, Abū Zayd ibn Muḥammad [d. 1406] 1967 *The Muqaddimah* [trans. Franz Rosenthal, abr. Nigel Dawood], Bollingen Series. Princeton, NJ: Princeton University Press.

Ingold, Timothy 1996 The Optimal Forager and Economic Man. Pp. 25–45 in P. Descola and G. Palsson, eds., *Nature and Society: Anthropological Perspectives*. London: Routledge.

   1982 *Hunters, Herders, and Ranchers*. Cambridge: Cambridge University Press.

Ingrams, W. Harold [1936, 1937] 1939 *A Report on the Social, Economic and Political Condition of the Hadhramaut*. London: His Majesty's Stationery Office. [reprinted twice]

   1936 Hadhramaut: A Journey to the Sei'ar Country and through the Wadi Maseila. *The Geographical Journal* 88: 524–551.

Inomata, Takeshi 2006 Plazas, Performers, and Spectators: Political Theaters of the Classic Maya. *Current Anthropology* 47: 805–842.

Ivory, C. S. 2005 Art and Aesthetics in the Marquesas Islands. Pp. 25–38 in E. Kjellgren and C. S. Ivory, eds., *Adorning the World: Art of the Marquesas Islands*. New York: Yale University Press and the Metropolitan Museum of Art.

Jamme, A. 1947 Le panthéon sudarabe préislamique d'après les sources épigraphiques. *Le Muséon* 60: 57–147.

Janzen, Jorg 1986 Nomads in the Sultanate of Oman. *Tradition and Development in Dhofar*. Boulder, CO: Westview Press.

Jasim, S. A. 1985 *The Ubaid Period in Iraq: Recent Excavations in the Hamrin Region*. British Archaeological Reports International Series 267. Oxford: British Archaeological Reports.

Jesse, Frederike 2004 The Neolithic. Pp. 35–45 in Derek A. Welsby and Julie R. Anderson, eds., *Sudan: Ancient Treasures: An Exhibition of Recent Discoveries from the Sudan National Museum*. London: The British Museum Press.

Joffe, Alexander H. 1998 Alcohol and Social Complexity in Ancient Western Asia. *Current Anthropology* 39: 297–322.

Johnson, Amber L. 2002 Cross-Cultural Analysis of Pastoral Adaptations and Organizational States: A Preliminary Study. *Cross-Cultural Research* 36(2): 151–180.

Johnson, Gregory 1988–1989 Late Uruk in Greater Mesopotamia: Expansion or Collapse? *Origini* 14: 595–613.

Johnston, Kevin and Nancy Gonlin 1998 What Do Houses Mean? Approaches to the Analysis of Classic Maya Commoner Residences. Pp. 141–186 in Stephen D. Houston, ed., *Function and Meaning in Classic Maya Architecture*. Washington, DC: Dumbarton Oaks.

Johnstone, T. M. 1975 The Modern South Arabian Languages. *Afroasiatic Linguisitics* 1: 93–121.

Jones, Andrew 2003 Technologies of Remembrance. Pp. 65–88 in Howard Williams, ed., *Archaeologies of Remembrance: Death and Memory in Past Societies*. New York: Kluwer Academic/Plenum Publishers.

Jordan, Peter 2001 The Materiality of Shamanism as a "World-View": Praxis, Artefacts and Landscape. Pp. 87–104 in Neil S. Price, ed., *The Archaeology of Shamanism*. London: Routledge.

Joyce, Rosemary A. 2000 Heirlooms and Houses: Materiality and Social Memory. Pp. 189–212 in Rosemary A. Joyce and Susan D. Gillespie, eds., *Beyond Kinship: Social and Material Reproduction in House Societies*. Philadelphia: University of Pennsylvania Press.

Joyce, Rosemary A. and Susan D. Gillespie, eds., 2000 *Beyond Kinship: Society and Material Reproduction in House Societies*. Philadelphia: University of Pennsylvania Press.

Kaeppler, Adrienne 1988 Hawaiian Tattoo: A Conjunction of Genealogy and Aesthetics. Pp. 157–170 in Arnold Rubin, ed., *Marks of Civilization*. Los Angeles: Museum of Cultural History, University of California Los Angeles.

Kafafi, Zeidan A. 2006 Domestic Activities at the Neolithic Site, 'Ain Ghazal. Pp. 81–89 in Edward B. Banning and Michael Chazan, eds., *Domesticating Space: Construction, Community, and Cosmology in the Late Prehistoric Near East*. Studies in Early Near Eastern Production, Subsistence, and Environment 12. Berlin: Ex Oriente.

Kamp, Kathryn A. and Norman Yoffee 1980 Ethnicity in Ancient Western Asia during the Early Second Millennium B.C.: Archaeological Assessments and Ethnoarchaeological Perspectives. *Bulletin of the American Schools of Oriental Research* 237: 85–104.

Kardulias, P. Nick, ed., 1999 *World-Systems Theory in Practice: Leadership, Production, and Exchange*. Lanham, MD: Rowman and Littlefield Publishers.

Keeley, Laurence 1995 Protoagricultural Practices among Hunter-Gatherers: A Cross-cultural Survey. Pp. 243–272 in Douglas T. Price and Anne B. Gebauer, eds., *Last Hunters – First Farmers*. Santa Fe: School of American Research Press.

Keith, Kathryn 2003 The Spatial Patterns of Everyday Life in Old Babylonian Neighborhoods. Pp. 56–80 in Monica L. Smith, ed., *The Social Construction of Ancient Cities*. Washington, DC: Smithsonian Press.

1999 *Cities, Neighborhoods and Houses: Urban Spatial Organization in Old Babylonian Mesopotamia*. Ph.D. dissertation, University of Michigan. Ann Arbor: University Microfilms.

Kelly, John D. and Martha Kaplan 1990 History, Structure, and Ritual. *Annual Review of Anthropology* 19: 119–150.

Kenyon, Kathleen 1981 The Architecture and the Stratigraphy of the Tell. Pp. 18–61 in Kathleen M. Kenyon and Thomas A. Holland, eds., *Excavations at Jericho. Volume III*. London: The British School of Archaeology in Jerusalem.

1957 *Digging up Jericho*. London: Ernest Benn.

Kertzer, David I. 1988 *Ritual, Politics, and Power*. New Haven, CT: Yale University Press.

Khalaily, H. Ofer Bar-Yosef, O. Barzilai, E. Boaretto, F. Bocquentin, A. Eirikh-Rose, Z. Greenhut, A. Nigel Goring-Morris, G. Le Dosseur, O. Marder, L. Sapir-Hen and M. Yizhaq 2007 Excavations at Motza in the Judean Hills and the Early Pre-Pottery Neolithic B in the Southern Levant. *Paléorient* 33(2): 5–38.

Khalidi, Lamya 2005 The Prehistoric and Early Historic Settlement Patterns on the Tihamah Coastal Plain (Yemen): Preliminary Findings of the Tihamah Coastal Survey 2003. *Proceedings of the Seminar for Arabian Studies* 35: 115–127.

Khan, Majeed 2000 *Wusum: The Tribal Symbols of Saudi Arabia*. Riyadh: Ministry of Education.

1993 *Prehistoric Rock Art of Northern Saudi Arabia*. Riyadh: Ministry of Education Department of Antiquities and Museums, Kingdom of Saudi Arabia.

King, Russel 1972 The Pilgrimage to Mecca: Some Geographical and Historical Aspects. *Erdkunde* 26: 61–73.

Kinglake, Alexander W. [1888] 1908 *Eothen*. New York: E. P. Dutton & Co.

Kirch, Patrick V. 1994 *The Wet and the Dry: Irrigation and Agricultural Intensification in Polynesia*. Chicago: University of Chicago Press.

Kirch, Patrick V. and Roger C. Green 2001 Hawaiki, Ancestral Polynesia. *An Essay in Historical Anthropology*. Cambridge: Cambridge University Press.

Kirch, Patrick V. and Terry L. Hunt 1997 *Historical Ecology in the Pacific Islands: Prehistoric Environmental and Landscape Change*. New Haven, CT: Yale University Press.

Kister, M. J. 1986 Mecca and the Tribes of Arabia. Pp. 33–57 in M. Sharon, ed., *Studies in Islamic History and Civilization in Honour of David Ayalon*. Jerusalem: Cana. [Reprinted as II in M. J. Kister 1990 *Society and Religion from Jahiliyya to Islam*. Aldershot, UK: Variorum Press.]

1982 On "Concessions" and Conduct: A Study in Early Hadith. Pp. 89–107, 214–230 in G. H. A. Juynboll, ed., *Studies on the First Century of Islamic Society*. Carbondale: Southern Illinois University Press. [Reprinted as XIII in M. J. Kister 1990 *Society and Religion from Jahiliyya to Islam*. Aldershot, UK: Variorum Press.]

1980 Labbayka, allahumma, labbayka . . .: On a Monotheistic Aspect of a Jahiliyya Practice. *Jerusalem Studies in Arabic and Islam* 2: 35–57. [Reprinted as I in M. J. Kister 1990 *Society and Religion from Jahiliyya to Islam*. Aldershot, UK: Variorum Press.]

Klejn, Leo S. 1994 Childe and Soviet Archaeology: A Romance. Pp. 75–93 in David R. Harris, ed., *The Archaeology of V. Gordon Childe: Contemporary Perspectives*. Chicago: University of Chicago Press.

Knapp, A. Bernard 1992 Archaeology and Annales: Time, Space, and Change. Pp. 1–21 in Bernard Knapp, ed., *Archaeology, Annales, and Ethnohistory*. Cambridge: Cambridge University Press.

Knysh, Alexander 1997 The Cult of Saints and Religious Reformism in Hadhramaut. Pp. 199–216 in Ulrike Freitag and W. Clarence-Smith, eds.,

Hadhrami Traders, Scholars, and Statesmen in the Indian Ocean, 1750s–1960s. London: E. J. Brill.

1993 The Cult of Saints in Hadramwt: An Overview. Pp. 137–153 in Robert J. Sergeant, Robin L. Bidwell and G. Rex Smith, eds., *New Arabian Studies* 1. Exeter: University of Exeter Press.

Korotayev, Andrey 2003 Religion and Society in Southern Arabia and among the Arabs in Arabia. *Revue de sabéologie* 1: 65–76.

1995 Were There Any Truly Matrilineal Lineages in the Arabian Peninsula? *Proceedings of the Seminar for Arabian Studies* 25: 83–98.

1994a Middle Sabaean Cultural-Political Area: Problem of Local Taxation and Temple Tithe ('S2R). *Le Muséon* 107: 15–22.

1994b Sabaean Cultural-Political Area in the 2nd and 3rd Centuries AD: Problem of Taxation at the Kingdom Level and Temple Tithe. *Annali dei Istituto Universitario Orientale di Napoli* 54: 1–14.

1994c Internal Structure of Middle Sabaean Bayt. *Arabian Archaeology and Epigraphy* 5: 174–183.

1993a Middle Sabaean Cultural-Political Area: Material Sources of Qaylite Political Power. *Abr-Nahrain* 31: 93–105.

1993b Bayt: Basis of Middle Sabaean Social Structure. *Rivista degli Studi Orientali* 67: 55–63.

Korotayev, Andrey, Vladimir Klimenko and Dmitry Proussakov 1999 Origins of Islam: Political-Anthropological and Environmental Context. *Acta Orientalia Academiae Scientiarum Hungaria* 52: 243–276.

Kouchoukos, Nicholas 1998 *Landscape and Social Change in Late Prehistoric Mesopotamia.* Ph.D. dissertation, Yale University. Ann Arbor: University Microfilms.

Kozlowski, Stefan K. and Olivier Aurenche 2005 *Territories, Boundaries and Cultures in the Neolithic Near East.* Oxford: British Archaeological Reports, International Series 1362.

Kroeber, Alfred L. 1944 *Configurations of Cultural Growth.* Berkeley: University of California Press.

Küchler, Susan 1993 Landscape as Memory: The Mapping of Process and Its Representation in a Melanesian Society. Pp. 85–106 in Barbara Bender, ed., *Landscape: Politics and Perspectives.* Oxford: Berg.

Kuhn, Steven L. and Mary C. Stiner 2006 What's a Mother to Do? The Division of Labor among Neanderthals and Modern Humans in Eurasia. *Current Anthropology* 47: 953–980.

Kuijt, Ian 2008 The Regeneration of Life: Neolithic Structures of Symbolic Remembering and Forgetting. *Current Anthropology* 49: 171–198.

2005 Comment: The Materiality of Ritual on the Social Landscape: Questions and Issues. *Neolithics* 2(5): 35–37.

2004 When the Walls Came Down: Social Organization, Ideology, and the "Collapse" of the Pre-Pottery Neolithic. Pp. 183–213 in H. D. Bienert, H. G. K. Gebel and R. Neef, eds., *Central Settlements in Neolithic Jordan.* Studies in Early Near Eastern Production, Subsistence, and Environment 5. Berlin: Ex Oriente.

2002 Reflections on Ritual and the Transmission of Authority in the Pre-Pottery Neolithic of the Southern Levant. Pp. 81–90 in Hans Georg Gebel, Bo Dahl Hermansen and Charlotte Hoffman Jensen, eds., *Magic Practices and Ritual in the Near Eastern Neolithic*. Studies in Early Near Eastern Production, Subsistence, and Environment 8. Berlin: Ex Oriente.

2001 Meaningful Masks: Place, Death, and the Transmission of Social Memory in Early Agricultural Communities of the Near Eastern Pre-Pottery Neolithic. Pp. 80–99 in Meredith Chesson, ed., *Social Memory, Identity, and Death: Intradisciplinary Perspectives on Mortuary Rituals*. Anthropological Papers 10. Washington, DC: American Anthropological Association.

2000a People and Space in Early Agricultural Villages: Exploring Daily Lives, Community Size, and Architecture in the Late Pre-Pottery Neolithic. *Journal of Anthropological Archaeology* 19: 75–102.

2000b Keeping the Peace: Ritual Skull Caching and the Community Integration in the Levantine Neolithic. Pp. 137–164 in Ian Kuijt, ed., *Life in Neolithic Farming Communities. Social Organization, Identity, and Differentiation*. New York: Kluwer Academic/Plenum Press.

1996 Negotiating Equality Through Ritual: A Consideration of Late Natufian and Pre-Pottery Neolithic A Period Mortuary Practices. *Journal of Anthropological Archaeology* 15(4): 313–336.

1994 Pre-Pottery Neolithic A Period Settlement Systems of the Southern Levant: New Data, Archaeological Visibility, and Regional Site Hierarchies. *Journal of Mediterranean Archaeology* 7(2): 165–192.

Kuper, Adam 1982a Lineage Theory: A Critical Retrospect. *Annual Review of Anthropology* 11: 71–95.

1982b Wives for Cattle. *Bridewealth and Marriage in Southern Africa*. London: Routledge and Kegan Paul.

Kuznar, Lawrence A. 2003 Sacred Sites and Profane Conflicts: The Use of Burial Facilities and Other Sacred Locations as Territorial Markers – Ethnographic Evidence. Pp. 270–286 in Robert J. Jeske and D. K. Charles, eds., *Theory, Method, and Practice in Modern Archaeology*. London: Praeger.

LaBianca, Oysten S., ed., 1990 *Sedentarization and Nomadization: Food System Cycles at Hesban and Vicinity in Transjordan*. Berrien Springs, MI: Andrews University Press.

Lahti, Minna 1994 Constructing Identities through Pilgrimage: Meanings and Masculinity in Naples. *Suomen Antropologia* 19: 22–33.

Lamberg-Karlovsky, C. C. 1989 Mesopotamia, Central Asia and the Indus Valley: So the Kings Were Killed. Pp. 241–267 in C. C. Lamberg-Karlovsky, ed., *Archaeological Thought in America*. Cambridge: Cambridge University Press.

Lammens, P. Henri 1926 Les sanctuaries préislamites dans l'Arabie occidentale. *Mélanges de l'Université Saint-Joseph, Beyrouth* 11: 39–169.

1919 Le culte des Bétyles et les processions religieuses chez les arabes préislamites. *Bulletin de l'Institut Français d'archéologie orientale du Caire* 17: 39–101.

Lancaster, W. and F. Lancaster 1999a *People, Land, and Water in the Arab Middle East*. Amsterdam: Harwood.

1999b Identities and Economics: Mountain and Coastal Ras Al-Khaimah. *Proceedings of the Seminar for Arabian Studies* 29: 89–94.

Landau, Misia 1984 Human Evolution as Narrative. *American Scientist* 72: 262–268.

Lapidus, Ira M. 1990 Tribes and State Formation in Islamic History. Pp. 25–47 in Philip S. Khoury and Joseph Kostiner, eds., *Tribes and State Formation in the Middle East*. Berkeley: University of California Press.

Larsen, Mogens Trolle 1994 *The Conquest of Assyria*. London: Routledge.

Leone, Mark P. 1984 Interpreting Ideology in Historical Archaeology. Using the Rules of Perspective in the William Paca Garden in Annapolis, Maryland. Pp. 25–35 in Daniel Miller and Christopher Tilley, eds., *Ideology, Power, and Prehistory*. New York: Cambridge University Press.

1982 Some Opinions about Recovering Mind. *American Antiquity* 47: 742–760.

Le Roy Ladurie, Emmanuel [1975] 1979 *Montaillou: The Promised Land of Error* [trans. Barbara Bray]. New York: Vintage Books.

Leslie, Paul W. and Rada Dyson-Hudson 1999 People and Herds. Pp. 232–247 in Michael A. Little and Paul W. Leslie, eds., *Turkana Herders of the Dry Savanna*. Oxford: Oxford University Press.

Lévi-Strauss, Claude [1979] 1982 *The Way of the Masks* [trans. Sylvia Modelski]. Seattle: University of Washington Press.

1966 *The Savage Mind*. London: Weidenfeld and Nicolson.

[1964] 1969 *The Raw and the Cooked* [trans. John and Doreen Weightman]. New York: Harper Row.

1963 *Structural Anthropology* [trans. Claire Jacobson and Brooke Grundfest Schoepf]. New York: Basic Books.

Levkovskya, G. M. and A. A. Filatenko 1992 Palaeobotanical and Palynological Studies in South Arabia. *Review of Palaeobotany and Palynology* 73: 241–257.

Lev-Yadun, Simcha, Avi Gopher and Shahal Abbo 2000 The Cradle of Agriculture. *Science* 288: 1602–1603.

Lewis-Williams, David and David Pearce 2005 *Inside the Neolithic Mind*. London: Thames and Hudson.

Lezine, A. M., J.-F. Saliège, C. Robert, F. Wertz and M.-L. Inizan 1998 Holocene Lakes from Ramlat as-Sab'atayn (Yemen) Illustrate the Impact of Monsoon Activity in Southern Arabia. *Quaternary Research* 50: 290–299.

Lippens, P. 1956 *Expédition en Arabie Centrale*. Paris: Adrien-Maisonneuve.

Liverani, Mario [1998] 2006 *Uruk: The First City* [trans. from Italian by Zainab Bahrani and Marc Van De Mieroop]. London: Equinox.

Llobera, Marcos 2005 New Paradigms and Methods for Landscape Research in Archaeology. Pp. 43–54 in Jean-François Berger, Frédérique Bertoncello, Frank Braemer, Gourguen Davtian and Michel Gazenbeek, eds., *Temps et Espaces de l'Homme en Société. Analyses et modèles spatiaux en archéologie*. Antibes: Éditions APDCA.

Lloyd, Seton and Fuad Safar 1943 Tell Uqair: Excavations by the Iraq Government Directorate of Antiquities in 1940 and 1941. *Journal of Near Eastern Studies* 2: 131–158.

Loudine, A. G. 1990 Le banquet ritual dans l'état de Saba. *Proceedings of the Seminar for Arabian Studies* 20: 95–100.

Lüling, G. 1981 *Die Wiederentdeckung des Propheten Muhammad. Ein Kritik am "chistlichen" Abenland.* Erlangen: Verlagsbuchhandlung Hannelore Lüling.

Lyon, B. 1987 Marc Bloch: Historian. *French Historical Studies* 15: 195–207.

Lyonnet, Bertille 2001 L'occupation des marges arides de la Djezire: pastoralisme et nomadisme aux débuts du 3e et du 2e millénaire. Pp. 15–26 in B. Geyer, ed., *Conquête de la Steppe.* Travaux Maison de l'Orient Mediterranéen 36. Lyon: Maison de l'Orient Mediterranéen.

Lyons, Diane 1996 The Politics of House Shape: Round vs. Rectilinear Domestic Structures in Déla Compounds, Northern Cameroon. *Antiquity* 70: 351–367.

Mack, Burton 1987 Introduction: Religion and Ritual. Pp. 1–70 in Robert G. Hamerton-Kelly, ed., *Violent Origins: Walter Burkert, René Girard and Jonathan Z. Smith on Ritual Killing and Cultural Formation.* Stanford, CA: Stanford University Press.

Maekawa, Kyazu 1980 Femal Weavers and Their Children in Lagash-Presargonic and Ur III. *Acta Sumerologica* 2: 81–125.

Maraqten, Mohammed 2008 Women's Inscriptions Recently Discovered by the AFSM at the Awām Temple/Maḥrām Bilqīs in Ma'rib, Yemen. *Proceedings of the Seminar for Arabian Studies* 38: 231–250.

1994 Typen altsüdarabischer Altäre. Pp. 160–177 in Rosemarie Richter, Ingo Kottsieper and Mohammed Maraqten, eds., *Arabia Felix: Beiträge zur Sprache und Kultur des vorislamischen Arabien (Festschrift Walter W. Müller).* Wiesbaden: Harrassowitz Verlag.

Marett, R. R. 1914 *The Threshold of Religion.* London: Methuen.

Margoliouth, David S. 1905 *Mohamed and the Rise of Islam.* New York: Putnam.

Margueron, Jean 1986 Quelques Remarques Concernant L'Architecture Monumentale À L'Époque d'Obeid. Pp. 349–377 in Jean-Louis Huot, ed., *Préhistoire de la Mésopotamie.* Colloques Internationaux CNRS. Paris: Éditions du CNRS.

Marshall, Fiona and Elisabeth Hildebrand 2002 Cattle before Crops: The Beginnings of Food Production in Africa. *Journal of World Prehistory* 16(2): 99–143.

Martin, Louise A. 1999 Mammal Remains from the Eastern Jordanian Neolithic and the Nature of Caprine Herding in the Steppe. *Paléorient* 25(2): 87–104.

Martin, Louise A., Joy McCorriston and Rémy Crassard 2009 The Earliest Arabian Domesticates: Faunal Remains from Manayzah, Yemen. *Proceedings of the Seminar for Arabian Studies* 39: 285–296.

Marx, Emmanuel 1992 Are There Pastoral Nomads in the Middle East? Pp. 255–261 in Ofer Bar-Yosef and Anatoly Khazanov, eds., *Pastoralism in the Levant: Archaeological Materials in Anthropological Perspectives.* Madison, WI: Prehistory Press.

1977 Communial and Individual Pilgrimage: The Region of Saints' Tombs in South Sinai. Pp. 29–54 in R. P. Werbner, ed., *Regional Cults.* London: Academic Press.

Marx, Karl 1973 *Grundrisse*. Hammondsworth: Penguin.

[1964] 1989 *Pre-Capitalist Economic Formations* [trans. F. Cohen]. Eleventh printing. New York: International Publishers.

Masry, Abdallah H. 1974 *Prehistory in Northeastern Arabia: The Problem of Interregional Interaction*. Miami: Field Research Projects, Coconut Grove.

McCabe, J. Terrence 2004 *Cattle Bring Us to Our Enemies*. Ann Arbor: University of Michigan Press.

McClure, Henry 1984 *Late Quaternary Palaeoenvironments of the Rub'al Khali*. Unpublished Ph.D. dissertation, University College, University of London.

McCorriston, Joy 2006 Breaking the Rainfall Barrier and the Tropical Spread of Near Eastern Agriculture into Southern Arabia. Pp. 217–236 in Douglas J. Kennett and Bruce Winterhalder, eds., *Behavioral Ecology and the Transition to Agriculture*. Berkeley: University of California Press.

1998 Landscape and Human Interaction in the Middle Habur Drainage from the Neolithic Period to the Bronze Age. P. 43–54 in M. Fortin and O. Aurenche, eds., *Espace naturel, espace habité en Syrie du Nord (10e–2e millénaires av J-C)*, Travaux de la Maison de l'Orient 28 and Canadian Society for Mesopotamian Studies 33. Lyon and Québec: Maison de l'Orient and Canadian Society for Mesopotamian Studies.

1997 The Fiber Revolution: Textile Extensification, Alienation, and Social Stratification in Ancient Mesopotamia. *Current Anthropology* 38: 517–549.

1992 *The Early Development of Agriculture in the Ancient Near East: An Ecological and Evolutionary Study*. Ph.D. dissertation, Yale University. Ann Arbor: University Microfilms.

McCorriston, Joy and Frank Hole 1991 The Ecology of Seasonal Stress and the Origins of Agriculture in the Near East. *American Anthropologist* 93: 46–69.

McCorriston, Joy and Louise Martin 2009 Chapter 23. Southern Arabia's Early Pastoral Population History: Some Recent Evidence. Pp. 237–250 in Michael D. Petraglia and Jeffrey I. Rose, eds., *Footprints in the Sand: Tracking the Evolution and History of Human Populations in Arabia*. New York: Springer Verlag.

McCorriston, Joy and Eric A. Oches 2001 Two Ancient Checkdams from Southern Arabia. *Antiquity* 75: 675–76.

McCorriston, Joy and Sanford Weisberg 2002 Spatial and Temporal Variation in Mesopotamian Agricultural Practices in the Khabur Basin, Syrian Jazira. *Journal of Archaeological Science* 29: 485–498.

McCorriston, Joy, Michael Harrower, Eric Oches and Abdalaziz Bin 'Aqil 2005 Foraging Economies and Population in the Middle Holocene Highland of Southern Yemen. *Proceedings of the Seminar for Arabian Studies* 35: 143–154.

McCorriston, Joy, Eric A. Oches, Dawn E. Walter and Kenneth Cole 2002 Holocene Paleoecology and Prehistory in Highland Southern Arabia. *Paléorient* 28(1): 61–88.

McGovern, Patrick, D. Glusker, L. Exner and Mary Voigt 1996 Neolithic Resinated Wine. *Nature* 381: 480–481.

Meinig, D. W. 1979 *The Interpretation of Ordinary Landscapes*. New York: Oxford University Press.

Méry, Sophie, Vincent Charpentier, G. Auxiette and E. Pelle 2009 A Dugong Bone Mound: The Neolithic Ritual Site on Akab in Umm al-Quwain. *Antiquity* 83: 696–708.

Méry, S., K. McSweeney, S. van der Leeuw and W. Y. Al Tikriti 2004 New Approaches to a Collective Grave from the Umm An-Nar Period at Hili (UAE). *Paléorient* 30(1): 163–178.

Méry, S., J. Rouquet, K. McSweeney, G. Basset, J.-F. Saliege and W. Y. Al Tikriti 2001 Re-excavation of the Early Bronze Age Collective Hili N Pit-grave (Emirate of Abu Dhabi, UAE): Results of the First Two Campaigns of the Emirati-French Project. *Proceedings of the Seminar for Arabian Studies* 31: 161–178.

Michalowski, Piotr 1987 Charisma and Control: On Continuity and Change in Early Mesopotamian Bureaucratic Systems. Pp. 5–58 in McGuire Gibson and Robert D. Biggs, eds., *The Organization of Power. Aspects of Bureaucracy in the Ancient Near East*. Studies in Ancient Oriental Civilization 46. Chicago: The Oriental Institute of the University of Chicago.

Miller, Naomi F. 1997 Farming and Herding along the Euphrates: Environmental Constraint and Cultural Choice (Fourth to Second Millennia BC). Pp. 123–132 in R. L. Zettler, *Subsistence and Settlement in a Marginal Environment: Tell es-Sweyhat, 1989–1995 Preliminary Report*. Masca Research Papers in Science and Archaeology 14. Philadelphia: University of Pennsylvania Museum.

Mitterauer, M. 1992 Peasant and Non-peasant Family Forms in Relation to the Physical Environment and the Local Economy. *Journal of Family History* 17: 139–159.

Monchambert, J.-Y. 1994 Prospection archéologiques sur l'emplacement du future lac du Moyen Khabur. *Akkadica* 39: 1–7.

Mooney, Harold A. and E. Lloyd Dunn 1970 Convergent Evolution of Mediterranean-Climate Evergreen Sclerophyll Shrubs. *Evolution* 24: 292–303.

Moore, Andrew, Gordon C. Hillman and Anthony J. Legge 2000 *Village on the Euphrates: From Foraging to Farming at Abu Hureyra*. Oxford: Oxford University Press.

Moore, Henrietta 1986 *Space, Text, and Gender. An Anthropological Study of the Marakwet of Kenya*. Cambridge: Cambridge University Press.

Moreland, John F. 1992 Restoring the Dialectic: Settlement Patterns and Documents in Medieval Central Italy. Pp. 112–129 in A. Bernard Knapp, ed., *Archaeology, Annales, and Ethnohistory*. Cambridge: Cambridge University Press.

Morgan, Lewis H. 1877 *Ancient Society*. Chicago: Charles H. Kerr & Co.

Morinis, Alan 1992a Introduction: The Territory of the Anthropology of Pilgrimage. Pp 4–30 in Alan Morinis, ed., *Sacred Journeys: The Anthropology of Pilgrimage*. Westport, CT: Greenwood Press.

1992b Persistent Peregrination: From Sun Dance to Catholic Pilgrimage among Canadian Prairie Indians. Pp. 101–113 in Alan Morinis, ed., *Sacred Journeys: The Anthropology of Pilgrimage*. Westport, CT: Greenwood Press.

1984 *Pilgrimage in the Hindu Tradition*. Delhi: Oxford University Press.

Morris, Ian 1991 The Archaeology of Ancestors: The Saxe/Goldstein Hypothesis Revisited. *Cambridge Archaeological Journal* 1: 147–169.

Morton, H. V. 1964 *In the Steps of the Master*. New York: Methuen.

Mouton, Michel, Anne Benoist, Jeremy Schiettecatte, Mounir Arbach and Vincent Bernard 2006 Makaynūn, an Ancient South Arabia Site in the Hadramawt. *Proceedings of the Seminar for Arabian Studies* 36: 229–242.

Müller, Walter W. 1979 Arabian Frankincense in Antiquity According to Classical Sources. Pp. 79-92 in Abdelgadir Mahmoud Abdalla, Sami Al-Sakkar and Richard T. Mortel, eds., *Studies in the History of Arabia I. Proceedings of the First International Symposium on Studies in the History of Arabia*. Riyadh: University of Riyadh.

    1976 Notes on the Use of Frankincense in South Arabia. *Proceedings of the Seminar for Arabian Studies* 9: 124–136.

Mumford, Lewis 1961 *The City in History: Its Origins, Its Transformations, and Its Prospects*. London: Secker and Warburg

Murdock, George P. 1981 *Atlas of World Cultures*. Pittsburgh: University of Pittsburgh Press.

Mytum, Harold 2007 Materiality and Memory: An Archaeological Perspective on the Popular Adoption of Linear Time in Britain. *Antiquity* 81: 381–396.

Nadel, Dani 2006 Residence Ownership and Continuity from the Early Epipalaeolithic into the Neolithic. Pp. 25–34 in Edward B. Banning and Michael Chazan, eds., *Domesticating Space: Construction, Community, and Cosmology in the Late Prehistoric Near East. Studies in Early Near Eastern Production, Subsistence, and Environment* 12. Berlin: Ex Oriente.

Naveh, Danny 2003 PPNA Jericho: A Socio-Political Perspective. *Cambridge Archaeological Journal* 13: 83–96.

Naveh, Zev 1975 The Evolutionary Significance of Fire in the Mediterranean Region. *Vegetatio* 29: 199–208.

Netting, Robert M. 1993 *Smallholders, Householders: Farm Families and the Ecology of Intensive, Sustainable Agriculture*. Stanford, CA: Stanford University Press.

Nichols, Deborah and Thomas Charlton, eds. 1997 *The Archaeology of City-States: Cross-Cultural Approaches*. Washington, DC: Smithsonian Institution Press.

Nissen, Hans J. 1988 *The Early History of the Ancient Near East 9000–2000 B.C.* [trans. Elizabeth Lutzeier with Kenneth J. Northcott]. Chicago: Chicago University Press.

Nissen, Hans J., Peter Damerow and Robert K. Englund 1993 *Archaic Bookkeeping*. Chicago: University of Chicago Press.

Noakes, Gregory 1999 The Servants of God's House. *Aramco World* 50: 48–67.

Noja, Sergio 1985 Une hypothèse sur l'origine du vêtement du Muhrim. *Annali di Istituto Universitario Orientale Napoli* 45: 405–408.

Nolan, Mary Lee and Sidney Nolan 1997 Regional Variations in Europe's Roman Catholic Pilgrimage Traditions. Pp. 61-94 in Robert H. Stoddard and Alan Morinis, eds., *Sacred Places, Sacred Spaces: The Geography of Pilgrimage*. Geoscience and Man 34. Baton Rouge: Louisiana State University.

Oates, David 1986 Different Traditions in Mesopotamian Temple Architecture in the Fourth Millennium B.C. Pp. 379–383 in Jean-Louis Huot, ed.,

Préhistoire de la Mésopotamie. Colloques Internationaux CNRS. Paris: Éditions du CNRS.

Obermeyer, Gerald 1999 Civilization and Religion in Ancient South Arabia. *Bulletin of the Royal Institute for Inter-Faith Studies* 1(1): 35–63.

Obeyesekere, Gananath 1966 The Buddhist Pantheon in Ceylon and Its Extensions. Pp 1–26 in Manning Nash, ed., *Anthropological Studies in Theravada Buddhism.* New Haven, CT: Yale University Southeast Asian Studies.

Ochsenschlager, Edward L. 2004 *Iraq's Marsh Arabs in the Garden of Eden.* Philadelphia: University of Pennsylvania Museum of Archaeology and Anthropology.

Orthmann, Winifred 1995 *Ausgrabungen in Tell Chuera in Nordost-Syrien 1 Vorbericht über die Grabungskampanien 1986–1992.* Saarbrücken: Saarbrücker Druckerei und Verlag.

Overpeck, J., D. Anderson, S. Trumbore, and W. Prell 1996 The Southwest Indian Monsoon over the Last 18,000 Years. *Climate Dynamics* 12: 213–225.

Özdoğan, Aslı 1999 Çäyönü. Pp. 35–64 in Mehmet Özdoğan and Nezih Başgelen, eds., *Neolithic in Turkey. The Cradle of Civilization: New Discoveries.* Istanbul: Arkeoloji ve Sanat Yayinlari.

Özdoğan, Mehmet and Nezih Başgelen, eds., 1999 *Neolithic in Turkey. The Cradle of Civilization: New Discoveries.* Istanbul: Arkeoloji ve Sanat Yayinlari.

Panchur, H.J. and P. Hoezlmann 1991 Paleoclimatic Implications of Late Quaternary Lacustrine Sediments in Western Nubia, Sudan. *Quaternary Research* 36: 257–276.

Panja, Sheena 2003 Monuments in a Flood Zone: "Builders" and "Recipients" in Ancient Varendri (Eastern India and Bangladesh). *Antiquity* 77: 497–504.

Park, Chris C. 1994 *Sacred Worlds: An Introduction to Geography and Religion.* London: Routledge.

Parker, S. Thomas 1987 Peasants, Pastoralists, and Pax Romana: A Different View. *Bulletin of the American Schools of Oriental Research* 265: 35–54.

Parker-Pearson, Michael 2000 *The Archaeology of Death and Burial.* College Station: Texas A&M University Press.

Parker-Pearson, M. and S. Ramilisonina 1998 Stonehenge for the Ancestors: The Stones Pass on the Message. *Antiquity* 72: 308–326.

Pauketat, Timothy R. and Susan M. Alt 2003 Mounds, Memory, and Contested Mississippian History. Pp. 151–179 in Ruth M. Van Dycke and Susan E. Alcock, eds., *Archaeologies of Memory.* Oxford: Blackwell.

Peasnall, Brian 2002 Appendix: Burials from Tepe Gawra, Levels VIII to XIA/B. Pp. 171–234 in Mitchell S. Rothman, *Tepe Gawra: The Evolution of a Small, Prehistoric Center in Northern Iraq.* University Museum Monograph 112, Philadelphia: University of Pennsylvania Museum of Archaeology and Anthropology.

Peltenburg, Edgar 2004 Cyprus – A Regional Component of the Levantine PPN. *Neolithics* 4(1): 3–7.

Peltenburg, Edgar, Sue Colledge, Paul Croft, Adam Jackson, Carole McCartney and Mary Anne Murray 2001 Neolithic Dispersals from the Levantine Corridor: A Mediterranean Perspective. *Levant* 33: 35–64.

Peters, F. E. 1994 *The Hajj: The Muslim Pilgrimage to Mecca and the Holy Places*. Princeton, NJ: Princeton University Press.

Peters, J. and Klaus Schmidt 2004 Animals in the Symbolic World of Pre-Pottery Neolithic Göbekli Tepe, South-Eastern Turkey: A Preliminary Assessment. *Anthropozoologica* 39(1): 179–218.

Peters, J. D. Helmer, A. von den Driesch and M. Saña Segui 1999 Early Animal Husbandry in the Northern Levant. *Paléorient* 25(2): 27–48.

Peterson, Jane 2002 *Sexual Revolutions: Gender and Labor at the Dawn of Agriculture*. Walnut Creek, CA: AltaMira Press.

Pfälzner, Peter. 2002 Modes of Storage and the Development of Economic Systems in the Early Jezireh Period. Pp. 259–286 in L. al-Gailani Werr, J. Curtis, H. Martin, A. McMahon, J. Oates and J. Reade, eds., *Of Pots and Plans: Papers on the Archaeology and History of Mesopotamia and Syria Presented to David Oates in Honour of His 75th Birthday*. London: Nabu Publications.

Phillips, Carl S. 2005 A Preliminary Description of the Pottery from al-Hāmid and Its Significance in Relation to Other Pre-Islamic Sites on the Tihāmah. *Proceedings for the Seminar for Arabian Studies* 35: 177–193.

1998 The Tihāmah c. 5000 to 500 BC. *Proceedings of the Seminar for Arabian Studies* 28: 233–237.

Piaget, J. 1970 *The Child's Conception of Time*. London: Routledge.

Pignatti, Sandro 1979 Plant Geographical and Morphological Evidences in the Evolution of the Mediterranean Flora (with Particular Reference to the Italian Representative). *Webbia* 34: 243–255.

Pillaud, Marin A. 2009 *Community Structure at Neolithic Çatalhöyük: Biological Distance Analysis of Household, Neighborhood and Settlement*. Ph.D. dissertation, The Ohio State University.

Pirenne, Jacqueline 1991 Les 'Arbay du dieu 'Amm de Labakh et Leur Sanctuaire Rupestre. Pp. 153–166 in Etudes Sud-Arabes. *Recueil offert à Jacques Ryckmans*. Publications de L'Institut Orientaliste de Louvain 39. Louvain la-Neuve: Université Catholique de Louvain.

1990 *Fouilles de Shabwa 1. Les Témoins Écrits de la région de SHABWA et l'Histoire*. Paris: Geuthner.

1976 La religion des Arabes preislamiques. Pp. 177–217 in *Al Bahit. Festschrift Joseph Henninger*. Studia Instituti Anthropos 28. Bonn: Verlag des Anthropos Instituts.

1972 RShW, RShWT, FDY, FDYT and the Priesthood in Ancient South Arabia. *Proceedings of the Seminar for Arabian Studies* 9: 137–143.

Pollock, Susan 2001 The Uruk Period in Southern Mesopotamia. Pp. 181–231 in Mitchell S. Rothman, ed., *Uruk Mesopotamia and Its Neighbors*. Santa Fe: School of American Research Press.

1999 *Ancient Mesopotamia: The Eden That Never Was*. Cambridge: Cambridge University Press.

Porter, Anne 2002 The Dynamics of Death: Ancestors, Pastoralism, and the Origins of a Third-Millennium City in Syria. *Bulletin of the American Schools of Oriental Research* 325: 1–36.

Postgate, J. Nicholas 1992 *Early Mesopotamia: Society and Economy at the Dawn of History*. London: Routledge.

Potts, Daniel T. 1997 *Mesopotamia: The Material Foundations*. Ithaca, NY: Cornell University Press.

Potts, Timothy 1994 *Mesopotamia and the East*. Oxford: Oxford University Committee for Archaeology Monograph 37.

Pred, Allan 1977 The Choreography of Existence: Comments on Hägerstrand's Time-Geography and Its Usefulness. *Economic Geography* 53: 207–221.

Preston, James J. 1992 Spiritual Magnetism: An Organizing Principle for the Study of Pilgrimage. Pp. 31–46 in Alan Morinis, ed. *Sacred Journeys. The Anthropology of Pilgrimage*. Westport, CT: Greenwood Press.

Prorok, Carolyn V. 1997 Becoming a Place of Pilgrimage: An Eliadean Interpretation of the Miracle at Ambridge, Pennsylvania. Pp. 117–139 in Robert H. Stoddard and Alan Morinis, eds., *Sacred Places, Sacred Spaces: The Geography of Pilgrimage*. Geoscience and Man 34. Baton Rouge: Louisiana State University.

Rachad, Madiha 2007 Chapitre VII Chronologie et styles de l'art rupestre. Chapitre VIII Thèmes de l'art rupestre. Pp. 73–94 in Marie-Louise Inizan and Madiha Rachad, eds., *Art rupestre et peuplements préhistoriques au Yémen*. Sana'a: CEFAS.

Radcliffe-Brown, A. R. 1958 *Method in Social Anthropology: Selected Essays*. Chicago: University of Chicago Press.

1952 *Structure and Function in Primitive Society: Essays and Addresses*. New York: Free Press.

1940 On Social Structure. Presidential Address. *Journal of the Royal Anthropological Institute* 70: 1–12. (Reprinted 1977 in Adam Kuper, ed., The Social Anthropology of Radcliffe-Brown. London: Routledge Kegan Paul.)

Rafeq, A.-K. 1987 New Light on the Transportation of the Damascene Pilgrimage during the Ottoman Period. Pp. 127–136 in R. Olson, ed., *Islamic and Middle Eastern Studies*. Brattleboro, VT: Amana Books.

Rapoport, Amos 1982 *The Meaning of the Built Environment: A Nonverbal Communication Approach*. Beverly Hills, CA: Sage Publications.

1969 *House Form and Culture*: Englewood Cliffs, NJ: Prentice Hall.

Ratnagar, Shireen 2003 Theorizing Bronze-Age Intercultural Trade: The Evidence of the Weights. *Paléorient* 29(1): 79–92.

2001 The Bronze Age, Unique Instance of a Pre-industrial World System. *Current Anthropology* 42: 351–365.

Raunig, Walter 1997 Die Suche nach dem Zentrum von Ausan. Pp. 145–152 in *Mare Erythraeum I*. München: Staatliches Museum für Völkerkunde.

Raven, Peter H. 1973 The Evolution of Mediterranean Floras. Pp. 213–224 in Francesco di Castri and Harold A. Mooney, eds., *Mediterranean-Type Ecosystems: Origin and Structure*. New York: Springer Verlag.

Reade, Julian and Daniel T. Potts 1993 New Evidence for Late Third Millennium Linen from Tell Abraq, Umm al-Qaiwain, UAE. *Paléorient* 19: 99–106.

Redfield, Robert [1955] 1967 The Social Organization of Tradition. Pp. 25–34 in Jack M. Potter, May N. Diaz and George M. Foster, eds., *Peasant Society, A Reader*. Boston: Little Brown.

Reinhold, Jacques 2000 *Archéologie au Soudan*. Paris: Editions Errance.

Renfrew, Colin 1998 Mind and Matter: Cognitive Archaeology and External Symbolic Storage. Pp. 1–6 in Colin Renfrew and Chris Scarre, eds., *Cognition and Material Culture: The Archaeology of Symbolic Storage*. Cambridge: McDonald Institute Monographs, McDonald Institute for Archaeological Research.

1976 Megaliths, Territories and Population. Pp. 198–220 in S. Laet, ed., *Acculturation and Continuity in Atlantic Europe*. Bruges: De Tempel.

1973 Monuments, Mobilization and Social Organization in Neolithic Wessex. Pp. 539–558 in Colin Renfrew, ed., *The Explanation of Culture Change: Models in Prehistory*. London: Duckworth.

Renger, Johannes M. 1995 Institutional, Communal, and Individual Ownership or Possession of Arable Land in Ancient Mesopotamia from the End of the Fourth to the End of the First Millennium B.C. *Chicago Kent Law Review* 71: 269–319.

1994 On Economic Structures in Ancient Mesopotamia. *Orientalia* 63: 157–208.

Richerson, Peter, Robert Boyd and Robert Bettinger 2001 Was Agricultures Impossible during the Pleistocene but Mandatory during the Holocene? A Climate Change Hypothesis. *American Antiquity* 66: 387–411.

Rinschede, Gisbert and Angelika Sievers 1987 The Pilgrimage Phenomenon in Socio-Geographical Research. *The National Geographical Journal of India* 33: 213–217.

Roaf, Michael 1986 The 'Ubaid Architecture of Tell Madhur. Pp. 425–429 in Jean-Louis Huot, ed., *Préhistoire de la Mésopotamie. Colloques Internationaux CNRS*. Paris: Éditions du CNRS.

Robertson Smith, William 1907a *Lectures on the Religion of the Semites*. London: Adam and Charles Black.

[1885] 1907b *Kinship and Marriage in Early Arabia*. London: Adam and Charles Black.

Robin, Christian 2000 Les "Filles de Dieu" de Saba à La Mecque: Réflexions sur l'Agencement des Panthéons dans l'Arabie Ancienne. *Semitica* 50: 113–192.

1984 La civilization de l'Arabie meridionale avant l'Islam. Pp 195–223 in J. Chelhod, ed., *L'Arabie du Sud: histoire et civilization: I. Le people Yémenite et ses racines*. Paris: G-P Maisonneuve et Larose.

1982a Esquisse d'une histoire de l'organisation tribale en Arabie du sud antique. Pp. 17–30 in P. Bonnenfant, ed., *La péninsuéle arabique d'aujourd'hui*. Paris: Centre National de la recherche scientifique.

1982b Les Hautes-Terres du Nord-Yemen avant L'Islam. Tome I. *Recherches sur la Géographie Tribale et Réligieuse de Ḥawlān Quda'a et du Pays de Hamdan*. Istanbul: Nederlands Historisch-Archaeologisch Instiuut.

Robin, Christian and Jean-François Breton 1982 Le sanctuaire préislamique du Ğabal al-Lawd (Nord-Yémen). *Comptes Rendus de l'Académie des Inscriptions et Belles-Lettres* 1982: 590–629.

Robin, Christian and Serge Frantsouzoff 1999 Une inscription Hadramawtique provenant du Temple de Siyan Dhū-Alīm à Shabwa (Yémen). *Semitica* 49: 155–160.

Rodinov, Mikhail A. 1997 Mawlā Matar and Other Awliyā': On Social Functions of Religious Places in Western Hadhramawt. Pp. 107–114 in *Mare Erythraeum I*. München: Staatliches Museum für Völkerkunde.

Rollefson, Gary O. 2005 Early Neolithic Ritual Centers in the Southern Levant. *Neolithics* 2(5): 3–13.

2000 Ritual and Social Structure at Neolithic 'Ain Ghazal. Pp. 165–190 in Ian Kuijt, ed., *Life in Neolithic Farming Communities. Social Organization, Identity, and Differentiation*. New York: Kluwer Academic/Plenum Press.

1997 Changes in Architecture and Social Organization at 'Ain Ghazal. Pp. 287–307 in Hans Georg Gebel, Zeidan Kafafi and Gary O. Rollefson, eds., *The Prehistory of Jordan, II. Perspectives from 1997*. SENEPSE 4. Berlin: ex oriente.

1990 The Uses of Plaster at Neolithic 'Ain Ghazal, Jordan. *Archaeomaterials* 40: 33–54.

Rollefson, Gary O. and Ilse Köhler Rollefson 1992 Early Neolithic Exploitation Patterns in the Levant: Cultural Impact on the Environment. *Population and Environment* 13: 243–254.

Röllig, W. and H. Kühne 1983 Lower Khabur: Second Preliminary Report on a Survey in 1997. *Les Annales Archéologiques Arabes Syriennes* 33(1): 187–199.

Ronen, A. and D. Adler 2001 The Walls of Jericho Were Magical. *Archaeology, Ethnology, and Anthropology of Eurasia* 2: 97–103.

Rosen, Steven A. 2002 The Evolution of Pastoral Nomadic Systems in the Southern Levantine Periphery. Pp. 23–44 in E. van den Brink and E. Yannai, eds., *Quest of Ancient Settlements and Landscapes: Archaeological Studies in Honour of Ram Gophna*. Tel Aviv: Ramot Publishing.

Rosen, Steven A., Fanny Bocquentin, Yoav Avni and Naomi Porat 2007 Investigations at Ramat Saharonim: A Desert Neolithic Sacred Precinct in the Central Negev. *Bulletin of the American Schools of Oriental Research* 346: 1–27.

Rosenberg, Michael 1999 Hallan Çemi. Pp. 25–33 in Mehmet Özdoğan and Nezih Başgelen, eds., *1999 Neolithic in Turkey. The Cradle of Civilization: New Discoveries*. Istanbul: Arkeoloji ve Sanat Yayinlari.

1998 Cheating at Musical Chairs: Territoriality and Sedentism in an Evolutionary Context. *Current Anthropology* 39: 653–664.

Rosenberg, Michael and Richard W. Redding 2000 Hallan Cemi and Early Village Organization in Eastern Anatolia. Pp. 39–61 in Ian Kuijt, ed., *Life in Neolithic Farming Communities: Social Organization, Identity, and Differentiation*. New York: Kluwer Academic Press/Plenum Publishers.

Rosenberg, Michael, Mark Nesbitt, Richard Redding and Brian Peasnall 1998 Hallan Çemi, Pig Husbandry, and Post-Pleistocene Adaptations Along the Taurus-Zagros Arc (Turkey). *Paléorient* 24: 25–41.

Rosenberg, Michael, Mark R. Nesbitt, Richard W. Redding and T. F. Strasser 1995 Hallan Çemi Tepesi: Some Preliminary Observations Concerning Early Neolithic Subsistence Behaviors in Eastern Anatolia. *Anatolica* 21: 1–12.

Rostovtzeff, M. 1932 *Caravan Cities* [trans. D. Talbot Rice and T. Talbot Rice]. Oxford: Clarendon Press.

Rowlands, M. 1993 The Role of Memory in the Transmission of Culture. *World Archaeology* 25: 141–151.

Rowley, Gwyn 1997 The Pilgrimage to Mecca and the Centrality of Islam. Pp. 141–159 in Robert H. Stoddard and Alan Morinis, eds., *Sacred Places, Sacred Spaces: The Geography of Pilgrimage*. Geoscience and Man 34. Baton Rouge: Louisiana State University.

Rowton, Michael B. 1976 Dimorphic Structure and Topology. *Oriens Antiquus* 15: 17–31.

1975 Enclosed Nomadism. *Journal of the Economic and Social History of the Orient* 17: 1–30.

1973 Autonomy and Nomadism in Western Asia. *Orientalia* 42: 247–248.

Rubin, U. [1990] 1999 Hanīfiyya and Ka'ba: An Inquiry into the Arabian Pre-Islamic Background of Dīn Ibrāhīm. Pp. 313–347 in F. E. Peters, ed., *The Arabs and Arabia on the Eve of Islam*. Aldershot, UK: Ashgate. [Reprinted from *Jerusalem Studies in Arabic and Islam* 13: 85–112. Max Schloessinger Memorial Foundation, Institute of Asian and African Studies, the Hebrew University of Jerusalem.]

Rubio, Gonzalo 2005 On the Linguistic Landscape of Early Mesopotamia. Pp. 316–332 in W. H. Van Soldt, ed., *Ethnicity in Ancient Mesopotamia. Papers Read at the 48th Rencontre Assyriologique Internationale Leiden 2002*. Istanbul: Nederlands Instituut voor het Nabije Oosten.

1999 On the Alleged Pre-Sumerian Substratum. *Journal of Cuneiform Studies* 51: 1–16.

Rudolph, R. L. 1992 The European Family and Economy: Central Themes and Issues. *Journal of Family History* 17: 119–138.

Russell, Kenneth W. 1988 After Eden. *The Behavioral Ecology of Early Food Production in the Near East and North Africa*. Oxford: British Archaeological Reports, International Series 391.

Russell, Nerissa and Louise Martin 2005 Çatalhöyük Mammal Remains. Pp. 33–98 in Ian Hodder, ed., *Inhabiting Çatalhöyük: Reports from the 1995–99 Seasons*. Cambridge: McDonald Institute Monographs/British Institute of Archaeology at Ankara.

Russell, Nerissa, Louise Martin and Hijlke Buitenhuis 2005 Cattle Domestication at Çatalhöyük Revisted. *Current Anthropology* 46 Supplement: S101–S108.

Rutter, Eldon 1929 The Muslim Pilgrimage. *The Geographical Journal* 74: 271–273.

Ryan, Kathleen, Karega Munene, Samuel M. Kahinju and Paul N. Kunoni 2000 Ethnographic Perspectives on Cattle Management in Semi-arid Environments: A Case Study from Maasailand. Pp. 462–477 in Roger M. Blench and Kevin C. MacDonald, eds., *The Origins and Development of African Livestock: Archaeology, Genetics, Linguistics, and Ethnography*. London: UCL Press.

Ryckmans, Gonzague 1951 *Les religions Arabes préislamiques*. Louvain: Publications Universitaires.

Ryckmans, Jacques 1983 Biblical and Old South Arabian Institutions: Some Parallels. Pp. 14–25 in Robin L. Bidwell and G. Rex Smith, eds., *Arabian and Islamic Studies*. Articles Presented to R. B. Serjeant. London: Longman.

1976 La chasse rituelle dans l'Arabie du sud ancienne. Pp. 259–308 in *Al-Bahit. Festschrift Joseph Henninger*. Studia Instituti Anthropos 28. Bonn: Verlag des Anthropos Instituts.

1975 Les inscriptions sud-arabes anciennes et les études arabes. *Annali dell'Istituto Orientale di Napoli N.S. 25*, 35: 443–463.

1973a Les Inscriptions Anciennes de L'Arabie du Sud: Point de Vue et Problemes Actuels. *Oosters Genootschap in Nederland*. Leiden: E. J. Brill.

1973b Ritual Meals in the Ancient South Arabian Religion. *Proceedings of the Seminar for Arabian Studies* 3: 36–39.

1973c Le repas ritual dans la réligion sud-arabe. Pp. 327–334 in M. A. Beek, A. A. Kampman, C. Nijland and J. Ryckmans, eds., *Symbolae Biblicae et Mesopotamicae: Francisco Mario Theodoro de Liagre Böhl Dedicatae*. Leiden: E. J. Brill.

Ryckmans, Jacques, Walter W. Müller and Yusuf M. Abdulla 1994 Textes du Yémen antique: inscrits sur bois (with an English Summary). *Publications del'Institut orientaliste de Louvain*, 43. Louvain la Neuve: Université catholique de Louvain.

Safar, Fouad and I. Ali 1981 *Eridu*. Baghdad: Ministry of Culture and Information, State Organization of Antiquities and Heritage.

Sahlins, Marshall 1995 *How "Natives" Think: About Captain Cook for Example*. Chicago: University of Chicago Press.

1985 *Islands of History*. Chicago: University of Chicago Press.

1981 *Historical Metaphors and Mythical Realities: Structure in the Early History of the Sandwich Islands Kingdom*. Ann Arbor: University of Michigan Press.

1976 *Culture and Practical Reason*. Chicago: University of Chicago Press.

1972 *Stone Age Economics*. Chicago: Aldine.

Sahlins, Marshall and Elman Service, eds., 1960 *Evolution and Culture*. Ann Arbor: University of Michigan Press.

Said, Edward W. 1979 *Orientalism*. New York: Random House [Vintage Books edition].

Sallnow, M. J. 1981 Communitas Reconsidered: The Sociology of Andean Pilgrimage. *Man* 16: 163–182.

Saxe, Arthur A. 1970 *Social Dimensions of Mortuary Practice*. Ph.D. dissertation, University of Michigan. Ann Arbor: University Microfilms.

Scagliarini, Fiorella 2007 The Word slm/snm and Some Words for "statue, idol" in Arabian and Other Semitic Languages. *Proceedings of the Seminar for Arabian Studies* 37: 253–262.

Schama, Simon 1995 *Landscape and Memory*. New York: Knopf.

Schloen, J. David 2001 The House of the Father as Fact and Symbol. *Harvard Semitic Museum Publications 2*. Winona Lake, WI: Eisenbrauns.

Schmidt, Klaus 2005a Ritual Centers and the Neolithisation of Upper Mesopotamia. *Neolithics* 2(5): 13–21.

2005b Die "Stadt" der Steinzeit. Pp. 25–38 in H. Falk, ed., *Wege zur Stadt: Entwicklung und Formen urbanen Lebens in der alten Welt*. Vergleichende Studien zu Antike und Orient 2. Bremen.

2001 Göbekli Tepe, Southeastern Turkey. A Preliminary Report on the 1995–1999 Excavations. *Paléorient* 26(1): 45–54.

Schoup, John 1990 Middle Eastern Sheep Pastoralism and the Hima System. Pp. 195–215 in John G. Galaty and Douglas L. Johnson, eds., *The World of Pastoralism: Herding Systems in Comparative Perspective*. New York: The Guilford Press.

Schwartz, Glenn and Steven E. Falconer 1994 *Archaeological Views from the Countryside: Village Communities in Early Complex Societies*. Washington, DC: Smithsonian Press.

Schwartz, Glenn M., Hans H. Curvers, Sally Dunham and Barbara Stuart 2003 A Third Millennium B.C. Elite Tomb and Other New Evidence from Tell Umm el-Marra, Syria. *American Journal of Archaeology* 107: 325–361.

Sedov, Alexander V. 2005 *Temples of Ancient Hadramawt*. Arabia Antica 3. Pisa: Edizione Plus.

2003 Notes on Stratigraphy and Pottery Sequence at Raybun I Settlement (Western Wadi Hadramawt) in Arabia. *Révue de sabéologie* 1: 173–196.

2000 Temples of Raybun Oasis in Wadi Hadramawt, Yemen. *Adumatu* 2: 15–26.

1998 *The Coinage of Ancient Hadramawt*. Moscow: Center for Strategic and International Research. [In Russian, with English summary]

1988. Raybun, a Complex of Archaeological Monuments in the Lower Reaches of Wadi Dau'an, and Certain Problems of Its Protection and Restoration. Pp. 61–66 in *Ancient and Mediaeval Monuments of Civilization of Southern Arabia*. Moscow.

1996 Monuments of the Wadi al-'Ayn. Notes on an Archaeological Map of the Hadramawt, 3. *Arabian Archaeology and Epigraphy* 7: 253–278.

Sergeant, Robert B. 1983 Early Arabic Prose. Pp. 114–153 in A. F. L. Beeston, T. M. Johnstone, R. B. Sergeant and G. R. Smith, eds., *Arabic Literature to the End of the Umayyad Period. Cambridge History of Arabic Literature*. London: Cambridge University Press.

1981 *Studies in Arabian History and Civilization*. London: Variorum Reprints.

1976 *South Arabian Hunt*. London: Luzac.

1971 The "White Dune" at Abyan: An Ancient Place of Pilgrimage in Southern Arabia. *Journal of Semitic Studies* 16: 74–83.

1962 Haram and Hawtah, the Sacred Enclave in Arabia. Pp. 41–58 in Abdurrahman Badawi, ed., *Mélanges Taha Husain*. Cairo: Dar al-Maaref.

1954 Hud and Other Pre-Islamic Prophets of Hadramawt. *Le Muséon* 67: 121–179.

Seri, Andrea 2005 *Local Power in Old Babylonian Mesopotamia*. London: Equinox.

Service, Elman R. 1962 Primitive Social Organization. *An Evolutionary Perspective*. New York: Random House.

Sewell, William H. Jr. 1996 Political Events as Structural Transformations: Inventing Revolution at the Bastille. *Theory and Society* 25: 841–881.

1992 A Theory of Structure: Duality, Agency, and Transformation. *American Journal of Sociology* 98: 1–29.

Shair, Issa 1979 Review of the English Literature on Spatial Pilgrim Circulation. *Journal of the College of Arts, University of Riyadh* 6: 1–7.

Shair, Issa and P. P. Karan 1979 Geography of the Islamic Pilgrimage. *GeoJournal* 3(6): 599–608.

Shirai, Noriyuki 2005 Walking with Herdsmen: In Search of the Material Evidence for the Diffusion of Agriculture from the Levant to Egypt. *Neolithics* 1/05: 12–17.

Shutova, Nadezhda 2006 Trees in Udmurt Religion. *Antiquity* 80: 318–327.

Simeone-Senelle, Marie-Claire 1991 Recents développements des recherches sur les langues sudarabiques modernes. Pp. 321–337 in *Proceedings of the Fifth International Hamito-Semitic Congress*. Volume 2. Vienna: Ver offentlichungen der Institut für Afrikanistik und Ägyptologie der Universität Wien.

Simmons, Alan H. 2007 *The Neolithic Revolution in the Near East*. Tucson: University of Arizona Press.

Singer, Milton 1974 Robert Redfield's Development of a Social Anthropology of Civilizations. Pp. 187–260 in John V. Murra, ed., *American Anthropology, The Early Years. 1974 Proceedings of the American Ethnological Society*. St. Paul: West Publishing Co.

Sirocko, Frank 1996 The Evolution of the Monsoon Climate over the Arabian Sea during the Last 24,000 Years. Pp. 53–69 in K. Heine, ed., *Palaeoecology of Africa*. Rotterdam: A. A. Balkema.

Sirocko, Frank, M. Sarnthein, H. Erlenkeuser, H. Lange, M. Arnold and J. C. Duplessy 1993 Century Scale Events in Monsoonal Climate over the Past 24,000 Years. *Nature* 364: 322–324.

Smith, Bruce D. 2001 Low Level Food Productions. *Journal of Archaeological Research* 9: 1–43.

Smith, Jonathan Z. 1982 *Imagining Religion: From Babylon to Jonestown*. Chicago: University of Chicago Press.

Smith, Michael E. 1987 Household Possessions and Wealth in Agrarian States: Implications for Archaeology. *Journal of Anthropological Archaeology* 6: 297–335.

Smith, Sidney 1954 Events in Arabia in the 6th Century A.D. *Bulletin of the School of Oriental and African Studies* 16: 425–468.

Sopher, David E. 1997 The Goal of Indian Pilgrimage: Geographical Considerations. Pp. 183–190 in Robert H. Stoddard and Alan Morinis, eds., *Sacred Places, Sacred Spaces: The Geography of Pilgrimages*. Geoscience and Man 34. Baton Rouge: Louisiana State University.

1987 The Message of Place in Hindu Pilgrimage. *The National Geographic Journal of India* 33: 353–369.

1967 *Geography of Religions*. New York: Prentice Hall.

Spengler, Oswald [1922] 1926 *The Decline of the West* [trans. Charles Atkinson]. New York: Alfred Knopf.

Sperling, Louise and John G. Galaty 1990 Cattle, Culture, and Economy: Dynamics in East African Pastoralism. Pp. 69–98 in John G. Galaty and Douglas L. Johnson, eds., *The World of Pastoralism: Herding Systems in Comparative Perspective*. New York and London: The Guildford Press and Belhaven Press.

Spooner, Brian 1973 *The Cultural Ecology of Pastoral Nomads*. Reading, MA: Addison-Wesley Publishing.

Stahl, Ann Brower 1993 Concepts of Time and Approaches to Analogical Reasoning in Historical Perspective. *American Antiquity* 58: 235–260.

Stark, Freya 1953 *The Coast of Incense*. London: John Murray.

Steimer-Herbet, Tara 2004 *Classification des sepultures à superstructures lithique dans le Levant et l'Arabie occidentale (IVe et IIIe millénaires avant J.-C.)*. Oxford: British Archaeological Reports International Series 1246.

1999 Jabal Ruwaik: Megaliths in Yemen. *Proceedings of the Seminar for Arabian Studies* 29: 179–182.

Stein, Gil J. 2004 Structural Parameters and Sociocultural Factors in the Economic Organization of North Mesopotamian Urbanism in the Third Millennium BC Pp. 61–78 in Gary M. Feinman and Linda M. Nicholas, eds., *Archaeological Perspectives on Political Economies*. Salt Lake City: University of Utah Press.

1999 Rethinking World Systems. *Diasporas, Colonies, and Interaction in Uruk Mesopotamia*. Arizona: University of Arizona Press.

1994 Economy, Ritual, and Power in 'Ubaid Mesopotamia. Pp. 35–46 in Gil Stein and Mitchell S. Rothman, eds., *Chiefdoms and Early States in the Near East: The Organizational Dynamics of Complexity*. Madison, WI: Prehistory Press.

1987 Regional Economic Integration in Early State Societies: Third Millennium BC Pastoral Production at Gritille, Southeast Turkey. *Paléorient* 13: 101–111.

Steward, Julian 1968 Cultural Ecology. Pp. 337–344 in David L. Sills, ed., *International Encyclopedia of the Social Sciences*. New York: Macmillan.

Stol, Marten 2004 Teil 3. Wirtschaft und Gesellschaft in altbabylonischer Zeit. Pp. 643–975 in Dominique Charpin, Dietz Otto Edzard and Marten Stol, eds., *Mesopotamien: Die altbabylonische Zeit. Orbis Biblicus et Orientalis 160/4*. Fribourg and Göttingen: Academic Press Fribourg/Vandenhoeck and Ruprecht Göttingen.

Stone, Elizabeth C. 2000 The Development of Cities in Ancient Mesopotamia. Pp. 235–248 in Jack M. Sasson, ed., *Civilizations of the Ancient Near East. Volumes I and II*. Peabody, MA: Hendrickson.

1999 The Constraints on State and Urban Form in Ancient Mesopotamia. Pp. 203–228 in Michael Hudson and Baruch A. Levine, eds., *Urbanization and Land Ownership in the Ancient Near East. Peabody Museum Bulletin 7*. Cambridge, MA: Peabody Museum of Archaeology and Ethnology, Harvard University.

1997 City-States and Their Centers: The Mesopotamian Example. Pp. 15–26 in D. L. Nichols and T. H. Charlton, eds., *The Archaeology of City-States: Cross-Cultural Approaches*. Washington, DC: Smithsonian Institution Press.

1987 Nippur Neighborhoods. *Studies in Ancient Oriental Civilization*. Volume 44. Chicago: Oriental Institute of the University of Chicago.

Stone, Glenn D. 1996 *Settlement Ecology: The Social and Spatial Organization of Kofyar Agriculture*. Tucson: University of Arizona Press.

Stordeur, Danielle 2004 New Insights and Concepts: Two Themes of the Neolithic in Syria and South-East Anatolia. *Neolithics* 1(4): 49–51.

2000 New Discoveries in Architecture and Symbolism at Jerf el Ahmar (Syria), 1997–1999. *Neolithics* 1(0): 1–4.

Tapper, Nancy 1990 Ziyarat: Gender, Movement, and Exchange in a Turkish Community. Pp. 236–255 in Dale F. Eickelman and James Piscatori, eds., *Muslim Travellers. Pilgrimage, Migration, and the Religious Imagination*. London: Routledge.

Tapper, Richard 1990 Anthropologists, Historians, and Tribespeople on Tribe and State Formation in the Middle East. Pp. 48–73 in Philip S. Khoury and Joseph Kostiner, eds., *Tribes and State Formation in the Middle East*. Berkeley: University of California Press.

Terray, Emmanuel 1972 *Marxism and "Primitive Societies." Two Studies* [trans. Mary Klopper]. New York: Monthly Review Press.

Terrell, John 1986 *Prehistory in the Pacific Islands*. Cambridge: Cambridge University Press.

Terrenato, Nicola and Albert J. Ammerman 1996 Visibility and Site Recovery in the Cecina Valley Survey, Italy. *Journal of Field Archaeology* 23: 91–110.

Testart, Alan 2008 Des cranes et des vautours ou la guerre oubliée. *Paléorient* 34(1): 33–38.

Thayer, James Steel 1992 Pilgrimage and Its Influence on West African Islam. Pp. 169–187 in Alan Morinis, ed., *Sacred Journeys. The Anthropology of Pilgrimage*. Westport, CT: Greenwood Press.

Thomas, Bertram 1938 *Arabia Felix*. London: Jonathan Cape.

Tilley, Christopher C. 1994 *A Phenomenology of Landscape: Places, Paths and Monuments*. Oxford: Berg.

Tilly, Charles 1984 *Big Structures, Large Processes, Huge Comparisons*. New York: Russell Sage Foundation.

Torrey, Charles C. 1933 *The Jewish Foundations of Islam*. New York: Jewish Institute of Religion Press.

Tosi, Maurizio 1986a The Emerging Picture of Prehistoric Arabia. *Annual Reviews in Anthropology* 15: 461–490.

1986b Archaeological Activities in the Yemen Arab Republic 1986: Survey and Excavations on the Coastal Plain (Tihamah). *East and West* 36: 400–415.

1985 Archaeological Activities in the Yemen Arab Republic, 1985: Tihamah Coastal Archaeology Survey. *East and West* 35: 363–369.

Toynbee, Arnold J. 1934–1954 *A Study of History. Volumes 1–12*. London: Oxford University Press.

Trabaud, L. 1981 Man and Fire: Impacts on Mediterranean Vegetation. Pp. 523–538 in Francesco di Castri, David W. Goodall and Raymond L. Specht, eds., *Mediterranean-type Shrublands. Ecosystems of the World 11*. Amsterdam: Elsevier Scientific.

Trigger, Bruce G. 2003 *Understanding Early Civilizations*. Cambridge: Cambridge University Press.

1993 *Early Civilizations. Ancient Egypt in Context*. Cairo: American University in Cairo Press.

Turner, Victor 1977 Death and the Dead in the Pilgrimage Process. Pp. 24–39 in Frank E. Reynolds and Earl Waugh, eds., *Religious Encounters with Death*. University Park: Pennsylvania State University Press.

1974a *Dramas, Fields, and Metaphors*. Ithaca, NY: Cornell University Press.

1974b Pilgrimage and Communitas. *Studia missionalia* 23: 305–327.

1969 The Ritual Process: Structure and Anti-Structure. *The Lewis Henry Morgan Lectures, 1966*. Ithaca, NY: Cornell University Press.

Turner, Victor and Edith Turner 1978 *Image and Pilgrimage in Christian Culture*. New York: Columbia University Press.

Twiss, Katheryn C. 2007 The Zooarchaeology of Tel Tf'dan (Wadi Fidan 001), Southern Jordan. *Paléorient* 33(2): 127–146.

Twiss, Katheryn C., Amy Bogaard, Doru Bogdan, Tristan Carter, Michael P. Charles, Shahina Farid, Nerissa Russell, Mirjana Stevanović, E. Nurcan Yalman and Lisa Yeomans 2008 Arson or Accident? The Burning of a Neolithic House at Çatalhöyük, Turkey. *Journal of Field Archaeology* 33: 59–84.

Uerpmann, Hans-Peder 1999 Camel and Horse Skeletons from Protohistoric Graves at Mleiha in the Emirate of Sharjah (U.A.E.). *Arabian Archaeology and Epigraphy* 10: 102–118.

Uerpmann, Hans-Peder and Margarethe Uerpmann 2008 Neolithic Faunal Remains from al-Buhais 18 (Sharjah, UAE). Pp. 97–132 in H.-P. Uerpmann, M. Uerpmann and S. Jasim, eds., The Natural Environment of Jebel al-Buhais: Past and Present. *The Archaeology of Jebel Al-Buhais, Sharjah, United Arab Emirates. Volume 2*. Tuebingen: Kerns Verlag.

2000 Faunal Remains of Al-Buhais 18: An Aceramic Neolithic Site in the Emirate of Sharjah (SE Arabia) – Excavations 1995–1998. Pp. 40–49 in M. Mashkour, A. M. Choyke, H. Buitenhuis and F. Poplin, eds., *Archaeozoology of the Near East IVb*. Groningen: ARC-Publicatie 32.

Uerpmann, Hans-Peder, Margarethe Uerpmann and S. Jasim 2000 Stone Age Nomadism in SE Arabia – Palaeo-Economic Considerations on the Neolithic Site of Al-Buhais 18 in the Emirate of Sharjah, U.A.E. *Proceedings of the Seminar for Arabian Studies* 30: 229–234.

Uerpmann, Margarethe 1992 Structuring the Late Stone Age of Southern Arabia. *Arabian Archaeology and Epigraphy* 3: 65–109.

Urban, Greg 2001 *Metaculture*. Minneapolis: University of Minnesota Press.

Urban, Günter and Michael Jansen, eds., 1984 *The Architecture of Mohenjo-Daro*. Delhi: Books and Books.

Valeri, Valerio 1985 *Kingship and Sacrifice: Ritual and Society in Ancient Hawaii*. Chicago: University of Chicago Press.

Van de Mieroop, Marc 1997 *The Ancient Mesopotamian City*. Oxford: Clarendon Press.

Van der Meulen, D. [1947] 1958 *Aden to the Hadramawt*. London: John Murray.

Van Dycke, Ruth M. 2003 Memory and the Construction of Chacoan Society. Pp. 180–200 in Ruth M. Van Dycke and Susan E. Alcock, eds., *Archaeologies of Memory*. Oxford: Blackwell.

Van Dycke, Ruth M. and Susan E. Alcock 2003 Archaeologies of Memory: An Introduction. Pp. 1–14 in Ruth M. Van Dycke and Susan E. Alcock, eds., *Archaeologies of Memory*. Oxford: Blackwell.

Van Gennep, M. Arnold 1909 *Rites de passage*. Paris: É. Nourry.

　　1902 Les "Wasm," ou marques de propriété des arabes. *Internationales Archiv für Ethnographie* 15: 85–98.

Van Soldt, W. H., ed., 2005 *Ethnicity in Ancient Mesopotamia*. Papers Read at the 48th Rencontre Assyriologique Internationale Leiden 2002. Istanbul: Nederlands Instituut voor het Nabije Oosten.

Verhoeven, Marc 2002a The Transformations of Society: The Changing Role of Ritual and Symbolism in the PPNB and the PN in the Levant, Syria and South-East Anatolia. *Paléorient* 28(1): 5–14.

　　2002b Ritual and Its Investigation in Prehistory. Pp. 5–40 in Hans Georg Gebel, Bo Dahl Hermansen and Charlotte Hoffman Jensen, eds., *Magic Practices and Ritual in the Near Eastern Neolithic*. Studies in Early Near Eastern Production, Subsistence, and Environment 8. Berlin: Ex Oriente.

　　2002c Ritual and Ideology in the Pre-Pottery Neolithic B of the Levant and Southeast Anatolia. *Cambridge Archaeological Journal* 12: 233–258.

Vermeersch, P. M., P. van Peer, J. Moyersons and Willem van Neer 1994 Sodmein Cave, Red Sea Mountains (Egypt). *Sahara* 6: 31–40.

Vogt, Burkhard 1994 Death, Resurrection, and the Camel. Pp. 279–290 in Rosemarie Richter, Ingo Kottsieper and Mohammed Maraqten, eds., *Arabia Felix: Beiträge zur Sprache und Kultur des vorislamischen Arabien*. (Festschrift Walter W. Müller). Wiesbaden: Harrassowitz Verlag.

　　1985 *Zur Chronologie und Entwicklung der Gräber des späten 4.-2. Jtsd. v. Chr. auf der Halbinsel Oman*. Ph.D. dissertation. Göettingen.

Vogt, Burkhard and Alexander Sedov 1998 The Sabir Culture and Coastal Yemen during the Second Millennium BC – The Present State of Discussion. *Proceedings of the Seminar for Arabian Studies* 28: 261–270.

Vogt, B. and C. Velde 1987 Ghalilah Tomb SH 103. Pp. 37–44 in B. Vogt and U. Franke-Vogt, eds., *Shimal 1985/1986, Excavations of the German Archaeological Mission in Ras al Khaimah, U.A.E. Berliner Beitrage zum Vorderen Orient*, 8. Berlin: Reimer Verlag.

Voigt, Mary M. 2000 Çatal Höyük in Context: Ritual at Early Neolithic Sties in Central and Eastern Turkey. Pp. 253–293 in Ian Kuijt, ed., *Life in Neolithic Farming Communities. Social Organization, Identity, and Differentiation*. New York: Kluwer Academic/Plenum Press.

Vosmer, Tom 2003 The Naval Architecture of Early Bronze Age Reed-Built Boats of the Arabian Sea. Pp. 152–157 in Daniel Potts, Hasan Al Naboodah and Peter Hellyer, eds., *Archaeology of the United Arab Emirates*. Trident Press.

Waardenburg, Jacques 1963 *L'Islam dans le miroir de l'Occident*. The Hague: Mouton and Co.

Waetzoldt, Hartmut 1972 *Untersuchungen zur neusumerischen Textilindustrie*. Studi Economici e Tecnologici I. Roma: Centro per le antichità e la storia dell'arte del Vicino Oriente.

1980–1983 Leinen (Flachs). *Reallexikon der Assyriologie* 6: 583–594.

Wagner, Roy 2001 Condensed Mapping. Myth and the Folding of Space/ Space and the Folding of Myth. Pp. 71–78 in Alan Rumsey and James Weiner, eds., *Emplaced Myth: Space, Narrative, and Knowledge in Aboriginal Australia and Papua New Guinea*. Honolulu: University of Hawaii Press.

1986 *Symbols that Stand for Themselves*. Chicago: University of Chicago Press.

Waterson, Roxana 2000 House, Place, and Memory in Tana Toraja (Indonesia). Pp. 177–188 in Rosemary A. Joyce and Susan D. Gillespie, eds., *Beyond Kinship: Society and Material Reproduction in House Societies*. Philadelphia: University of Pennsylvania Press.

Watkins, Trevor 2006 Architecture and the Symbolic Construction of New Worlds. Pp. 15–24 in Edward B. Banning and Michael Chazan, eds., *Domesticating Space: Construction, Community, and Cosmology in the Late Prehistoric Near East*. Studies in Early Near Eastern Production, Subsistence, and Environment 12. Berlin: Ex Oriente.

2004 Building Houses, Framing Concepts, Constructing Worlds. *Paléorient* 30(1): 5–24.

Watson, Patty-Jo 1979 *Archaeological Ethnography in Western Iran*. Viking Fund Publications in Anthropology 57. Tucson: University of Arizona Press.

Wattenmaker, Patricia 1998 *Household and State in Upper Mesopotamia: Specialized Economy and the Social Uses of Goods in an Early Complex Society*. Washington, DC: Smithsonian Press.

Weber, Max 1952 *Ancient Judaism* [trans. Hans H. Gerth and Don Marindale]. Glencoe: Free Press.

Weingrod, Alex 1990 Saints and Shrines, Politics, and Culture: A Morocco-Israel Comparison. Pp. 217–235 in Dale F. Eickelman and James Piscatori, eds., *Muslim Travellers. Pilgrimage, Migration, and the Religious Imagination*. London: Routledge.

Weisgerber, Gerd 1983 Copper Production during the Third Millennium BC in Oman and the Question of Makan. *Journal of Oman Studies* 6: 269–276.

Weiss, Harvey 1986 The Origins of Tell Leilan and the Conquest of Space in 3rd Millennium Mesopotamia. Pp. 71–108 in Harvey Weiss, ed., *The Origins of Cities in Dry-Farming Syria*. Guilford, CT: Four Quarters Press.

Wellhausen Julius 1887 *Reste Arabischen Heidentums*. Berlin: Georg Reimer.

Wendorf, Fred 1968 Late Paleolithic Sites in Egyptian Nubia. Pp. 954–995 in F. Wendorf, ed., *The Prehistory of Nubia*. Dallas: Fort Burgwin Research Center and Southern Methodist Press.

Wendorf, Fred, Angela E. Close and Romuald Schild 1987 Early Domestic Cattle in the Eastern Sahara. Pp. 441–448 in J. A. Coetzee, ed., *Palaeoecology of Africa*. Rotterdam: A. A. Balkema.

Wengrow, David 2006 *The Archaeology of Early Egypt. Social Transformations in North-East Africa, 10,000–2650 BC*. Cambridge: Cambridge University Press.

2003 On Desert Origins for the Ancient Egyptians. Review article in *Antiquity* 77: 597–601.

2001a Rethinking "Cattle Cults" in Early Egypt: Toward a Prehistoric Perspective on the Narmer Palette. *Cambridge Archaeological Journal* 11(1): 94–104.

2001b The Evolution of Simplicity: Aesthetic Labour and Social Change in the Neolithic Near East. *World Archaeology* 32: 168–188.

1998 The Changing Face of Clay: Continuity and Change in the Transition from Village to Urban Life in the Near East. *Antiquity* 72: 783–795.

Wenke, Robert J. 1975–1976 Imperial Investment and Agricultural Development in Parthian and Sasanian Khuzestan: 150 B.C.–A.D. 640. *Mesopotamia* 10–1: 31–221.

Wensinck, A. J. 1914 Die Entstebung der muslimischen Reinheitsgesetzgebung. *Der Islam* 5: 62–79.

Wheatley, Paul 1971 *Pivot of the Four Quarters*. Chicago: Aldine.

Wheeler, Bonnie 1999 Models of Pilgrimage: From Communitas to Confluence. *Journal of Ritual Studies* 13(2): 26–41.

Whitehouse, H. 1992 Memorable Religions: Transmission, Codification and Change in Divergent Melanesian Contexts. *Man (new series)* 27: 777–799.

Whittaker, Gordon 2005 The Sumerian Question: Reviewing the Issues. Pp. 409–429 in W. H. Van Soldt, ed., *Ethnicity in Ancient Mesopotamia. Papers Read at the 48th Rencontre Assyriologique Internationale Leiden 2002*. Istanbul: Nederlands Instituut voor het Nabije Oosten.

Wilk, Richard R. 1983 Little House in the Jungle: The Causes of Variation in House Size among Modern Kekchi Maya. *Journal of Anthorpological Archaeology* 2: 99–116.

Wilk, Richard R. and William L. Rathje 1982 Household Archaeology. *American Behavioral Scientist* 25: 617–639.

Wilken, George A. 1884 *Das Matriarchat (das Mutterrecht) bei den alten Arabern*. Leipzig: O. Schulze.

Wilkinson, Tony J. 2003 *Archaeological Landscapes of the Near East*. Tucson: University of Arizona Press.

2000 Regional Approaches to Mesopotamian Archaeology: The Contribution of Archaeological Surveys. *Journal of Archaeological Research* 8: 219–267.

1999 Settlement, Soil Erosion and Terraced Agriculture in Highland Yemen: A Preliminary Statement. *Proceedings of the Seminar for Arabian Studies* 29: 183–191.

1997 Holocene Environments of the High Plateau, Yemen. Recent Geoarchaeological Investigations. *Geoarchaeology* 12: 833–864.

Wilkinson, Tony J. and D. J. Tucker 1995 *Settlement Development in the Northern Jazira, Iraq: A Study of the Archaeological Landscape*. Iraq Archaeological Reports 3. Warminster: Aris and Phillips.

Wilkinson, Tony J., Christopher Edens and Glynn Barratt 2001 Hammat al Qa': An Early Town in Southern Arabia. *Proceedings of the Seminar for Arabian Studies* 31: 249–259.

Wilkinson, T. J., Jason Ur and Jesse Casana 2004 From Nucleation to Dispersal: Trends in Settlement Pattern in the Northern Fertile Crescent. Pp. 189–205 in Susan E. Alcock and John F. Cherry, eds., *Side by Side Survey:*

Comparative Regional Studies in the Mediterranean World. Oxford: Oxbow Books.

Willcox, George 2002 Charred Plant Remains from a 10th Millennium B.P. Kitchen at Jerf el Ahmar (Syria). *Vegetation History and Archaeobotany* 11: 55–60.

Willcox, George, S. Fornite and L. Herveux 2008 Early Holocene Cultivation before Domestication in Northern Syria. *Vegetation History and Archaeobotany* 17: 313–325.

Wilson, Peter J. 1988 *The Domestication of the Human Species.* New Haven, CT: Yale University Press.

Winkelman, Michael and Jill Dubisch 2005 Introduction: The Anthropology of Pilgrimage. Pp. ix–xxxvi in Jill Dubisch and Michael Winkelman, eds., *Pilgrimage and Healing.* Tucson: University of Arizona Press.

Winterhalder, Bruce and Douglas J. Kennett 2006 Behavioral Ecology and the Transition from Hunting and Gathering to Agriculture. Pp. 1–21 in Douglas J. Kennett and Bruce Winterhalder, eds., *Behavioral Ecology and the Transition to Agriculture.* Berkeley: University of California Press.

Wiseman, James 2000 Barbarians at the Gate: Roman Frontiers from Britain to Arabia. *Archaeology* 53 (6): 12–14.

Wittfogel, Karl A. 1957 *Oriental Despotism.* New Haven, CT: Yale University Press.

Wolf, Eric 1958 The Virgin of Guadeloupe: A Mexican National Symbol. *Journal of American Folklore* 71: 34–39.

1951 The Social Organization of Mecca and the Origins of Islam. *Southwestern Journal of Anthropology* 7: 329–356.

Wright, Henry T., and Susan Pollock 1986 Regional Socio-Economic Organization in Southern Mesopotamia: The Middle and Later Fifth Millennium. Pp. 317–329 in Jean-Louis Huot, ed., *Préhistoire de la Mésopotamie. Colloques Internationaux CNRS.* Paris: Éditions du CNRS.

Wright, Katherine I. 2000 The Social Origins of Cooking and Dining in Early Villages of Western Asia. *Proceedings of the Prehistoric Society* 66: 89–121.

Wüstenfeld, F., ed., 1866–1873 *Mu'jam al-Buldan (Jacut's Geographisches Wörterbuch aus den Handschriften zu Berlin, St. Petersburg, Paris, und London).* 6 vols. Leipzig: in Commission bei F.A. Brockhaus.

Yartah, Thaer 2005 Les bâtiments communautaires de Tell 'Abr 3 (PPNA, Syrie). *Neolithics* 1(5): 3–9.

2004 Tell 'Abr 3, un village du néolithique précéramique (PPNA) sur le moyen Euphrate. Première approche. *Paléorient* 30(2): 141–158.

Yoffee, Norman 2005 *Myths of the Archaic State.* Cambridge: Cambridge University Press.

1995 Political Economy in Early Mesopotamian States. *Annual Reviews in Anthropology* 24: 281–311.

1993 The Late Great Tradition in Ancient Mesopotamia. Pp. 300–308 in Mark E. Cohen, Daniel C. Snell and David B. Weisberg, eds., *The Tablet and the Scroll.* Near Eastern Studies in Honor of William W. Hallo. Bethesda, MD: CDL Press.

1988 The Collapse of Mesopotamian States and Civilization. Pp. 44–68 in Norman Yoffee and George L. Cowgill, eds., *The Collapse of Ancient States and Civilizations*. Tucson: University of Arizona Press.

Yoffee, Norman and George L. Cowgill, eds., 1988 *The Collapse of Ancient States and Civilizations*. Tucson: University of Arizona Press.

Zarins, Juris 2001 The Land of Incense. *Archaeological Work in the Governate of Dhofar, Sultanate of Oman 1990–1995*. Sultan Qaboos University Publications Arcaheology and Cultural Heritage Series Volume 1. Sultanate of Oman: The Project of the National Committee for the Supervision of Archaeological Survey in the Sultanate. Ministry of Information.

1992 Pastoral Nomadism in Arabia: Ethnoarchaeology and the Archaeological Record – A Case Study. Pp. 219–240 in Ofer Bar-Yosef and Anatoly Khazanov, eds., *Pastoralism in the Levant: Archaeological Materials in Anthropological Perspectives*. Madison, WI: Prehistory Press.

Zeder, Melinda 2009 The Neolithic Macro-(R)evolution: Macroevolutionary Theory and the Study of Cultural Change. *Journal of Archaeological Research* 17: 1–63.

1998 Environment, Economy, and Subsistence on the Threshold of Urban Emergence in Northern Mesopotamia. Pp. 55–67 in M. Fortin and O. Aurenche, eds., *Espace naturel, espace habité en Syrie du Nord (10e–2e millénaires av J-C)*. Travaux de la Maison de l'Orient 28 and Canadian Society for Mesopotamian Studies 33. Lyon and Québec: Maison de l'Orient and Canadian Society for Mesopotamian Studies.

1994 After the Revolution: Post-Neolithic Subsistence Strategies in Northern Mesopotamia. *American Anthropologist* 96: 97–126.

Zeder, Melinda A., Daniel G. Bradley, Eve Emshwiller and Bruce D. Smith, eds., 2006 *Documenting Domestication. New Genetic and Archaeological Paradigms*. Berkeley: University of California Press.

Zettler, Richard 1992 *The Ur III Temple of Inanna at Nippur: The Operation and Organization of Urban Religious Institutions in Mesopotamia in the Later Third Millennium BC* Berliner Beiträge zum Vorderen Orient Band 11. Berlin: Dietrich Reimer Verlag.

Znaniecki, F. 1936 *The Method of Sociology*. New York: Farrar and Rinehart.

Zohar, Mattanyah 1992 Pastoralism and the Spread of the Semitic Languages. Pp. 165–180 in Ofer Bar-Yosef and Anatoly Khazanov, eds., *Pastoralism in the Levant: Archaeological Materials in Anthropological Perspectives*. Madison, WI: Prehistory Press.

Zohary, Daniel and Maria Hopf 1988 *Domestication of Plants in the Old World: The Origin and Spread of Cultivated Plants in West Asia, Europe, and the Nile Valley*. Oxford: Clarendon Press.

INDEX

Made in the USA
Columbia, SC
28 April 2020